Jean-Jacques Rousseau

International Library of Essays in the History of Social and Political Thought
Series Editor: Tom Campbell

Titles in the Series:

Hannah Arendt
Amy Allen

Friedrich Hayek
Norman Barry

Charles-Louis de Secondat Montesquieu
David Carrithers

Emile Durkheim
Roger Cotterrell

Vilfredo Pareto
Joseph Femia

Jean Bodin
Julian H. Franklin

Edmund Burke
Iain Hampsher-Monk

Talcott Parsons
John Holmwood

David Hume
Knud Haakonssen

Thomas Aquinas
John Inglis

Aristotle
George Klosko

Thomas Paine
Bruce Kuklick

Max Weber
Peter Lassman

T.H. Green
John Morrow

Martin Heidegger
Stephen Mulhall

Jean-Jacques Rousseau
Timothy O'Hagan

John Rawls
David Reidy

Jeremy Bentham
Frederick Rosen

Theodor Adorno
James Schmidt

Thomas Hobbes
Gabriella Slomp

Friedrich Nietzsche
Tracy Strong

Isaiah Berlin
Scott Veitch

Jean-Jacques Rousseau

Edited by

Timothy O'Hagan

University of East Anglia, UK

ASHGATE

Published by
Ashgate Publishing Limited
Gower House
Croft Road
Aldershot
Hampshire GU11 3HR
England

Ashgate Publishing Company
Suite 420
101 Cherry Street
Burlington, VT 05401-4405
USA

Ashgate website: http://www.ashgate.com

British Library Cataloguing in Publication Data
Jean-Jacques Rousseau. – (International library of essays
  in the history of social and political thought)
  1. Rousseau, Jean-Jacques, 1712–1778
  I. O'Hagan, Timothy
  194

Library of Congress Cataloging-in-Publication Data
Jean-Jacques Rousseau / edited by Timothy O'Hagan.
        p.cm. – (The international library of essays in the history of social and
political thought)
   Includes index
   ISBN: 978-0-7546-2717-3 (alk. paper)
  1. Rousseau, Jean-Jacques, 1712–1778. I. O'Hagan, Timothy.

  B2137 .J4113 2007
  300 .92–dc22

                                                                    2007002953

ISBN: 978-0-7546-2717-3

Printed in Great Britain by TJ International Ltd, Padstow, Cornwall

Contents

PART IV ANTICIPATIONS OF GAME THEORY

PART V   STRATEGIES OF REDEMPTION

Acknowledgements

The editor and publishers wish to thank the following for permission to use copyright material.

American Philosophical Association for the essay: Brian Skyrms (2001), 'The Stag Hunt', *Proceedings and Addresses of the American Philosophical Society*, **75**, pp. 31–41.

Blackwell Publishing for the essay: Joshua Cohen (1986), 'Reflections on Rousseau: Autonomy and Democracy', *Philosophy and Public Affairs*, **15**, pp. 275–97, 297a–b.

Cambridge University Press for the essay: Arthur M. Melzer (1983), 'Rousseau's Moral Realism: Replacing Natural Law with the General Will', *American Political Science Review*, **77**, pp. 633–51, 651a–c. Copyright © 1983 American Political Science Association.

Copyright Clearance Center for the essay: W.T. Jones (1987), 'Rousseau's General Will and the Problem of Consent', *Journal of the History of Philosophy*, **25**, pp. 105–30, 130a. Copyright © 2001 Bell and Howell Information and Learning Company.

Duke University Press for the essay: Frederick Neuhouser (1993), 'Freedom, Dependence, and the General Will', *The Philosophical Review*, **102**, pp. 363–95, 395a.

Harvard University Press for the essay: Jean Starobinski (1993), 'The Antidote in the Poison: The Thought of Jean-Jacques Rousseau', in *Blessings in Disguise, or the Morality of Evil*, trans. Arthur Goldhammer, Cambridge, MA: Harvard University Press, pp. 118–68, 223–28, 228a–b.

Journal of Philosophy, Inc. for the essay: Victor Gourevitch (1972), 'Rousseau on the Arts and Sciences', *Journal of Philosophy*, **69**, pp. 737–54, 754a–c. Copyright © 1972 Journal of Philosophy, Inc.

Oxford University Press for the essay: W.G. Runciman and Amartya K. Sen (1965), 'Games, Justice and the General Will', *Mind*, **74**, pp. 554–62.

Palgrave Macmillan for the essay: Robert Wokler (1987), 'Rousseau's Two Concepts of Liberty', in G. Feaver and F. Rosen (eds), *Lives, Liberties and the Public Good: Essays in Political Theory for Maurice Cranston*, London: Macmillan, pp. 61–100, 100a–b.

Penguin Group (UK) for the essay: Claude Lévi-Strauss (1977), 'Jean-Jacques Rousseau, Founder of the Sciences of the Man', in Claude Lévi-Strauss, *Structural Anthropology*, **2**, London: Allen Lane, pp. 33–43. Copyright © 1977 Claude Lévi-Strauss.

Series Preface

The International Library of Essays in the History of Social and Political Thought brings together collections of important essays dealing with the work of major figures in the history of social and political thought. The aim is to make accessible the complete text with the original pagination of those essays that should be read by all scholars working in that field. In each case, the selection is made from the extensive available literature by an established expert who has a keen sense of the continuing relevance of the history of social and political thought for contemporary theory and practice. The selection is made on the basis of the quality and enduring significance of the essays in question. Every volume has an introduction that places the selection made in the context of the wider literature, the historical period, the contemporary state of scholarship and the editor's particular interests.

TOM CAMPBELL
Series Editor
Centre for Applied Philosophy and Public Ethics (CAPPE)
Charles Sturt University
Canberra

In memory of

ROBERT WOKLER
1942–2006

'*a great cosmopolitan soul*'

Introduction

When the Series Editor Tom Campbell asked me to select 14 key essays on Rousseau's political and social philosophy, I accepted blithely. After more than 20 years living and breathing Jean-Jacques' work and having reviewed a good proportion of the books recently published on him in English, I thought this would be an easy task. But it turned out to be remarkably difficult. The first problem was the daunting scale of the secondary literature. Biographers, philosophers, political theorists, psychologists, intellectual historians, lettrists, educationalists, feminists, theologians, musicologists and botanists all find in Rousseau's paradoxical and multifaceted work material that is as provocative and arresting today as it was in the eighteenth century.

My brief was to limit the selection to *political and social theory*. Yet Rousseau's refusal to observe conventional demarcation lines between disciplines rendered that limitation problematic. In the *Emile* Rousseau declared: 'It is necessary to study society by men and men by society; those who would like to treat politics and morals separately will never understand anything about either of the two' (*OC*4.524/*Em*.235).[1] This epigram is borne out in each of his major works, and all the essays in the present collection address points of intersection between the moral and the political, the personal and the social.

Many of the authors also follow Rousseau's injunction to observe the close connection between the major works that make up his œuvre. In his famous account of the 'illumination' he experienced on the road to Vincennes in the summer of 1749, Rousseau condensed the leitmotiv of all his thought into a single epigram: 'Man is naturally good; it is only through their institutions that men become wicked.' The truths revealed to him at that moment were to be found 'scattered' in his 'three principal writings', the First and Second *Discourses* and 'the treatise on education' (the *Emile*). 'These works', we are told, 'are inseparable and form a whole' (Letter to Malesherbes, 12 January 1762, *OC*1.1136).

Obliged to narrow the focus and concentrate on the strictly *social and political* dimension of Rousseau's thought, I have omitted any essays devoted specifically to the *Emile*, despite Rousseau's Vincennes declaration, and despite the fact that this educational treatise embodies the author's deepest reflections on human nature. Rousseau emphasized its importance on more than one occasion. In the posthumous *Rousseau, Judge of Jean-Jacques* (Third Dialogue, *OC*1.933/*CW*1.211), he advised readers that his works formed a 'system' within which they should treat the *Emile* as the apex, with which they should start their reading.

It is with a heavy heart therefore that I have responded to constraints of space by excluding essays devoted specifically to the *Emile* or to the key concept of *amour-propre* which lies at its heart. Nonetheless, both text and concept are discussed by many authors in the collection.

---

[1]   For referencing conventions, please see the 'Note on References' at the end of the Introduction.

Many, too, bring out the systematic nature of Rousseau's work, while never ignoring the irreducible but creative tensions which lie within it.[2]

The Critique of Progress and the Speculative Anthropology: Rousseau's First Two *Discourses*

The two opening essays are addressed to the pessimistic vision of civilization expounded in Rousseau's first two major works, the *Discourse on the Sciences and the Arts* and the *Discourse on the Origin of Inequality among Men*.

The Critique of Progress (Discourse on the Sciences and the Arts)

As we have observed, Rousseau listed the *Discourse on the Sciences and the Arts* among his 'principal works', but he later wrote of it: 'This work, full of warmth and strength, is absolutely lacking in logic and order; of all the ones that have come from my pen it is the weakest in reasoning and the poorest in unity and harmony' (*Confessions*, Book VIII, *OC*1.352/*CW*5.295). Paradoxically, both of Rousseau's verdicts on the *First Discourse* may be correct. The text contains a powerful, provocative negative answer to the Prize essay question set by the Academy of Dijon, 'whether the restoration of the sciences and the arts has contributed to the purification of morals' (*OC*3.3/*CW*2.1). In answering 'No' to the question, Rousseau marshalled a proliferation of examples, both historical and contemporary, to illustrate the damaging effects of high culture on social mores. His target was the widespread optimism which dominated Enlightenment thinking, later summed up by the Marquis de Condorcet in these words: 'Truth, virtue and happiness are bound together by an indissoluble chain.' In his brief rhetorical *tour de force* Rousseau set out to destroy each link in this chain.

Despite its weaknesses, which Rousseau so candidly acknowledged, the *Discourse* went to the heart of the Enlightenment project. Over a century later, in his *Essay on Liberty* (1859), John Stuart Mill was impressed by Rousseau's boldness: 'With what a salutary shock did the paradoxes of Rousseau explode in our midst, dislocating a mass of one-sided opinion and forcing its elements to recombine in a new form and with additional ingredients.' The paradoxes stemmed from Rousseau's questioning of the universal 'admiration of what is called civilization, and of the marvels of modern science, literature and philosophy'.[3] It was in this *Discourse* that Rousseau first tried out the idea of the *remedy in the evil* to explain how it might be possible to break through an apparently closed, self-reinforcing cycle of corruption and power, and find an escape route to a new, higher order of things. We shall return to this in a moment.[4]

---

[2]   The philosopher who has revolutionized our thinking about amour-propre and subtly analysed its lineaments is Nicholas Dent. In order to do justice to Dent's work, I should have had to gouge out long sections from his books, but unfortunately that was impossible. All I can do is guide readers to his work via the Bibliography.

[3]   John Stuart Mill (1962), *Essay on Liberty* (1859), ed. M. Warnock, London: Fontana, p. 174.

[4]   In Part V of this collection, Jean Starobinski presents an extended investigation of the *remedy in the evil*.

In the opening essay of the collection, Victor Gourevitch uses the *Discourse* to highlight several important themes which will reappear at many points in Rousseau's later work, in particular those of citizen virtue and the debasement of taste which undermines it. He identifies a fascinating ambivalence at the heart of Rousseau's thought. Is Rousseau's argument that the arts are good for good societies and bad for bad ones or, to the contrary, that they are bad for good societies and good for bad ones? The latter version, which would emerge clearly in the Preface to *Julie*, would be the key to the *remedy in the evil*: the idea that if snake venom can be used to treat snake bites, so too elements of our corrupt culture can, under carefully controlled conditions, be used to treat the ills of that culture.

Gourevitch observes another ambiguity in the *Discourse*. The essay question referred to 'the sciences and the arts', and Rousseau addressed both elements equally in his comprehensive critique of modernity. Yet by the end of the *Discourse*, he passed rather different verdicts on the two. In short, he seems to have allowed that the greatest minds might pursue the sciences for their own sake and for the public good, whereas the arts attract only those ambitious for personal glory and indifferent to duty.

The Speculative Anthropology (Discourse on the Origin of Inequality among Men)

The occasion for Rousseau's second major work was once again an essay question set by the Academy of Dijon: 'What is the source of inequality among men and whether it is authorized by natural law?' (*OC*3.129/*CW*3.17).

Where the *First Discourse* had been mainly provocation, this *Second Discourse* was a work of genius. Yet, unlike its predecessor, it failed to win the prize, perhaps just because it was a work of genius (that at any rate was Rousseau's view!).

Instead of responding directly to the two-part question, Rousseau conducted an audacious thought-experiment. He aimed to strip away from human beings everything that comes from society and to construct a model of Homo sapiens in what he calls the *pure state of nature*, the ideal laboratory conditions of total isolation. The laboratory – imaginary, but graphically described – is the *Forest*. There, nature is bountiful. People's needs are easily satisfied. Without the *spur of necessity* individuals are not driven together in order to survive. They are idle, lacking imagination, ambition or anxiety. They are hard-wired to preserve themselves and to feel compassion – *an innate repugnance to see a fellow creature suffer*. Rousseau was struck by descriptions of the recently discovered orang-utan, and his savage in the Forest is closer to the higher primates than to contemporary civilized man.[5]

How, then, did we get to where we are now from where we were then? To the salon from the Forest? Since our ancestors could have lived for ever unchanging in the Forest, it can only have been because environmental changes – 'barren years, long and hard winters, scorching summers' – drove them together to survive. Once that process had set in, then humankind began its process of development, as human beings, endowed, unlike other animals, with free will and the power of self-improvement over generations (*perfectibility*), adapted to further changes in their environment. Rousseau traces the evolution of humankind through a series of stages, each initiated by 'the chance combination of several external events' (*OC*3.162/ *CW*3.42), ending up in the disordered 'civilized' world we now inhabit. The happiest stage

---

[5]   See Robert Wokler's masterly studies, including Wokler (1978).

was the *Youth of the World*, the life of simple hunting and gathering people, equipped with stone tools, living in huts, organized in kinship groups without formal political authority (see Hobson, 1992).

Rousseau's vision appealed to Claude Lévi-Strauss, the doyen of twentieth-century ethnologists, who hailed Rousseau as the 'founder of the sciences of man' in his 1962 lecture delivered to commemorate the 200th anniversary of the publication of the *Social Contract*. In this lecture, which forms Chapter 2 of our collection, Lévi-Strauss declares that 'Rousseau did not restrict himself to anticipating ethnology: he founded it' (p. 27). The *Discourse on the Origin of Inequality* provides the starting point for Lévi-Strauss's reflections. In it he finds an original and radical investigation of the distinction between nature and culture, constituting 'the first treatise of general ethnology' and the first clear distinction between the 'object' of the social scientist and those of the moralist and historian.

But Lévi-Strauss does not restrict himself to the *Discourse*. He ranges over the whole of Rousseau's corpus, finding it to be unified by a preoccupation with his own self. Paradoxically, Lévi-Strauss declares, it is just that preoccupation which triggered Rousseau's deepest insights in the social sciences. And that is because for Rousseau, more than any writer before him, the self is always elusive and veiled, and most importantly because culture always intervenes between the self and consciousness of the self. In short, the self is always a culturally mediated self.

The Naturalizing of Natural Law and the General Will and Totalitarianism

Uniting the essays in Parts II and III is the question of what, if any, theory of political legitimacy can be constructed from the remnants of natural law theory, the destruction of which was begun by Hobbes and completed by Rousseau. The two essays in Part II start from Rousseau's ruthless dispatch of traditional models of man. The six essays in Part III circle round the elements of his own stark alternative: the sovereign people, issue of the foundational moment of the social contract, exercising absolute power through the general will. Whether this is a vision of liberation or totalitarian despotism is the recurring question which haunts every one of these essays.

To allow readers to keep their bearings in these two parts, I display a number of key passages from the *Social Contract* and elsewhere.

The passages in question fall into two groups. The first group is drawn from *Social Contract* Book I, chapters 6, 7 and 8, and Book II, chapter 7. These contain the terms of the contract, the mechanism of its enforcement and the ways in which human nature is transformed in the passage from the state of nature to civil society.

Terms of the Contract
> *Each of us puts his person and all his power in common under the supreme direction of the general will ['sous la suprême direction de la volonté générale'] and we receive as a body each member as an indivisible part of the whole.* (SCI, 6: *OC*3.361/*CW*4.139)

Total Alienation
> These clauses, properly understood, may be reduced to one – the total alienation of each associate, together with all his rights, to the whole community. (SCI, 6: *OC*3.360/*CW*4.138)

Forced to be Free

In fact, each individual can, as a man, have a particular will contrary to or differing from the general will which he has as a Citizen. His particular interest can speak to him quite differently from the common interest ... he might wish to enjoy the rights of the citizen without being ready to fulfil the duties of a subject, an injustice whose spread would cause the ruin of the body politic. In order then that the social compact may not be an empty formula, it tacitly includes the following undertaking, which alone can give force to the others, that whoever refuses to obey the general will shall be compelled to do so by the whole body: which means nothing else than that he will be forced to be free. (SCI, 7: *OC*3.363–64/*CW*4.140–41)

Remarkable Change in Man

The passage from the state of nature to the civil state produces a very remarkable change in man, by substituting justice for instinct in his conduct, and giving his actions the morality they previously lacked. Only then, when the voice of duty replaces physical impulse and right replaces appetite, does man, who until then had considered only himself, find that he is forced to act on different principles, and to consult his reason before listening to his inclinations. Although in this state he deprives himself of several advantages given him by nature, he gains such great ones, his faculties are exercised and developed, his ideas broadened, his feelings ennobled, and his whole soul elevated to such a point that if the abuses of this new condition did not often degrade him beneath the condition he left, he ought ceaselessly to bless the happy moment that tore him away from it forever, and that changed him from a stupid, limited animal into an intelligent being and a man. (SCI, 8: *OC*3.364/*CW*4. 141)

The Lawgiver

In Book II, chapter 7, Rousseau attributes this transformation process to a *législateur*, by which he meant a founding father, like Moses or Lycurgus, who in codifying a system of laws thereby formed a people:

The same reasoning Caligula used with respect to fact was used by Plato with respect to right in defining the civil or royal man he seeks in the *Statesman*. But if it is true that a great prince is a rare man, what about a great Legislator? The former only has to follow the model that the latter should propose. The latter is the mechanic who invents the machine; the former is only the workman who puts it together and starts it running. At the birth of societies, says Montesquieu, the leaders of republics create the institutions; thereafter, it is the institutions that form the leaders of republics. (SCII, 7: *OC*3.381/*CW*4.154–55)

In the second group of passages Rousseau describes the way in which the general will can emerge and be expressed in the rule of law in a civil society set up according to the conditions of legitimacy specified above.

General Will

When a law is proposed in the assembly of the people, what the people is asked is not exactly whether it approves or rejects the proposal, but whether it is in conformity with the general will, which is their will. Each man, in giving his vote, states his opinion on that point; and the general will is found, therefore, by counting votes. When therefore the opinion that is contrary to my own prevails, this proves neither more or less than that I was mistaken, and that what I thought to be the general will was not so. (SCIV, 2: *OC*3.440–41/*CW*4.200–201)

The Rule of Law

There is no liberty where there are no Laws or where someone is above the Laws ... A free people obeys, but it does not serve; it has leaders (*chefs*) and not masters. It obeys the Laws, but it obeys only the Laws, and it is by the force of the Laws that it does not obey men ... Any condition imposed on each by all can be burdensome to no one, and the worst of Laws is worth more than the best master; for every master has preferences, whereas the Law never has any. (*Lettres écrites de la montagne*, VIII: *OC*3.842–43/*CW*9.261)

Public and Private

Finally, one passage in which Rousseau appears to reserve an area of private life immune to public intervention, but in a fashion that may arouse further anxieties in the mind of the liberal reader:

But, besides the public person, we have to consider the private persons composing it, whose life and liberty are naturally independent of it. We are bound then to distinguish clearly between the respective rights of the citizens and the sovereign, and the duties the former have to fulfil as subjects, and the natural rights they should enjoy as men.

  Each man alienates, I admit, by the social compact, only such part of his powers, goods and liberty as it is important for the community to control; but it must also be granted that the sovereign is sole judge of what is important. (SCII, 4: *OC*3.373/*CW*4.148)

The Naturalizing of Natural Law

Leo Strauss opens the first essay in Part II (Chapter 3 – a chapter from his book *Natural Right and History*) with a dramatic declaration: 'The first crisis of modernity occurred in the thought of Jean-Jacques Rousseau' (p. 39).

  The crisis came about as Rousseau returned to the ancients for a model of virtue flourishing within a patriotic city state, but at the same time abandoned assumptions about human nature which had been common currency in antiquity, and which had survived, despite Hobbes's withering onslaught, well into the eighteenth century. The most important of these was a belief in the innate rationality and sociability of human beings. Rousseau abandoned that assumption and replaced reason with passion as the key element of his philosophical anthropology.

  For Strauss, Rousseau's critique of modernity embodies an unresolved tension between two nostalgic aspirations: on the one hand, a desire to recover from antiquity the ideal of active citizenship and, on the other hand, an equally strong yearning for a return to a state of nature which would mean a withdrawal from all political engagement.

  Strauss is dismissive of the view that Rousseau's model of a novel social order, exercising popular sovereignty through the general will, constitutes a *solution* to the conflict between individual and society. This is because, for Rousseau, even the best society would be 'a burden to man'.

  Strauss uncovers unsettling themes in the *First Discourse*, particularly the idea that since civil society is healthy only if it is closed, the sciences and the search for knowledge are socially dangerous insofar as they undermine that closure and introduce cosmopolitan values incompatible with patriotism and civic virtues.

  Strauss passes this judgement on the *Second Discourse*: 'There is no natural constitution of man to speak of ' (p. 58). From that he concludes that because Rousseau's model of the state of nature was 'undefined and undefinable', it could no longer provide a coherent objective standard against which one could measure the merits and defects of any particular society or form of government. Previous natural law theory had provided such a standard with a philosophical anthropology. Rousseau finally destroyed that programme and left a vacuum, to be filled by an unrestrained legal voluntarism, infused by a utopian vision of citizenly virtue. In Chapter 8 Robert Wokler identifies a similar lack of content in Rousseau's model of man, but Wokler concludes that it is a liberating, rather than an enslaving, vision.

In his 1983 essay 'Rousseau's Moral Realism: Replacing Natural Law with the General Will' (Chapter 4), Arthur Melzer highlights three recurring themes in Rousseau's work: the natural goodness of man, the critique of progress and enlightenment, and the theory of the sovereign people exercising its absolute power through the general will. He draws attention to the kinship between Hobbes and Rousseau, who both denied that natural sociability was the source of legitimacy, and who both propounded a version of absolutism as the only alternative to a now discredited theory of natural law. The most important difference between the two philosophers was that Rousseau's model of man was more 'realist' than Hobbes's.

Melzer stresses the importance of the rule of law in Rousseau's system. In this respect his Rousseau would be in agreement with traditional natural lawyers (as well as with later liberals). But the agreement is superficial, masking a deeper gulf between the two positions. For, as Melzer presents Rousseau's system, the function of the general will, expressed in the rule of law, is not to embody justice, but to replace it. Popular sovereignty is to be accepted not because it is just, but because it protects individual citizens against oppression, which is in turn defined as personal dependence.

Melzer's essay thus leads us into the theme of the next section, opening up the still unresolved question of whether Rousseau's system can ever be consistent with liberal values.

The General Will and Totalitarianism

The 'liberal' attack on Rousseau, inaugurated by Constant and Tocqueville, was carried through into the twentieth century by a legion of critics, including most notably Isaiah Berlin. Of these, it was Lester G. Crocker who engaged most closely with the whole corpus of Rousseau's work in a systematic, scholarly fashion. At the heart of Rousseau's doctrine of the general will Crocker (Chapter 5) finds two different entities: 'empirical men' on the one hand and an idealized person on the other. The latter presupposes that there is a 'rational unity among all men, consisting of what their reason would desire if all individual passions and desires could be stilled' (p. 112). For Crocker, Rousseau 'mingles in one concept a real empirical situation and a purely metaphysical postulate' (p. 112).

The key to totalitarianism then lies in the fusion of the figure of the divided self with the elimination of natural law as a critical standard applicable to the procedures of a sovereign people, consisting of citizens who have submitted to the 'total alienation' of their individual wills to the collectivity.[6]

In a densely argued essay, Joshua Cohen in Chapter 6 traces a series of dilemmas running through Rousseau's political thought. These stem from a tension between the two elements which lie at its heart. On the one hand there is the view that legitimacy depends on the promotion

---

[6]   The themes of totalitarianism and the divided self recur in many of the essays in this collection.

of the common good, and on the other hand the view that it depends on endorsement by the general will: 'common good morality' versus voluntarism.

Cohen argues that the two can be reconciled only if we accept as a starting point that 'social interdependence' is 'a basis for that [general] will in the nature of human beings' (p. 130). The social contract thus does not offer a reason why atomized, asocial creatures should leave the pure state of nature and enter civil society. Rather, it offers a model of a desirable form of social order to individuals already involved in, and aware of, their social ties. In that context, we should interpret the common good morality as a '*substantive moral conception* that one ought to act to advance the common good' (p. 133). Thus interpreted, agents are not inconsistent if they endorse a common good morality for reasons of autonomy. Everything hinges on the assumption that the 'remarkable change in man' described in *Social Contract* I, 8 has taken place. This transforms the individual from someone who thinks instrumentally, advancing the common good only when it serves his selfish interest, into one who regards the general will 'not ... [as] a means to autonomy ... [but as] what autonomy consists in' (p. 133).

After illuminating reflections on Rousseau's reasons for limiting direct democracy, Cohen concludes that his reading of Rousseau's social contract theory as 'autonomy under conditions of interdependence' (p. 143) remains the best normative programme available to us today.

W.T. Jones in Chapter 7 brings out Rousseau's debt to Hobbes in his treatment of a central problem of political philosophy, that of reconciling freedom and compulsion. The general will, he argues, is Rousseau's solution to that problem. For Jones, Rousseau's general will is complex, combining normative and descriptive dimensions. On the normative side, Rousseau maintains that political morality depends on citizens' consent and that their consent depends on there being a general will to express it. On the empirical side, he makes a series of empirical assertions which are more or less susceptible to empirical testing. These include the view that a general will is most likely to emerge in a small, relatively homogeneous group. Jones investigates the procedural conditions which Rousseau holds to be necessary for the emergence of a general will.

The conflict between liberalism and totalitarianism had receded into the background of Cohen's and Jones's reflections, but with Robert Wokler it regains centre stage. The title of his essay, 'Rousseau's Two Concepts of Liberty' (Chapter 8) echoes Isaiah Berlin's famed lecture of 1952. In taking up arms on behalf of Rousseau, Wokler starts by placing the argument of the *Social Contract* in its historical context. His claim here is not that Rousseau was a liberal, but rather that he was simply not faced by a choice between two opposing doctrines, since *liberalism*, both the term and the concept, did not exist before the nineteenth century. 'As a political ideology', claims Wokler, 'liberalism is ... as absent from the periods in which Hobbes and Rousseau lived as it is alien to their writings' (p. 181). In this opening section Wokler thus radically historicizes the debate and appears to debunk the charge of totalitarianism.

However, this debunking move raises yet more questions. It is true that Rousseau's first great *liberal* critic, Benjamin Constant, was writing in the aftermath of the French Revolution, a generation later. But one might wonder whether Rousseau and his contemporaries, while lacking the later terminology, were also unaware of the risks involved in 'the total alienation of each associate, together with all his rights, to the community' (SCI, 6). Wokler responds that Constant confused Rousseau with Robespierre, who interpreted 'total alienation ... to the *community*' as 'total alienation ... to the *government*'. It is the latter, rather than the former, that would lead to totalitarianism. But it is incompatible with Rousseau's own systematic distinction between the sovereign people and its government. Therefore the charge of being even an unwitting herald of an ideology yet to be born is unfounded.

What we have outlined here is merely the opening salvo in Wokler's complex strategy. In the following sections Wokler moves on to engage with Rousseau's own elusive images of freedom, united only by their extreme lack of content. He contrasts Rousseau not only with the natural lawyers, but also with Hobbes in virtue of his 'emptier, more formal, more strictly negative conception of our distinguishing behavioural traits' (p. 191). Thus where Leo Strauss had also found a content-free model of man in Rousseau, only to be filled by a sinister legal voluntarism, Wokler judges this 'negative conception' to be liberating.

There still remains the notorious formula 'whoever refuses to obey the general will shall be compelled to do so by the whole body: which means nothing else than that he will be forced to be free' (SCI, 7: *OC*3.363–64/*CW*4.140–41). If the words are given an Orwellian reading, they carry the sinister message that recalcitrant individuals, even while (apparently) being constrained, are (really) being liberated. Against that, Wokler sees recalcitrants as being 'protected against personal dependence which invariably *does* deprive them of their freedom'. In terms of Isaiah Berlin's polar opposites, this political freedom would be *negative*, while moral freedom, overcoming domination by one's own passions, would be *positive*. Rousseau's original *double* conception of freedom, combining Berlin's two poles, would be united by the idea that to be free is to emancipate oneself from *dépendance personnelle*. At neither pole should we look for any teleologically prescribed desirable goals. Nor should the two poles be confused. They share 'a certain range of meanings in the light of which their differences … [yield] direct opposition and conflict'.

John Hope Mason in Chapter 9 locates Rousseau in the tradition of civic republicanism stretching from Machiavelli and Montesquieu and inspired by an image of the ancient city state, in which active, engaged citizens would live lives infused by patriotic virtues. That much Rousseau shared with his predecessors. What marked him out from them was his insistence on difference and rupture. Starting with the *Second Discourse*, Rousseau stressed that people in the pure state of nature were qualitatively different creatures from those in civil society. By the same token, the inhabitants of corrupt contemporary societies were radically different from the citizens of antiquity. A radical transformation of human nature would therefore be needed in order to realize the 'republican vision' in the modern world.

If that transformation is to be carried out, it will be necessary to rechannel the ruling passion of socialized man, *amour-propre*. Only then can individuals become parts of a new social whole. The dominant image of the seventeenth century had been the *mechanism*: atoms entered into mechanically ordered wholes and were not altered in the process. The eighteenth-century image, in contrast, was the *organism*. With this came a new understanding of the part–whole relationship in terms of a dynamic interactive system which produces qualitative changes in its components.

When applied to society, this organic imagery seems to bring the spectre of totalitarianism ever closer. It is not evidently better to be a cell in the social organism than to be a cog in the social machine. Against that, Hope Mason argues that, when citizens are absorbed into the social whole, their individuality is 'not eradicated' thereby. Their 'identification' with the city is not analogous to the mystical believer's 'identification' with God.

As we have seen already, Rousseau offers a multilayered political theory. It incorporates not only a normative core, defining legitimate authority, but also extended reflections on the conditions necessary for its attainment. It is in the articulation between these two dimensions of Rousseau's thought that Hope Mason locates its 'totalitarian drift'. Rousseau, he argues, was driven by empirical evidence to hold that human feelings were now universally and irredeemably corrupted. In the light of that pessimistic conclusion, he saw no alternative to measures designed to restrict the meaningful political activity of the sovereign people, limiting legislative power to the formal approval or rejection of bills formulated by their so-called *commissaires*, the magistrates composing the government.

Part III concludes with an essay by the distinguished Hegel scholar Frederick Neuhouser (Chapter 10), who notes certain continuities between themes in Rousseau and Hegel, in particular the central role which both allot to the will, but here his focus, until the last few pages, is strictly on Rousseau.

At the heart of the *ancien régime* lay relations of *dépendance personnelle*, founded on unequal power between individuals, whether inherited or acquired. In such a society, isolated, passive individuals were excluded from engagement in public life – in short, from the life of the citizen. It is important to mark off this undesirable form of dependence from dependence in general, since 'Rousseau starts from the supposition that dependence is a fundamental, ineliminable feature of human existence' (p. 256). All human beings have needs, and even savages in the pure state of nature are dependent. But they, according to Rousseau's distinction in the *Emile*, would be dependent only on *things*, not on *men*. Once we become socialized, both forms of dependence become inevitable. Understood in this way, the function of the general will is to keep citizens free from *dependence on men*, not from dependence on *things*.

Within society, the assertion of freedom is 'an inherently moral phenomenon' involving a plurality of wills, in which individuals strive for recognition in a play of amour-propre. Rousseau's aim therefore, at least in his mature political works, is not to eliminate dependence, but to 'restructure' it. The general will can fulfil that aim if it guarantees citizens' freedom by transforming *dépendance personnelle* into *dépendance de la cité*. For Neuhouser, this means simply that 'relations of dependence between individuals are [now] *mediated* by a system of well-founded law' (p. 268). Such a system must embody not only procedural 'equality before the law', but also uphold a level of economic equality sufficient to ensure a real, not merely formal, freedom for all citizens.

So far, so good. But Neuhouser still needs to defuse the paradox of the recalcitrant citizen who will be *forced to be free*. To the question: 'In what sense do the dictates of the general will constitute one's own will even when one fails to recognize them as such?' Neuhouser responds that the individual 'necessarily and most fundamentally wills its own freedom' (p. 273). This means that, when not mistaken, he wills the objective conditions of its realization. Neuhouser distinguishes this version of freedom as absence of *dépendance personnelle* from Cohen's social autonomy model, while recognizing that the two could be seen as but two sides of the single core notion of freedom as obedience to a law one prescribes to oneself.

At the end of the essay, Neuhouser's Hegelian affiliations come into the open. The social autonomy model, he maintains, is 'subjective', depending on the attitude individuals adopt to the general will; whereas freedom as personal independence is 'objective', so that the general will expresses 'a set of conditions' guaranteeing personal independence 'independent of one's subjective relation to the principles that structure the social world' (p. 275). As a good

Hegelian, Neuhouser does not conflate the subjective and objective aspects of freedom, but seeks a synthesis between them. Both aspects are necessary, but neither is sufficient without the other. The recalcitrant citizen is *forced to be free* when and only when the two aspects fail to coincide.

Anticipations of Game Theory

The two short essays in Part IV bring out elements of game theory to be found in Rousseau's work.

In their classic 'Games, Justice and the General Will' (Chapter 11), W.G. Runciman and Amartya Sen proceed in two phases. In the first phase, they take issue with Kenneth Arrow, who had attributed to Rousseau the view that:

> ... each individual has two orderings, one which governs him in his everyday actions and one which would be relevant under some ideal conditions and which is in some sense truer than the first ordering. (p. 284)

Against Arrow, Runciman and Sen use the prisoner's dilemma to argue that Rousseau is not committed to the thesis of 'two orderings', that he

> ... does not require us to impute to each person more than a single set of orderings ... [since] each person has ... a single and consistent aim. The conflict between the will of all and the general will arises not because the individual must be required to change his preference orderings, but because of the difference between the outcome of individual strategy and of enforced collusion. (p. 284)

As Runciman and Sen read the *Social Contract*, when the will of all fails to correspond to the general will, there is a 'conflict between what seems individually better and what seems to produce the best over-all result' (p. 282), rather than a conflict between two selves endowed with different preference orderings. So at the heart of Rousseau's contract are rational individuals, who sign up to a system of enforceable rules and thereby to the existence of an enforcement agency. The function of the latter would be to override decisions taken by individuals in their short-term interest when the result of those decisions would be to the long-term detriment of all. That, they argue, is what Rousseau meant by being *forced to be free*. They modestly deny that they are contributing to the debate about Rousseau's status as liberal or totalitarian. But if we contrast their interpretation with Arrow's, their Rousseau looks strikingly more liberal than his.

In the second phase of their essay, Runciman and Sen draw attention to the absence of any substantive theory of distributive justice in Rousseau's *Social Contract*. In particular, they point out, the general will requires only that decisions must be Pareto-optimal – that is, they must leave no one worse off than he would have been without civil society. It does not tell us how to choose between two alternatives, which were both Pareto-optimal but had different distributive outcomes. They conclude that Rousseau's account would need to be supplemented by a theory such as John Rawls's *justice as fairness*, which would lay the basis of principled decision-making in the real world.

The 'stag hunt' in Brian Skyrms' essay (Chapter 12) is the name now attached to a game-theoretic model of social interaction. It is derived from Rousseau's throw-away discussion at the beginning of Part II of the *Second Discourse*:

> That is how men could imperceptibly acquire some crude idea of mutual engagements and of the advantages of fulfilling them, but only insofar as present and perceptible interest would require; for foresight meant nothing to them, and far from being concerned about a distant future, they did not even think about the next day. Was it a matter of catching a Deer, everyone clearly felt that for this purpose he ought faithfully to keep his post; but if a hare happened to pass within reach of one of them, there can be no doubt that he pursued it without scruple, and that having obtained his prey, he cared very little about having caused his Companions to miss theirs. (*Second Discourse, OC*3.166–67/*CW*3.45)

The lesson of Rousseau's story is that the deer hunt fails because the hunters are 'perfect strangers to foresight', and they are also unreliable, since they do not 'abide faithfully by [their] post'. On that assumption, the rational hunter, knowing that his neighbours are unreliable, will, if presented with a certain hare, be driven by instrumental reason to abandon his post. The same will go for each member of the group if confronted by an available hare. Each will be driven to make a decision that is rational for him under the circumstances, but less than optimal for him (and for everyone else) in the long run. The deer hunt, then, seems to be doomed, though it is to everyone's advantage that it should succeed.

It is hard to see how the people described in Rousseau's vignette could ever move to a more rational way of ordering their lives. 'The transition from non-cooperation to cooperation seems impossible' (p. 295). Yet somehow it happens. Society as we know it turns out to be what Rawls has called a 'cooperative venture', however imperfect. In seeking a solution, the author turns from Rousseau to Hume, who explained that 'the stability of possession' (the fundamental cooperative institution) 'arises gradually, and acquires force by a slow progression' (p. 295). For the game theorist that means that when people move from games involving one play to those involving repeated plays, the mechanism of 'replicator dynamics' sets in. Agents simply learn by experience that they are better off if they cooperate. Here, chance is important. A group may become stuck in a cycle of non-cooperation. But just because social groups do not form closed systems, when one non-cooperative group interacts with another, more successful, cooperative group, that contact can transform the behaviour of the former group. Equally, chance factors can reverse the process. Rousseau's thinking in the *Second Discourse* is remarkably close to this. 'That is how men could *imperceptibly acquire* some crude idea of mutual engagements and of the advantages of fulfilling them', he tells us, and 'the chance combination of several external events' (*OC*3.162/*CW*3.42) runs as a guiding thread through the second part of the *Discourse*. The empirical work of contemporary game theorists suggests that Rousseau's insights are more than flights of fancy.

Strategies of Redemption

The authors of the two essays in Part V both interweave biography and textual exegesis to uncover recurring themes in Rousseau's work, which I have grouped under the heading *Strategies of Redemption.*[7]

In Chapter 13, his magisterial essay 'The Antidote in the Poison', Jean Starobinski takes us back to our starting point, the *Discourse on the Sciences and the Arts.* Before presenting Starobinski's miniature *magnum opus*, I shall provide a rapid overview of some of Rousseau's key texts and arguments.

The message of the *First Discourse* appeared to be wholly pessimistic. Modern society, Rousseau maintained, was irredeemably corrupt, and its culture was both the product and the instrument of the prevailing political despotism. What escape can there be from this mire of complicity? Here is Rousseau's surprising answer:

> ... the evil is not as great as it could have become. By placing salutary herbs beside various harmful plants, and by placing within several injurious animals the antidote for their wounds, eternal providence has taught sovereigns, who are its ministers, to imitate its wisdom. (*OC*3.26/*CW*2.19)

The solution would be to encourage enlightened despots to found academies in which *savants* of genius would be able to promote science and culture in a protected environment.

Gourevitch has already alerted us to Rousseau's ambivalent attitude to the possible benefits of high culture. Starobinski makes the most persuasive case for thinking that it is the image of the remedy in the evil which sheds most light not only on the *First Discourse*, but also on much of Rousseau's subsequent work.

Here, for instance, Rousseau deploys the image in the first version of the *Social Contract* of 1760:

> ... although men become unhappy and wicked in becoming sociable ... far from thinking that there is neither virtue nor happiness for us and that heaven has abandoned us without resources to the depravation of the species, let us attempt to draw from the evil itself the remedy that should cure it. (*OC*3.288/*CW*4.81)

In other words, the only available cure for our disordered society must be generated from within society itself. To effect the cure the therapist must re-order, though not replace, the egotistic drives of individuals within society. The therapy would address the way in which individuals understand themselves and their interests. The 'remedy' is already present in society. People already engage with one another in ways which transcend elementary selfishness. The trick is to enlarge people's sense of self-interest rather than to replace it. This will lead them to identify themselves with the new social order and find themselves in it. Their very egotism, thus transformed and expanded, will provide the remedy in the evil.

Starobinski identifies an underlying pessimism in Rousseau's thought, which is subject only to intermittent relief when the remedy in the evil becomes a *cure* rather than a mere *palliative* for an incurable disease. As Gourevitch would do later, Starobinski poses the same dilemma at the heart of the *First Discourse*: is high culture good for good societies and bad for

---

[7]   This title is taken from a chapter in Gauthier (2006).

bad ones, or is it on the contrary bad for good societies and good for bad ones? It is the latter alternative that informs the more optimistic versions of the remedy in the evil.

For Starobinski this elusive image is the key to much of Rousseau's thinking about education and politics. In both, *timing* is crucial. The remedy must be applied at precisely the right time. If it is too early, then the remedy may precipitate the very condition it was designed to exclude. If it is too late, then the condition will be beyond remedy.

Over even the last moment of Rousseau's œuvre, the final, unfinished, *Rêverie*, the remedy in the evil casts its shadow: '[W]hen the malady disappears along with the concomitant need to search for a remedy, it is because vital energy has all but run dry' (p. 336). The very sickness which has constantly threatened the life of the individual and society turns out to be the engine of their growth and transformation.

These are but a few of the moments of Starobinski's multifaceted work. It also contains psychoanalytic insights into Rousseau's life and imagery, as well as an extended account of the relationship between music and society.

In Chapter 14, the final essay of the collection, David Gauthier provides a brief sketch of the whole of Rousseau's life and thought through the prism of Jean-Jacques' passionate involvement with Madame de Warens – *maman*. This essay now forms a key element, though not the final conclusion, of Gauthier's luminous monograph *The Sentiment of Existence*.

For Gauthier, if there is a totalitarian element in both the *Social Contract* and the *Emile*, it is to be found in the role played by dependence in those works. The citizen, it will be recalled, exchanges *dépendance personnelle* for dependence on the sovereign people. Emile, on the other hand moves from absolute dependence on the tutor to autonomy, but that can be achieved by the 'savage educated to live in the city' only so long as he remains protected from corrupting social influences. Faced by the choice between the two models of existence elaborated in 1762, the citizen's 'fractional existence' in an unrealized political order on the one hand, and Emile's anomalous existence as the savage in the city on the other, Rousseau in his late, posthumously published works moved to a third conception of human existence. As a conception, this is no less a 'construction' than the others. Rousseau reached it only through intense reflection on his own experience of passionate love and its transcendence. The latter, as described so vividly in *Julie*, involves a ceaseless play of dominance and dependence – in short, the very *dépendance personnelle* from which both the *Social Contract* and the *Emile* sought vainly to protect us. Yet that same passion, which starts as a desire to *possess* the beloved's affections, can be transformed into a sense of *shared* existence. If that 'sentiment of [shared] existence' can be carried through into the present social world we inhabit, then it may be the key to our survival in that world, in which our irreducible dependence on others, and indeed on particular others, may be experienced as *identification* with them, rather than a form of oppression.

***

It would be fruitless to attempt a *summary* of the contents of the collection. I hope that the essays form a kind of picaresque *narrative*, in which tropes and themes emerge, disappear and return, only to be transformed in the light of fresh strategies of interpretation. I hope, too, that the collection will offer something to old Rousseau hands and also to social scientists who are relative newcomers to his work.

***

It only remains to acknowledge the contribution of three collaborators. Mike Gough worked tirelessly in the initial stages, assembling the extracts and standardizing the references. Alexandre Erler carefully oversaw the middle stages. Finally Richard Hibbitt engaged all his editorial skills and experience to ensure the successful completion of the project. Mavis Reynolds was a constant standby throughout. I should like to thank all four for their invaluable help.

A Note on References

The authors of these essays have used many different editions of Rousseau's works, both French and English. In the Introduction I have referred to the *Œuvres complètes*, the *Collected Writings* and Bloom's translation of *Emile* (for details, see below). Where possible, I have added similar references to individual essays in the collection. These are appended as Addenda following the relevant essays.

Bibliography

This bibliography is anything but comprehensive. It is restricted to Rousseau's own work, some reference books and some of the secondary literature from which I have learnt most.

Rousseau's Texts (French)

Rousseau, Jean-Jacques (1959–95), *Œuvres complètes*, 5 vols, general eds Bernard Gagnebin and Marcel Raymond, Paris: Gallimard (Bibliothèque de la Pléiade) (abbreviated *OC*).

Many authors still refer to this classic collection:

Rousseau, Jean-Jacques (1915), *The Political Writings of Jean-Jacques Rousseau*, 2 vols, ed. C. E. Vaughan, Cambridge: Cambridge University Press (repr. Oxford: Blackwell, 1962).

Rousseau's Correspondence (French)

The standard edition is now Ralph Leigh's magisterial work of scholarship:

Correspondance complète de Jean-Jacques Rousseau (1965–91), 50 vols, ed. R. A. Leigh, vols 1–15, Geneva: Institut et Musée Voltaire, 1965–71; vols 16–50, Banbury: The Voltaire Foundation, 1972–91 (abbreviated *CC*).

It has now replaced the earlier:

Correspondance générale de Jean-Jacques Rousseau (1924–34), 20 vols, ed. Théophile Dufour, Paris: Colin (abbreviated *CG*).

Rousseau's Texts (English translations)

The standard English translation is now:

Rousseau, Jean-Jacques (1990–), *Collected Writings*, 11 volumes to date, series eds Roger D. Masters and Christopher Kelly, various translators, Hanover, NH: University Press of New England (abbreviated *CW*).

The *Emile* has not yet appeared in the *Collected Writings*. The best English translation is:

Rousseau, Jean-Jacques (1979), *Emile, or on Education*, trans. Allan Bloom, New York: Basic Books (abbreviated *Em*).

Meanwhile, Victor Gourevitch has produced a series of excellent translations for Cambridge University Press.

Collections of Essays

Cranston, Maurice and Peters, Richard S. (eds) (1972), *Hobbes and Rousseau: A Collection of Critical Essays*, Garden City, NY: Anchor Books.
Riley, Patrick (ed.) (2001), *Cambridge Companion to Rousseau*, Cambridge: Cambridge University Press.
Scott, John T. (ed.) (2005), *Jean-Jacques Rousseau: Critical Assessments of Leading Political Philosophers*, 4 vols, London: Routledge.

This collection contains a vast number of essays, including some which have been translated into English for the first time.

Wokler, Robert (ed.) (1995), *Rousseau and Liberty*, Manchester: Manchester University Press.

Glossaries-cum-Encyclopaedias

Dent, N.J.H. (1992), *A Rousseau Dictionary*, Oxford: Blackwell (contains one of the best bibliographies available).
Eigeldinger, Frédéric S. and Trousson, Raymond (eds) (2001), *Dictionnaire de Jean-Jacques Rousseau*, Paris: Champion (first published 1996).

Biographies

There are two great twentieth-century biographies. The first is:

Guéhenno, Jean (1966), *Jean-Jacques Rousseau*, trans. J. and D. Weightman, London: Routledge and Kegan Paul (first published 1962).

The Weightmans' sensitive translation brings out the passion and commitment of an author who identified with his subject, while maintaining a healthy scepticism about the accuracy of the main source of his information, Jean-Jacques' own voluminous autobiographical writings.

Guéhenno was one of the most admirable figures of the intellectual resistance movement during the Second World War. After the liberation he completed the two volumes of the biography, which were published in 1948 and 1952 respectively.

Cranston, Maurice (1983), *Jean-Jacques: Early Life and Work of Jean-Jacques Rousseau, 1712–1754*, London: Allen Lane.
Cranston, Maurice (1991), *The Noble Savage: Jean-Jacques Rousseau, 1754–1762*, London: Allen Lane.
Cranston, Maurice (1997), *The Solitary Self: Jean-Jacques Rousseau in Exile and Adversity*, London: Allen Lane.

Sadly the third and final volume of Cranston's biography was left uncompleted at his death, although it has been edited and brought to press by Stanford Lakoff. Stylistically, Cranston's work stands in marked contrast to Guéhenno's. Where Cranston is meticulous in attributing his every claim to a precise page and sentence in the sources, Guéhenno's narrative flows unimpeded, without pausing for references. Yet the two biographies are complementary, and both are immensely enjoyable.

A Micro-masterpiece

Finally, if I were to recommend just one book to beginners and old hands alike, it would be:

Wokler, Robert (2001), *Rousseau: A Very Short Introduction*, Oxford: Oxford University Press.

This tiny volume is filled with wit, erudition and illumination. It also contains exquisite illustrations, many from the author's own collection.

Voyage intérieur

Two outstanding works which combine biography, psychoanalysis and philosophical insights are:

Gauthier, David (2006), *Rousseau: The Sentiment of Existence*, Cambridge: Cambridge University Press.
Starobinski, Jean (1970), *Jean-Jacques Rousseau: La transparence et l'obstacle*, Paris: Gallimard (translated by Arthur Goldhammer as *Transparency and Obstruction*, Chicago: University of Chicago Press, 1988).

Amour-propre *and the* Emile

On this key topic, Nicholas Dent has transformed the landscape of Rousseau scholarship:

Dent, N.J.H. (1988), *Rousseau: An Introduction to his Psychological, Social and Political Theory*, Oxford: Blackwell.
Dent, Nicholas (2005), *Rousseau*, London: Routledge.

Rousseau in Context

Rousseau has been depicted as the heir to, and ancestor of, countless other philosophers and philosophies. From this plethora of scholarship, the following titles can be recommended:

Cassirer, Ernst (1954), *The Question of Jean-Jacques Rousseau*, trans. Peter Gay, New York: Columbia University Press (original German edition, 1932).

Cassirer, Ernst (1963), *Rousseau, Kant and Goethe*, trans. J. Gutmann, P. O. Kristeller and J. H. Randall, introduction by Peter Gay, New York: Harper & Row (first published 1945 by Princeton University Press).

Gouhier, Henri (1984), *Les méditations philosophiques de Jean-Jacques Rousseau*, Paris: Vrin.

Hulliung, Mark (1994), *The Autocritique of Enlightenment: Rousseau and the Philosophes*, Cambridge, MA: Harvard University Press.

Rousseau's Political and Social Thought in Toto

Derathé, Robert (1988), *Jean-Jacques Rousseau et la science politique de son temps*, Paris: Vrin (first published in 1950) (French scholarship of the highest order).

Masters, Roger (1968), *The Political Philosophy of Rousseau*, Princeton, NJ: Princeton University Press (heir to Leo Strauss, doyen of US political theory and master of the Rousseau corpus).

Masters, Roger (1972), 'The Structure of Rousseau's Political Thought', in Maurice Cranston and Richard S. Peters (eds), *Hobbes and Rousseau: A Collection of Critical Essays*, Garden City, NY: Anchor Books.

O'Hagan, Timothy (2003), *Rousseau* (Arguments of the Philosophers), London: Routledge (first published 1999). (An account of all the topics treated in this collection, and many more that lie beyond its remit.)

Monographs

The following monographs stand out in that each identifies with admirable clarity a fundamental dichotomy within Rousseau's political and social thought:

Baczko, Bronisław (1971), *Rousseau: solitude et communauté*, trans. from Polish by C. Brendhel-Lamhout, Paris: Mouton.

Goldschmidt, Victor (1983), *Anthropologie et politique: les principes du système de Rousseau*, Paris: Vrin.

Melzer, Arthur M. (1990), *The Natural Goodness of Man: On the System of Rousseau's Thought*, Chicago: University of Chicago Press. (One of the most influential works of modern American Rousseau scholarship.)

Shklar, Judith (1969), *Men and Citizens: A Study of Rousseau's Social Theory*, Cambridge: Cambridge: Cambridge University Press.

General Will, Totalitarianism

The classic statement of 'liberal' disquiet with Rousseau's political thought is to be found in:

Berlin, Isaiah (2002), 'Rousseau', in *Freedom and its Betrayal*, ed. Henry Hardy, London: Chatto & Windus. (Lecture first delivered on the BBC Third Programme in 1952. An early, clear statement of Berlin's critique.)

Constant, Benjamin (1997), 'De la liberté des anciens comparée avec celle des modernes' (1819), in *Œuvres politiques*, ed. M. Gauchet, Paris: Gallimard (trans. by B. Fontana in B. Constant, *Political Writings*, Cambridge: Cambridge University Press, 1988).

Crocker, Lester G. (1968), *Rousseau's Social Contract: An Interpretive Essay*, Cleveland, OH: Press of Case Western Reserve University.

Waldron, Jeremy (1989), 'Rights and Majorities: Rousseau Revisited', in J.W. Chapman and A. Wertheimer (eds), *Majorities and Minorities*, New York: NYU Press (*Nomos*, **32**), pp. 44–75 (incisive and wide-ranging essay).

On the first two *Discourses* the following papers combine deep scholarship with philosophical insight:

First Discourse

Hope Mason, John (1987), 'Reading Rousseau's *First Discourse*', in *Studies on Voltaire and the Eighteenth Century*, **249**, pp. 251–66.

Second Discourse

Hobson, Marian (1992), '"Nexus effectivus" and "nexus causalis" in the *Inégalité* and in the *Essai sur l'origine des langues*', in M. Hobson, J. T. A. Leigh and R. Wokler (eds), *Rousseau and the Eighteenth Century: Essays in Memory of R. A. Leigh*, Oxford: The Voltaire Foundation, pp. 225–50.

Wokler, Robert (1978), 'Perfectible Apes in Decadent Cultures: Rousseau's Anthropology Revisited', *Daedalus*, **107** (3), pp. 107–34.

On the *Social Contract* the most recent introduction to the text is:

Bertram, Christopher (2004), *Rousseau and the Social Contract*, London: Routledge.

Part I
The Critique of Progress and the Speculative Anthropology: Rousseau's First Two *Discourses*

[1]

ROUSSEAU ON THE ARTS AND SCIENCES *

VICTOR GOUREVITCH

ROUSSEAU consistently argued that the arts and sciences tend to corrupt morals (*moeurs, Sitten*) and that they are at odds with the requirements for a free and just political society.

The issue is not what the arts and sciences may be in themselves but what role they play in the public life, or what the relations are between what we now call "culture" and political society. Rousseau considers this problem from the perspective of a plain man who knows nothing and yet esteems himself none the less for it, a member of a political community who, as such, shares its concerns and aspirations (*First Disc.* iii,5,30; *à d'Alembert* 126).† That is the "natural" perspective of man in society (*Emile* iv,468f,509), just as the perspective of man in society is "natural" once political societies are established. Men are, after all, not free to choose whether to live in political society and to submit to the inexorable logic of social relations (*Inégalité* (n ix), iii,207f). That is why, even if man is not by nature a political animal—indeed especially if he is not —the political problem assumes precedence and defines the horizon within which all other problems must be viewed. Thus Rousseau clearly also considers the problem of culture from the enlarged perspective of a man who sees beyond his own society and who has

* To be presented in an APA symposium of the same title, December 28, 1972. Commentators will be Thomas Scanlon and Judith Shklar; their comments are not available at this time.

† All references to the works contained in the four volumes of the *Oeuvres Complètes* so far published under the general editorship of B. Gagnebin and M. Raymont (Paris: Pléiade, 1959–) are to that edition; roman numerals indicate the volume, arabic numerals the page; where larger works are divided into sections, these are indicated in parentheses immediately following the title of the work. References to the *Letter to d'Alembert* are to the edition of the *Contrat Social* and other writings (Paris: Garnier, 1962); to the *Essay on the Origin of Languages* in the critical edition by C. Porset (Bordeaux: Ducros, 1970); and to the *Letter to Mirabeau* in C. E. Vaughan, *J. J. Rousseau, The Political Writings* 2 vols. (2nd ed., Oxford: Blackwell, 1962). To save space, references and citations have been kept to a minimum and incorporated into the body of the text as much as possible.

given thought to the foundations of any political order *(First Disc.*
iii,3; *Préf. seconde lettre* iii,106). Political·society is based on men's
inability to satisfy their needs each by himself alone *(C.S.* (1,6) iii,
360). Since in this condition each seeks out others primarily to profit
from them and at their expense, what brings and holds men together is what divides them *(Geneva ms.* iii,282–289; *Inég.* iii,187–
194). All the political solutions that Rousseau criticizes and rejects
are attempts to police—and hence to perpetuate and even to
aggravate—this state of affairs instead of altering it. The central
political problem as he sees it is, therefore, to specify the conditions
that will establish or restore the balance between everyone's needs
and the resources he can command in a manner such that none can
—let alone must—satisfy his needs at the expense of another. In
the state of civil society where all depend on all, this can be
achieved only if man's activities and pursuits are constantly gauged
in terms of whether they contribute to the good of all without
injuring anyone. The most distinctive feature of the social contract,
as Rousseau conceives of it, is the moral and psychological change
every individual undergoes as he comes to conceive of himself as a
member of his political community; it is first and foremost a change
in men's relation to themselves. Hence its defining characteristic is
that it fosters habits and dispositions that enable men to live together without being divided between the dictates of private and
of public interest or of the individual and the general will. Rousseau's rejection of the Hobbesian and Lockean social contract goes
hand in hand with his rejection of the bourgeois in the name of
the citizen and of citizen virtue. For all intents and purposes citizen
virtue is one and the same as public spirit or patriotism. It consists not so much in the private pursuit of the private good of one's
fellows as in the public pursuit of the public good. Hence virtue,
which might appear to tighten the bonds of dependence on others
because it places one in the position of striving to do what others
need or wish, really loosens such bonds to a considerable extent,
because it places one in the position of doing what is good for
all. It is less concerned with persons and propriety than with the
quality of public life. It requires and develops vigor and greatness
of soul. Virtue so conceived does not erase the distinction between
the private and the public; instead it reduces as far as possible the
areas of conflict between them, that is to say, between what interest
dictates and justice requires. In a well-ordered civil society, in a
society of citizens, virtue is the perfection of morals. Rousseau's
thought on this point is perhaps best expressed by speaking of

morals as the middle term between the laws and virtue. Morals is not primarily a matter of individual actions; most people act well or decently most of the time. But even though we may, in any given case, have acted with good will, even though we may have attempted to avoid injuring anyone and succeeded in benefiting or at least dealing justly with those most immediately affected by what we happen to do, the more far-reaching effects of our actions may prove harmful not merely to some one person or other but to entire groups of people, as when, for example, the things we do are, viewed in a narrow compass, perfectly fair, decent, and correct, and yet establish or perpetuate practices or institutions that are unjust *(Obs.* iii,50; *Frgs. politiques* iii,555; *Geneva ms.* iii,329f). These difficulties are not adequately overcome by the laws. The laws cannot possibly be sufficiently detailed to deal with all possible circumstances, and, indeed, to put the issue in terms of law would be to structure man's conduct altogether too much in terms of external criteria. The laws only channel men's actions and, for the most part, state only the minimum conditions of men's living together. Nor are these difficulties adequately overcome by generalizing the maxims of our actions, that is to say, by invoking the general will, because the problem to which Rousseau is addressing himself here is one of establishing routines, habits, and social perceptions rather than reasoned judgments about the relations between any given action and the well-being of the community or even mankind as a whole. Wills and dispositions, morals, are fashioned by authoritative traditions, practices, and beliefs, in short by public opinion. It is through opinion that societies typically guide and instruct us about what they praise, honor, reward—and thus foster —or blame, censure, condemn—and thus discourage—not only as regards specific kinds of actions, but as regards ways of life and types of character. Morals are the laws that are "inscribed neither on marble nor on brass, but in the hearts of the citizens . . . a dimension ignored by our political thinkers but on which depends the success of all others" *(C.S.* (ii,12) iii,394; cf. *Poland* iii,955). That is why politics cannot but be concerned with morals and why political justice can never be solely procedural or a virtue of institutions alone. That is also why morals in the sense in which Rousseau is concerned with them are far less a matter of cultivated reason than of sound opinion and good taste.

II

In a society where culture enjoys considerable esteem, where developments in the arts are followed with interest by large numbers of persons in positions of prestige and authority, where sophistication and taste are prized and manners polished to the point of artful naturalness, men feel required either to possess these accomplishments or to pretend that they do. The slavish adherence to the dictates of "the art of pleasing reduced to principles" brings about a "vile and deceiving uniformity" of manners and tastes. No one dares show himself for what he is, and, in the process, individuality, spontaneity, sincerity, true friendships—and enmities—are sacrified. All the contrasts Rousseau draws in this connection: between the gracious and the boorish, city and farm, civilized nations and barbarians, Athens and Sparta, are, of course, not intended to establish that to be uncouth or laconic is to have good morals or to be virtuous, but to show rather that, contrary to the dominant belief of enlightened opinion, the absence of culture is perfectly compatible with even the most common criteria of moral and political excellence, freedom, and empire; and that, again contrary to the dominant belief of enlightened opinion, a high premium on culture is not compatible with the preservation of freedom and empire, let alone with justice. He considers this relationship to be as binding as any law of nature. Manners, taste, sophistication contribute nothing to the fulfillment of a society's needs or aspirations; on the contrary, they obstruct it. The greater the rewards for useless occupations, the smaller are those for occupations that are useful, and, since men are drawn to what promises rewards, society as a whole is the loser (*Emile* (III) IV,456f, *Inég.* (n IX), III,206). It is not merely that someone who might have made a decent craftsman becomes, instead, an indifferent poetaster, nor that the literary and artistic life in all of its forms unfits men for hardships, sacrifice, and valor. These are but symptoms of a deeper and more pervasive injury done to opinion and to morals inasmuch as the care and concern for the agreeable—which is ultimately private—crowds out the care and concern for the useful or the public good (*Dernière Réponse* III,74).

The aim of the arts is to please and of artists to be applauded (*First Disc.* III,21; *Dernière Réponse* III,73f, *à d'Alembert* 135,143). Since we find pleasing what conforms to our tastes, artists must appeal to them or fail. Allowing for individual differences, most people who exercise independent judgment tend to agree in matters of taste, that is to say, about what is and what is not agreeable, beautiful or fitting, when they are considering objects that do not directly affect their well-being. Perceptions of taste are so much influenced by experience and opinion and hence so closely related to morals that Rousseau sometimes uses the terms interchangeably. Admittedly, good taste is not the same as good morals, nor are they always found together; but whenever morals are corrupt, so is taste. In societies where judgments are under the sway of public opinion and private interests, people cease to trust their taste and defer, instead, to what is approved by those who are supposed to know better: the great, the rich, the artists. For the great and the rich, art is largely a means to gratify vanity and the desire for ostentation; for the artists to achieve status and wealth by flattering their patrons' and their public's passions (*Emile* (IV) IV,671–677; *Lang.* (XV),163–167; *à d'Alembert* 136n 2). Thus the arts are both an effect and a cause of luxury. Indeed, a taste for the arts is always found together with a taste for luxury, and a taste for luxury is commonly accompanied by a taste for the arts (*First Disc.* III,19; *Observations* III,49f, *Dernière Réponse* III,74). Rich and poor being relative notions, great disparities of wealth inevitably engender feelings of deprivation and envy in those who have less, and this knowledge is the source of the greatest pleasure that those who have more derive from their wealth (*Inég.* III,175f,189). In this way luxury and the arts corrupt rich and poor alike (*Observations* III,51). At the same time the artists, being dependent on their patrons and their public, corrupt their tastes and hence their morals. For in order to keep the interest of their audiences alive they will have to be constantly either more precious or more outrageous. Rousseau charges that they are both and that under cover of ever subtler refinements they become increasingly shocking (*First Disc.* III,21f,28, *Dernière Réponse* III,73n 2). As the gulf between manners and morals widens and the public grows distracted by nuances and subtleties, men lose the capacity and the will to deal with great objects greatly. "It is not possible for minds debased with endless futile cares ever to rise to something great; and even if they had the required strength, they would lack the courage" (*First Disc.* III,20; cf. *à Grimm* III,64). Petty care make for petty souls, and petty souls are fit for nothing but servitude (*First Disc.* III,7n,29; *N.H.* (I,12) II,59; *Narcisse* II,967f).

Yet the arts are said to enlarge and ennoble by exhibiting grand models and purging the baser passions. Rousseau discusses theater in greater detail than any of the other arts because he judges it—as we might the movies or television—to be the most completely absorbing of the arts (*Lang.* 35, *à d'Alembert* 135). He agrees with Aristotle that tragedy both arouses and purges pity. But he is not primarily concerned with classical drama, and he places an altogether different estimate on pity than did the ancients. Besides, nowadays even an educated audience is seldom deeply moved by the performance of an ancient play. As for modern tragedies, we do not leave them feeling more intransigent toward transgression and hardened in the face of danger than we did when we came in. We leave them having wept at the sham suffering of imaginary characters, satisfied with ourselves at this proof of our humanity, and purged, if at all, of any urge to alleviate the real suffering around us (à d'Alembert 140f,152,137). Nor does comedy elevate by arousing us to hate what is mean and vicious. Comedy merely mocks such things, making them appear ridiculous and unseemly. Comedy is a school of manners, not of morals (à d'Alembert 142). In any event, virtue rarely triumphs on stage, and when we see transgression punished we are often more deeply moved by the grandeur or the horror of the crimes committed than by the retribution visited upon them. Besides, it is a mistake to judge the effect of a play by its outcome. By and large the two are entirely independent (à d'Alembert 166). The deepest and most lasting impressions are made on us by villains and villainies, especially when we discover a secret sympathy or affinity with them, and their punishment merely permits us to indulge that fascination without shame or guilt (à d'Alembert 149,159). At best most plays flatter us into feeling that we possess all the virtues we lack (*Lang.* 35n, *à d'Alembert* 142f).

If the arts merely gratify and confirm an audience's ruling moral tastes and opinions and if artists are the slaves of their public, it would seem to follow that the arts are good for societies with good morals and bad for societies whose morals are bad (à d'Alembert 137). But the arts not only affect men by what they portray; they distract them from other pursuits, the good from attending to the round of their duties, to their families and their friends, the wicked from their mischief. In this light, it would seem that the arts are bad for good societies and good for bad ones (à Alembert 133,168f; *Narcisse* ii,972f). The arguments for and against appear to cancel each other, and art to be a matter of indifference in a society. But Rousseau does not leave it at that. He seeks a way to preserve the benefits and avoid the drawbacks of the arts. In societies with corrupt morals the arts, by keeping alive a public pretense and show of virtue and by maintaining standards of propriety, may shame men into at least the semblance of decency; better to live among knaves than bandits (*Narcisse* ii,972). Certainly the arts cannot restore good morals, nor is it possible to arrest their corruption. Rousseau doubts that anything can, "short of a great revolution almost as much to be feared as the evil it might cure" *(Observations* iii,56). But it may be possible to slow its progress and to reach a few individuals even if one cannot affect a whole society. Addiction to the arts develops a constant craving for novelty. Jaded tastes are apt to find portrayals of the naive and natural more startling than the most outrageous excesses *(à d'Alembert* 136). An artist who combines talent and humanity may here find a way to be both pleasing and useful by awakening a desire for excellence in his audience *(à d'Alembert* 126; *N.H.* (2nd Pref.) ii,17,20 (ii,18), ii,261; (ii,21) ii,277). Certainly these considerations consistently guided Rousseau in his own extraordinarily sophisticated subversions of sophistication.[1]

The closest he comes to a suggestion about the role the arts might play in a society with good morals is the recommendation that Geneva, instead of introducing a permanent theater, establish public festivals in which all would participate and which would provide joyous occasions on which everyone is both actor and spectator, fully himself and fully a member of the community, where all class distinctions are forgotten and all do and hold everything in common *(à d'Alembert* 225f). In reading his evocation of these festivals one cannot help being reminded both of the festivals he, on a different occasion, had called "the cradles of society" *(Lang.* (ix),123; cf. *Inég.* iii,169,171) and of the citizen in the precise and emphatic sense he attaches to that term, who is both sovereign and subject. The festivals he recommends as the appropriate art for a good society are as much the dramatic equivalents of the just political order as they are the political equivalents of a privileged natural condition. Festivals allow the communal spirit to express itself. But they could not impart a communal spirit to a political society whose laws and morals do not also embody it. Festivals can only confirm citizenship where it exists; they cannot make citizens (cf. also *Poland* iii,955,962f).

III

Rousseau's discussion of the sciences deals primarily with philosophy and philosophers and, more briefly, with intellectuals and with scholars. His treatment of these is, on the whole, more modulated

[1] Upon being refused his request for a copy of Rousseau's *Confessions* by the prison authorities, the Marquis de Sade is said to have told them: "Rousseau may be a dangerous writer for massive bigots like yourselves, but . . . for me he is an excellent author. Jean-Jacques is for me what an *Imitation of Jesus Christ* is for you." The incident is reported by R. Barthes, *Sade, Fourier, Loyola* (Paris: Seuil, 1971), p. 185.

than is his treatment of art and artists. The major difference between the arts and the sciences, when they are viewed in the political context, is that the arts are essentially public, whereas philosophy, science, and scholarship are more restricted in their immediate appeal. They are certainly less dependent on general applause than are the arts. Indeed it makes sense to distinguish between those who pursue philosophy, science, or scholarship primarily for the acclaim attendant upon a reputation for them and those who pursue them primarily for their own sakes. It makes less sense, if it makes any sense at all, to draw such a distinction in the case of the arts *(Narcisse* ii,967f). This basic distinction between the arts and the sciences guides Rousseau's critique of them and his proposals for reform. While he calls for arts that are more popular, he calls for a conception of science that is decisively less popular.

In speaking of philosophy and philosophers Rousseau criticizes more severely and also praises more generously than he ever does in speaking of the arts. He quotes Socrates and Montaigne with approval. He calls Bacon "perhaps the greatest philosopher" and refers to him, Descartes, and Newton as "teachers of mankind." He exhorts princes to enlist the aid of such men in the conduct of public affairs, although only a few pages earlier he had raised questions about the value of Descartes's as well as of Newton's physics. He charges the teachings of Leucippus and Diagoras with impiety and invites men to reject "the dangerous dreams" of Hobbes, and Spinoza *(First Disc.* iii,13,9n,11n,24n,29,18,27f). To reconcile these judgments they must, as we said, be viewed from the vantage points from which Rousseau arrives at them: the citizen of a Republic who knows nothing, esteems himself none the less for it, and speaks out on behalf of virtue against vain knowledge; and a man free of the prejudices of his society and of his age whose ambition it is to live beyond his century *(First Disc.* iii,3,17n). In other words he assumes the stance of a citizen-philosopher or of a civil philosopher. The philosophers whose opinions he endorses Socrates and Montaigne, take a similar stance. They reconciled knowledge of ignorance with the rule that one ought to abide by the laws and morals of one's country (Xenophon, *Mem.* I,ii,64; cf. *Frg. sur la révélation* iv,1053; Montaigne, *Essais* ii,12; cf. the first maxim of the "provisional" morality in Descartes, *Discourse on Method* iii), and although they were alive to the tension between the requirements for a just and stable political order on the one hand, and the requirements of truth, comprehensiveness, and clarity on the other, or between the requirements of virtue or justice and the requirements of knowledge, they satisfied the claims of citizenship in their conduct and in their teaching. Yet as citizens they fell short. When compared to Cato or to Cicero they are seen to have remained essentially private persons (*Econ. Pol.* III, 255; *Héros* II,1263; *First Disc.* III,9n; cf. *Emile* (IV) IV,598f). Indeed, philosophy loosens one's attachment to those with whom one lives, and the philosopher tends to forsake his own community for the more dispersed and general community of like-minded inquirers (*Inég.* III,156,133,213; *à Philopolis* III,234). Inquiry becomes an end in itself and in itself pleasant and thus diverts one from attending to what is useful or required. "The contemplative life disgusts one with action (*Dialogues* I,822; *Narcisse* II,967). Philosophy fosters cosmopolitanism.

In contrast to Socrates or Montaigne or Cicero, Leucippus, Hobbes, and Spinoza, as well as Bacon, Descartes, and Newton appear to press their inquiries beyond the confines of ordinary experience and discourse. They come closer to being what Hume called "accurate and abstruse" philosophers. They are also natural rather than civil philosophers. Now, in praise of those he calls "the teachers of mankind," Rousseau says that they were not themselves in need of teachers; they owed their achievements to their genius and their own endeavours alone, and did not depend for their insights and discoveries on public support of scientific inquiry or on a climate of opinion favorable to it. But, insofar as this can be said of them, it can be said with as much justice of Leucippus, the teacher of Democritus, of Hobbes, or of Spinoza. It would seem, then, that what sets the teachers of mankind apart is that, although at least some of their inquiries may lead to results that are very much at odds with ordinary experience, they are also far removed from ordinary concerns. Their studies and results do not appear to bear directly on men's moral and political opinions or conduct. They do not directly affect morals, for good or ill. But in order to pursue their inquiries they, like all philosophers, must enjoy leisure. They can, therefore, not possibly take an active part in the common enterprise. As such they, once again like all philosophers, are, from the point of view of the citizen, useless; hence harmful. For the citizen does not acknowledge the distinction between leisure and idleness; "in politics as in ethics, not to do good is a great evil; and every useless citizen may be regarded as a pernicious person" (*First Disc.* III,18). A well-ordered society will, therefore, not reward even great and disinterested men

who pursue inquiries into matters remote from the practical concerns and affairs of men. But only a badly ordered society will
ignore them. Being men of large views, they are free of vulgar
yearnings for approbation or gain; but they are not insensitive
to honor. A well-ordered society will know how to appeal to their
desire for worthy honor by calling upon them to contribute to the
well-being of their people.

It may seem surprising to have Rousseau look for advisers to
princes among philosophers who devote themselves primarily to
physics and metaphysics rather than to look for them among those
who strive to combine such inquiries with studies of morals and
politics and even take pains to instruct political men, as Hobbes
and Spinoza, for example, did. Such men seem to have more in
common with Socrates and Montaigne than with Descartes and
Newton. Rousseau's judgment of them seems to be guided by different considerations, however. The abstruse researches of the
teachers of mankind may, from the point of view of the citizen, be
useless because far removed from what affects the well-being of his
society; but they are, for that very reason, also comparatively
innocuous. The remoteness of their inquiries from the objects of
ordinary concern leaves the realm of morals, opinions, customs,
the political realm in short, comparatively untroubled. That is the
point of contact between them and the civil philosophers who,
though presumably for different reasons, also do not seek to
change the character of the political realm. In contrast, men like
Hobbes and Spinoza presumably do seek to effect such a change
by assigning to philosophy a central role in the economy of civil
society. They presumably attempted to place civil society on a
strictly rational basis. But society cannot rest on reason or insight
(*C.S.* (ii,7) iii,383), not because virtue and knowledge are, in the
last analysis, incompatible, but because it is given only to a very
few to combine them. Men like Socrates, who can attain virtue by
reason alone, are rare exceptions (*Inég.* iii,156). The majority of
men acquire virtue, the fiber and vigor of soul that enable one to
subject self-interest to considerations of the common good, by
being brought up to be good citizens of a good civil society, to be
patriots (*Geneva ms.* iii,286f,328f; cf. *Emile* (v) iv,858–860). Rousseau is, of course, well aware that arguments for public enlightenment may be based on considerations about the public good. The
demands of civic virtue may be thought too restrictive of the desire
for commodious living or of private freedoms to serve as the realistic fundations of a just and stable civil order. Such reflections

may lead to a search for ways to minimize or to eliminate altogether the need for an austere civil virtue by devising structures and institutions that will channel men's self-interested actions into publicly innocuous or even profitable outcomes. The model for such arguments is the eventually successful attempt to replace political by economic considerations. "The ancient political thinkers forever spoke of morals and virtue; ours speak only of commerce and money." [2] To tell people that private vice furthers public virtue, encourages private vice; "what will become of virtue once men are obliged to get rich at any price?" To claim that there is no need to heed the public interest because no conflict can arise between it and one's self-interest is to play into the hands of those whom the laws favor, that is to say of the rich (*C.S.* (1,9) III 367n, *Emile* (IV), IV 524n; cf. *on Helvétius* IV,1130; *Inég.* (n IX) III,202–208). To add that the public interest should be given precedence if and when conflicts do arise is of no avail because by then men's habits are formed, their thought has not been exercised in that direction, and, if they should discover what they ought to do, they are likely to be too weak-willed to act on their judgment *(Geneva ms.* III,284f). The attempt to rationalize politics by replacing patriotism with calculations of enlightened self-interest succeeds only in removing all curbs on men's passions and, in particular, frees the powerful and the rich to engage in the unbridled pursuit of their self-interest. The only alternative to the most austere democracy is the most ruthless Hobbesism (*à Mirabeau,* Vaughan II,161; cf. *Guerre* III,511).

Not incidentally, Leucippus, Hobbes, and Spinoza were—or were generally thought to be—materialists and atheists. Rousseau consistently equates philosophy with atheism. He does not restrict this judgment to the *philosophes* of his day, but includes in it the entire tradition from Pythagoras to our own time (*First Disc.* III,3,9; *Obs.* III,44,48; *Emile* (Sav.Vic.) IV,643; *à Voltaire* IV,634; *à Francquières* IV,1135,1137,1138; on philosophical esotericism as atheism: *Obs.*

---

[2] Further: "One will tell you that in some places a man is worth what he would be sold for in Algiers; another, pursuing this calculation, will find countries where a man is worth nothing, and others still will find one where he is worth less than nothing," *First Disc.* III,19f; cf. Montesquieu, *Esprit* III,3; XXIII,17; and "The *value,* or WORTH of a man is, as of all other things, his price; that is, so much as he would be given for the use of his power: and therefore is not absolute, but a thing dependent on the need and judgment of another. . . . And as in other things, so in men, not the seller, but the buyer determines the price. For let a man, as most men do, rate themselves at the highest rate they can; yet their true value is no more than it is esteemed by others" (Hobbes, *Leviathan,* ch. 10); see also B. Constant, *Conquête et usurpation* II,6.

III,46n; *Dialogues* I,695; *Rêveries* (3) I,1022). Now Rousseau regarded atheism as incompatible with a stable political order and
with citizen virtue *(Inég.* III,186; *C.S.* (II,7) III,383, (IV,8) III,467f; *à
d'Alembert* 201n), because men are ruled not by reason but by
opinion, pleasure, and passion, by the prospect of rewards and
punishments much more than by the knowledge of their good.
The abandonment of religious beliefs deprives the just and unfortunate of an innocent hope and removes a salutary restraint on
the powerful and privileged. "Philosopher, your moral laws are
excellent, but pray show me their sanction" *(Emile* (IV)IV,635n; cf.
Dialogues I,968–972). Yet religious beliefs, while they lend an indispensable support to moral laws, at the same time fan fanaticism
and, under the banner of God and righteousness, lead to excesses.
Rousseau nevertheless holds that, on balance, real and passionate
convictions are preferable to the kind of prudence and self-seeking fostered by a so-called philosophic spirit *(Lang.* 135,137). It is
better to be led to excess out of conviction about the good than
to be moderate out of indifference for it *(C.S.* (III,9) III,420n). In
his political defense of religion, i.e., his teaching regarding civil
religion, he does, however, make every effort to mitigate the worst
features of what used to be called "enthusiasm." The civil religion
is, of course, not Christianity. On the contrary. His critique of
philosophy in essential respects overlaps with his critique of
Christianity. Both are universal; both cause men to become detached from the cares for this world. "True Christians are made to
be slaves" *(C.S.* (IV,8) IV,467), since the Christian's loyalty is to
another realm. Still, it would seem that philosophy is less at odds
with the claims of citizenship than is Christianity, for, whereas
philosophy leads to detachment, Christianity divides men's alle-
giances *(Inég.* (Ep.Ded.) III,119; *C.S.* (IV,8) III,463).

Rousseau does not criticize the "dangerous reveries" of Hobbes,
Spinoza or of others he sometimes adds to their list (e.g., *Narcisse*
I,965) because they may ultimately have been wrong—anymore
than he regards those he calls the teachers of mankind to have been
right—nor because they are wicked or lacking in civic spirit, but
because their teachings are bound to be misused and are thus
bound to injure the prospects for a free and just, or at least a
decent political order.[3] It is perfectly clear that the politics he ex-

---

[3] Hobbes was "one of the finest geniuses who ever lived: *(Guerre* III,611); he
"correctly saw the defect of all modern definitions of natural right," namely that
natural right cannot be based on reason *(Inég.* III,153,124f); he alone of all
Christian writers saw the need to "re-unite the two heads of the eagle," namely
to subordinate the authority of the Church to the civil authority; hence "It is

pects from the teachers of mankind, if they should ever be called to the councils of princes, will be guided by the clear awareness of difference between the requirements of science and the requirements of civil society and will emphatically not be a politics "deduced" or derived from their physics or metaphysics. It is not qua philosophers that they should be rulers or citizens; rather, they may be tolerated as philosophers on condition of remaining fully mindful of the requirements of citizenship. If they do, it will be to the advantage of the political community to have them, as it were, pay for the privilege of pursuing their private good by taking a large share of responsibility in the pursuit of the common good (cf. Plato, *Republic* 591D–521B).

Rousseau's critique of philosophy is, then, a critique not of this or that doctrine, but of the conception of the place of philosophy or science in the public realm that is typically associated with enlightenment. Whereas it scarcely matters whether philosophers are materialists, atheists, or cosmopolites, it greatly matters what the public believes and does once such views are disseminated and, more generally, once philosophy or science comes to enjoy wide public credit. The teachers of mankind who had no need of teachers, the rare men who can attain virtue by their own reason alone or preserve it as they acquire knowledge, cannot be our models because the overwhelming majority of men do not seek knowledge disinterestedly and their morals are a matter of mindless habit. In most respects we do not exercise independent judgment but are guided in what we believe and do by the opinions of our society; "opinions are transmitted by opinions, not by reason, and whoever yields to another's reasoning, which is rare enough, does so by prejudice, authority, affection, laziness; rarely, perhaps never, by his own judgment" (*à Francquières* IV,1134; cf. *à d'Alembert* 176). Reason is a creature of the passions, and for the most part it only exacerbates them (*Inég.* III,143); knowledge or philosophy as commonly understood become their instruments rather than their rulers and profit the wicked far more than the good (*Dernière Réponse* III,73).

---

not so much what is awful and false as what is correct and true in his politics that has made it so odious" (*C.S.* (IV,8) III,463); but he failed to see that "the cause that prevents savages from using their reason . . . at the same time prevents them from misusing their faculties" (*Inég.* III,154), and the resulting teaching about the relations between reason and the passions plays into the hands of despotism and a passively obedient citizenry (*Guerre* III,611). On Spinoza, cf. especially *à Beaumont* IV,931. Note, in this context, Rousseau's praise of *The Prince*, "the book of Republicans (*C.S.* (III,6) III,409; cf. Spinoza, *Tract. Pol.* v,7); to my knowledge Rousseau's frequent references to Machiavelli are invariably approving.

Indeed, most of those who profess a devotion to knowledge would lose all interest in its pursuit if they found themselves in a setting where it enjoyed no credit and served no useful purpose. Precisely because it is so largely an instrument—and a cause—of vanity, philosophy leads to detachment from the communal cares, weakens fellow feeling, blunts courage, and makes for indifference to virtue and vice alike. If philosophy is taken to consist in justifying and demonstrating, the spirit of philosophy at large in a society will foster and reward ingenuity in argument more than good deeds (*First Disc.* III,12f,24,25,30; *Dernière Réponse* III,73,83; cf. *Lettres morales* (2) IV,1090). If philosophy is understood to consist in challenging and questioning what is generally accepted, then the spirit of philosophy will move men to show that they are not duped by the common beliefs rather than to try to discover what is the case. "Some men are nowadays free-thinkers and philosophers who, with as much reason, would have been but fanatics at the time of the League"; "not that they at bottom hate virtue or our dogmas; their enemy is public opinion and all it would take to bring them back to the feet of the altars is to banish them among atheists" (*First Disc.* III,3,19; cf. *Emile* (IV), IV,569). More generally, the spirit of philosophy leads to the denial of whatever cannot be explained and thus inevitably engenders dogmatism (*Emile* (IV) IV,59n; *N.H.* (V,3) II,565). It might be objected that knowledge is progressive, that today's truths are tomorrow's errors, or at least that they will be superseded by tomorrow's truths, that the awareness of this fact will restrain people from unreservedly embracing any claim to the truth and that, indeed, the greatest merit of public enlightenment is that it immunizes against the ever-present threat of dogmatism. It is at the very least an open question whether experience bears out such sanguine claims and whether, even if it did, a widespread and pervasive skepticism about the bases of our moral and political life is, in the long run, compatible with a stable, just, and free society. Rousseau, in any event, denies both contentions. Except in the case of some few individuals it is not true that the more men learn, the more acutely do they become aware of their ignorance and hence the more moderate do they become in putting forward claims to knowledge (*First Disc.* III,18; *Obs.* III,41f). Once morals are corrupted and freedom lost, they cannot be restored. As for the belief in progress, it fails to take into account that men's capacities are comparatively narrow and unchanging, that any gains are balanced by equal losses, so that what we call progress is but the substitution of new prejudices for old (*à Mirabeau,*

Vaughan II,159, *Emile* (IV) IV,676). In fine, public enlightenment leads to a dogmatism far more stubborn than that of unenlightened opinion or prejudice precisely because it claims the authority of knowledge or science;⁴ it does not lead to public knowledge of ignorance. For "among the people to doubt is as rare as to be categorical is among true philosophers" (*Héros* II,1265).

Ignorance is preferable to the cultivation of knowledge, since that cultivation is likely to lead to more errors than truths—"surely there are more errors in the Academy of Sciences than in a whole nation of Hurons" (*Emile* (III) IV,483)—and these errors are more likely to prove harmful than the truths profitable. By ignorance Rousseau, of course, does not mean some universal *tabula rasa* nor, in spite of his occasionally hyperbolic praise of them, is he speaking about a condition to be found only among primitive peoples. Ignorance was the condition of all nations in their beginning, it remained that of Sparta throughout, of Russia until the reign of Peter the Great and beyond, of the Geneva in which Rousseau grew up, of Poland, Corsica. . . . It is, then, the condition of nations where philosophy or science, if they are pursued, are pursued by individuals and in private but do not become a required element in what that nation would regard as the proper education of a citizen, and where they are not especially rewarded as such by public opinion. Ignorance is compatible with virtue, but all learned nations have invariably been corrupt (*First Disc.* III,16; *Obs.* III,54n; *à Grimm* III,62; *Dernière Réponse* III,74–76,89). Rousseau recognizes the difficulties that surround any attempt to establish such very general propositions. But to shy away from the attempt and to refuse to try to reach a fair judgment about the

---

⁴ Consider in this connection the following reflections: "The implications of Marx's theory called for a proletarian movement. But the intellectual achievements of Marx's philosophy cannot provide without modifications an ideological basis for a political movement possessing organizational continuity and experiencing the normal ups and downs of political life. The vulgarization of Marx's theory thus becomes a necessary component in the make-up of those historical movements brought to life by Marx's own philosophical speculation and historical analysis. It is therefore more than a mere side effect of Marx's theory that the various Marxist movements, social democratic or communist, had to emancipate themselves from many of the most outstanding and most brilliant of Marx's intellectual achievements and replace them by simplified vulgarizations and a wholly uncritical reverence towards the founding fathers of the movement. Thus a popularizing emasculation of his theory went hand in hand with an idolatrous attitude towards a mythical image of the person of Marx. Kautsky and Bebel were guilty of this not less than Lenin and Stalin, though the methods of course differed. Marxist theory may thus be denied by the very historical processes he foresaw" [S. Avineri, *The Social and Political Thought of Karl Marx* (New York: Cambridge, 1968), p. 251].

morals of a people would leave us in the absurd position of not
being able to reach any politically significant conclusions about
different regimes and ways of life. "When one wants to study men
one must look around one; but to study man one must learn to cast
one's glance afar" (*Lang.* (VIII) 89; cf. *Obs.* III,53n; *Inég.* (n x) III,
212–214). In order to escape some of the objections to comparisons
between different peoples, Rousseau prefers, whenever possible, to
contrast early and late periods in a given nation's history: the
Greeks victorious at Troy and subjugated by Philip and Alexander, Athens at the time of Solon and Periclean Athens, Rome as
a Republic and under the Emperors (*First Disc.* III,10; *Dernière
Réponse* III,76). Further, in arguing that the corruption of morals
invariably goes hand in hand with the progress of the arts and
sciences, he is always careful to distinguish between nations and
individuals (*à Beaumont* IV,967). His thesis is that no nation has
ever successfully and over the long run combined good morals with
the culture of the arts and sciences. That is not to maintain that
ignorance in nations, or in individuals, is a guarantee of virtue
(*Obs.* III,54; *Dernière Réponse* III,78f), nor to deny that there may
always be individuals who are both learned or cultivated and virtuous (*First Disc.* III,29; *Obs.* III,39,52f,55; *à Grimm* III,60f; *Dernière
Réponse* III,72f; *Narcisse* II,970f). If it were not for the distinction
between the morals of a people and the morals of individuals,
Rousseau's thesis would, for all practical purposes, have been
refuted by being awarded an Academy Prize. As it is he was clearly
somewhat surprised and perhaps even slightly vexed by it (*First
Disc.* III,3). The same distinction comes into play whenever
Rousseau has to reply to the charge that he uses much learning
and art to attack learning and the arts (*Obs.* III,38f, *Narcisse* II,972–
974). Again, it is the distinction to which he appeals when he
maintains that it does not matter how many learned and cultivated
persons take issue with his argument, since they are interested
parties in the dispute (*à Grimm* III,61). On the other hand, those
who do agree with him and who, like himself, combine a love of
knowledge and of the arts (*à d'Alembert*, 229f,n) with an awareness of the danger they pose for morals and who are, therefore,
prepared to defend morals against what might seem to be their self-
interest, men who, in other words, are capable of freeing themselves of the authoritative opinions or prejudices of their societies
and to place their wisdom and their art in the service of the
public interest are "true" philosophers, scholars and artists (*First
Disc.* III,5; *Obs.* III,39; *Inég.* (n x) III,212f).

IV

The political critique of the arts and sciences is but a corollary of more comprehensive studies (*Préf. seconde lettre* III,106). Rousseau always regarded as his most important single teaching the doctrine of man's natural goodness, the view that man is by nature inclined to do his own good with the least possible harm to others (*Inég.* III,156) and that, therefore, most, if not all the evils men visit upon one another are the result of remediable political arrangements. The confirmation of this view of man's natural goodness, together with the account of its vicissitudes in the development of the race and of every individual, which he claims to have provided in the body of his work, is intended to establish both the fundamentally problematic character of any civil society and the conditions for as free and just a civil society as can be achieved, to establish, in other words, the relations between what he understands by natural right and by political right or between man and citizen. The fundamentally problematic character of civil society is most succinctly indicated by the thesis that it is conventional, that it rests, to a greater or lesser extent, on an irreducibly arbitrary or nonnatural foundation. The conventional foundation of a civil society that would combine freedom and justice is particularly precarious because freedom and justice require equality, and the equality of men in civil society is at odds with their irreducible natural inequality (*C.S.* (II,11) III,391; (I,9) III,367; *Inég.* III,131). In a condition where men depend on one another for the satisfaction of their needs, the ascendancy of some by virtue of their natural superiority increases the dependency of all the others. The function of civil society is to redress this imbalance. If, in the state of civil society, natural inequalities are permitted to earn authority in any of its forms which is not freely awarded by all for contributions to the common good, there results a combination of the worst features of the state of nature with the worst features of civil society. For in the state of civil society superiorities in strengths of mind or body soon become superiorities of power, privilege, and wealth that redound to the benefit of those who have at the expense of the rest, and thus the destruction of equality brings about the destruction of freedom and justice (*Inég.* III,174–176,186–190,193f; cf. *First Disc.* III,25; *Obs.* III,49f). The laws cannot, by themselves, keep in check the tendency of natural inequalities from asserting themselves. They cannot, in particular, control that alliance of talents, wealth, and power that manifests itself most seductively in a flourishing culture of the arts and sciences. Although the laws can do much to influence morals, only opinion can sustain them, just as only sound opinions and good morals, not the laws, make for the precision of discernment that enables a body of citizens to reward their fellows solely in proportion to their contribution to the common good, that is to say, always to judge according to the principles of distributive justice that inform a just and free political society.

VICTOR GOUREVITCH

Wesleyan University

Addenda 754a

References within the text:

p. 737, §2, l. 7: *OC*3.5, 30/*CW*2.4, 22; *OC*5.6/*CW*10. 255
  Ibid., §2, l. 8: *OC*4.468ff, 509/ *Em*.194ff, 225
  Ibid., §2, l. 12: *OC*3.207–08/*CW*3.79–80
p. 738, §2, ll. 1–2: *OC*3.3/*CW*2.3; *OC*3.6/*CW*2.184–85
  Ibid., §1, ll. 3–4: *OC*3.360/*CW*4.138
  Ibid., §1, ll. 6–7: *OC*3.282–89/*CW*4.77–82; *OC*3.187–94/*CW*3.62–67
p. 739, §1, l. 12: *OC*3.50/*CW*2.48–49; *OC*3.555/*CW*4.71; *OC*3.329ff/
  *CW*4.113ff
  Ibid., §1, l. 34: *OC*3.394/*CW*4.164–65; cf. *OC*3.955/*CW*11.170–71
p. 740, §1, ll. 25–26: *OC*4.456ff/.*Em*.185ff; *OC*3.206/*CW*3.78–79
  Ibid., §1, l. 33: *OC*3.74/*CW*2.112
  Ibid., §2, l. 2: *OC*3.21/*CW*2.15; *OC*3.73ff/*CW*2. 111ff; *OC*5.16–17, 25/*CW*10.
263, 270
p. 741, §1, ll. 10–11: *OC*4.671–77/*Em*.339–44; *OC*5.417–19/*CW*7.323–25;
  *OC*5.18 n.2/*CW*10.264 n.2
  Ibid., §1, ll. 14–15: *OC*3.19/*CW*2.14; *OC*3.49f/*CW*2. 48ff; *OC*3.74/
  *CW*2. 112
  Ibid., §1, l. 19: *OC*3.175ff, 189/*CW*3.52ff, 63
  Ibid., §1, ll. 20–21: *OC*3.51/*CW*2.49
  Ibid., §1, l. 27: *OC*3.21ff, 28/*CW*2.15ff, 20–21; *OC*3. 73 n. 2/*CW*2. 112 n. 1
  Ibid.,, §1, l. 33: *OC*3.20/*CW*2.15; cf. *OC*3.64/*CW*2.87–88
  Ibid., §1, l. 35: *OC*3. 7 n, 29/*CW*2.5 n, 21–22; *OC*2.59/*CW*6.47–48; *OC*2.967
ff/*CW*2. 192ff
  Ibid., §2, l. 5: *OC*5.377–78/*CW*7.291–92; *OC*5.16–17/*CW*10.263–64
p. 742, §1, l. 9: *OC*5.22/*CW*10.267ff; *OC* 5.35ff/*CW*10.278ff; *OC*
  5.19ff/*CW*10.265ff
  Ibid., §1, l. 12: *OC*5.24–25/*CW*10.269–70
  Ibid., §1, l. 18: *OC*5.50/*CW*10.290–91
  Ibid., §1, l. 22: *OC*5.32–33/*CW*10.275–56; *OC* 5.43/*CW*10.284–85
  Ibid., §1, ll. 23–24: *OC*5.378 n. 1/*CW*7.292 n. 1; *OC*5.24ff/*CW*10. 269ff
  Ibid., §2, ll. 4–5: *OC*5.19/*CW*10.265
  Ibid., §2, ll. 9–10: *OC*5.14–15/*CW*10.261–62; *OC*5.52ff/*CW*10.292ff;
  *OC*2.972f/*CW*2.196ff
  Ibid., §2, l. 17: *OC*2.972/*CW*2.196
p. 743, §1, l. 3: *OC*3.56/*CW*2.53
  Ibid., §1, ll. 7–8: *OC*5.18–19/*CW*10.264–65
  Ibid., §1, ll. 10–11: *OC*5.6–7/*CW*10.255–56; *OC*2.17, 20/*CW*6.11–12, 14;
  *OC*2.261/*CW*6.214; *OC*2.277/*CW*6.227
  Ibid., §2, l. 8: *OC*5.115ff/*CW*10.344ff
  Ibid., §2, l. 11: *OC*5.406/*CW*7.314; *OC*3. 169, 171/*CW*3.47, 49
  Ibid., §2, l. 20: *OC*3.955, 962ff/*CW*11.170–71, 176ff
p. 744, §1, l. 11: *OC*2.967ff/*CW*2.192ff
  Ibid., §2, l. 11: *OC*3.13, 9n, 11n, 24n, 29, 18, 27ff/*CW*2. 10, 7n, 9n, 18n.
2, 21, 13, 20ff
  Ibid., §2, ll. 17–18: *OC*3.3, 17n/*CW*2.3, 12n
  Ibid., §2, ll. 22–25: *OC*4.1053/–
p. 745, §1, ll. 5–6: *OC*3.255/*CW*3.151; *OC*2.1263/*CW*4.2; *OC*3.9n/*CW*2.7n;
  cf *OC*4.598ff/.289ff
  Ibid., §1, l. 10: *OC*3.156, 133, 213/*CW*3.37, 19–20, 85–86;
*OC*3.324/*CW*3.130
  Ibid., §1, l. 13: *OC*1.822/*CW*1.125; *OC*2.967/*CW*2.192–93
  Ibid., §2, l. 27: *OC*3.18/*CW*2.13

754 b

p. 746, §2, l. 23: *OC*3.383/*CW*4.156
  Ibid., §2, l. 26: *OC*3.156/*CW*3.38
  Ibid., §2, l. 30: *OC*3.286ff, 328ff/*CW*4.80ff, 112ff; cf. *OC*4.858–60/.473–75
p. 747, §1, ll. 13–15: *OC*3.367n/*CW*4.144n; *OC*4.524n/.236n; cf. *OC*4.1130/–;
  *OC*3.202–08/*CW*3.74–80
  Ibid., §1, ll. 19–20: *OC*3.284ff/*CW*4.78ff
  Ibid., §1, ll. 25–26: –/–; cf. *OC*3.611 (not 511)/*CW*11.63
pp. 747 –78, §2, ll. 5–7: *OC*3.3, 9/*CW*2.3, 7; *OC*3.44, 48/*CW*2.43–44, 47;
  *OC*4.643 (not 634)/*Em*.319–20; –/–; *OC*4.1135, 1137,
  1138/*CW*8.260–61, 262–63, 263–64; *OC*3.46n/*CW*2.45n; *OC*1.695/*CW*1.
  28–29; *OC*1.1022/*CW*8.26
p. 748, §1, ll. 3–4: *OC*3.186/*CW*3.61; *OC*3.383/*CW*4.156
*OC*3.467ff/*CW*4.221ff;
  *OC*5.89n/*CW*10.322 n. 2
  Ibid., §1, ll. 10–11: *OC*4.635n/.314n; cf. *OC*1.968–72/*CW*1.239–42
  Ibid., §1, l. 16: *OC*5.409–10/*CW*7.316–17
  Ibid., §1, l. 18: *OC*3.420n/*CW*4.185–86n
  Ibid., §1, l. 26: *OC*3.467/*CW*4.221
  Ibid., §1, l. 30: *OC*3.119/*CW*3.9–10; *OC*3.463/*CW*4.218–19
  §2, ll. 2–3: *OC*2.965 (not *OC*1)/*CW*2.191
p. 749, §2, l. 18: *OC*4.1134/*CW*8.259; cf. *OC*5.61–62/*CW*10.300
  Ibid., §2, l. 20: *OC*3.143/*CW*3.27
  Ibid., §2, l. 22: *OC*3.73/*CW*2.111
p. 750, §1, ll. 10–11: *OC*3.12ff, 24, 25, 30/*CW*2.9ff, 17–18, 18–19, 22; *OC*3.73,
  83/*CW*2.111–12, 119; *OC*4.1090/–
  Ibid., §1, l. 20: *OC*3.3, 19/*CW*2.3, 14; cf. *OC*4.569/.268–69
  Ibid., §1, ll. 22–23: *OC*4.595n (not 59n)/.286n; cf. *OC*2.565/*CW*6.463
  Ibid., §1, l. 37: *OC*3.18/*CW*2.13; *OC*3.41ff/*CW*2.41ff
  Ibid., §1, l. 42: –/–; cf. *OC*4.676/.*Em*.343
p. 751, §1, l. 6: *OC*2.1265/*CW*4.4
  Ibid., §2, l. 4: *OC*4.483/.204
  Ibid., §2, ll. 18–19: *OC*3.16/*CW*2.12; *OC*3.54n/*CW*2.51n. 2; *OC*3.62/*CW*2.86;
  *OC*3.74–76, 89/*CW*2.112–14, 123–24
p. 752, §1, ll. 5–6: *OC*5.394/*CW*7.305; cf. *OC*3.53n/*CW*2.51n. 1; *OC*3.212–
  14/*CW*3.84–86
  Ibid., §1, ll. 11–12: *OC*3.10/*CW*2.7–8; *OC*3.76/*CW*2.114
  Ibid., §1, l. 15: *OC*4.967/*CW*9.52
  Ibid., §1, l. 19: *OC*3.54/*CW*2.51–52; *OC*3.78ff/*CW*2.115ff
  Ibid., §1, ll. 21–22: *OC*3.29/*CW*2.21–22; *OC*3.39, 52ff, 55/*CW*2.39–40, 50ff,
  52–53; *OC*3.60ff/*CW*2.85ff; *OC*3.72ff/*CW*2.110ff; *OC*2.970ff/*CW*2.194ff
  Ibid., §1, ll. 26–27: *OC*3.3/*CW*2.3
  Ibid., §1, ll. 29–30: *OC*3.38ff/*CW*2.39ff; *OC*2.972–74/*CW*2.196–98
  Ibid., §1, l. 33: *OC*3.61/*CW*2.85–86
  Ibid., §1, l. 35: *OC*5.120n/*CW*10.348n
  Ibid., §1, ll. 41–42: *OC*3.5/*CW*2.4; *OC*3.39/*CW*2.39–40; *OC*3.212ff/*CW*3.84ff
p. 753, §1, l. 2: *OC*3.106/*CW*2.184–85
  Ibid., §1, l. 6: *OC*3.156/*CW*3.37–38
  Ibid., §1, ll. 23–24: *OC*3.391/*CW*4.162; *OC*3.367/*CW*4.143–44;
  *OC*3.131/*CW*3.18
  Ibid., §1, ll. 36–37: *OC*3.174–76, 186–90, 193ff/*CW*3.51–53, 61–64, 67; cf.
  *OC*3.25/*CW*2.18–19; *OC*3.49ff/*CW*2.48–49

754c

Endnotes:

2. *OC*3.19–20/*CW*2.14
3. Rousseau's references to Hobbes appear in, respectively:
     *OC*3.611f.1/*CW*11.62–64
     *OC*3.153,124f.4/*CW*3.35,14f.15
     *OC*3.463/*CW*4.218–219
     *OC*3.154/*CW*3.35
     *OC*3.611/*CW*11.62–63
The Sparta reference is at *OC*4.931/*CW*9.24.
Rousseau's précis of *The Prince* is at *OC*3.409/*CW*4.177

[2]

Jean-Jacques Rousseau, Founder of the Sciences of Man

Claude Lévi-Strauss

B<small>Y INVITING</small> an ethnologist to this celebration, you do him a signal honor, an honor for which he is personally grateful to you. You also present an opportunity for a young science to testify to the genius of a man who could be considered glorified in all aspects by an already numerous group, which includes individuals in literature, poetry, philosophy, history, ethics, political science, pedagogy, linguistics, music, botany—to mention only a few. For Rousseau was not only an acute observer of peasant life, an impassioned reader of travel books, a knowledgeable analyst of exotic customs and beliefs. Without fear of con-

Chapter II was originally presented as a speech delivered in Geneva on June 28, 1962, at the ceremonies marking the two hundred twenty-fifth anniversary of the birth of Jean-Jacques Rousseau. First published under the title "Jean-Jacques Rousseau, fondateur des sciences de l'homme," in *Jean-Jacques Rousseau* by the Université ouvrière and the Faculté des Lettres de l'Université de Genève (Neufchâtel: La Baconnière, 1962).

tradiction, it can be affirmed that—a whole century before it made its appearance—he had conceived, willed, and announced this very ethnology which did not yet exist, placing it first among the already established natural and human sciences. He had even guessed at the particular form in which—thanks to individual or collective patronage—it was to take its first steps.

This prophecy, which is both a justification and a program, takes up a long note in the *Discourse on the Origin and Foundations of Inequality* (Rousseau 1964) from which I would like to quote some passages, if only to justify the presence of my discipline at today's ceremony.

"I have difficulty conceiving," wrote Rousseau, "how in a century taking pride in splendid knowledge, there are not to be found two closely united men . . . one of whom would sacrifice twenty thousand crowns of his wealth and the other ten years of his life to a celebrated voyage around the world, in order to study, not always stones and plants, but for once men and morals." He exclaimed, a little further,

> The whole world is covered with nations of which we know only the names, yet we dabble in judging the human race! Let us suppose a Montesquieu, a Buffon, a Diderot, a d'Alembert, a Condillac, or men of that stamp traveling in order to inform their compatriots by observing and describing, as they know how, Turkey, Egypt, Barbary, the empire of Morocco, Guinea, the land of the Bantus, the interior of Africa and its eastern coasts, the Malabars, the Mogul, the banks of the Ganges, the kingdom of Siam, Pegu, and Ava, China, Tartary, and especially Japan; then, in the other hemisphere, Mexico, Peru, Chile, the straits of Magellan, not forgetting the Patagonias true or false, Tucuman, Paraguay, if possible Brazil, and finally the Caribbean islands, Florida, and all the savage countries—the most important voyage of all and the one that must be undertaken with the greatest care. Let us suppose that these new Hercules, back from these memorable expeditions, then wrote at leisure the natural, moral, and political history of what they would have seen; we ourselves would see a new world come from their pens, and we would thus learn to know our own . . . (Rousseau 1964, pp. 212–213).

Is it not contemporary ethnology, with its program and methods, which we see emerging here? And the famous names cited by Rousseau remain those which today's ethnographers assign themselves as models, without presuming to be their equals, but convinced that only by following their example will they earn for their science a respect long begrudged it.

Rousseau did not restrict himself to anticipating ethnology: he founded it. First, in a practical way, by writing the *Discourse on the Origin and Foundations of Inequality*, which poses the problem of the relation between nature and culture and in which one can see the first treatise of general ethnology. Next, on the theoretical plane, by distinguishing, with admirable clarity and concision, the object proper of the ethnologist from that of the moralist and the historian: "When one wants to study men, one must look around oneself; but to study man, one must first learn to look into the distance; one must first see differences in order to discover characteristics" (Rousseau 1967, Chap. VIII).

This methodological rule which Rousseau assigns to ethnology and which marks its advent also makes it possible to overcome what, at first glance, one would take for a double paradox: that Rousseau could have, simultaneously, advocated the study of the most remote men, while mostly given himself to the study of that particular man who seems the closest—himself; and secondly that, throughout his work, the systematic will to identify with the other goes hand in hand with an obstinate refusal to identify with the self. These two apparent contradictions, which resolve themselves into a single reciprocal implication, must be resolved, at one time or other, in every ethnological career.

The ethnologist's debt toward Rousseau is increased because, not content to place a science yet unborn with extreme precision in the scheme of human knowledge, he has—by his work, by the temperament and character expressed in it, by each of his accents, by his person and his being—provided for the ethnologist the fraternal comfort of an image in which he recognizes himself and which helps him to understand himself better; not as a purely contemplative intelligence, but as the involuntary agent of a transformation conveyed through him. In Jean-Jacques Rousseau, the whole of mankind learns to feel this transformation.

Every time he is in the field, the ethnologist finds himself open to a world where everything is foreign and often hostile to him. He has only this self still at his disposal, enabling him to survive and to pursue his research. But it is a self physically and morally battered by weariness, hunger, discomfort, the shock to acquired habits, the sudden appearance of unsuspected prejudices. It is a self which, in this strange conjuncture, is crippled and maimed by all the blows of a personal history responsible at the outset for his vocation, but which will affect its future course. Hence, in ethnographic experience the observer apprehends himself as his own instrument of observation. Clearly, he must learn to know himself, to obtain, from a *self* who reveals himself as *another* to the *I* who uses him, an evaluation which will become an integral part of the observation of other selves. Every ethnographic career finds its principle in "confessions," written or untold.

But if we can throw light on this experience through that of Rousseau, is it not because his temperament, his particular past and circumstances, placed him in a situation whose ethnographic character is clear to see? A situation from which he at once draws personal consequences: "Here they are," he says of his contemporaries, "unknown strangers, non-beings to me since they so wished it! But I, detached from them and from everything, what am I? This is what remains for me to seek" (First Walk). Paraphrasing Rousseau, the ethnographer could exclaim as he first sets eyes on his chosen savages, "Here they are, then, unknown strangers, non-beings to me, since *I* wished it so! And I, detached from them and from everything, what am I? This is what I *must* find out *first*."

To attain acceptance of oneself in others (the goal assigned to human knowledge by the ethnologist), one must first deny the self in oneself.

To Rousseau we owe the discovery of this principle, the only one on which to base the sciences of man. Yet it was to remain inaccessible and incomprehensible as long as there reigned a philosophy which, taking the *Cogito* as its point of departure, was imprisoned by the hypothetical evidences of the self; and which could aspire to founding a physics only at the expense of founding a sociology and even a biology. Descartes believes that he proceeds directly from a man's interiority to the exteriority of the world, without seeing that societies, civilizations—in other words, worlds of men—place themselves between these two extremes. Rousseau, by so eloquently speaking of himself in the third person (sometimes even going as far as to split it, as in the *Dialogues*, for instance), anticipates the famous formula "I is another." Ethno-

Jean-Jacques Rousseau, Founder of the Sciences of Man   37

graphic experience must establish this formula before proceeding to its demonstration: that the other is an I. Indeed, he claims to be the great inventor of this radical reification which, he indicates during the First Walk, is his aim: "to become aware of the modifications of my soul and their successive states." He adds: "I will perform on myself in every respect the operations which physicists perform on the air to test its daily state." What Rousseau means is that there exists a "he" who "thinks" through me and who first causes me to doubt whether it is I who am thinking (a surprising truth, before psychology and ethnology made us more familiar with it). To Montaigne's "What do I know?" (from which everything stems), Descartes believed it possible to answer that "I know that I am, since I think." To this Rousseau retorts with a "What am I?" without a definite solution, since the question presupposes the completion of another, more essential one: "Am I?" Intimate experience provides only this "he" which Rousseau discovered and which he lucidly undertook to explore.

Let us not make a mistake. Even the conciliatory intention of the Savoyard vicar does not succeed in concealing the fact that for Rousseau the notion of personal identity is acquired by inference, and that its ambiguity remains unmistakable: "I exist . . . this is the first truth which strikes me and *with which I am forced to agree.* . . . Do I have a separate feeling of my existence, or do I only feel it through my sensations? This is my first doubt, which is, for the present, impossible to resolve" (italics added). But it is in Rousseau's strictly anthropological teaching—that of the *Discourse on the Origin of Inequality*—that one discovers the foundation of this doubt. It lies in a conception of man which places the other before the self, and in a conception of mankind which places life before men.

If it is possible to believe the demonstration of the *Discourse* —that a threefold passage (from nature to culture, from feelings to knowledge, from animality to humanity) occurred with the appearance of society—it can only be by attributing to man, even in his primitive state, an essential faculty which moves him to get over these three obstacles. It is a faculty which possesses originally and immediately some contradictory attributes, although not precisely within itself; which is both natural and cultural, affective and rational, animal and human; and which (provided only that it become conscious) can transform itself from one plane to the other.

This faculty—Rousseau did not neglect to repeat—is compassion, deriving from the identification with another who is not only a parent, a relative, a compatriot, but any man whatsoever, seeing that he is a man, and much more: any living being, seeing that it is living. Thus man begins by experiencing himself as identical to all his fellows. And he will never forget this primitive experience, despite demographic expansion, which plays Rousseau's anthropological thought the role of a contingent event, one which could have not happened but which we must admit did happen since society is. This demographic expansion will have forced him to diversify his ways of life, adapting himself to the different environments through which his increased numbers forced him to spread. It will also have forced him to know how to differentiate himself, but only inasmuch as a laborious apprenticeship instructed him to discern the others, that is, animals by species, humanity from animality, my self from other selves. The total apprehension of men and of animals as sensitive beings (in which identification consists) precedes the awareness of oppositions—oppositions first between common characteristics, and only later between human and nonhuman.

It is veritably the end of the *Cogito* which Rousseau proclaims in putting forward this bold solution. For until his time, the question was mostly to put man out of the question, to be assured, from humanism, of a "transcendental retreat." Rousseau is able to remain a theist, since this was the least demand made by his upbringing and his times. He unequivocally ruins his attempt by putting man in question again.

If this interpretation is correct, if by the ways of anthropology Rousseau as radically upsets philosophical tradition as we believe he does, we can better understand the underlying unity of the many aspects of his work and the really essential place of his so imperious preoccupations. (This despite the fact that they are at first glance foreign to the toil of the philosopher and the writer—I mean linguistics, music, and botany.)

As described by Rousseau in *On the Origin of Language* (1967) the process of language reproduces, in its way and on its plane, the process of humanity. The first stage is that of identi-

Jean-Jacques Rousseau, Founder of the Sciences of Man   39

fication, here that of the literal sense and the figurative sense; the true name gradually comes out of the metaphor which merges each being with other beings. As for music, no other form of expression is better suited, it seems, to impugn the double Cartesian opposition between material and spiritual, body and soul. Music is an abstract system of oppositions and relations—alterations in ways of range which, when brought into play, have two consequences: firstly, the reversal in the relationship of the self and the other, since, when *I hear* music, *I listen to myself* through it. And secondly, by a reversal of the relationship between soul and body, music *lives itself* in me. A "chain of relations and combinations" (*Confessions*, Book XII) but which nature presents as incarnate in "sensitive objects" (*Rêveries*, Seventh Walk). It is in these terms, finally, that Rousseau defines botany, confirming that by this roundabout way he also aspires to rediscover the union of the sensitive and the intelligible, because it constitutes for man a first state which accompanied the awakening of consciousness and was not to survive it except in rare and precious instances.

Thus the expansion of Rousseau's thought stems from a double principle: firstly, of identification with others and even with the most "other" of all others, be it an animal; and secondly, of refusal to identify with oneself—in other words, refusal of all that can make the self "acceptable." These two attitudes complement each other, and the latter even forms the basis of the former: in truth, I am not "me," but the weakest, the most humble of "others." Such is the discovery of the *Confessions*.

What does the ethnologist write but confessions? In his own name first (as I have shown), since it is the driving force of his vocation and his work; and, through this very work, in the name of his society which, through the ethnologist, its emissary, chooses for itself other societies, other civilizations, precisely among those which appear to it the weakest and the most humble. Society does this in order to verify how "inacceptable" it is itself. It recognizes that it is not at all a privileged form, but only one of these "other" societies which have succeeded each other throughout the millennia, or whose precarious diversity still attests that—in his collective being also—man must recognize himself as a "he" before daring to lay claim to also being a "me."

Rousseau's revolution, preshaping and initiating the ethnologi-

cal revolution, consists of refusing forced identifications, whether
of a culture with that culture, or of an individual member of a
culture with a character or social function that this same culture
tries to impose on him. In both cases, the culture or the individual claims the right to free identification, which can only
realize itself *beyond* man with all that is alive and, consequently,
suffers; an identification also *before* the function or the character,
with a being not yet shaped but given. Then, freed from an antagonism which philosophy alone sought to stimulate, the self and
the other recover their unity. A primordial alliance, revived at last,
enables them together to found the *we* against the *him*. It is an
alliance against a society hostile to man, and which man feels all
the more prepared to challenge since Rousseau, by his example,
teaches him how to elude the unbearable contradictions of civilized
life. For, if it is true that nature has rejected man and that society persists in oppressing him, man can at least reverse the poles
of the dilemma to his benefit and *seek the society of nature to
meditate there on the nature of society*. Here, it seems to me, is
the indissoluble message of *Le Contrat social*, of *Lettres sur la
Botanique*, and of *Les Rêveries*.

We must not see in this the manifestation of a timid will,
giving a quest for wisdom as pretext for its abdication. Rousseau's
contemporaries were not deceived and his successors even less.
The former perceived that this proud thinking, this solitary and
wounded existence, radiated a subversive force the likes of which
no society had yet felt. His successors made this thought and the
example of this life the levers with which to shake ethics, law,
and society.

But it is today, for those of us who feel (as Rousseau pre-
dicted to his reader) "the fear of those who will have the misfortune to live after you" (*Discourse*) that his thought takes on a
supreme magnitude and acquires all its significance. In this world,
more cruel to man than it perhaps ever was, all the means of
extermination, massacre, and torture are raging. We never dis-
avowed these atrocities, it is true, but we liked to think that they
did not matter just because we reserved them for distant populations which underwent them (we maintained) for our benefit and,
in any case, in our name. Now, brought together in a denser
population which makes the universe smaller and shelters no por-
tion of humanity from abject violence, we feel the anguish of

Jean-Jacques Rousseau, Founder of the Sciences of Man 41

living together weighing on each of us. It is now, I repeat, by
exposing the flaws of a humanism decidedly unable to establish
the exercise of virtue among men, that Rousseau's thinking can
help us to reject an illusion whose lethal effects we can observe
in ourselves and on ourselves. For is it not the myth of the exclusive dignity of human nature, which subjected nature itself to a
first mutilation, one from which other mutilations were inevitably
to ensue?

We started by cutting man off from nature and establishing
him in an absolute reign. We believed ourselves to have thus
erased his most unassailable characteristic: that he is first a living
being. Remaining blind to this common property, we gave free
rein to all excesses. Never better than after the last four centuries
of his history could a Western man understand that, while assuming the right to impose a radical separation of humanity and
animality, while granting to one all that he denied the other, he
initiated a vicious circle. The one boundary, constantly pushed
back, would be used to separate men from other men and to claim
—to the profit of ever smaller minorities—the privilege of a
humanism, corrupted at birth by taking self-interest as its principle
and its notion.

Rousseau alone rebelled against this egoism. He preferred to
accept—in the note of the *Discourse* which I have quoted—that
the great apes of Africa and Asia, awkwardly described by the
travelers, were men of an unknown race, rather than to risk
challenging the human nature of beings which could possess it.
The first error would have been less serious, since respect for others
knows only a natural basis, sheltered from reflection and its
sophisms because anterior to it; a respect which Rousseau per-
ceives in man in "an innate repugnance to see his equal suffer"
(*Discourse*). But its discovery forces him to see an equal in any
being exposed to suffering and, by the same token, indefeasibly
entitled to pity. The only hope, for each of us not to be treated
as an animal by his fellow men is that all his fellow men (and himself first) feel themselves immediately as suffering beings. Thus
they cultivate inwardly this aptitude for pity which, in nature,
takes the place of "laws, customs, and virtue," and without whose
exercise we realize that there can be neither laws, customs, nor
virtues.

Far from offering itself to man as a nostalgic refuge, identification with all the forms of life (beginning with the most humble ones) proposed to today's humanity—through Rousseau's voice— the principle for all collective wisdom and action. It is the only principle which, in a world so encumbered that reciprocal *consideration* is rendered more difficult but all the more necessary, can enable men to live together and to build a harmonious future.

These teachings were perhaps already contained in the great religions of the Far East. But we were confronted with an occidental tradition that held since antiquity that one could gamble on all counts and falsify the evidence that man is a living and suffering being, like all other beings before, being distinguished from them only by subordinate criteria. Who else then, except Rousseau, could have given these teachings to us? "I have a violent aversion," he wrote in the fourth letter to Malesherbes, "for the estates which dominate others. I loathe the Great, I hate their estate." Does this declaration not first apply to man himself, who claimed to dominate the other beings and to enjoy a separate estate? Did this not leave a clear field to the least worthy men, to avail themselves of the same advantage against other men, and to twist to their benefit a line of argument as exorbitant in this particular form as it already was in its general form? In an organized society there could be no excuse for the only crime which man cannot expiate: the belief in his lasting or temporary superiority and his treating other men like objects, be it in the name of race, of culture, of conquest, of mission, or simply of expediency.

We know of a minute in the life of Rousseau—a second, perhaps—whose significance in his eyes, in spite of its tenuousness, orders all the rest. It explains why at the end of his life it is that moment which obsesses him, which he lingers to describe in his last work, and to which, in his random walks, he comes back constantly. What is it, though, but a commonplace recovery of consciousness after a fall and a fainting spell? But the feeling of existing is "precious" beyond all others, undoubtedly because it is so rare and so debatable. "I felt as if I was filling with my light existence all the objects which I perceived . . . I had no distinct notion of my person . . . I felt in my whole being a ravishing calm to which, every time I recall it, I find nothing comparable in the whole experience of known pleasures." This famous text of the Second Walk is echoed by a passage from the Seventh Walk, where

Jean-Jacques Rousseau, Founder of the Sciences of Man   43

he gives the reason for it: "I feel ecstasies, inexpressible ravishings to melt myself, as it were, into the system of beings, to identify myself with all of nature."

Living in a society, man is denied the opportunity for this primitive feeling of identification, and, made forgetful of his essential virtue, he no longer comes to feel it, except in a fortuitous manner and by the play of paltry circumstances. Rousseau's precious moment gives us access to the very core of his works. And if we give these a special place among the great productions of human genius, it is because their author not only discovered, with identification, the real principle of the human sciences and the only possible basis for ethics. It is because he also restored for us its ardor, burning for the last two centuries and forever in this crucible, a crucible uniting beings whom the interests of politicians and philosophers are everywhere else bent on rendering incompatible: me and the other, my societies and other societies, nature and culture, the sensitive and the rational, humanity and life.

Part II
The Naturalizing of Natural Law

[3]

THE CRISIS OF MODERN NATURAL RIGHT

Leo Strauss

A. ROUSSEAU

THE first crisis of modernity occurred in the thought of Jean-Jacques Rousseau. Rousseau was not the first to feel that the modern venture was a radical error and to seek the remedy in a return to classical thought. It suffices to mention the name of Swift. But Rousseau was not a "reactionary." He abandoned himself to modernity. One is tempted to say that only through thus accepting the fate of modern man was he led back to antiquity. At any rate, his return to antiquity was, at the same time, an advance of modernity. While appealing from Hobbes, Locke, or the Encyclopedists to Plato, Aristotle, or Plutarch, he jettisoned important elements of classical thought which his modern predecessors had still preserved. In Hobbes, reason, using her authority, had emancipated passion; passion acquired the status of a freed woman; reason continued to rule, if only by remote control. In Rousseau, passion itself took the initiative and rebelled; usurping the place of reason and indignantly denying her libertine past, passion began to pass judgment, in the severe accents of Catonic virtue, on reason's turpitudes. The fiery rocks with which the Rousseauan eruption had covered the Western world were used, after they had cooled and after they had been hewn, for the imposing structures which the great thinkers of the late eighteenth and early nineteenth centuries erected. His disciples clarified his views indeed, but one may wonder whether they preserved the breadth of his vision. His passionate and forceful attack on modernity in the name of what was at the same time

classical antiquity and a more advanced modernity was repeated, with no less passion and force, by Nietzsche, who thus
ushered in the second crisis of modernity—the crisis of our
time.

Rousseau attacked modernity in the name of two classical
ideas: the city and virtue, on the one hand, and nature, on the
other.[1] "The ancient politicians spoke unceasingly of manners and virtue; ours speak of nothing but trade and money."
Trade, money, enlightenment, the emancipation of acquisitiveness, luxury, and the belief in the omnipotence of legislation are characteristic of the modern state, be it the absolute
monarchy or the representative republic. Manners and virtue
are at home in the city. Geneva is a city, indeed, but it is less a
city than the cities of classical antiquity, especially Rome: in
his very eulogy of Geneva, Rousseau calls, not the Genevans,
but the Romans, the model of all free peoples and the most
respectable of all free peoples. The Romans are the most respectable of all peoples because they were the most virtuous,
the most powerful, and the freest people that ever were. The
Genevans are not Romans or Spartans or even Athenians, because they lack the public spirit or the patriotism of the ancients. They are more concerned with their private or domestic
affairs than with the fatherland. They lack the greatness of
soul of the ancients. They are bourgeois rather than citizens.
The sacred unity of the city has been destroyed in postclassical
times by the dualism of power temporal and power spiritual,

1. In the notes to this section, the following abbreviated forms of the titles are used:
"*D'Alembert*" = *Lettre à d'Alembert sur les spectacles*, ed. Léon Fontaine; "*Beaumont*" =
Lettre à M. de Beaumont (Garnier ed.); "*Confessions*" = *Les Confessions*, ed. Ad. Van
Bever; "*C.S.*" = *Contrat social*; "*First Discourse*" = *Discours sur les sciences et sur les arts*,
ed. G. R. Havens; "*Second Discourse*" = *Discours sur l'origine de l'inégalité* (Flammarion
ed.); "*Émile*" = *Émile* (Garnier ed.); "*Hachette*" = *Œuvres complètes*, Hachette ed.;
"*Julie*" = *Julie ou la Nouvelle Héloïse* (Garnier ed.); "*Montagne*" = *Lettres écrites de la
Montagne* (Garnier ed.); "*Narcisse*" = *Préface de Narcisse* (Flammarion ed.); "*Rêveries*" = *Les Rêveries du promeneur solitaire*, ed. Marcel Raymond.

and ultimately by the dualism of the earthly and the heavenly fatherland.[2]

The modern state presented itself as an artificial body which comes into being through convention and which remedies the deficiencies of the state of nature. For the critic of the modern state, therefore, a question arose as to whether the state of nature is not preferable to civil society. Rousseau suggested the return to the state of nature, the return to nature, from a world of artificiality and conventionality. Throughout his entire career, he never was content merely to appeal from the modern state to the classical city. He appealed almost in the same breath from the classical city itself to "the man of nature," the prepolitical savage.[3]

There is an obvious tension between the return to the city and the return to the state of nature. This tension is the substance of Rousseau's thought. He presents to his readers the confusing spectacle of a man who perpetually shifts back and forth between two diametrically opposed positions. At one moment he ardently defends the rights of the individual or the rights of the heart against all restraint and authority; at the next moment he demands with equal ardor the complete submission of the individual to society or the state and favors the most rigorous moral or social discipline. Today most serious students of Rousseau incline to the view that he eventually succeeded in overcoming what they regard as a temporary vacillation. The mature Rousseau, they hold, found a solution which he thought satisfied equally the legitimate claims of the

2. *First Discourse*, p. 134; *Narcisse*, pp. 53–54, 57 n.; *Second Discourse*, pp. 66, 67, 71–72; *D'Alembert*, pp. 192, 237, 278; *Julie*, pp. 112–13; *C.S.*, IV, 4, 8; *Montagne*, pp. 292–93. No modern thinker has understood better than Rousseau the philosophic conception of the *polis:* the *polis* is that complete association which corresponds to the natural range of man's power of knowing and of loving. See especially *Second Discourse*, pp. 65–66, and *C.S.*, II, 10.

3. *First Discourse*, pp. 102 n., 115 n., 140. "On me reproche d'avoir affecté de prendre chez les anciens mes examples de vertu. Il y a bien de l'apparence que j'en aurais trouvé encore davantage, si j'avais pu remonter plus haut" (Hachette, I, 35–36).

individual and those of society, the solution consisting in a certain type of society.[4] This interpretation is exposed to a decisive objection. Rousseau believed to the end that even the right kind of society is a form of bondage. Hence he cannot have regarded his solution to the problem of the conflict between the individual and society as more than a tolerable approximation to a solution—an approximation which remains open to legitimate doubts. The farewell to society, authority, restraint, and responsibility or the return to the state of nature remains therefore for him a legitimate possibility.[5] The question is, then, not how he solved the conflict between the individual and society but rather how he conceived of that insoluble conflict.

Rousseau's *First Discourse* provides a key to a more precise formulation of this question. In that earliest of his important writings he attacked the sciences and the arts in the name of virtue: the sciences and the arts are incompatible with virtue, and virtue is the only thing which matters.[6] Virtue apparently requires support by faith or theism, although not necessarily by monotheism.[7] Yet the emphasis rests on virtue itself. Rousseau indicates the meaning of virtue clearly enough for his purpose by referring to the examples of the citizen-philosopher Socrates, of Fabricius, and, above all, of Cato: Cato was "the greatest of men."[8] Virtue is primarily political virtue, the

4. The classic formulation of this interpretation of Rousseau is to be found in Kant's "Idee zu einer allgemeinen Geschichte in weltbürgerlicher Absicht," Siebenter Satz (*The Philosophy of Kant*, ed. Carl J. Friedrich ["Modern Library" ed.], pp. 123–27).

5. *C.S.*, I, 1; II, 7, 11; III, 15; *Émile*, I, 13–16, 79–80, 85; *Second Discourse*, pp. 65, 147, 150, 165.

6. *First Discourse*, pp. 97–98, 109–10, 116. Hachette, I, 55: Morality is infinitely more sublime than the marvels of the understanding.

7. *First Discourse*, pp. 122, 140–41; *Émile*, II, 51; *Julie*, pp. 502 ff., 603; *Montagne*, p. 180.

8. *First Discourse*, pp. 120–22; *Second Discourse*, p. 150; *Julie*, p. 325. Hachette, I, 45–46: Original equality is "the source of all virtue." *Ibid.*, p. 59: Cato has given the human race the spectacle and the model of the purest virtue which has ever existed.

virtue of the patriot or the virtue of a whole people. Virtue presupposes free society, and free society presupposes virtue: virtue and free society belong together.[9] Rousseau deviates from his classical models at two points. Following Montesquieu, he regards virtue as the principle of democracy: virtue is inseparable from equality or from the recognition of equality.[10] Secondly, he believes that the knowledge which is required for virtue is supplied, not by reason, but by what he calls the "conscience" (or "the sublime science of the simple souls") or by sentiment or by instinct. The sentiment which he has in mind will prove to be originally the sentiment of compassion, the natural root of all genuine beneficence. Rousseau saw a connection between his inclination toward democracy and his preference for sentiment above reason.[11]

Since Rousseau assumed that virtue and free society belong together, he could prove that science and virtue are incompatible by proving that science and free society are incompatible. The reasoning underlying the *First Discourse* can be reduced to five chief considerations, which are indeed only insufficiently developed in that work but which become sufficiently clear if, in reading the *First Discourse*, one takes into account Rousseau's later writings.[12]

9. *Narcisse*, pp. 54, 56, 57 n.; *Émile*, I, 308; *C.S.*, I, 8; *Confessions*, I, 244.

10. Hachette, I, 41, 45–46; *Second Discourse*, pp. 66, 143–44; *Montagne*, p. 252. Compare the quotation from Plato's *Apology of Socrates* (21^b ff.) in the *First Discourse* (pp. 118–20) with the Platonic original: Rousseau fails to quote Socrates' censure of the (democratic or republican) statesmen; and he substitutes for Socrates' censure of the artisans a censure of the artists.

11. *First Discourse*, p. 162; *Second Discourse*, pp. 107–10; *Émile*, I, 286–87, 307; *Confessions*, I, 199; Hachette, I, 31, 35, 62–63.

12. This procedure is unobjectionable, since Rousseau himself said that he did not yet reveal his principles fully in the *First Discourse* and that that work is inadequate also for other reasons (*First Discourse*, pp. 51, 56, 92, 169–70); and, on the other hand, the *First Discourse* reveals more clearly than do the later writings the unity of Rousseau's fundamental conception.

THE CRISIS OF MODERN NATURAL RIGHT   257

According to Rousseau, civil society is essentially a particular or, more precisely, a closed society. Civil society, he holds, can be healthy only if it has a character of its own, and this requires that its individuality be produced or fostered by national and exclusive institutions. These institutions must be animated by a national "philosophy," by a way of thinking that is not transferable to other societies: "the philosophy of each people is little apt for another people." On the other hand, science or philosophy is essentially universal. Science or philosophy necessarily weakens the power of the national "philosophies" and therewith the attachment of the citizens to the particular way of life, or the manners, of their community. In other words, whereas science is essentially cosmopolitan, society must be animated by a spirit of patriotism, by a spirit which is by no means irreconcilable with national hatreds. Political society being a society that has to defend itself against other states, it must foster the military virtues, and it normally develops a warlike spirit. Philosophy or science, on the contrary, is destructive of the warlike spirit.[13] Furthermore, society requires that its members be fully devoted to the common good or that they be busy or active on behalf of their fellows: "Every idle citizen is a scoundrel." On the other hand, the element of science is admittedly leisure, which is falsely distinguished from idleness. In other words, the true citizen is devoted to duty, whereas the philosopher or scientist selfishly pursues his pleasure.[14] In addition, society requires that its members adhere without question to certain religious beliefs. These salutary certainties, "our dogmas" or "the sacred dogmas authorized by the laws," are endangered by

13. *First Discourse*, pp. 107, 121–23, 141–46; *Narcisse*, pp. 49 n., 51–52, 57 n.; *Second Discourse*, pp. 65–66, 134–35, 169–70; *C.S.*, II, 8 (toward the end); *Émile*, I, 13; *Gouvernement de Pologne*, chaps. ii and iii; *Montagne*, pp. 130–33.

14. *First Discourse*, pp. 101, 115, 129–32, 150; Hachette, I, 62; *Narcisse*, pp. 50–53; *Second Discourse*, p. 150; *D'Alembert*, pp. 120, 123, 137; *Julie*, p. 517; *Émile*, I, 248.

science. Science is concerned with truth as such, regardless of its utility, and thus by reason of its intention is exposed to the danger of leading to useless or even harmful truths. In fact, however, the truth is inaccessible, and therefore the quest for truth leads to dangerous error or to dangerous skepticism. The element of society is faith or opinion. Therefore, science, or the attempt to replace opinion by knowledge, necessarily endangers society.[15] Moreover, free society presupposes that its members have abandoned their original or natural freedom in favor of conventional freedom, that is, in favor of obedience to the laws of the community or to uniform rules of conduct, to the making of which everyone can have contributed. Civil society requires conformity or the transformation of man as natural being into the citizen. But the philosopher or scientist must follow his "own genius" with absolute sincerity or without any regard to the general will or the communal way of thinking.[16] Finally, free society comes into being through

15. *First Discourse*, pp. 107, 125–26, 129–33, 151, 155–57; *Narcisse*, pp. 56, 57 n.; *Second Discourse*, pp. 71, 152; *C.S.*, II, 7; *Confessions*, II, 226. Hachette, I, 38 n.: "Ce serait en effet un détail bien flétrissant pour la philosophie, que l'exposition des maximes pernicieuses et des dogmes impies de ses diverses sectes ... y-a-t-il une seule de toutes ces sectes qui ne soit tombée dans quelque erreur dangereuse? Et que devons-nous dire de la distinction des deux doctrines, si avidement reçu de *tous* les philosophes, et par laquelle ils professaient en secret des sentiments contraires à ceux qu'ils enseignaient publiquement? Pythagore fit le premier qui fut usage de la doctrine intérieure; il ne la découvrait à ses disciples qu'après de longues épreuves et avec le plus grand mystère. Il leur donnait en secret des leçons d'athéisme, et offrit solennellement des hécatombes à Jupiter. Les philosophes se trouvaient si bien de cette méthode, qu'elle se répandit rapidement dans la Grèce, et de là dans Rome, comme on le voit par les ouvrages de Cicéron, qui se moquait avec ses amis des dieux immortels, qu'il attestait avec tant d'emphase sur le tribunal aux harangues. La doctrine intérieure n'a point été portée d'Europe à la Chine; mais elle y est née aussi avec la philosophie; et c'est à elle que les Chinois sont redevables de cette foule d'athées ou de philosophes qu'ils ont parmi eux. L'histoire de cette fatale doctrine, faite par un homme instruit et sincère, serait un terrible coup porté à *la philosophie ancienne et moderne*." (The italics are not in the original.) Cf. *Confessions*, II, 329.

16. *First Discourse*, pp. 101–2, 105–6, 158–59; *Second Discourse*, p. 116; *C.S.*, I, 6, 8; II, 7; *Émile*, I, 13–15.

THE CRISIS OF MODERN NATURAL RIGHT   259

the substitution of conventional equality for natural inequality. The pursuit of science, however, requires the cultivation of talents, that is, of natural inequality; its fostering of inequality is so characteristic of it that one is justified in saying that concern with superiority, or pride, is the root of science or philosophy.[17]

It was by means of science or philosophy that Rousseau established the thesis that science or philosophy is incompatible with free society and hence with virtue. In so doing, he tacitly admitted that science or philosophy can be salutary, i.e., compatible with virtue. He did not leave it at this tacit admission. In the very *First Discourse*, he bestowed high praise upon the learned societies whose members must combine learning and morality; he called Bacon, Descartes, and Newton the teachers of the human race; he demanded that scholars of the first rank should find honorable asylum at the courts of princes, in order from there to enlighten the peoples concerning their duties and thus contribute to the peoples' happiness.[18]

Rousseau has suggested three different solutions to this contradiction. According to the first suggestion, science is bad for a good society and good for a bad society. In a corrupt society, in a society ruled despotically, the attack on all sacred opinions or prejudices is legitimate because social morality cannot become worse than it already is. In such a society, only science can provide man with a measure of relief: the discussion of the foundations of society may lead to the discovery of palliatives for the prevailing abuses. This solution would suffice if Rousseau had addressed his works only to his contemporaries, i.e., to members of a corrupt society. But he wished to live as a writer beyond his time, and he foresaw a revolution. He wrote, therefore, also with a view to the requirements of a

17. *First Discourse*, pp. 115, 125–26, 128, 137, 161–62; *Narcisse*, p. 50; *Second Discourse*, p. 147; *C.S.*, I, 9 (end); Hachette, I, 38 n.

18. *First Discourse*, pp. 98–100, 127–28, 138–39, 151–52, 158–61; *Narcisse*, pp. 45, 54.

good society and, in fact, of a more perfect society than had ever existed before, which might be established after the revolution. This best solution to the political problem is discovered by philosophy and only by philosophy. Hence philosophy cannot merely be good for a bad society; it is indispensable for the emergence of the best society.[19]

According to Rousseau's second suggestion, science is good for "the individuals," i.e., for "some great geniuses" or "some privileged souls" or "the small number of true philosophers," among whom he counts himself, but bad for "the peoples" or "the public" or "the common men" (*les hommes vulgaires*). Hence he attacked in the *First Discourse*, not science as such, but popularized science or the diffusion of scientific knowledge. The diffusion of scientific knowledge is disastrous not only for society but for science or philosophy itself; through popularization, science degenerates into opinion, or the fight against prejudice becomes itself a prejudice. Science must remain the preserve of a small minority; it must be kept secret from the common man. Since every book is accessible not only to the small minority but to all who can read, Rousseau was forced by his principle to present his philosophic or scientific teaching with a great deal of reserve. He believed, indeed, that in a corrupt society, like the one in which he lived, the diffusion of philosophic knowledge can no longer be harmful; but, as was said before, he wrote not merely for his contemporaries. The *First Discourse* must be understood in the light of these facts. The function of that work is to warn away from science, not all men, but only the common men. When Rousseau rejects science as simply bad, he speaks in the character of a common man addressing common men. But he intimates that, far from being a common man, he is a philosopher

19. *First Discourse*, p. 94 (cf. 38, 46, 50); *Narcisse*, pp. 54, 57–58, 60 n.; *Second Discourse*, pp. 66, 68, 133, 136, 141, 142, 145, 149; *Julie*, Preface (beginning); C.S., I, 1; *Beaumont*, pp. 471–72.

THE CRISIS OF MODERN NATURAL RIGHT   261

who merely appears in the guise of a common man and that, far from ultimately addressing "the people," he addresses only those who are not subjugated by the opinions of their century, of their country, or of their society.[20]

It might then seem that it was Rousseau's belief in the fundamental disproportion between science and society (or "the people") which was the primary reason for his belief that the conflict between the individual and society is insoluble or for his making an ultimate reservation on behalf of "the individual," i.e., of the few "privileged souls" against the claims of even the best society. This impression is confirmed by the fact that R ）usseau finds the foundations of society in the needs of the bo ly and that he says of himself that nothing related to the interest of his body could ever truly occupy his soul; he himself finds in the joys and raptures of pure and disinterested contemplation—for example, the study of plants in the spirit of Theophrastus—perfect happiness and a godlike self-sufficiency.[21] Thus the impression grows that Rousseau sought to restore the classical idea of philosophy as opposed to the En-

20. *First Discourse*, pp. 93–94, 108 n., 120, 125, 132–33, 152, 157–62, 227; Hachette, I, 23, 26, 31, 33, 35, 47 n. 1, 48, 52, 70; *Second Discourse*, pp. 83, 170, 175; *D'Alembert*, pp. 107–8; *Beaumont*, p. 471; *Montagne*, pp. 152–53, 202, 283. A critic of the *First Discourse* had said: "On ne saurait mettre dans un trop grand jour des vérités qui heurtent autant de front le goût général...." Rousseau replied to him as follows: "Je ne suis pas tout-à-fait de cet avis, et je crois qu'il faut laisser des osselets aux enfants" (Hachette, I, 21; cf. also *Confessions*, II, 247). Rousseau's principle was to say the truth "en toute chose *utile*" (*Beaumont*, pp. 472, 495; *Rêveries*, IV); hence one may not only suppress or disguise truths devoid of all possible utility but may even be positively deceitful about them by asserting their contraries, without thus committing the sin of lying. The consequence regarding harmful or dangerous truths is obvious (cf. also *Second Discourse*, end of the First Part, and *Beaumont*, p. 461). Compare Dilthey, *Gesammelte Schriften*, XI, 92: "[Johannes von Mueller spricht] von der sonderbaren Aufgabe: 'sich so auszudrücken, dass die Obrigkeiten die Wahrheit lernen, ohne dass ihn die Untertanen verstünden, und die Untertanen so zu unterrichten, dass sie vom Glück ihres Zustandes recht überzeugt sein möchten.' "

21. *First Discourse*, p. 101; *Montagne*, p. 206; *Confessions*, III, 205, 220–21; *Rêveries*, V–VII.

lightenment. It is certainly in opposition to the Enlightenment
that he reasserts the crucial importance of the natural inequality of men in regard to intellectual gifts. But one must add at
once that the instant Rousseau takes hold of the classical view
he succumbs again to the powers from which he sought to
liberate himself. The same reason which forces him to appeal
from civil society to nature forces him to appeal from philosophy or science to nature.[22]

The contradiction of the *First Discourse* regarding the value
of science is solved as completely as Rousseau ever solved it by
his third suggestion, of which the first and second suggestions
are parts. The first and second suggestions solve the contradiction by distinguishing between two kinds of addressees of science. The third suggestion solves the contradiction by distinguishing between two kinds of science: a kind of science which
is incompatible with virtue and which one may call "metaphysics" (or purely theoretical science) and a kind of science
which is compatible with virtue and which one may call
"Socratic wisdom." Socratic wisdom is self-knowledge; it is
knowledge of one's ignorance. It is therefore a kind of skepticism, an "involuntary skepticism" but not a dangerous one.
Socratic wisdom is not identical with virtue, for virtue is "the
science of the simple souls," and Socrates was not a simple
soul. Whereas all men can be virtuous, Socratic wisdom is the
preserve of a small minority. Socratic wisdom is essentially
ancillary; the humble and silent practice of virtue is the only
thing that matters. Socratic wisdom has the function of defending "the science of the simple souls," or the conscience,
against all kinds of sophistry. The need for such defense is not
accidental and not limited to times of corruption. As one of
Rousseau's greatest disciples put it, simplicity or innocence is a
wonderful thing indeed, but it can easily be misled; "therefore

22. *First Discourse*, p. 115 n.; *Narcisse*, pp. 52–53; *Second Discourse*, pp. 89, 94, 109,
165; *Julie*, pp. 415–17; *Émile*, I, 35–36, 118, 293–94, 320–21. Hachette, I, 62–63: "osera-t-
on prendre le parti de l'instinct contre la raison? C'est précisément ce que je demande."

THE CRISIS OF MODERN NATURAL RIGHT   263

wisdom which otherwise consists in doing or in forbearing to do rather than in knowing, is in need of science." Socratic wisdom is needed, not for the sake of Socrates, but for the sake of the simple souls or of the people. The true philosophers fulfil the absolutely necessary function of being the guardians of virtue or of free society. Being the teachers of the human race, they, and they alone, can enlighten the peoples as to their duties and as to the precise character of the good society. In order to fulfil this function, Socratic wisdom requires as its basis the whole of theoretical science; Socratic wisdom is the end and crown of theoretical science. Theoretical science, which is not intrinsically in the service of virtue and is therefore bad, must be put into the service of virtue in order to become good.[23] It can become good, however, only if its study remains the preserve of the few who are by nature destined to guide the peoples; only an esoteric theoretical science can become good. This is not to deny that, in times of corruption, the restriction on the popularization of science can and must be relaxed.

This solution might be regarded as final if the virtuous citizen and not "natural man" were Rousseau's ultimate standard. But according to him, the very philosopher comes closer to natural man in certain respects than does the virtuous citizen. It suffices here to refer to the "idleness" which the philosopher shares with natural man.[24] In the name of nature, Rousseau questioned not only philosophy but the city and virtue as well. He was forced to do so because his Socratic wisdom is ultimately based on theoretical science or, rather on a particular kind of theoretical science, namely, modern natural science.

23. *First Discourse*, pp. 93, 97, 99–100, 107, 118–22, 125, 128, 129, 130 n., 131–32, 152–54, 161–62; Hachette, I, 35; *Narcisse*, pp. 47, 50–51, 56; *Second Discourse*, pp. 74, 76; *Émile*, II, 13, 72, 73; *Beaumont*, p. 452. Cf. Kant, *Grundlegung zur Metaphysik der Sitten*, Erster Abschnitt (toward the end).

24. *First Discourse*, pp. 105–6; *Second Discourse*, pp. 91, 97, 122, 150–51, 168; *Confessions*, II, 73; III, 205, 207–9, 220–21; *Rêveries*, VI (end) and VII.

To understand Rousseau's theoretical principles, one must turn to his *Discourse on the Origin of Inequality*. Contrary to the inclinations of most present-day students, he always regarded this work (the *Second Discourse*) as "a work of the greatest importance." He claimed that in it he had developed his principles "completely," or that the *Second Discourse* is the writing in which he had revealed his principles "with the greatest boldness, not to say audacity."[25] The *Second Discourse* is indeed Rousseau's most philosophic work; it contains his fundamental reflections. In particular, the *Social Contract* rests on the foundations laid in the *Second Discourse*.[26] The *Second Discourse* is decidedly the work of a "philosopher." Morality is regarded there, not as an unquestioned or unquestionable presupposition, but as an object or as a problem.

The *Second Discourse* is meant to be a "history" of man. That history is modeled on the account of the fate of the human race which Lucretius gave in the fifth book of his poem.[27] But Rousseau takes that account out of its Epicurean context and puts it into a context supplied by modern natural and social science. Lucretius had described the fate of the human race in order to show that that fate can be perfectly understood without recourse to divine activity. The remedies for the ills which he was forced to mention, he sought in philosophic withdrawal from political life. Rousseau, on the other hand, tells the story of man in order to discover that political order which is in accordance with natural right. Furthermore, at least at the outset, he follows Descartes rather than Epicurus: he assumes that animals are machines and that man transcends

25. *Confessions*, II, 221, 246.

26. Cf. especially *C.S.*, I, 6 (beginning), which shows that the *raison d'être* of the social contract is set forth, not in the *C.S.*, but in the *Second Discourse*. Cf. also *C.S.*, I, 9.

27. *Second Discourse*, p. 84; cf. also *Confessions*, II, 244. See Jean Morel, "Recherches sur les sources du discours de l'inégalité," *Annales de la Société J.-J. Rousseau*, V (1909), 163–64.

the general mechanism, or the dimension of (mechanical) necessity, only by virtue of the spirituality of his soul. Descartes had integrated the "Epicurean" cosmology into a theistic framework: God having created matter and established the laws of its motions, the universe with the exception of man's rational soul has come into being through purely mechanical processes; the rational soul requires special creation because thinking cannot be understood as a modification of moved matter; rationality is the specific difference of man among the animals. Rousseau questions not only the creation of matter but likewise the traditional definition of man. Accepting the view that brutes are machines, he suggests that there is only a difference of degree between men and the brutes in regard to understanding or that the laws of mechanics explain the formation of ideas. It is man's power to choose and his consciousness of this freedom which cannot be explained physically and which proves the spirituality of his soul. "It is then not so much the understanding which constitutes the specific difference of man among the animals as his quality of a free agent." Yet, whatever Rousseau might have believed concerning this subject, the argument of the *Second Discourse* is not based on the assumption that freedom of the will is of the essence of man, or, more generally expressed, the argument is not based on dualistic metaphysics. Rousseau goes on to say that the cited definition of man is subject to dispute, and he therefore replaces "freedom" by "perfectibility"; no one can deny the fact that man is distinguished from the brutes by perfectibility. Rousseau means to put his doctrine on the most solid ground; he does not want to make it dependent on dualistic metaphysics, which is exposed to "insoluble objections," to "powerful objections," or to "insurmountable difficulties."[28] The argument of the *Second Discourse* is meant to be acceptable

28. *Second Discourse*, pp. 92–95, 118, 140, 166; *Julie*, p. 589 n.; *Émile*, II, 24, 37; *Beaumont*, pp. 461–63; *Rêveries*, III. Cf. *First Discourse*, p. 178.

to materialists as well as to others. It is meant to be neutral with regard to the conflict between materialism and antimaterialism, or to be "scientific" in the present-day sense of the term.[29]

The "physical" investigation[30] of the *Second Discourse* is meant to be identical with a study of the basis of natural right and therewith of morality; the "physical" investigation is meant to disclose the precise character of the state of nature. Rousseau takes it for granted that, in order to establish natural right, one must return to the state of nature. He accepts Hobbes's premise. Dismissing the natural right teaching of the ancient philosophers, he says that "Hobbes has seen very well the defect of all modern definitions of natural right." "The moderns" or "our jurists" (as distinguished from "the Roman jurists," i.e., Ulpian) erroneously assumed that man ·is by nature capable of the full use of his reason, i.e., that man as man is subject to perfect duties of natural law. Rousseau obviously understands by "the modern definitions of natural right" the traditional definitions which still predominated in the academic teaching of his time. He agrees, then, with Hobbes's attack on the traditional natural law teaching: natural law must have its roots in principles which are anterior to reason, i.e., in passions which need not be specifically human. He further agrees with Hobbes in finding the principle of natural law in the right of self-preservation, which implies the right of each to be the sole judge of what are the proper means for his self-preservation. This view presupposes, according to both thinkers, that life in the state of nature is "solitary," i.e., that it is characterized by the absence not only of society but even of sociability.[31] Rousseau expresses his loyalty to the

29. As regards the prehistory of this approach, see above, pp. 173–74 and 203–4.

30. *Second Discourse*, pp. 75, 173.

31. *Ibid.*, pp. 76, 77, 90, 91, 94–95, 104, 106, 118, 120, 151; *Julie*, p. 113; *C.S.*, I, 2; II, 4, 6; cf. also *Émile*, II, 45.

THE CRISIS OF MODERN NATURAL RIGHT   267

spirit of Hobbes's reform of the natural law teaching by substituting for "that sublime maxim of reasoned justice 'Do unto
others as you would have them to do unto you' . . . this much
less perfect, but perhaps more useful maxim 'Do good to yourself with as little evil as possible to others.' " He tries no less
seriously than Hobbes to find the basis of justice by "taking
men as they are," and not as they ought to be. And he accepts
Hobbes's reduction of virtue to social virtue.[32]

Rousseau deviates from Hobbes for the same two reasons for
which he deviates from all previous political philosophers. In
the first place, "the philosophers who have examined the
foundations of society, have all of them felt the necessity to go
back to the state of nature, but not one of them has arrived
there." All of them have painted civilized man while claiming
to paint natural man or man in the state of nature. Rousseau's

32. *Second Discourse*, p. 110; cf. also *C.S.*, I (beginning); *D'Alembert*, pp. 246, 248; and
Confessions, II, 267. Rousseau was fully aware of the antibiblical implications of the
concept of the state of nature. For this reason, he originally presented his account of the
state of nature as altogether hypothetical; the notion that the state of nature was once
actual contradicts the biblical teaching which every Christian philosopher is obliged
to accept. But the teaching of the *Second Discourse* is not that of a Christian; it is the
teaching of a man addressing mankind; it is at home in the Lyceum at the time of
Plato and of Xenocrates, and not in the eighteenth century; it is a teaching arrived at
by applying the natural light to the study of man's nature, and nature never lies. In
accordance with these statements, Rousseau asserts later on that he has proved his
account of the state of nature. What remains hypothetical, or less certain than the
account of the state of nature, is the account of the development leading from the state
of nature to despotism, or "the history of governments." At the end of the First Part
of the bipartite work, Rousseau calls the state of nature a "fact": the problem consists
in linking "two facts given as real" "by a sequence of intermediate and actually or
supposedly unknown facts." The given facts are the state of nature and contemporary
despotism. It is to the intermediate facts, and not to the characteristics of the state of
nature, that Rousseau refers when he says in the first chapter of the *C.S.* that he does
not know them. If Rousseau's account of the state of nature were hypothetical, his
whole political teaching would be hypothetical; the practical consequence would be
prayer and patience and not dissatisfaction and, wherever possible, reform. Cf. *Second
Discourse*, pp. 75, 78–79, 81, 83–85, 104, 116–17, 149, 151–52, 165; cf. also the reference
to the "thousands of centuries" required for the development of the human mind (*ibid.*,
p. 98) with the biblical chronology; see also Morel, *op. cit.*, p. 135.

predecessors attempted to establish the character of natural man by looking at man as he is now. This procedure was reasonable as long as it was assumed that man is by nature social. Making this assumption, one could draw the line between the natural and the positive or the conventional by identifying the conventional with what is manifestly established by convention. One could take it for granted that at least all those passions which arise in man independently of the fiat of society are natural. But once one denies, with Hobbes, man's natural sociality, one must regard it as possible that many passions which arise in man as we observe him are conventional in so far as they originate in the subtle and indirect influence of society and hence of convention. Rousseau deviates from Hobbes because he accepts Hobbes's premise; Hobbes is grossly inconsistent because, on the one hand, he denies that man is by nature social and, on the other hand, he tries to establish the character of natural man by referring to his experience of men which is the experience of social man.[33] By thinking through Hobbes's critique of the traditional view, Rousseau was brought face to face with a difficulty which embarrasses most present-day social scientists: not the reflection on man's experience of men, but only a specifically "scientific" procedure, seems to be able to lead one to genuine knowledge of the nature of man. Rousseau's reflection on the state of nature, in contradistinction to Hobbes's reflection, takes on the character of a "physical" investigation.

Hobbes had identified natural man with the savage. Rousseau frequently accepts this identification and accordingly makes extensive use of the ethnographic literature of the age. But his doctrine of the state of nature is, in principle, independent of this kind of knowledge, since, as he points out, the savage is already molded by society and therefore no longer a natural man in the strict sense. He also suggests some experi-

33. *Second Discourse*, pp. 74–75, 82–83, 90, 98, 105–6, 137–38, 160, 175.

THE CRISIS OF MODERN NATURAL RIGHT   269

ments which might be helpful for establishing the character of natural man. But these experiments, being entirely a matter of the future, cannot be the basis of his doctrine. The method which he uses is a "meditation on the first and most simple operations of the human soul"; those mental acts which presuppose society cannot belong to man's natural constitution, since man is by nature solitary.[34]

The second reason why Rousseau deviates from Hobbes can be stated as follows. Hobbes had taught that if natural right is to be effectual, it must be rooted in passion. On the other hand, he had conceived of the laws of nature (of the rules prescribing man's natural duties), apparently in the traditional manner, as dictates of reason; he had described them as "conclusions or theorems." Rousseau draws the conclusion that, since Hobbes's criticism of the traditional view is sound, one must question Hobbes's conception of the laws of nature: not only the right of nature but the laws of nature or man's natural duties or his social virtues must be rooted directly in passion; they must have a much more powerful support than reasoning or calculation. By nature, the law of nature "must speak immediately with the voice of nature"; it must be prerational, dictated by "natural sentiment" or by passion.[35]

Rousseau has summed up the result of his study of natural man in the statement that man is by nature good. This result can be understood as the outcome of a criticism of Hobbes's doctrine which is based on Hobbes's premises. Rousseau argues as follows: Man is by nature asocial, as Hobbes admitted. But pride or *amour-propre* presupposes society. Hence natural man cannot be proud or vain, as Hobbes had contended that he is. But pride or vanity is the root of all viciousness, as Hobbes had also contended. Natural man is therefore free from all

34. *Ibid.*, pp. 74–77, 90, 94–95, 104, 124, 125, 174; cf. also Condorcet, *Esquisse d'un tableau historique des progrès de l'esprit humain*, Première Époque (beginning).

35. *Second Discourse*, pp. 76–77, 103, 107–10; cf. also *Émile*, I, 289.

viciousness. Natural man is swayed by self-love or the concern with self-preservation; he will therefore hurt others if he believes that by doing so he will preserve himself; but he will not be concerned with hurting others for its own sake, as he would be if he were proud or vain. Furthermore, pride and compassion are incompatible; to the extent to which we are concerned with our prestige, we are insensitive to the sufferings of others. The power of compassion decreases with the increase of refinement or convention. Rousseau suggests that natural man is compassionate: the human race could not have survived prior to the existence of any conventional restraints if the powerful promptings of the instinct of self-preservation had not been mitigated by compassion. He seems to assume that the instinctive desire for the preservation of the species bifurcates into the desire for procreation and compassion. Compassion is the passion from which all social virtues derive. He concludes that man is by nature good because he is by nature swayed by self-love and compassion and free from vanity or pride.[36]

For the same reason for which natural man lacks pride, he also lacks understanding or reason and therewith freedom. Reason is coterminous with language, and language presupposes society: being presocial, natural man is prerational. Here again Rousseau draws a necessary conclusion from Hobbes's premises which Hobbes had not drawn. To have reason means to have general ideas. But general ideas, as distinguished from the images of memory or imagination, are not the products of a natural or unconscious process; they presuppose definitions; they owe their being to definition. Hence they presuppose language. Since language is not natural, reason is not natural. From this we can understand best why Rousseau replaces the traditional definition of man as a rational animal by a new definition. Furthermore, since natural man is prerational, he is utterly incapable of any knowledge of the law of nature which

36. *Second Discourse*, pp. 77, 87, 90, 97–99, 104, 107–10, 116, 120, 124–25, 147, 151, 156–57, 160–61, 165, 176–77.

is the law of reason, although "he attributes to himself [in accordance] with reason the right to the things which he needs." Natural man is premoral in every respect: he has no heart. Natural man is subhuman.[37]

Rousseau's thesis that man is by nature good must be understood in the light of his contention that man is by nature subhuman. Man is by nature good because he is by nature that subhuman being which is capable of becoming either good or bad. There is no natural constitution of man to speak of: everything specifically human is acquired or ultimately depends on artifice or convention. Man is by nature almost infinitely perfectible. There are no natural obstacles to man's almost unlimited progress or to his power of liberating himself from evil. For the same reason, there are no natural obstacles to man's almost unlimited degradation. Man is by nature almost infinitely malleable. In the words of the Abbé Raynal, the human race is what we wish to make it. Man has no nature in the precise sense which would set a limit to what he can make out of himself.[38]

37. *Ibid.*, pp. 85, 89, 93–94, 98–99, 101, 102, 105–6, 109, 111, 115, 118, 157, 168. Morel (*op. cit.*, p. 156) points in the right direction by saying that Rousseau "substitue à la fabrication naturelle des idées générales, leur construction scientifiquement réfléchie" (cf. above, pp. 172–74). In Rousseau's model, Lucretius' poem (v. 1028–90), the genesis of language is described without any reference to a genesis of reason: reason belongs to man's natural constitution. In Rousseau, the genesis of language coincides with the genesis of reason (*C.S.*, I, 8; *Beaumont*, pp. 444, 457).

38. Rousseau's contention that man is by nature good is deliberately ambiguous. It expresses two incompatible views—a rather traditional view and a thoroughly anti-traditional one. The first view can be stated as follows: Man is by nature good; he is bad through his own fault; almost all evils are of human origin: almost all evils are due to civilization; civilization has its root in pride, i.e., in the misuse of freedom. The practical consequence of this view is that men ought to bear the now inevitable evils of civilization in a spirit of patience and prayer. According to Rousseau, this view is based on belief in biblical revelation. In addition, natural man or man in the state of nature, as Rousseau describes him, is incapable of pride; hence pride cannot have been the reason for his leaving the state of nature (a state of innocence) or for his embarking on the venture of civilization. More generally expressed, natural man lacks freedom of will; hence he cannot misuse his freedom; natural man is characterized, not by freedom, but by perfectibility. Cf. *Second Discourse*, pp. 85, 89, 93–94, 102, 160; *C.S.*, I, 8; cf. above, n. 32.

272   NATURAL RIGHT AND HISTORY

If man's humanity is acquired, that acquisition must be explained. In accordance with the requirements of a "physical investigation," man's humanity must be understood as a product of accidental causation. This problem had hardly existed for Hobbes. But it arose necessarily on the basis of his premises. He had distinguished between the natural or mechanical production of natural beings and the voluntary or arbitrary production of human constructs. He had conceived of the world of man as a kind of universe within the universe. He had conceived of man's leaving the state of nature and establishing civil society as a kind of revolt of man against nature. His notion of the whole required, however, as Spinoza had indicated, that the dualism of the state of nature and the state of civil society, or the dualism of the natural world and the world of man, be reduced to the monism of the natural world or that the transition from the state of nature to civil society, or man's revolt against nature, be understood as a natural process.[39] Hobbes had concealed from himself this necessity, partly because he erroneously assumed that presocial man is already a rational being, a being capable of making contracts. The transition from the state of nature to civil society therefore coincided for him with the conclusion of the social contract. But Rousseau was forced by his realization of the necessary implications of Hobbes's premises to conceive of that transition as consisting in, or at least as decisively prepared by, a natural process: man's leaving the state of nature, his embarking on the venture of civilization, is due not to a good or a bad use of his freedom or to essential necessity but to mechanical causation or to a series of natural accidents.

Man's humanity or rationality is acquired. Reason comes later than the elementary wants of the body. Reason emerges in the process of satisfying these wants. Originally, these simple and uniform wants are easily satisfied. But this very

39. Cf. Spinoza's criticism of Hobbes in *Ep.* 50 with *Tr. theol.-pol.*, chap. iv (beginning) and *Ethics* III praef.; cf. above, chap. v, A, n. 9.

THE CRISIS OF MODERN NATURAL RIGHT   273

fact leads to an enormous increase in population and thus renders difficult the satisfaction of the elementary wants. Man is therefore forced to think—to learn to think—in order to survive. Furthermore, the elementary wants are satisfied in different manners under different climatic and other conditions. The mind develops, therefore, in exact proportion to the particular manner in which the basic wants or their satisfaction are modified by particular circumstances. These circumstances mold men's thinking. Once thus molded, men develop new wants, and, in attempting to satisfy them, the mind develops further. The progress of the mind is then a necessary process. It is necessary because men are forced to invent by changes (formation of islands, eruption of volcanoes, and the like) which, although not directed toward an end and hence accidental, are yet the necessary effects of natural causes. Accident forces understanding and its development upon man. This being the character especially of the transition from the state of nature to civilized life, it is perhaps not surprising that the process of civilization should have been destructive of the subhuman bliss of the state of nature or that men should have committed grave errors in organizing societies. Yet all this misery and all these blunders were necessary; they were the necessary outcome of early man's lack of experience and lack of philosophy. Still, in and through society, however imperfect, reason develops. Eventually, the original lack of experience and of philosophy is overcome, and man succeeds in establishing public right on solid grounds.[40] At that moment, which is Rousseau's moment, man will no longer be molded by fortuitous circumstances but rather by his reason. Man, the product of blind fate, eventually becomes the seeing master of his fate. Reason's creativity or mastership over the blind forces of nature is a product of those blind forces.

In Rousseau's doctrine of the state of nature, the modern

40. *Second Discourse*, pp. 68, 74–75, 91, 94–96, 98–100, 116, 118–19, 123, 125, 127, 128, 130, 133, 135, 136, 141, 142, 145, 179; *Narcisse*, p. 54; *Julie*, p. 633 n.

natural right teaching reaches its critical stage. By thinking through that teaching, Rousseau was brought face to face with the necessity of abandoning it completely. If the state of nature is subhuman, it is absurd to go back to the state of nature in order to find in it the norm for man. Hobbes had denied that man has a natural end. He had believed that he could find a natural or nonarbitrary basis of right in man's beginnings. Rousseau showed that man's beginnings lack all human traits. On the basis of Hobbes's premise, therefore, it became necessary to abandon altogether the attempt to find the basis of right in nature, in human nature. And Rousseau seemed to have shown an alternative. For he had shown that what is characteristically human is not the gift of nature but is the outcome of what man did, or was forced to do, in order to overcome or to change nature: man's humanity is the product of the historical process. For a moment—the moment lasted longer than a century—it seemed possible to seek the standard of human action in the historical process. This solution presupposed that the historical process or its results are unambiguously preferable to the state of nature or that that process is "meaningful." Rousseau could not accept that presupposition. He realized that to the extent to which the historical process is accidental, it cannot supply man with a standard, and that, if that process has a hidden purpose, its purposefulness cannot be recognized except if there are trans-historical standards. The historical process cannot be recognized as progressive without previous knowledge of the end or purpose of the process. To be meaningful, the historical process must culminate in perfect knowledge of the true public right; man cannot be, or have become, the seeing master of his fate if he does not have such knowledge. It is, then, not knowledge of the historical process but knowledge of the true public right which supplies man with the true standard.

It has been suggested that Rousseau's predicament was due

THE CRISIS OF MODERN NATURAL RIGHT   275

to mere misunderstanding. In the academic teaching of his
time, the state of nature was understood not as the condition
in which man had actually lived in the beginning but as a
mere "supposition": man in the state of nature is man with all
his essential faculties duly developed but "considered" as subject only to the natural law, and therefore as the bearer of all
those duties and rights and of only those duties and rights
which derive from natural law; whether man actually ever
lived in such a state in which he was not subject to any positive law is irrelevant. In the *Second Discourse* Rousseau himself
alludes to this conception of the state of nature and seems to
accept it. At the beginning of the *Social Contract* he seems to say
that knowledge of the "historical" state of nature is irrelevant
for the knowledge of natural right. Accordingly, his teaching
about the state of nature would seem to have no other merit
than that of having made abundantly clear the necessity of
keeping completely separate from each other the two wholly
unrelated meanings of the state of nature: the state of nature as
man's original condition (and hence as a fact of the past) and
the state of nature as the legal status of man as man (and hence
as an abstraction or a supposition). In other words, Rousseau
seems to be a somewhat unwilling witness to the fact that the
academic natural right teaching was superior to the teachings
of men like Hobbes and Locke.[41] This criticism disregards the
necessary connection between the question concerning the existence, as well as the content, of natural right and the question concerning the sanctions for natural right, the latter
question being identical with the question of the status of man
within the whole, or of man's origin. Rousseau is therefore
not altogether wrong in saying that all political philosophers
have felt the necessity to go back to the state of nature, i.e., to
man's original condition; all political philosophers are forced

41. Moses Mendelssohn, *Gesammelte Schriften* (Jubilaeums-Ausgabe), II, 92; cf.
Second Discourse, p. 83, and above, pp. 230–31.

to reflect upon whether and how far the demands of justice
have a support which is independent of human enactments.
Rousseau could not have returned to the academic natural
right teaching of his time except by simply adopting the traditional natural theology on which that teaching was explicitly
or implicitly based.[42]

The character, as well as the content, of natural right may
be decisively affected by the way in which the origin of man is
conceived. This does not do away with the fact that natural
right is addressed to man as he is now and not to the stupid
animal which lived in Rousseau's state of nature. It is therefore difficult to understand how Rousseau could have based his
natural right teaching on what he believed he knew of natural
man or man in the state of nature. His conception of the state
of nature points toward a natural right teaching which is no
longer based on considerations of man's nature, or it points
toward a law of reason which is no longer understood as a law
of nature.[43] Rousseau may be said to have indicated the character of such a law of reason by his teaching concerning the general will, by a teaching which can be regarded as the outcome
of the attempt to find a "realistic" substitute for the traditional natural law. According to that teaching, the limitation
of human desires is affected, not by the ineffectual requirements of man's perfection, but by the recognition in all others
of the same right which one claims for one's self; all others
necessarily take an effective interest in the recognition of their
rights, whereas no one, or but a few, take an effective interest
in human perfection of other men. This being the case, my
desire transforms itself into a rational desire by being "generalized," i.e., by being conceived as the content of a law which
binds all members of society equally; a desire which survives

42. Cf. *C.S.*, II, 6 (see chap. iii, n. 18, above). As for the connection between the
C.S. and the *Second Discourse*, see nn. 26 and 32 above.

43. Cf. *C.S.*, II, 4, and *Second Discourse*, p. 77

the test of "generalization" is, by this very fact, proved to be rational and hence just. By ceasing to conceive of the law of reason as a law of nature, Rousseau could have made his Socratic wisdom radically independent of natural science. Yet he did not take that step. The lesson which he had learned from Montesquieu counteracted in his thought the doctrinaire tendencies inherent in natural constitutional law; and extreme doctrinairism was the outcome of the attempt to make the law of reason radically independent of the knowledge of man's nature.[44]

The conclusions regarding the state of nature which Rousseau drew from Hobbes's premises seemed to suggest a return to the conception of man as a social animal. There was a further reason why Rousseau might have returned to that conception. According to Hobbes, all virtues and duties arise from the concern with self-preservation alone and hence immediately from calculation. Rousseau, however, felt that calculation or self-interest is not strong enough as the bond of society and not profound enough as the root of society. Yet he refused to admit that man is by nature a social being. He thought that the root of society can be found in human passions or sentiments as distinguished from a fundamental sociality of man. His reason can be stated as follows: If society is natural, it is not essentially based on the wills of the individuals; it is essentially nature, and not a man's will, which makes him a member of society. On the other hand, the primacy of the individ-

44. Rousseau agrees with the classics by explicitly agreeing with the "principle established by Montesquieu" that "liberty not being a fruit of all climates, is not within the reach of all peoples" (*C.S.*, III, 8). Acceptance of this principle explains the moderate character of most of Rousseau's proposals which were meant for immediate application. Deviating from Montesquieu and the classics, Rousseau teaches, however, that "every legitimate government is republican" (II, 6) and hence that almost all existing regimes are illegitimate: "very few nations have laws" (III, 15). This amounts to saying that in many cases despotic regimes are inevitable, without becoming, by this fact, legitimate: the strangling of a sultan is as lawful as all governmental actions of the sultan (*Second Discourse*, p. 149).

ual in relation to society is preserved if the place which Hobbes had assigned to calculation or self-interest is assigned to passion or sentiment. Rousseau refused, then, to return to the conception of man as a social animal because he was concerned with the radical independence of the individual, i.e., of every human being. He retained the notion of the state of nature because the state of nature guaranteed the individual's radical independence. He retained the notion of the state of nature because he was concerned with such a natural standard as favored in the highest possible degree the independence of the individual.[45]

Rousseau could not have maintained the notion of the state of nature if the depreciation or ex-inanition of the state of nature which he unintentionally effected had not been outweighed in his thought by a corresponding increase in the importance of independence or freedom, i.e., of the most characteristic feature of man in the state of nature. In Hobbes's doctrine, freedom, or the right of everyone to be the sole judge of the means conducive to his self-preservation, had been subordinate to self-preservation; in the case of conflict between freedom and self-preservation, self-preservation takes precedence. According to Rousseau, however, freedom is a higher good than life. In fact, he tends to identify freedom with virtue or with goodness. He says that freedom is obedience to the law which one has given to one's self. This means, in the first place, that not merely obedience to the law but legislation itself must originate in the individual. It means, secondly, that freedom is not so much either the condition or the consequence of virtue as virtue itself. What is true of virtue can also be said of goodness, which Rousseau distinguished from virtue: freedom is identical with goodness; to be free, or to be one's self, is to be good—this is one meaning of his thesis that man is by nature good. Above all, he suggests that the traditional defini-

45. Hachette, I, 374; *Émile*, I, 286-87, 306, II, 44-45.

THE CRISIS OF MODERN NATURAL RIGHT   279

tion of man be replaced by a new definition according to which not rationality but freedom is the specific distinction of man.[46] Rousseau may be said to have originated "the philosophy of freedom." The connection between the developed form of "the philosophy of freedom," i.e., German idealism, and Rousseau, and hence Hobbes, was realized by no one more clearly than by Hegel. Hegel noted the kinship between Kant's and Fichte's idealism and "the anti-socialistic systems of natural right," i.e., those natural right doctrines which deny man's natural sociality and "posit the being of the individual as the first and highest thing."[47]

"The anti-socialistic systems of natural right" had emerged by virtue of a transformation of Epicureanism. According to the Epicurean doctrine, the individual is by nature free from all social bonds because the natural good is identical with the pleasant, i.e., fundamentally with what is pleasant to the body. But, according to the same doctrine, the individual is by nature kept within definite bounds because there is a natural limit to pleasure, namely, the greatest or highest pleasure: endless striving is against nature. Hobbes's transformation of Epicureanism implied the liberation of the individual not only from all social bonds which do not originate in his will but also from any natural end. Rejecting the notion of a natural end of a man, he no longer understood by the "good life" of the individual his compliance with, or assimilation to, a universal pattern which is apprehended before it is willed. He

46. *Second Discourse*, pp. 93 (cf. Spinoza, *Ethics*, III, 9 schol.), 116, 130, 138, 140–41, 151; *C.S.*, I, 1 (beginning), 4, 8, 11 (beginning); III, 9 n. (end). Cf. the headings of the first two parts of Hobbes's *De cive;* also Locke, *Treatises*, II, secs. 4, 23, 95, 123.

47. "Wissenschaftliche Behandlungsarten des Naturrechts," *Schriften zur Politik und Rechtsphilosophie*, ed. Lasson, pp. 346–47: "In einer niedrigern Abstraktion ist die Unendlichkeit zwar auch als Absolutheit des Subjekts in der Glückseligkeitslehre überhaupt, und im Naturrecht insbesondere von den Systemen, welche anti-sozialistisch heissen und das Sein des einzelnen als das Erste und Höchste setzen, herausgehoben, aber nicht in die reine Abstraktion, welche sie in dem Kantischen oder Fichteschen Idealismus erhalten hat." Cf. Hegel's *Encyclopädie*, secs. 481–82.

conceived of the good life in terms of man's beginnings or of man's natural right as distinguished from his duty or perfection or virtue. Natural right, as he understood it, canalizes rather than limits infinite desire: that infinite desire for power after power which originates in the concern with self-preservation becomes identical with the legitimate pursuit of happiness. Natural right thus understood leads only to conditional duties and to mercenary virtue. Rousseau was satisfied that happiness as Hobbes understood it is indistinguishable from constant misery[48] and that Hobbes's and Locke's "utilitarian" understanding of morality is inadequate: morality must have a more solid support than calculation. In trying to restore an adequate understanding of happiness and of morality, he had recourse to a considerably modified version of traditional natural theology, but he felt that even that version of natural theology was exposed to "insoluble objections."[49] To the extent to which he was impressed by the power of these objections, he was compelled to attempt to understand human life by starting from the Hobbesian notion of the primacy of right or of freedom as distinguished from the primacy of perfection or virtue or duty. He attempted to graft the notion of unconditional duties and of nonmercenary virtue onto the Hobbesian notion of the primacy of freedom or of rights. He admitted, as it were, that duties must be conceived of as derivative from rights or that there is no natural law, properly speaking, which antedates the human will. Yet he sensed that the basic right in question cannot be the right of self-preservation, i.e., a right which leads only to conditional duties and which is itself derivative from an impulse that man shares with the brutes. If morality or humanity were to be understood adequately, they had to be traced to a right or a freedom which is radically and specifically human. Hobbes had implicitly ad-

48. *Second Discourse*, pp. 104–5, 122, 126, 147, 160–63; cf. also *Émile*, I, 286–87.
49. Cf. n. 28 above.

mitted the existence of such a freedom. For he had implicitly admitted that if the traditional dualism of substances, of mind and of body, is abandoned, science cannot be possible except if meaning, order, or truth originates solely in man's creative action, or if man has the freedom of a creator.[50] Hobbes was, in fact, compelled to replace the traditional dualism of body and mind, not by materialistic monism, but by the novel dualism of nature (or substance) and freedom. What Hobbes had, in fact, suggested in regard to science was applied by Rousseau to morality. He tended to conceive of the fundamental freedom, or of the fundamental right, as such a creative act as issues in the establishment of unconditional duties and in nothing else: freedom is essentially self-legislation. The ultimate outcome of this attempt was the substitution of freedom for virtue or the view that it is not virtue which makes man free but freedom which makes man virtuous.

It is true that Rousseau distinguishes true freedom or moral freedom, which consists in obedience to the law that one has given to one's self and which presupposes civil society, not only from civil freedom but, above all, from the natural freedom which belongs to the state of nature, i.e., to a state characterized by the rule of blind appetite and hence by slavery in the moral sense of the term. But it is also true that he blurs these distinctions. For he also says that in civil society everyone "obeys only himself and remains as free as he was before," i.e., as he was in the state of nature. This means that natural freedom remains the model for civil freedom, just as natural equality remains the model for civil equality.[51] Civil freedom, in its turn, being in a way obedience to one's self alone, certainly comes very close to moral freedom. The blurring of the distinctions between natural freedom, civil freedom, and moral

50. See pp. 172–74 above.

51. *C.S.*, I, 6, 8; *Second Discourse*, p. 65. As for the ambiguity of "freedom," cf. also *Second Discourse*, pp. 138–41.

freedom is no accidental error: the novel understanding of moral freedom originated in the notion that the primary moral phenomenon is the freedom of the state of nature. At any rate, the enhancement of the status of "freedom" gives the almost exploded notion of the state of nature a new lease on life in Rousseau's doctrine.

In Hobbes's and Locke's doctrines, the state of nature had been, as one might say, a negative standard: the state of nature is characterized by such a self-contradiction as points to one and only one sufficient solution, which is "the mighty leviathan" whose "blood is money." Rousseau, however, thought that civil society as such, to say nothing of civil society as Hobbes and Locke had conceived of it, is characterized by a fundamental self-contradiction and that it is precisely the state of nature which is free from self-contradiction; man in the state of nature is happy because he is radically independent, whereas man in civil society is unhappy because he is radically dependent. Civil society must therefore be transcended in the direction not of man's highest end but of his beginning, of his earliest past. Thus the state of nature tended to become for Rousseau a positive standard. Yet he admitted that accidental necessity had forced man to leave the state of nature and has transformed him in such a manner as to incapacitate him forever for a return to that blessed state. Hence Rousseau's answer to the question of the good life takes on this form: the good life consists in the closest approximation to the state of nature which is possible on the level of humanity.[52]

On the political plane that closest approximation is achieved by a society which is constructed in conformity with the requirements of the social contract. Like Hobbes and Locke, Rousseau starts from the premise that in the state of nature all men are free and equal and that the fundamental desire is the

---

52. *Second Discourse*, pp. 65, 104–5, 117–18, 122, 125–26, 147, 151, 160–63, 177–79; *Julie*, p. 385; *C.S.*, II, 11; III, 15; *Émile*, II, 125.

THE CRISIS OF MODERN NATURAL RIGHT   283

desire for self-preservation. Deviating from his predecessors, he contends that at the beginning, or in the original state of nature, the promptings of the desire for self-preservation were tempered by compassion and that the original state of nature was considerably changed through accidental necessity, prior to man's entering civil society; civil society becomes necessary or possible only in a very late stage of the state of nature. The decisive change which took place within the state of nature consisted in the weakening of compassion. Compassion was weakened because of the emergence of vanity or pride and ultimately because of the emergence of inequality and therefore of the dependence of man on his fellows. As a consequence of this development, self-preservation became increasingly difficult. Once the critical point is reached, self-preservation demands the introduction of an artificial substitute for natural compassion, or of a conventional substitute for that natural freedom and that natural equality which existed at the beginning. It is the self-preservation of everyone which requires that the closest possible approximation to original freedom and equality be achieved within society.[53]

The root of civil society must then be sought exclusively in the desire for self-preservation or in the right of self-preservation. The right to self-preservation implies the right to the means required for self-preservation. Accordingly, there exists a natural right to appropriation. Everyone has by nature the right to appropriate to himself what he needs of the fruits of the earth. Everyone may acquire through his labor, and only through his labor, an exclusive right to the produce of the land which he has cultivated, and therewith an exclusive right to the land itself, at least until the next harvest. Continuous cultivation may even legitimate continuous possession of the land cultivated, but it does not create property right in that

53. *Second Discourse*, pp. 65, 75, 77, 81, 109–10, 115, 118, 120, 125, 129, 130, 134; C.S., I, 6 (beginning); I, 2.

land; property right is the creation of positive law; prior to the sanction by positive law, land is usurped, i.e., acquired by force, and not truly owned. Otherwise, natural right would hallow the right of the first occupier to the detriment of the right of self-preservation of those who, perhaps through no fault of their own, failed to take possession of land; the poor retain the natural right to acquire as free men what they need for self-preservation. If they are unable to appropriate what they need by cultivating a plot of their own because everything has already been appropriated by others, they may use force. Thus a conflict arises between the right of the first occupiers and the right of those who must rely on force. The need for appropriation of the necessities of life transforms the latest stage of the state of nature into the most horrible state of war. Once this point has been reached, it is to the interest of everyone, of the poor as well as of the rich, that right should succeed to violence, i.e., that peace be guaranteed through convention or compact. This amounts to saying that "according to the maxim of the wise Locke, there could not be injustice where there is no property" or that in the state of nature everyone has "an unlimited right to everything which tempts him and which he can get." The compact which is at the basis of factual societies transformed men's factual possessions as they existed at the end of the state of nature into genuine property. It therefore sanctioned earlier usurpation. Factual society rests on a fraud perpetrated by the rich against the poor: political power rests on "economic" power. No improvement can ever cure this original defect of civil society; it is inevitable that the law should favor the haves against the have-nots. Yet, in spite of this, the self-preservation of everyone requires that the social contract be concluded and kept.[54]

The social contract would endanger the individual's self-preservation if it did not allow him to remain the judge of the

54. *Second Discourse*, pp. 82, 106, 117, 118, 125, 128–29, 131–35, 141, 145, 152; *C.S.*, I, 2, 8, 9; II, 4 (toward the end); *Émile*, I, 309; II, 300.

THE CRISIS OF MODERN NATURAL RIGHT   285

means required for his self-preservation or to remain as free as
he was before. On the other hand, it is of the essence of civil
society that private judgment be replaced by public judgment.
These conflicting demands are reconciled, as far as they can be
reconciled, if those public judgments which issue in executive
action conform strictly with law, if those public judgments
which are laws are the work of the citizen body, and if every
adult male who is subject to the laws can have influenced their
content through his vote. Voting on a law means to conceive
of the object of one's private or natural will as the object of a
law which is binding on all equally and benefits all equally, or
to restrict one's selfish desire by considering the undesirable
consequences which would follow if everyone else indulged
his selfish desire as well. Legislation by the all-inclusive citizen body is therefore the conventional substitute for natural
compassion. The citizen is indeed less free than man in the
state of nature, since he cannot follow his unqualified private
judgment, but he is freer than man in the state of nature, since
he is habitually protected by his fellows. The citizen is as free
as man in the (original) state of nature, since, being subject
only to the law or to the public will or to the general will, he
is not subject to the private will of any other man. But if every
kind of personal dependence or of "private government" is to
be avoided, everyone and everything must be subject to the
general will; the social contract requires "the total alienation
of each associate, with all his rights, to the whole community" or the transformation of "every individual who by himself is a perfect and solitary whole into a part of a greater
whole from which, in a sense, that individual receives his life
and his being." In order to remain as free in society as he was
before, man must become completely "collectivized" or "de-
naturalized."[55]

55. *C.S.*, I, 6, 7; II, 2–4, 7; *Émile*, I, 13. The discussion of the social contract in the
Second Discourse is admittedly provisional (p. 141).

Freedom in society is possible only by virtue of the complete surrender of everyone (and in particular of the government) to the will of a free society. By surrendering all his rights to society, man loses the right to appeal from the verdicts of society, i.e., from the positive law, to natural right: all rights become social rights. Free society rests and depends upon the absorption of natural right by positive law. Natural right is legitimately absorbed by the positive law of a society which is constructed in accordance with natural right. The general will takes the place of the natural law. "By the very fact that he is, the sovereign is always what he ought to be."[56]

Rousseau sometimes called the free society as he conceived of it a "democracy." Democracy is closer to the equality of the state of nature than is any other regime. Yet democracy must be "wisely tempered." While everyone must have a vote, the votes must be "arranged" in such a manner as to favor the middle class and the rural population as against *la canaille* of the big towns. Otherwise, those who have nothing to lose might sell freedom for bread.[57]

The absorption of natural right by the positive law of a properly qualified democracy would be defensible if there were a guaranty that the general will—and this means, for all practical purposes, the will of the legal majority—could not err. The general will or the will of the people never errs in so far as it always wills the good of the people, but the people do not always see the good of the people. The general will is therefore in need of enlightenment. Enlightened individuals may see the good of society, but there is no guaranty that they will espouse it if it conflicts with their private good. Calculation

56. *C.S.*, I, 7; II, 3, 6. Cf. *ibid.*, II, 12 ("Division of Laws") with the parallels in Hobbes, Locke, and Montesquieu, to say nothing of Hooker and Suarez; Rousseau does not even mention natural law.

57. *Second Discourse*, pp. 66, 143; *Julie*, pp. 470–71; *C.S.*, IV, 4; *Montagne*, pp. 252, 300–301. Cf. Rousseau's criticism of the aristocratic principle of the classics in *Narcisse*, pp. 50–51, and in the *Second Discourse*, pp. 179–80.

THE CRISIS OF MODERN NATURAL RIGHT   287

and self-interest are not strong enough as social bonds. Both
the people as a whole and the individuals are then equally in
need of a guide; the people must be taught to know what it
wills, and the individual, who as a natural being is concerned
exclusively with his private good, must be transformed into a
citizen who unhesitatingly prefers the common good to his
private good. The solution of this twofold problem is supplied
by the legislator, or the father of a nation, i.e., by a man of
superior intelligence, who, by ascribing divine origin to a code
which he has devised or by honoring the gods with his own
wisdom, both convinces the people of the goodness of the laws
which he submits to its vote and transforms the individual
from a natural being into a citizen. Only by the action of the
legislator can the conventional acquire, if not the status, at
least the force, of the natural. It goes without saying that the
arguments by which the legislator convinces the citizens of
his divine mission or of the divine sanction for his code are
necessarily of doubtful solidity. One might think that, once
the code were ratified, a "social spirit" developed, and the
wise legislation accepted on account of its proved wisdom
rather than its pretended origin, the belief in the superhuman
origin of the code would no longer be required. But this suggestion overlooks the fact that the living respect for old laws,
"the prejudice of antiquity" which is indispensable for the
health of society, can only with difficulty survive the public
questioning of the accounts regarding their origin. In other
words, the transformation of natural man into a citizen is a
problem coeval with society itself, and therefore society has a
continuous need for at least an equivalent to the mysterious
and awe-inspiring action of the legislator. For society can be
healthy only if the opinions and sentiments engendered by
society overcome and, as it were, annihilate the natural sentiments. That is to say, society must do everything possible to
render the citizens oblivious of the very facts that political

philosophy brings to the center of their attention as the foundations of society. Free society stands or falls by a specific obfuscation against which philosophy necessarily revolts. The problem posed by political philosophy must be forgotten if the solution to which political philosophy leads is to work.[58]

It is true, no doubt, that Rousseau's doctrine of the legislator is meant to clarify the fundamental problem of civil society rather than to suggest a practical solution, except in so far as that doctrine adumbrates Rousseau's own function. The precise reason why he had to abandon the classical notion of the legislator was that that notion is liable to obscure the sovereignty of the people, i.e., to lead, for all practical purposes, to the substitution of the supremacy of the law for the full sovereignty of the people. The classical notion of the legislator is irreconcilable with Rousseau's notion of freedom which leads to the demand for periodic appeals from the whole established order to the sovereign will of the people or from the will of past generations to the will of the living generation. Rousseau, therefore, had to find a substitute for the action of the legislator. According to his final suggestion, the function originally intrusted to the legislator must be discharged by a civil religion described from somewhat different points of view in the *Social Contract*, on the one hand, and the *Émile*, on the other. Only the civil religion will engender the sentiments required of the citizen. We need not go into the question of whether Rousseau himself fully subscribed to the religion which he presented in the profession of faith of the Savoyard vicar, a question that cannot be answered by reference to what he said when he was persecuted on account of that profession. What is decisive is the fact that, according to his explicit views about the relation of knowledge, faith, and the people,

58. *Narcisse*, p. 56; *Second Discourse*, pp. 66–67, 143; *C.S.*, II, 3, 6–7; III, 2, 11. Compare the reference to miracles in the chapter on the legislator (*C.S.*, II, 7) with the explicit discussion of the problem of miracles in *Montagne*, ii–iii.

THE CRISIS OF MODERN NATURAL RIGHT   289

the people cannot have more than opinion regarding the truth of this or any other religion. One may even wonder whether any human being can have any genuine knowledge in this respect, since the religion preached by the Savoyard vicar is exposed to "insoluble objections." Therefore, every civil religion would seem, in the last analysis, to have the same character as the legislator's account of the origin of his code, at least in so far as both are essentially endangered by the "dangerous pyrrhonism" fostered by science; the "insoluble objections" to which even the best of all religions is exposed are dangerous truths. Precisely a free society cannot exist if he who doubts the fundamental dogma of the civil religion does not outwardly conform.[59]

Apart from the civil religion, the equivalent to the action of the early legislator is custom. Custom, too, socializes the wills of the individuals independently of the generalization of the wills which takes place in the act of legislation. Law is even preceded by custom. For civil society is preceded by the nation or the tribe, i.e., a group which is kept together by customs arising from the fact that all members of the group are exposed to, and molded by, the same natural influences. The prepolitical nation is more natural than civil society, since natural causes are more effective in its production than in the genesis of civil society, which is produced by contract. The nation is closer to the original state of nature than is civil society, and therefore it is in important respects superior to civil society. Civil society will approximate the state of nature on the level of humanity to a higher degree, or it will be more healthy, if it rests on the almost natural basis of nationality or if it has a national individuality. National custom or national cohesion is a deeper root of civil society than are calculation and self-interest and hence than the social contract. National

59. *Julie*, pp. 502–6; *C.S.*, IV, 8; *Beaumont*, p. 479; *Montagne*, pp. 121–36, 180; cf. also n. 28 above.

custom and national "philosophy" are the matrix of the general will, just as feeling is the matrix of reason. Hence the past, and especially the early past, of one's own nation tends to become of higher dignity than any cosmopolitan aspirations. If man's humanity is acquired by accidental causation, that humanity will be radically different from nation to nation and from age to age.[60]

It is not surprising that Rousseau did not regard the free society as he conceived of it as the solution to the human problem. Even if that society met the requirements of freedom more nearly than did any other society, what would follow would simply be that true freedom must be sought beyond civil society. If civil society and duty are coextensive, as Rousseau suggests, human freedom must be sought even beyond duty or virtue. With a view to the connection between virtue and civil society, as well as to the problematic character of the relation between virtue and happiness, Rousseau made a distinction between virtue and goodness. Virtue presupposes effort and habituation; it is primarily a burden, and its demands are harsh. Goodness, i.e., the desire to do good or at least the complete absence of a desire to do harm, is simply natural; the pleasures of goodness come immediately from nature; goodness is immediately connected with the natural sentiment of compassion; it belongs to the heart rather than to conscience or reason. Rousseau taught, indeed, that virtue is superior to goodness. Yet the ambiguity of his notion of freedom, or, in other words, his longing for the happiness of prepolitical life, makes that teaching questionable from his own point of view.[61]

60. *Narcisse*, p. 56; *Second Discourse*, pp. 66–67, 74, 123, 125, 150, 169–70; *C.S.*, II, 8, 10, 12; III, 1; *Émile*, II, 287–88; *Pologne*, chaps. ii–iii; cf. also Alfred Cobban, *Rousseau and the Modern State* (London, 1934), p. 284.

61. Cf. especially *C.S.*, I, 8, and II, 11; *Second Discourse*, pp. 125–26, 150; *Julie*, pp. 222, 274, 277; *Émile*, II, 48, 274–75; *Confessions*, II, 182, 259, 303; III, 43; *Rêveries*, vi.

THE CRISIS OF MODERN NATURAL RIGHT   291

From this we can understand Rousseau's attitude toward the family or, more precisely, toward conjugal and paternal love as well as toward heterosexual love simply. Love is closer to the original state of nature than is civil society, duty, or virtue. Love is simply incompatible with compulsion and even self-compulsion; it is free or it is not. It is for this reason that conjugal and paternal love can be "the sweetest sentiments," or even "the sweetest sentiments of nature," "which are known to man" and that heterosexual love simply can be "the sweetest of passions" or "the most delicious sentiment which can enter the human heart." These sentiments give rise to "rights of the blood" and "rights of love"; they create bonds which are more sacred than any man-made bonds. Through love, man achieves a closer approximation to the state of nature on the level of humanity than he does through a life of citizenship or virtue. Rousseau returns from the classical city to the family and the loving couple. Using his own language, we may say that he returns from the concern of the citizen to the noblest concern of the bourgeois.[62]

Yet, at least according to that writing of Rousseau in which he revealed his principles "with the greatest boldness, not to say audacity," there is an element of the conventional or of the factitious even in love.[63] Love being a social phenomenon and man being by nature asocial, it becomes necessary to consider whether the solitary individual is not capable of the closest approximation to the state of nature which is possible on the level of humanity. Rousseau has spoken in glowing terms of the charms and raptures of solitary contemplation. By "solitary contemplation" he does not understand philosophy or the culmination of philosophy. Solitary contemplation, as he understands it, is altogether different from, not to say hostile to,

62. *Second Discourse*, pp. 122, 124; *D'Alembert*, pp. 256–57; *Julie*, pp. 261, 331, 392, 411 (cf. also pp. 76, 147–48, 152, 174 n., 193, 273–75); *Rêveries*, x (p. 164).

63. *Second Discourse*, pp. 111, 139.

thinking or observation. It consists of, or it leads up to, "the feeling of existence," i.e., the pleasant feeling of one's own existence. If man has withdrawn from everything outside himself, if he has emptied himself of every affection other than the feeling of existence, he enjoys the supreme felicity—godlike self-sufficiency and impassibility; he finds consolation only in himself by being fully himself and by belonging fully to himself, since the past and the future are extinguished for him. It is in giving himself completely to this feeling that civilized man completes the return to the primitive state of nature on the level of humanity. For, whereas sociable man derives the feeling of his existence, as it were, exclusively from the opinions of his fellows, natural man—indeed even the savage— feels his existence naturally; he gives himself "to the sole feeling of his present existence without any idea of the future." The feeling of existence is "man's first feeling." It is more fundamental than the desire for self-preservation; man is concerned with the preservation of his existence because existence itself, mere existence, is by nature pleasant.[64]

The feeling of existence as Rousseau experienced and described it has a rich articulation which must have been lacking in the feeling of existence as it was experienced by man in the state of nature. Here at last civilized man or those civilized men who have returned from civil society to solitude reach a degree of happiness of which the stupid animal must have been utterly incapable. In the last analysis it is only this superiority of civilized man, or of the best among civilized men, which permits Rousseau to contend without hesitation that, while the emergence of civil society was bad for the human species or for the common good, it was good for the individual.[65] The ultimate justification of civil society is, then, the fact that it allows a certain type of individual to enjoy the supreme felicity by withdrawing from civil society, i.e., by living at its

64. *Ibid.*, pp. 96, 118, 151, 165; *Émile*, I, 286; *Rêveries*, V and VII. See above, pp. 261–62.

65. *Second Discourse*, pp. 84, 116, 125–26; *Beaumont*, p. 471.

THE CRISIS OF MODERN NATURAL RIGHT   293

fringes. Whereas in the earliest of his important writings the citizen of Geneva had said that "every useless citizen may be regarded as a pernicious man," he says in his last writing that he himself always was indeed a useless citizen, yet that his contemporaries have done wrong in proscribing him from society as a pernicious member, instead of merely removing him from society as a useless member.[66] The type of man foreshadowed by Rousseau, which justifies civil society by transcending it, is no longer the philosopher but what later came to be called the "artist." His claim to privileged treatment is based on his sensitivity rather than on his wisdom, on his goodness or compassion rather than on his virtue. He admits the precarious character of his claim: he is a citizen with a bad conscience. Yet, since his conscience accuses not merely himself but at the same time the society to which he belongs, he is inclined to regard himself as the conscience of society. But he is bound to have a bad conscience for being the bad conscience of society.

One must contrast the dreamlike character of Rousseau's solitary contemplation with the wakefulness of philosophic contemplation. In addition, one must take into consideration the insoluble conflict between the presuppositions of his solitary contemplation and his natural theology (and therewith the morality based on that theology). Then one realizes that the claim which he raises on behalf of the individual, or of some rare individuals, over against society lacks clarity and definiteness. More precisely, the definiteness of the act of claiming contrasts sharply with the indefiniteness of the content of the claim. This is not surprising. The notion that the good life consists in the return on the level of humanity to the state of nature, i.e., to a state which completely lacks all human traits, necessarily leads to the consequence that the individual claims such an ultimate freedom from society as lacks any definite human content. But this fundamental defect of the

66. *First Discourse*, p. 131; *Rêveries*, VI (end).

state of nature as the goal of human aspiration was in Rousseau's eyes its perfect justification: the very indefiniteness of the state of nature as a goal of human aspiration made that state the ideal vehicle of freedom. To have a reservation against society in the name of the state of nature means to have a reservation against society without being either compelled or able to indicate the way of life or the cause or the pursuit for the sake of which that reservation is made. The notion of a return to the state of nature on the level of humanity was the ideal basis for claiming a freedom from society which is not a freedom for something. It was the ideal basis for an appeal from society to something indefinite and undefinable, to an ultimate sanctity of the individual as individual, unredeemed and unjustified. This was precisely what freedom came to mean for a considerable number of men. Every freedom which is freedom for something, every freedom which is justified by reference to something higher than the individual or than man as mere man, necessarily restricts freedom or, which is the same thing, establishes a tenable distinction between freedom and license. It makes freedom conditional on the purpose for which it is claimed. Rousseau is distinguished from many of his followers by the fact that he still saw clearly the disproportion between this undefined and undefinable freedom and the requirements of civil society. As he confessed at the end of his career, no book attracted and profited him as much as the writings of Plutarch.[67] The solitary dreamer still bowed to Plutarch's heroes.

67. *Rêveries,* IV (beginning).

[4]

Rousseau's Moral Realism:
Replacing Natural Law with the General Will

ARTHUR M. MELZER
Michigan State University

The Social Contract *is reinterpreted by emphasizing its relation to Rousseau's other writings and doctrines. In the spirit of Hobbesian realism, Rousseau regards natural law and other forms of "private morality" as ineffectual, invalid, and in practice dangerous tools of oppression and subversion. But, still more realistic than Hobbes, Rousseau thinks it impossible to build a nonoppressive state on men's selfish interests alone and embraces the classical view that morality or virtue is politically necessary (as well as intrinsically good). Rousseau's doctrine of the natural goodness of man, however, which traces all vice to the effects of oppression, leads him to conclude that the non-oppression more or less guaranteed by the absolute rule of general laws is also sufficient to make men virtuous. Thus Rousseau can declare law as such (General Will) infallible and "sovereign"—and he* must *do so in order to protect rule of law from its greatest danger, the subversive appeal to "natural law."*

Rousseau's political philosophy may be said to comprise three characteristic elements: the theory of the natural goodness of man described in the *Second Discourse* and *Emile;* the critique of progress and enlightenment in the *First Discourse,* or, more generally, the skeptically "realistic" assessment of the worth and power of reason; and the elaborate juridical doctrine of the *Social Contract,* which calls for the absolute sovereignty of the General Will. How these three elements relate to one another is rarely discussed, and when the *Social Contract,* in particular, is related to the other two elements, as often as not the purpose is to demonstrate its inconsistency with Rousseau's previous ideas.

Rousseau stated expressly, however, that his thought formed a single, consistent whole, that his writings must be understood with reference to one another, and specifically that the *Social Contract* "should be considered as a kind of appendix to [*Emile*]" (Letter to Duchesne, May 23, 1762; *R. Juge de J.-J.,* pp. 932-935; *Works,* III, pp. 106-107).[1] Indeed, as I hope to show, the fundamental intention and presuppositions of the *Social Contract* are not stated or defended in that work. Consequently, the attempt to interpret it in isolation falls into various misunderstandings, the most important being the view that Rousseau's

doctrine is moralistic and utopian, and the view that its primary purpose is to combat the danger to the people posed by rulers. This article attempts to reinterpret the *Social Contract* by showing how its doctrines grow directly out of the other two elements of Rousseau's thought.

The Goal of Politics

In a crucial passage of the *Confessions* Rousseau summarizes the overall goal and strategy of his political thought.

> This great question of the best possible Government seemed to me to reduce to this one. What is the nature of the Government suited to make a People the most virtuous, the most enlightened, the wisest, and, in short, the best, to take this word in its largest sense? I thought I saw that this question was closely tied to this other one, if indeed it was different from it. What is the Government which by its nature always adheres most closely to the law? (*Confessions,* pp. 404-405)

The goal of politics is not merely to secure preservation and wealth, but to produce virtuous, healthy human beings. Revolted by the degrading consequences of modern politics and philosophy which "talk only of business and money," Rousseau consciously returns to the "ancient politicians [who] incessantly talked about morals and virtue" (*First Discourse,* p. 51).

The means to the end of virtue, Rousseau adds without explanation, is to "adhere most closely to the law." To understand why rule of law as such will produce virtue, one must begin from what Rousseau calls the fundamental principle of his

---

This study was undertaken during the tenure of a Duke Mellon Fellowship. The author would like to thank the Mellon Foundation and Duke University for their generous assistance.

[1]References for *Confessions, Héloïse, Rousseau Juge de Jean-Jacques,* and *Montagne* are to *Works* (1959-1969); translations are my own.

thought: "nature made man happy and good, but society depraves him and makes him miserable" (*R. Juge de J.-J.*, p. 934). By nature man already possesses "virtue, which is the strength and vigor of the soul" (*First Discourse*, p. 37); he loses it in society through the effects of "personal dependence," that is, all social relations in which one man is dependent on the will of another (hence also "inequality" or "oppression," broadly construed). Men's ever-shifting relations of domination and servitude destroy their inner unity and strength and make them cowardly, spiteful, vain, and deceitful. Thus freedom from dependence on others is needed to maintain man's natural health of soul, and such freedom is produced by the absolute rule of law. This chain of reasoning is presented most clearly in a passage from *Emile* that "resolves all the contradictions of the social system":

> There are two sorts of dependence: dependence on things, which is from nature; dependence on men, which is from society. Dependence on things, since it has no morality, is in no way detrimental to freedom and engenders no vices. Dependence on men, since it is without order, engenders all the vices, and by it, master and slave are mutually corrupted. If there is any means of remedying this ill in society, it is to substitute law for man and to arm the general wills with a real strength superior to the action of every particular will. If the laws of nations could, like those of nature, have an inflexibility that no human force could ever conquer, dependence on men would then become dependence on things again. (*Emile*, p. 85)

The absolute rule of law creates freedom from personal dependence, and freedom preserves man's natural virtue or health of soul; therefore, "This is . . . the great problem of statecraft: to find a form of government that puts law above man" (Letter to Mirabeau, July 26, 1767).[2]

The crucial importance assigned to the rule of law might seem to be another aspect of Rousseau's return to classical thought. One thinks of the famous reply of the Pythagorean to a man who asked him the best means of educating his son to virtue: "Let him be born in a city with good laws" (Diogenes, Laertius, VIII-1.15). But the strictness and urgency of Rousseau's demand for rule of law reveals rather his break with

classical thought. In the saying from Diogenes, as in the thought of Plato and Aristotle, it is not law as such but substantively good or just law that is praised. Ultimately, Plato considered the form or "generality" of law an obstacle to justice and regarded the absolute, lawless rule of the wise as the best form of government. Rousseau's praise of law is greater, extending to law as such, regardless of content. And for him, "the worst of laws is still better than the best master" (*Montagne*, pp. 842-843).

The root of this difference is Rousseau's assertion of the natural goodness of man. He claims that all human vices derive not from nature, but from the effects of personal dependence, servitude, oppression: "I hate servitude as the source of *all the evils* of the human race"—a remarkable statement (*Works*, p. 1019, emphasis added). All classical thinkers would certainly have agreed that servitude and oppression are among the evils men face, but there are other and greater evils. In general, corruption of the soul is worse than enslavement of the body. Rousseau agrees, but maintains that the latter causes the former: "Dependence on men . . . engenders all the vices." The problem of depravity of soul is thus reduced to that of servitude. In short, through the "natural goodness of man" Rousseau accomplishes a revolutionary simplification of the human problem: he reduces it to the problem of oppression.

If oppression is the source of all evil or imperfection, it follows that freedom from dependence—and law, which by its very form, produces such freedom—will be the condition of all good. They guarantee not only preservation but also virtue or health of soul. That is why Rousseau can assert that "the first of all goods is . . . freedom," and that law is "the most sublime of all human institutions" (*Emile*, p. 84; *Political Economy*, p. 214). Rousseau is the first philosopher to have found in freedom and law as such the means to the most comprehensive human good, to men's highest as well as most elementary ends.

With this understanding of Rousseau's general ends and means, we may turn to the *Social Contract* to examine the detailed political doctrine he built on them. In doing so, however, we are met with a surprise: none of the foregoing arguments is to be found in the *Social Contract*. The book contains little mention of virtue, and none of the natural goodness of man. Although it stresses the importance of freedom and law, the reasoning is different from that given above. We do not find a full statement of the goal of politics followed by a discussion and ranking of the various forms of government. Instead, we find what the subtitle to the *Social Contract* calls the "principles of political right," that is, a juridical doctrine, a

---

[2] These simple points get obscured in Rousseau by the following complication. Putting "law above man" requires that men be made into patriotic citizens, which in turn requires the radical redirection of their natural affections. Thus, in society, virtue, or the unity and strength natural to men's souls, can be preserved only in the unnatural form of patriotic "citizen virtue."

rigid, abstract, and legalistic definition of "legitimate" government, deduced from the right to self-preservation. No wonder then that Rousseau's writings have been thought to lack consistency. If his ends are virtue and happiness, why does his major political work argue from self-preservation? And if the crucial task of politics is to preserve man's natural virtue or goodness through the absolute rule of law, why does Rousseau fail to say so in that work? In light of Rousseau's stated ends and means, then, what is the meaning and purpose of this elaborate juridical doctrine based on self-preservation and culminating in the theory of the General Will?

The Purpose of Hobbes's Doctrine

A brief glance at Hobbes helps to answer these questions. The doctrine of the *Social Contract* takes the form of a juridical deduction beginning from a "state of nature" and proceeding through a "social contract" to the establishment of the "sovereignty" of the General Will. Theories of contract and of man's early state have existed since classical times, whereas most would agree that the doctrine of sovereignty was first formulated in the sixteenth century by Bodin. Thomas Hobbes first put these three elements together in the specific form used by Rousseau. Of course, Hobbes's doctrine presents the same difficulty as Rousseau's. Its abstract and legalistic form obscures its moral and political significance; consequently, he too is commonly misunderstood. But if we are willing to listen, Hobbes explains the purpose of his doctrines in his prefaces, and these statements also provide a clue to Rousseau's purposes.

According to the conventional understanding, the key to Hobbes's political thought is his view that man is naturally evil and contentious. Because of men's unruliness, the danger of anarchy is ever present; government has been instituted to maintain the peace and to do so must be absolute and all-powerful. On this reading of Hobbes, however, it has always been difficult to explain the specific form of his juridical doctrine. C. E. Vaughan, the distinguished Rousseau scholar, finds it "a strange irony" that Hobbes, "the first writer to formulate in any detail [the theory of social contract], should have perverted it to ends the direct contrary of those for which it was manifestly devised" (Vaughan, 1925, pp. 22, 12). Why did Hobbes use, indeed invent, the modern doctrine of the state of nature and social contract—which are generally regarded as liberal and liberating—when he sought to strengthen the authority of the state? Why did he scorn the more authoritarian premise of traditional natural law that man was born for society and enthusiastically adopt the individualist principle that man was born for himself alone, hence free?

I believe this dilemma arises from a basic misunderstanding of Hobbes's juridical doctrine and especially of the purposes "for which it was manifestly devised." While asserting that men are selfish, Hobbes denies they are malicious or evil, and only a small minority of men are even strongly ambitious or contentious (*De Cive*, pp. 100-101, 114; *Leviathan*, pp. 99, 101). The ever-present danger of anarchy does not arise from individual lawlessness and crime or from general disobedience, but from political subversion by the ambitious few. By inducing others to follow them, such men form clans, armies, parties, sects, and other associations that resist the government's power and, in some cases, endeavor to supplant it. Thus anarchy threatens not because most men are too unruly and disobedient, but rather because they are too obedient. Being superstitious, fearful, and knavishly ambitious, the mass of men are followers, too easily led by rabble rousers of all kinds, by local heroes, demagogic moralists, and, above all, ambitious priests. Rousseau, agreeing with this interpretation of Hobbes and of the political problem, writes: "Of all Christian authors, the philosopher Hobbes is the only one who correctly saw the evil and the remedy." The evil is the "internal divisions that have never ceased to stir up Christian peoples," the "perpetual conflict of jurisdiction that has made any good polity impossible in Christian states" where "no people has ever been able to figure out whom it was obligated to obey, the [political] master or the priest" (*Social Contract*, pp. 126-127). The people's *misplaced obedience*, by empowering the ambitious, is what leads to anarchy.

Accordingly, two opposite means of strengthening the government and restoring peace present themselves. Hobbes rejects as unrealistic the first and more traditional: to make the ambitious more obedient. The second means is to disarm the ambitious by making the people less obedient, less receptive to authority. That is the avowed purpose of Hobbes's individualistic juridical doctrine. It aims to make men "the less subject to serve the ambition of a few discontented persons, in their purposes against the state" (*Leviathan*, p. 511). More specifically, Hobbes's doctrine of the *state of nature*—where men are equal, selfish, and unable to trust one another—serves to sweep away all traditional forms of authority, all natural claims to rule. Men owe no obedience to the old, the wise, the virtuous, the great, the holy, the customary. Hobbes weakens the claim of family, guild, class, province, church, and tradition, of all mediating institutions and subpolitical associations, leaving a liberated and naked "individual" alone to face the state—the resulting nonauthoritarian but homogeneous, centralized, and absolute state. As Tocqueville would warn the Americans two hundred years later, individualism and tyranny go hand in hand. Hobbes's new doctrine liberates men the better to control them (*Leviathan,* pp. 169-179, 152-153).

Having refuted all natural and supernatural titles to rule, Hobbes then refounds the title and authority of the rulers by the doctrine of *social contract:* men have irrevocably, if tacitly, consented to the rule of the established sovereign. Let others be wiser, holier, or morally superior; only the established sovereign can claim men's (tacit) consent.

But title to rule or legitimacy is one thing, substantive justice another. Hobbes thought it unavailing to try to end conflict over the former without also settling the question of the latter. A man's title to rule may be perfectly clear, but if a natural or transcendent standard of justice is acknowledged by which his particular laws and actions may be judged, then secular and religious ideologues will use it to subvert his rule. Through the call to "justice" or "morality" the people will be induced once again to "join with ambitious and hellish spirits, to the utter ruin of their state" (*De Cive,* p. 97). A further doctrine is needed.

> If any man shall . . . by most firm reasons demonstrate that there are no authentical doctrines concerning right and wrong, good and evil, besides the constituted laws in each realm and government . . . surely he will not only show us the highway to peace, but will also teach us how to avoid the close, dark, and dangerous by-paths of faction and sedition; than which I know not what can be thought more profitable. (*De Cive,* p. 98)

Hobbes aspired to be that man by virtue of his doctrine of *sovereignty.*

He argued that the total war prevailing in man's natural state sweeps away not only all natural titles to rule, but also all morality, all substantive natural law in the traditional sense. Where all are enemies, everything is permitted. (The immoralism of *raison d'état* is, in this way, at the root of the doctrine of sovereignty.) Men themselves must create order and morality by creating the sanctioning power nature lacks, and to do so they must promise to obey this power whatever it commands. Such a promise is rational because any well-enforced command or law, regardless of content, will produce peace, and peace is the whole of the common good. Justice becomes identical to obedience to law, law being understood as the sovereign's command or will. That is the core of the doctrine of sovereignty. The natural law tradition had defined law as rational command to in-

dicate that the essence and obligation of law comes not from the command of authority as such, but from the intrinsic justice of what is commanded. Hobbes's doctrine reverses the relation of justice to command or law:

> Before there was any government, *just* and *unjust* had no being. Legitimate kings therefore make the things they command just, by commanding them, and those which they forbid, unjust, by forbidding them. (*De Cive;* pp. 244-245, italics in the original)

Sovereign command or will is the source of the rules of justice.

In sum, Hobbes invented his new juridical doctrine in order to end misplaced obedience, hence to disarm the ambitious, by liberating the people from all authority and morality outside the will of the established sovereign. Hobbes writes his books

> for your sakes, readers, who I persuaded myself, when you should rightly apprehend and thoroughly understand this doctrine . . . that, weighing the justice of those things you are about, not by the persuasion and advice of private men, but by the laws of the realm, you will no longer suffer ambitious men through the streams of your blood to wade to their own power. (*De Cive,* p. 103)

The purpose of the doctrine Rousseau elaborates in the *Social Contract* is essentially the same, I will argue. We have seen that the goal of virtue, when understood in light of the natural goodness of man, leads him to the view that "this is . . . the great problem of statecraft: to find a form of government that puts law above man." Hobbes and Rousseau share, then, the same political task, the same radical opposition to all challenges to the law (albeit for the sake of different ultimate goals). As we will see, Rousseau also shares Hobbes's understanding of the enemy: the ambitious ideologues and moralists who escape and subvert the law through appeals to supposedly higher standards. To fight the same battle, Rousseau uses the same general doctrine. He replaces all natural titles to rule with one based on social contract, and all natural law or morality with the commands of the sovereign (General) Will. In other words, to understand Rousseau's juridical doctrine—and especially its specific form borrowed from Hobbes—one must go beyond the conventional interpretation that sees only the intention of limiting the power of rulers through popular sovereignty. (After all, there are many ways to argue for democracy.) The doctrine's specific purpose is to disarm the "moralizing" enemies of law.

The remainder of the article will attempt to

elaborate and substantiate this interpretation and to respond to several of the obvious objections to which it is exposed. One such objection is best treated at the outset.

Rousseau and Hobbesian Realism

The difficulty concerns this partial assimilation of Rousseau to Hobbes. Although it is generally conceded that the major concepts of Rousseau's doctrine were borrowed from Hobbes, this fact has not been taken as a sign of any deeper similarity between the two thinkers, a similarity of reasoning and purpose. It appears that no two thinkers could be more dissimilar. Hobbes is the skeptic and realist, limiting his political goals to preservation or peace. Rousseau seems to be the anti-Hobbesian, the utopian moralist who longs for virtue and pure democracy. In order to appreciate the full extent of Rousseau's debt to Hobbes, and therewith the plausibility of the above interpretation, one must see how generally "Hobbesian" Rousseau is, how realistic and cynically hard-headed.[3]

This tough side of Rousseau actually becomes most visible in his disagreements with Hobbes, for these stem not from utopianism but from Rousseau's superior realism. Although he regards Hobbes as "one of the greatest geniuses that has ever existed," Rousseau also finds much to hate in the "horrible system of Hobbes," beginning with the defense of absolute monarchy (*Works*, III, pp. 610-611). Rousseau considers it *unrealistic* to believe that a monarch

> guarantees civil tranquility to his subjects. Perhaps so, but what have they gained if the wars that his ambition brings on them, if his insatiable greed, if the harassment of his ministers are a greater torment than their dissensions would be? (*Social Contract*, p. 49)

Of course, not all monarchs are bad, but

> to see what this government is in essence, it must be considered under stupid or wicked princes, for either they are like this when they ascend the throne, or the throne makes them so. (*Social Contract*, p. 90)

Locke and Montesquieu, who eliminate this difficulty by limiting and dividing the sovereign power, are still unrealistic, in Rousseau's view, because they share with Hobbes the more fundamental faith that a stable or nonoppressive society can be built on men's selfish interests. These

[3]On this theme, see also Masters (1968) and Goldschmidt (1974).

modern thinkers—so proud of their realism in acknowledging the weakness of reason and the power of men's baser passions—demonstrate an underlying optimism, not to say utopianism, in their expectations for a society built upon such passions. For example, beneath the hard-headed doctrine of Hobbes lies the hope that after its publication

> mankind should enjoy such an immortal peace, that unless it were for habitation, on supposition that the earth should grow too narrow for her inhabitants, there would hardly be left any pretence for war. (*De Cive*, p. 91)

Rousseau could not share these hopes, nor the more open faith in progress that emerged among his contemporaries. He was more suspicious of men. If they are naturally selfish and materialistic, as the "realists" are all agreed, then encouraging them to follow their own interests must lead to a small amount of cooperation and a great deal of treachery, crime, exploitation, hypocrisy, violence, and treason (*Works*, II, pp. 968-969; *Second Discourse*, pp. 156, 172-175; *Political Economy*, pp. 216-217; see Keohane, 1980, pp. 420-432). It is claimed that honesty is in one's genuine self-interest, "yet who follows his truest interests? Only the wise man, if he exists." Addressing the Physiocrats, Rousseau writes:

> Sirs, permit me to say it to you; you give too much force to your calculations, and not enough to the inclinations of the human heart, and to the play of the passions. Your system is very good for the men of Utopia, it is worth nothing for the children of Adam. (Letter to Mirabeau, July 26, 1767)

All the modern thinkers, these crypto-idealistic realists, labor under the utopian delusion that good politics is possible without good—that is, public spirited—men.

With superior realism, Rousseau argues as follows: men are by nature asocial and selfish; therefore, they cannot be employed as they are, nor can they be "exhorted" to virtue. If a decent society is to be possible, men must be utterly denatured and collectivized, a course of action difficult but possible as proved by the examples of Rome and Sparta. Precisely because social men tend to be as bad as Hobbes claims, rigorous virtue or patriotism is needed to guarantee peace and order. Nothing less will do. When thought through, Hobbesian realism, paradoxically enough, returns one to the concern for virtue.

Of course, in calling for Spartan virtue Rousseau was proposing a solution he knew to be impossible in most times and places, but in so doing he was not being unrealistic, only pessimistic.

> "Propose what can be done," they never stop repeating to me. It is as if I were being told "Propose doing what is done," or at least, "Propose some good which can be allied with the existing evil." Such a project, in certain matters, is much more chimerical than mine. (*Emile*, p. 34)

They are the utopians who assume that a universally practicable solution must exist.

Thus if Rousseau broke with Hobbes, as well as with the more liberal thinkers, arguing that peace and order are possible only in an "austere democracy" of ardent and virtuous patriots, he did so not out of utopian moralism but rigorous realism and a more consistent Hobbesism. And given this kinship of spirit, it is not implausible to suggest that in borrowing Hobbes's juridical doctrines, Rousseau had the same realistic purpose as Hobbes had in inventing them.

Incidentally, these considerations provide an answer for the question of why the argument of the *Social Contract* is based on self-preservation when Rousseau's goal is virtue. Rousseau argues that public virtue is necessary to secure the minimum Hobbesian goals of preservation and nonoppression. He also argues that since oppression is the source of all vice, the mere elimination of oppression is sufficient to foster or preserve virtue. The political requirements of preservation and of virtue therefore coincide perfectly. Rousseau collapses the distinction between the lowest and highest goals of politics or between legitimate and ideal government, which explains why Rousseau's political doctrine is so strict or dogmatic and why he could present it in terms of preservation in some of his works and in terms of virtue and happiness in others.

The Refutation of Natural Law

Having treated these initial questions, we turn to a detailed analysis of Rousseau's juridical doctrine. Although it must be understood in light of its purpose, the doctrine should not be seen as mere rhetoric, for the same considerations that make it useful also make it true in Rousseau's eyes. Rousseau's argument begins with an account of the state of nature, which as in Hobbes accomplishes the crucial task of moral "liberation" by dismissing all natural titles to rule and also all substantive natural law. By nature, no one rules, and nothing is just or unjust.

Rousseau easily dismisses all natural titles to rule by showing that men in the state of nature are entirely selfish and solitary. He also refutes the particular claims of Divine Right, paternal authority and the right of the strongest, using

familiar arguments that need not be repeated here (*Social Contract*, pp. 46-49; *Second Discourse*, pp. 161-166). He concludes that "since no man has any natural authority over his fellow man ... there remain only conventions [social contracts] as the basis of all legitimate authority among men" (*Social Contract*, p. 49).

Rousseau's refutation of substantive natural law, of all natural rules of right and wrong, is less familiar and a great deal more complicated. He treats the issue in the preface to the *Second Discourse* by means of a terse and elliptical refutation of "our jurists" (p. 129), meaning Grotius, Barbeyrac, Burlamaqui, Pufendorf, and others—the School of Natural Law as it came to be called. These writers were the main authorities on moral and political matters for the Encyclopedists, and Diderot, chief among the latter, vigorously attacked Rousseau's position in the article "Natural Right." Rousseau then defended and enlarged upon his views in an introductory chapter of the *Geneva Manuscript* (the first draft of the *Social Contract*).

We may take Pufendorf as representative of the natural law doctrine Rousseau attacks.[4] It is explicitly a compromise between Hobbes and more traditional natural law. Pufendorf follows Hobbes in seeking to end feudal anarchy by fostering a centralized, secular political authority based on contract. Seeing, however, that the newly strengthened state can be dangerous as well as useful, he seeks a way to limit its actions although without dividing or diminishing its power. His solution is to formulate and popularize a detailed, secular code of natural law. Thus Pufendorf accepts Hobbes's individualistic, contractual doctrine of the right to rule but emphatically rejects his doctrine of sovereignty in favor of a substantive natural law. Legitimacy derives from consent, but the rules of right and wrong are fixed by nature.

According to Pufendorf's argument, all men originally lived in a "state of nature" in which they were free, equal, and without rule; hence, all rule arises from a social contract as Hobbes had taught. However, although naturally apolitical, men are not naturally selfish but sociable, so their natural state was a social and peaceful one in which they could and did practice the law of nature as discovered by reason. Since they did so imperfectly, however, states and rulers were established precisely to enforce and follow that natural law and not freely to create law with absolute sovereignty. Justice, then, is natural, although the state and rule are not (*Droit de la*

---

[4] I follow Derathé's suggestion (1950, pp. 83-84) that Rousseau seems to have the most respect for Pufendorf.

Nature, II-2, II-3, VII-1, VIII-1.5; see Rommen, 1947, pp. 77-88; Derathé, 1950, pp. 36-41).

Against Pufendorf Rousseau argues that justice is not natural, thus rejecting the compromise with traditional natural law—and wholly returning to "Hobbes [who] saw very clearly the defect of all modern definitions of natural right," albeit before the fact (*Second Discourse,* p. 129). Rousseau argues that in the original state of nature, these rational principles of natural law are not known; later, when they may be known, they are not by nature enforced.

The first half of the argument follows directly from Rousseau's description of natural man, who is not sociable by nature but rather selfish and solitary. Since reason cannot develop without society and language, solitary natural man could not possibly have known the supposed laws of nature. Nevertheless, even if one grants to Pufendorf and the others that man was sociable and rational in the primitive state of nature, the difficulty still remains because

they all establish [natural] law upon such metaphysical principles . . . that it is impossible to understand [it] and consequently to obey it without being a great reasoner and a profound metaphysician; which means precisely that men must have used, for the establishment of [civil] society, enlightenment which only develops with great difficulty and in very few people in the midst of society itself. (*Second Discourse,* p. 94)

The facts of history also confirm that primitive man lacked such knowledge:

one easily sees that the healthy ideas of natural right and the brotherhood of all men were disseminated rather late and made such slow progress in the world that it was only Christianity that generalized them sufficiently. (*Geneva Manuscript,* p. 162; see *Droit de la Nature,* II-2.10)

But even if these supposed laws of justice were known, the argument continues, they would be neither obeyed nor valid because they are not by nature enforced. To appreciate this argument concerning the sanctions for morality it is important that one not "Kantianize" the essentially eudaemonistic natural law tradition. Rousseau and his opponents all agree that to be valid, the demands of natural law must be rooted in the inclinations and fulfillment of human nature (*Second Discourse,* p. 93; *Droit de la Nature,* II-2.14; Grotius, *Law of War and Peace,* I-1). As Burlamaqui puts it, natural law is the collection of

those rules which nature alone prescribes to man, in order to conduct him safely to the end, which everyone has, and indeed ought to have, in view, namely true and solid happiness. (*Principes du Droit Naturel,* I-1.1)

For a rule of justice to be valid it must promote the natural good of each when all follow it. But in addition, it must have a force or sanction—stemming from the power of reason, from a benevolent passion or from some external agent—which can guarantee to each that the others will follow it. If "natural law" is not by nature enforced and generally obeyed, and if it is thus harmful to those who do obey, then this law cannot be naturally valid or binding.

Rousseau argues that in the later stages of the state of nature reason does develop along with extended desires and (nonpolitical) society. Theoretically, men could then form a rational conception of justice or of a common good. But we find that

the development of society stifles humanity in men's hearts by awakening personal interest, and that concepts of the natural law . . . begin to develop only when the prior development of the passions renders all its precepts impotent. (*Geneva Manuscript,* p. 159)

After the development of reason Rousseau's state of nature becomes the same as Hobbes's, a "most horrible state of war" (*Second Discourse,* p. 157), and the objection to natural law is also the same:

Everything you tell me about the advantages of the social law would be fine if while I were scrupulously observing it toward others, I were sure that all of them would observe it toward me. But what assurances of this can you give me? . . . Either give me guarantees against all unjust undertakings or do not expect me to refrain from them in turn. (*Geneva Manuscript,* p. 160; see *Social Contract,* p. 66)

Lacking a natural sanction, the rules of "justice" were harmful to follow and therefore not obligatory or valid.

Rousseau thus rejects the natural law compromise of Pufendorf, Diderot, and the others—that justice is natural, although the state artificial—by showing that the supposed natural law known and followed in the state of nature "is truly an illusion, since the conditions for it are always either unknown or impracticable and men must necessarily be in ignorance of them or violate them" (*Geneva Manuscript,* p. 159).

The argument is quite clear and plausible, yet its relevance is unclear. After all, traditional natural law doctrines did not explicitly base themselves on the claim that natural law was known and followed in a prepolitical state of nature. What significance, then, have Pufendorf's claim and Rousseau's denial?

640   The American Political Science Review   Vol. 77

The Significance of the State of Nature

Pufendorf and Rousseau agree in adopting Hobbes's view that the state is not natural but is a human invention. This premise is what gives rise to the radical division of human history into a pre-political "state of nature" and the artificial, civilized condition following the invention of the state. Now if the state is artificial, then justice, to be natural, must exist independently of, hence before, the state. To maintain the existence of a *natural* law, then, Pufendorf has to go beyond traditional claims and argue that it was already found in the "state of nature." Conversely, by showing that the justice now known and practiced did not exist in the state of nature, Rousseau proves that it is not something natural, but wholly a creature of the artificial state. The real issue between Rousseau and Pufendorf, then, concerns the relative priority of justice and the (artificial) state.

In other words, unlike a contemporary relativist or ancient Sophist, Rousseau does not deny altogether the existence of an objective standard of justice. He acknowledges that

> whatever is good and in accordance with order is so by the nature of things, independently of human conventions . . . there is without doubt a universal justice emanating from reason alone. (*Social Contract*, p. 65)

Men have, or rather can be made to have, a common good, and there are rules which, if generally known and followed, will promote the common good. To be truly valid and binding, however, these rules must be, in fact, generally known and enforced (*Second Discourse*, p. 95). The question is whether that condition is ever met, and if it is, as Pufendorf and Rousseau both agree, whether directly through the natural force of the rules themselves, or only indirectly through the agency of a human invention, the (legitimate) state.

Hobbes, for example, takes the latter position. Justice lacks a natural sanction, does not exist in the state of nature, and owes such existence as it ever attains to the (legitimate) state's power. This state cannot be built upon men's natural obedience to justice since by hypothesis such obedience does not exist; it must be built on nonmoral foundations, on the passion of fear, and the agreement to obey the sovereign *whatever* he commands. It follows that the direct appeal to justice, the demand that it be the basis and condition of obedience, must destroy the state and, with it, all justice. Thus justice cannot constitute a "natural law," a binding standard independent of the state and its laws.

Conversely, Pufendorf, seeking to subordinate the state to justice or natural law, replies:

> It is not to be conceived that civil governments could ever have been established, or after their establishment, preserved, if there had not been something just and unjust antecedent to their existence. (*Droit de la Nature*, VIII-1.5)

The objective standard of justice, having a natural force in men's reason and inclinations, is known and enforced by nature and therefore constitutes a direct guide for men and an obligatory moral law. It does not owe its existence or binding power to the state. On the contrary, natural law justice predated the state, gave rise to it, and now maintains it. Consequently, positive laws violating the natural law are not binding (*Droit de la Nature*, VII-8.2, VIII-1).

Rousseau, by claiming that justice is not enforced by nature, returns to the position of Hobbes. By claiming that it is also not known by nature, and that the state is needed to teach justice as well as enforce it, Rousseau also anticipates the views of the Historical School. Pufendorf's error lies in being unhistorical. He attributes to men in the state of nature qualities—including the knowledge and practice of justice—which they only acquired in the state. He then claims that these qualities caused or founded the state. But

> In order for an emerging people to feel the noble maxims of justice . . . the effect would have to become the cause; the social spirit, which should be the result of the institution [of the state] would have to preside over the founding of the institution itself, and men would have to be prior to laws what they should become by means of laws. (*Geneva Manuscript*, p. 182; see *Second Discourse*, pp. 133, 94; *Social Contract*, p. 69)

The famous teaching of the *Second Discourse*—that previous thinkers have underestimated the formative role of history or society while overestimating that of nature—is meant to demonstrate the social origin of man's wickedness, but also the social origin of his morality. The legitimate state has—and it alone—

> produced a remarkable change in man by substituting justice for instinct in his behavior . . . [and] changed him from a stupid, limited animal into an intelligent being and a man. (*Social Contract*, pp. 55-56; see *Second Discourse*, pp. 148-181; *Confessions*, pp. 404-405; *Works*, III, pp. 664-665; *Emile*, p. 473)

In short, "Law comes before justice and not justice before law" (*Geneva Manuscript*, p. 191).

Thus, although Rousseau acknowledges the existence of an objective standard of order or justice, discoverable by the wise, he thinks that "considering things from a human point of view, the laws of justice are ineffectual among men" (*Social Contract*, pp. 65-66). This standard does not constitute a "natural law" in the sense of a direct guide for men or a binding code of morality. It is not binding prior to the state, because it is not known or enforced, and it is not in the (legitimate) state because there it must yield to the state's laws. Natural law—and the "moralists" like Pufendorf—asserts: "Here is the standard of justice; you must obey it." But this command is self-contradictory, for justice cannot be obeyed without the state to teach and enforce it, and the state (which therefore must be based on something other than the force of justice) is destroyed by the command to obey only justice. Natural law cannot obligate men without destroying the condition of all obligation. There is a standard of justice then, but it cannot be realized "morally" through direct appeal to it, but only politically and indirectly through the effects of the (legitimate) state, which is obeyed for reasons other than its substantive justice. A doctrine of sovereignty must replace the theory of natural law.

Rousseau's argument, however, is open to an obvious objection. Mankind has progressed beyond the state of nature, beyond the ignorance and savagery of primitive times. Justice, which may at first have had no support but the state, has now taken root in men's reason and inclinations. This progress and moral development has freed justice from its utter dependence on the state while also potentially supplying the state with a new source of support. Consequently, the utter subordination of natural law to the state has become unnecessary and unreasonable.

The Critique of Progress and Enlightenment

The well-known message of the *First* and *Second Discourses,* that there is no progress, constitutes Rousseau's defense of his arguments and of the relevance of the state of nature. The fundamental relation of the state to justice appears most clearly at the beginning. Later developments do much to obscure that relation, but little to alter it. If one examines with hard-headed realism the historical development of reason, rational morality, and the nonlegitimate state, one will see the perpetuation of the two original obstacles to a valid and binding natural law: as in the state of nature, justice is not adequately known or enforced. (Where a wise legislator has founded a legitimate state, appeal to natural law—in addition to being unnecessary—remains destructive of the state, as I will show later.)

Treating first the problem of moral knowledge, it is obvious that reason has made immense progress since primitive times and that elaborate concepts of justice and natural law have developed in society. Nevertheless, Rousseau denies that the

mass of men have a true understanding of justice. The people "often does not know what it wants because it rarely knows what is good for it" (*Social Contract,* p. 67). And since "the art of generalizing ideas . . . is one of the most difficult and belated exercises of human understanding, will the average man ever be capable of deriving his rules of conduct from this manner of reasoning" (*Geneva Manuscript,* p. 161; see p. 182)? Even if he could form general principles of conduct, that would not be sufficient.

> For the science of government is only a science of combinations, applications and exceptions, according to times, places and circumstances. The public will never truly understand the relations and the play of all that. (Letter to Mirabeau, July 26, 1767)

Lack of intelligence or education is only half the problem, for "good sense depends more on the sentiments of the heart than the enlightenment of the mind" (*Works,* IV, p. 11). Ignorance and prejudice grow from the vices, moral wisdom from virtue or health of soul. Now peoples' virtue and vice stem from the character of their state: "It is certain that the people are in the long run what the government makes them. Warriors, citizens, men when it so pleases; mob, and rabble when it wishes" (*Political Economy,* p. 216). Unjust states make men corrupt, prejudiced, and irrational; just states make men honest and clear-sighted. It follows that the people's moral knowledge (as distinguished from that of gifted individuals) can never substantially surpass the actual justice of their state or political culture. That is why "once peoples are accustomed to masters, they are no longer able to do without them" (*Second Discourse,* p. 80; see *Social Contract,* p. 71). Thus natural law cannot function as a corrective to the fundamental abuses of the state, because where the state is corrupt, so will be men's opinions of the natural law.

Pufendorf and other moralists would respond that this political "relativism" of moral knowledge is overcome by the guidance of moral philosophers who, liberated from the prejudices of their time and political condition, show men the timeless truths of morality. Pufendorf thought this was particularly true in his own time, thanks to the spread of enlightenment and to progress in the science of natural law. According to the *Encyclopedia,* this science was "known only imperfectly to the ancients, their wise men and their philosophers have spoken of it most often in a very superficial way" ("Right of Nature," p. 194). As Barbeyrac explains in the introduction to his translation of Pufendorf, all natural law doctrines before Grotius failed to "contain a complete body of morality such as descends to the utmost degree of particularity and where everything is digested into the very best order and method possible" (Sec. 28). The Natural Law School has now constructed such a rigorous and detailed *code de nature* to serve as a direct guide for the conduct of life and affairs. Moreover, philosophers have now abandoned their traditional seclusion, assuming a role in society that enhances their public effect. As Voltaire boasts in the *Encyclopedia:*

> The spirit of the century has made most [men of letters] as much at ease in society as in their study. This is the great advantage they hold over men of letters of preceding centuries. Up to the time of [J.-L. Guez de] Balzac and Voiture they were not admitted to society; since then they have become a necessary part of it. The profound and clear reasoning which many have infused into their books and their conversation has done much to instruct and polish the nation. ("Men of Letters," p. 248)

Through its promulgation in the books of philosophers, natural law can be an effective standard and guide for politics.

Rousseau, however, thinks it far more difficult to introduce wisdom and truth into human affairs. Men do not listen to reason, shedding their illusions when shown the truth. They resist and deny the truth, or more likely fail to understand it in the first place. Rousseau possesses what came to be called the "historical sense" (as his predecessors, he claims, did not). He knows that men differ from one time and place to another, and that this difference affects what they can understand. "I know the delights of your country, said Brasidas to the satrap who compared the life of Sparta to that of Persepolis; but you cannot know the pleasures of mine." Cato knew and practiced justice as perhaps no other man has, yet "he was out of place in his century; and . . . only astonished the world, which he would have governed five hundred years earlier" (*Second Discourse*, pp. 164, 178). Corrupt peoples are simply incapable of comprehending the truth; hence, the epigraph of both the *First Discourse* and *Rousseau Juge de Jean-Jacques*, and the central theme of the autobiographical writings: "Here I am the barbarian because no one understands me."

Furthermore, even if the people could understand, they would not know who to listen to since the philosophers do not agree among themselves.

> It is not without surprise and scandal that one notes the little agreement which prevails on . . . [natural law] among the various authors who have discussed it. Among the most serious writers one can hardly find two who are of the same opinion on this point. (*Second Discourse*, p. 94; see *Emile*, pp. 268-269)

The insufficiency of human reason prevents the unanimity necessary for philosophy to be a salutary political guide.

This difficulty is particularly great due to the influence of sophists and counterfeit philosophers. Given the weakness of reason—both in its power to attain the truth and to rule over passion—a genuine philosopher is the rarest of men. "As beautiful and sublime as it is, [philosophy] is not made for man . . . his mind is too limited to make much progress in it and his heart too full of passions to avoid misusing it" (*Works*, III, p. 36). It must remain the preserve of the few "sublime geniuses who know how to penetrate the veils in which the truth envelops itself, the few privileged souls capable of resisting the stupidity of vanity, base jealously and other passions engendered by the taste for letters" (*Works*, II, p. 970; see *First Discourse*, p. 62). But wherever philosophy is in a position to teach the people justice, wherever it is most accepted and publicly admired, it is also most counterfeited. Men without genius, or more important, men with no love of truth, will pursue philosophy for the love of honor. And since they cannot easily be told apart, where a philosopher is honored a hundred sophists share the glory. Thus, of the guidance offered by the "philosophers," Rousseau writes:

> I sought for the truth in books; I found there only falsehood and error. I consulted authors; I found only charlatans who make a game of fooling men, who have no other law than their interest, no other God than their reputation; who are quick to decry the rulers who do not treat them to their liking, and quicker still to praise the wickedness that pays them. (*Works*, IV, p. 967; see *Emile*, p. 458)

Such "philosophers" cannot help the people to acquire genuine knowledge of justice.

Realistically considered, then, the progress of reason has not provided men with adequate moral knowledge, for prejudice and deceit have progressed at an equal pace with reason. As in the state of nature, natural law remains invalid because insufficiently known.

Nor has progress remedied the second obstacle to the existence of natural law, the lack of sanctions. Given the immense progress made by the productive arts, one might first expect that the dangerous and warlike condition of the late state of nature, which had made justice impossible, would have disappeared along with the economic scarcity producing it. That would indeed have been the result if men's desires had remained limited to the natural and necessary goods. But the magnificent progress of man's reason and productive capacities has been dwarfed by the progress of his needs and desires; hence, overflowing with goods, society is yet filled with labor, competition, and strife. The problem of distribution is another fruit of progress. By separating possession from need, the establishment of private property creates an artificial scarcity, allowing "a handful of men [to] be glutted with superfluities while the starving multitude lacks necessities" (*Second Discourse*, pp. 181, 197).

While thus increasing scarcity and conflict, the progress of the arts has also made that conflict more dangerous. The invention of metallurgy, then of gunpowder, vastly increased men's power for evil. And the art of fraud was added to these instruments of force. Men discovered the surprising power to be gained by speaking one way while acting another. "Before art had moulded our manners . . . human nature, basically, was no better, but men found their security in the ease of seeing through each other." In becoming civilized, men became more dangerous, for "suspicions, offenses, fears, coldness, reserve, hate, betrayal will hide constantly under that uniform and false veil of politeness" (*First Discourse*, pp. 37-38).

The "progressivists" and moralists might perhaps agree that the progress of reason and the arts has increased men's desires, their need to harm each other, and their power to do so. They would, nevertheless, deny that the war Rousseau describes continues to exist in society. For reason and justice, whatever their power in the state of nature, are now a real force in men's souls, a force that suppresses immoderate desires and creates harmony among men, a force supporting the state and in turn supported by it. Contemporary society, with its civility, morality, and cultivation, bears no resemblance to the conflict and savagery of Rousseau's late state of nature. Civilized man may indeed have more desires and craft than the savage; he also has more principles.

To Rousseau, the pride and folly of this position is once again the pride of reason.

> The error of most moralists has always been to take man for an essentially reasonable being. Man is only a sensitive being, who consults solely his passions in acting, and uses his reason merely to mitigate the errors they have led him to commit. (*Works*, III, p. 554)

Reason is a late, weak, and superficial faculty, powerless to control the passions. Again, Rousseau does not deny the obvious progress made by reason and moral ideas since primitive times, but he makes here the same two points he made against the progress of the arts. Far from controlling the unjust passions, the ideas of justice or morality that grow up in most societies actually stimulate them—and they give them new weapons as well.

The advent of moral concepts and beliefs has stimulated the passions by greatly strengthening that which underlies all passion: the hope of success. "Wishes without hope do not torment us. A beggar is not tormented by the desire to be a king. A king wants to be God only when he believes he is no longer a man" (*Emile*, p. 446). All the unnecessary desires—whether stemming from pleasure, habit, foresight, imagination, or vanity—owe their growth to that of man's hopes for getting and keeping, and these hopes have grown through man's creation, in fact and in his mind, of a moralized world. The passion for great wealth could not appear in human history until the creation of the moral idea and institution of private property, nor the passion for rule before the idea of authority. These passions, once aroused, take control of the moral thoughts that created them, leading men to project onto the world an illusory moral order supportive of their hopes and desires. "The first sentiment of justice does not come to us from the justice we owe but from that which is owed us" (*Emile*, p. 97). All the great passions and ambitions (even the immoral ones) are founded on such moral claims, on a superstitious faith in oneself: my physical powers are limited but my worth is not, and ultimately the latter will prevail.

> Vice is the love of order taken in a different sense. There is some moral order wherever there is sentiment and intelligence. The difference is that the good man orders himself in relation to the whole, and the wicked one orders the whole in relation to himself (*Emile*, pp. 291-292; see letter to Carondolet, March 4, 1764).

Even the tyrant is a twisted moralist in his faith that the world can be formed into a stable and responsive order around himself. It is precisely morality, then, that has made men's desires infinite.

If men saw the world as it truly is, they would have no passions and few desires. Wisely disillusioned and dispirited, they would see that "your power extend[s] only as far as your natural strength and not beyond. All the rest is only slavery, illusion and deception"; that "everything on earth is only transitory. All that we love will escape us sooner or later, and we hold on to it as if it were going to last eternally" (*Emile*, pp. 83-84, 444). But since the development of moral ideas, man has been lost in a world of illusions, and "in his senseless desires, he puts in the rank of the possible what is not possible" (*Emile*, p. 445). Only the philosopher, through genius and strength of soul, and natural man, through stupidity, are ever truly free of these illusions. Already in the late state of nature, "between the *right* of the stronger and the *right* of the first occupant there arose a perpetual conflict": war arose from moral ideas (*Second Discourse*, p. 157, emphasis added).

One might respond that eventually men learn their duties as well as their rights, and if the idea of their rights has increased men's passions, that of their duties has taught them to combat and suppress them. Thanks to justice and the state, we no longer experience that savage war of all against all that Rousseau describes. Look around. Can one seriously deny the fact of moral progress in light of "the decency of our entertainments, the politeness of our manners, the affability of our speech [and] our perpetual demonstrations of good will" (*First Discourse*, p. 39)?

This objection brings us to the heart of Rousseau's view, which he summarizes in the second epigraph to the *First Discourse:* "We are deceived by the appearance of right" (p. 34). We are deceived in the first place because, as compared with the late state of nature, the social state is an "epoch, less horrible at first sight, but more deadly in reality" (*Works*, III, p. 478). The present appearance of justice is false and ineffectual. But more important, the deceptive appearance of justice, like the use of gunpowder, has made men and their conflicts more dangerous.

> Whoever, renouncing in good faith all the prejudices of human vanity, seriously reflects on all these things, will discover at length that all these grand words of society, of justice, of law, of mutual defense, of help for the weak, of philosophy, and of the progress of reason are only lures invented by clever politicians or by cowardly flatterers to impose themselves on the simple. (*Works*, III, p. 475; see pp. 478, 54, 610, 606, 518; IV, p. 937 and b; *Emile*, p. 236)

Justice or morality, as it has developed, is the most fearsome invention of the art of fraud.

The "appearance of right" is indeed greater among civilized men than savages, yet not because justice has taken root in their souls, but because it is more useful to enslave a man than kill him, and "justice" provides the means for enslaving him. "Man was born free, and everywhere he is in chains. . . . How did this change occur" (p. 46)? The famous question, left unanswered in the *Social Contract*, is the true topic of the *Second Discourse:*

> Precisely what, then, is at issue in this Discourse? To indicate in the progress of things the moment when right taking the place of violence, nature was subjected to law; to explain by what sequence of marvels the strong [i.e. the great mass of men] could resolve to serve the weak, and the people to buy imaginary repose at the price of real felicity. (p. 102)

The central purpose of this work is to explain how mankind was enslaved through the invention of "justice" and the state.

These were invented, Rousseau argues, to put an end to the state of war resulting from the growth of men's selfish desires. The inventor proclaimed:

> Let us institute regulations of justice and peace to which all are obliged to conform . . . let us gather [our forces] into one supreme power which governs us according to wise laws, protects and defends all the members of the association, repulses common enemies, and maintains us in an eternal concord. (*Second Discourse*, p. 159)

These are fine and true principles, Rousseau explains, but one must consider their effect and significance in the historical circumstances in which they arose. The inventors of justice and the state could not themselves have been just or public-spirited, since these qualities arise only within the (legitimate) state. Moreover, justice and rule were needed and invented precisely because men had become so bad. In such conditions "social laws are a yoke that each wants to impose on the other without having to bear himself" (*Geneva Manuscript*, p. 160). In other words, the idea of justice and the common good can only arise from selfish motives, hence only as a tool of exploitation. Thus, according to the *Second Discourse*, the state was invented by the rich as a means of enslaving and exploiting the poor. Too easily led, the latter agreed to this arrangement. The noble words of justice and the common good won their trust, and they "all ran to meet their chains thinking they secured their freedom" (*Second Discourse*, p. 159). From the start, then, "justice" and the state were nothing but a ruse and a trap, and "as it began badly, time in discovering faults and suggesting remedies could never repair the vices of the constitution" (*Second Discourse*, p. 162). Through history, the original deception was continually repeated: laws, magistrates, punishments, armies were added, but "the vices that make social institutions necessary are the same ones that make their abuse inevitable" (*Second Discourse*, p. 173). Unable to suppress men's unjust passions, they soon became tools of them; hence each new institution only strengthened the very evils it was meant to control. Thus did moral and political "progress"—of which the moralists are so proud—enslave the world. Born free, men are in chains forged by the "appearance of right."

Looking past appearances, then, one sees no progress regarding sanctions for justice. In essence, the state of war persists, for all men are still "forced to flatter and destroy one another" (*Second Discourse*, p. 194).

Through his critique of progress, his skeptically realistic account of the historical development of reason and rational morality, Rousseau has shown that the original obstacles to natural law remain: men cannot know or afford justice. Although, in heaven as it were, there is an objective, rational standard of order discoverable by the wise, it does not reach down to men's reason or inclinations; it does not bind and obligate men, or in any way solicit its own fulfillment. Mankind is simply abandoned to the conflict of its collective passions and prejudices.

Rousseau grants, of course, that in civilized times moral ideas and doctrines of natural law have come into being which claim to be the timeless truth; yet if not "deceived by the appearance of right," one will see that they are not above the great war of interests, capable of settling it, but rather the most potent weapons invented for use within that war. "Morality" and "natural law" are not the solution; they are precisely the most dangerous part of the problem.[5]

Rousseau's Doctrine of Sovereignty: The Argument of the Social Contract

Having used the "state of nature" and the denial of progress to clear the ground of all natural titles to rule and all substantive natural law, Rousseau then erects in their place the positive doctrines of the *Social Contract*, the doctrines of contract and sovereignty, the "principles of political right." One must ask at the outset, however, how Rousseau could think his own doctrine would be any more effectual than the doctrines of natural law just rejected. Indeed, Rousseau seems to agree with Plato that men really have only one means of escaping the strife and oppression resulting from the weakness of their reason and the conflict of their interests: a philosopher must be king or legislator. "So long as power is alone on the one side, intellect and wisdom alone on the other . . . the people will continue to be vile, corrupt and unhappy" (*First Discourse*, p. 64; *Social Contract*, p. 67). The true principles of justice cannot reach the world directly through a natural law, but only indirectly through the political activity of a wise man. He alone can bring order,

justice, and virtue into the world as Lycurgus did in Sparta, not by "moralizing" or proclaiming doctrines, but by legislating, by wisely arranging the laws and institutions, the concrete social and political relations that shape men's characters (*Works*, III, p. 948). No book or doctrine can replace such political activity by the legislator, nor can it teach or command the people to recognize the true legislator when he arises. At most a book can help to educate future legislators, and that is surely one purpose of Rousseau's political writings (*Works*, III, p. 474; see Masters, 1968, pp. 306-313). His books give private advice to legislators as distinguished from public proclamations of universal principles.

But the "principles of political right" proclaimed in the *Social Contract* are just such a universal doctrine addressed to the people. Yet they differ in a crucial respect from a natural law doctrine because they establish not an elaborate code of morality but a simple rule defining legitimate government and sovereign command. Moreover, the doctrine is not truly addressed to all states but only to the few remaining republics, especially Geneva. There, where the main tasks of founding and legislation had already been accomplished, Rousseau could aspire, through a doctrine, simply to improve and complete the job. As he states in the *Confessions,* the Genevans lacked "correct and clear enough notions of the laws and liberty," so he wrote the *Social Contract* as "an indirect means of giving them to them" (p. 405; see *R. Juge de J.-J.,* p. 935).

Rousseau's doctrine proclaims the following. All legitimate rule derives from a social contract, which to be binding must leave to the people the law-making power. In such a state the will of the people as expressed in law is sovereign in the strict sense. It is not to be measured against a higher standard of justice but is itself the standard of justice and makes what it commands just, by commanding it. Like Hobbes, Rousseau replaces the nonexistent natural law with a theory of sovereignty. The traditional definition of law as just or rational command is replaced by the voluntaristic one of pure command or will (whence the term General Will). Rousseau illustrates the meaning of sovereignty by asserting that one cannot treat "as theft the cunning prescribed to Spartan children for obtaining their frugal meal, as if everything that is required by law could fail to be legitimate" (*Political Economy*, p. 212). The natural law, which is neither publicly known nor enforced, is wholly replaced by duly enacted positive law, which is both.

Rousseau establishes this doctrine in the first book of the *Social Contract*. In the warlike condition of the late state of nature, men are driven by their desire for preservation to establish a com-

[5]Rousseau's position on natural law has long been a subject of debate. See Vaughan (1915, vol. 1, pp. 16-18), Hubert (1928), Hendel (1934, vol. 1, pp. 97-99, 182), Cobban (1934, pp. 115, 147-150), Gough (1936, pp. 156-157), Haymann (1943-1945), Crocker (1961-1962), Hall (1973, pp. 25-28), and Goldschmidt (1974, pp. 133-155). The interpretation suggested here owes the most to Masters (1968, pp. 76-89, 158-165, 316-322), Plattner (1979, chap. 5), and Strauss (1953, pp. 252-294).

mon power to rule them. Since no natural law exists, they are free to create through contract any political arrangements and any "rules of justice" they please—so long as these promote their goal of preservation. But since they cannot rely on men's "morality," they can obligate themselves to obey *only* such a power as cannot oppress them. The latter requirement narrows the terms of a legitimate contract to these: "the total alienation of each associate with all his rights to the whole community" or to "the supreme direction of the General Will" (p. 53). Such an arrangement guarantees the security and nonoppression of each because

> since each one gives his entire self, the condition is equal for everyone, and since the condition is equal for everyone, no one has an interest in making it burdensome for the others. (p. 53)

Because of the total alienation of each, the community can have a General Will, a will that applies to all members equally, a will that has the form of "law." This General Will can be made sovereign because it cannot harm one without harming all. In other words, the social contract establishes the sovereignty of the people's will when expressed in the form of general laws, or the sovereignty of law as such, properly understood.

> When the entire people enacts something concerning the entire people . . . then the subject matter of the enactment is general like the will that enacts. It is this I call a law. (p. 66)

Taken in this sense, law is sovereign—again, because it cannot oppress.

The argument is in need of immediate qualification, however, for Rousseau was not so foolish as to think that "public deliberations are always equitable," that the will of all is always the General Will (*Political Economy*, p. 213; see *Social Contract*, p. 61). When the people have become corrupt and selfish and "the basest interest brazenly adopts the sacred name of the public good, then the general will becomes mute . . . and iniquitous decrees whose only goal is the private interest are falsely passed under the name of laws" (p. 109). The sovereignty of popularly enacted law is not meant as an "institutional solution" that can work anywhere and automatically; it will work only if men have been made into virtuous and patriotic citizens. (Hence, it does not eliminate the need for a wise legislator.) Rousseau's solution is not democracy, but "austere democracy" (Letter to Mirabeau, July 26, 1767).

Yet, if this is so, it must be acknowledged that the presentation of Rousseau's doctrine in the *Social Contract* is somewhat misleading. The argument seems to be institutional and universally applicable. Rousseau downplays the fact that the people must be virtuous in order for the laws they make to be just. He encourages the identification of the General Will with the will of the majority and indeed states that "the will of the majority *always* obligates all the others. This is a consequence of *the contract itself*" (p. 110, emphasis added; see p. 52).

This famous and obvious difficulty is not a sign of Rousseau's confusion as is often argued. He defends the last point as follows:

> This presupposes, it is true, that all the characteristics of the General Will are still in the majority. When they cease to be, there is no longer any freedom regardless of the side one takes. (p. 111)

In other words, where men are virtuous the (popularly enacted) laws will indeed be just; where they are corrupt the laws will be unjust, but public questioning of the laws will not lead to justice either. Thus Rousseau's doctrine of sovereignty *exaggerates* the necessary justice of popularly enacted law to discourage questioning of the law, for in any given society such law will constitute the most just standard possible.

The Purpose of Rousseau's Doctrine

This line of argument forces us to distinguish systematically between the truth of Rousseau's doctrine and its effect or usefulness. Indeed, even if the doctrine were true without exaggeration, we would still need to ask why the public proclamation of it is useful.

For Rousseau, the great task of statecraft consists in putting "law above man" because law more or less guarantees nonoppression, and because law eliminates personal dependence, thus preserving men's virtue or health of soul. The ends of preservation and virtue converge in rule of law. It does not necessarily follow, however, that the best way to promote rule of law is to proclaim these arguments as a public doctrine. Indeed, the argument from virtue is not a part of Rousseau's public doctrine. Moreover, Sparta and Rome, Rousseau's great models, succeeded in establishing the absolute rule of law without the use of any part of Rousseau's doctrine. Their laws were scrupulously respected as ancestral and divine. Rousseau himself admits that such a claim of divine support is always necessary to foster reverence for the law (*Social Contract*, pp. 124-131). What, then, is the specific purpose of Rousseau's public doctrine?

To establish rule of law, the crucial task is not so much to demonstrate its benefits as to disarm its enemies. The purpose of the doctrines proclaimed in the *Social Contract* must be understood, above all, in terms of the latter task. The most obvious enemies are, of course, the rulers, who always want to be above the law and masters of it. "All the governments of the world . . . sooner or later usurp the sovereign [legislative] authority" (*Social Contract*, p. 106). Rousseau's doctrine combats them "institutionally" by calling for annual popular assemblies to review the tenure of the government. It combats them ideologically by proving that sovereignty is inalienable and indivisible and by establishing with precision a distinction between the "sovereign"—the legislative power residing in the people—and the "government" or "prince" —the executive power established by the people's revocable decree (*Social Contract*, pp. 106-107, 59-61, 78-81). Addressing the Genevans in *Letters from the Mountain*, Rousseau explains:

> This distinction [between sovereign and government] is very important in these matters. To form a good idea of it one must read with some care the first two chapters of the third book of the *Social Contract*, where I tried to fix with a precise meaning some expressions which men artfully have left uncertain in order to give them whatever meaning they want as the need arises. (p. 771)

The precise distinctions made by Rousseau's doctrine are intended to help the people to understand and protect their legislative rights against the rulers.

Yet rulers are by no means the only ones with the ambition to be superior to the laws. Owing to a failure to look beyond the familiar conflict between rulers and peoples in this context, the full purpose of the *Social Contract* has never been grasped. For example, the clergy, by asserting that the will of God is a standard above the laws and by making itself the sole interpreter of that will, has carved out a lawless kingdom of its own within the state. Rousseau agrees with Hobbes that by this means Christianity has virtually ruined the politics of the West.

> Communion and excommunication are the social compact of the clergy, a compact by means of which it will always be master of peoples and kings. . . . This invention is a political masterpiece. (*Social Contract*, p. 127n)

To oppose this lawless power, Rousseau joins with the *philosophes* in their virulent attack on the Christian clergy.

But Rousseau also opposes the *philosophes,* the secular moralists, the natural lawyers proliferating in his time, for essentially the same reason. They, like other men, have their interests and ambitions. As Rousseau was among the first to see, these intellectuals constitute a new party, a "new class," a new church of secular priests seeking lawless power. While supporting their antifeudal and anticlerical mission, he sees that they act not for the people's interest but their own. In fact, by interest, the intellectual class is opposed to the people and the truth, "for truth does not lead to fortune, and the people does not confer embassies, professorships or pensions" (*Social Contract*, p. 61). Always seeking to distinguish themselves, they must "always think otherwise than the people," hence always "cast ridicule on the objects of their veneration" (*Works*, III, p. 557). In the short-term they serve the rich and powerful, but like the priests, they help to strengthen the power of others with the intention of eventually acceding to it themselves. As for their opposition to the Church, it is a simple case of rivalry.

> The Jesuits make themselves all powerful in exercising divine authority over consciences, and in making themselves in the name of God the arbiters of good and evil. The philosophers, unable to usurp the same authority applied themselves to destroying it; and then, in appearing to explain Nature to their docile sectarians, and in making themselves its supreme interpreters, they established in its name an authority no less absolute than that of their enemies. . . . These two groups, both imperious, both intolerant are consequently incompatible, since the fundamental system of the one and of the other is to reign despotically. (*R. Juge de J.-J.*, p. 967; see pp. 890, 964-965; and Shklar, 1969, pp. 96-99).

In sum, the priests and the intellectuals, who seek power through the appeal to God and Nature, are as great a danger to rule of law as the rulers.

Rousseau's attack on natural law and his doctrine of sovereignty must be understood in the light of this fact. Philosophical doctrines of natural law are not only false and useless but also destructive of the one thing that can replace them; they are powerful tools of ambition that endanger the one institution that can save man, the absolute rule of law. In other words, Rousseau confronts essentially the same political problem as Hobbes. Both want the absolute rule of law and find the major obstacle to such rule in the abuse of justice and religion by ambitious ideologues. Consequently, both use a juridical doctrine of state of nature, social contract, and absolute sovereignty for the purpose expressly stated by Hobbes: to end the people's misplaced obedience, hence to disarm the enemies of law, by sweeping away all supposedly higher standards of morality. Both seek to demonstrate "that there are no authentical doctrines concerning right and wrong, good and evil, besides the constituted laws in each realm and government" (*De Cive*, p. 98). In the post-Christian and post-Enlightenment world, the establishment of rule of law requires a doctrine of the *sovereignty* of law.

Rousseau's public doctrine (as opposed to his lessons for legislators) would not have been necessary in an earlier time. He shares Hobbes's lament for the passing of the prephilosophic age "before such questions began to be moved" when "subjects did not measure what was just by the sayings and judgments of private men, but by the laws of the realm." The sages of this early period "rather chose to have the science of justice wrapped up in fables, than openly exposed to disputations" (*De Cive*, p. 97; see *Works*, III, p. 505; *Social Contract*, p. 124; *Geneva Manuscript*, pp. 182-183). Hobbes, like Nietzsche, blames Socrates for destroying customary political morality and replacing it with a rational or philosophical one. In Rousseau's view, Socrates came after this change and, through his opposition to the Sophists, played the same "antiphilosophic" role as Rousseau himself, for already in Socrates' time "Athens was not in fact a democracy, but a highly tyrannical aristocracy, governed by learned men and orators" (*Political Economy*, p. 213; *First Discourse*, pp. 43-45; *Works*, III, p. 73n). At any rate, Rousseau agrees with his contemporaries that decisive progress in the development and dissemination of philosophical morality had occurred in the eighteenth century. The Natural Law School was indeed the first, as Barbeyrac says, to descend "to the utmost degree of particularity." Enthusiasm for such doctrines had become so great that, as one scholar has written, "eight or more new systems of natural law made their appearance at every Leipzig bookseller's fair since 1780" (Rommen, 1947, p. 106).

Rousseau's public doctrine was made necessary by this proliferation of harmful public doctrines. As he explains (with perhaps some exaggeration):

> The best use which one can make of philosophy is to employ it to destroy the evils which it has caused. . . . I plan to attack errors rather than to establish new truths, and I confess in good faith that when the works of my adversaries no longer exist, mine will be perfectly useless. Without wishing to be the guide of my contemporaries I content myself with warning them when I observe someone misleading them, and I would not need to tire them with my opinions if no one else undertook to lead them. (*Works*, III, pp. 516-517; see pp. 609-610).

Through his doctrine of sovereignty Rousseau attempts to restore the world to the prephilosophic age when peoples "did not measure what was just by the sayings and judgments of private men, but by the laws of the realm." The doctrine eliminates all higher standards above the law, standards that have always been the exclusive property and weapon of the intellectual class in all its various guises. It is at least as important to eliminate such private moralities as it is to abolish

private armies and to moderate private property. Through the sovereignty of the General Will, Rousseau tries to establish public ownership of the means of evaluation.

In sum, Rousseau's *Social Contract* proclaims a public doctrine as does the School of Natural Law that he refutes. They are nevertheless doing opposite things. Rousseau's doctrine is not that of a moralist who teaches what justice or natural law is and exhorts men to follow it, but that of a realistic political thinker who regards such moralizing and moral doctrines as pathetically ineffectual and, in fact, as weapons of the unjust passions they claim to control. Men cannot be made virtuous or secure by doctrines but only by living under the rule of law. Yet Rousseau's doctrine of sovereignty will make men virtuous and secure (in a few small republics) by preventing the moral doctrines of others from destroying the rule of law. It does not exhort men to be good but to ignore the exhortations of others and to avoid misplaced obedience.

Two Objections

Perhaps the greatest obstacle to a proper understanding of Rousseau's doctrine of sovereignty has been that he addresses an entirely different doctrine to France and the other over-large and corrupt states of Europe—a doctrine of natural law. A very brief discussion of it must suffice here. For the few states where legitimate rule is possible, such as Geneva and Corsica, Rousseau proposes that natural law be wholly replaced by the sovereignty of the General Will or duly enacted positive law. But where the size and decadence of the state renders legitimate rule impossible, Rousseau has to propose the opposite.

> Laws! Where are there laws and where are they respected? Everywhere you have seen only individual interest and men's passions reigning under this name. But the eternal laws of nature and order do exist. For the wise man, they take the place of positive law. (*Emile*, p. 473)

In light of what we have seen, Rousseau's hopes for the popular efficacy of these "eternal" laws could not have been very great. The two defects of natural law—that it is not sufficiently sanctioned or known—are "remedied" by two novel doctrines in *Emile*, the religion of the Savoyard Vicar and the theory of conscience. (There is a civil religion in the *Social Contract*, but it sanctions the positive laws; the book makes virtually no mention of conscience.) God as the sanction for natural law is a possibility Rousseau had already considered in the *Geneva Manuscript*.

The sublime concepts of a God of the wise, the gentle laws of brotherhood He imposes upon us, the social virtues of pure souls—which are the true cult He desires of us—will always escape the multitude. Gods as senseless as itself will always be made for the multitude, which will sacrifice worthless things in honor of these Gods in order to indulge in a thousand horrible, destructive passions. (p. 160)

By writing the "Profession of Faith of the Savoyard Vicar" Rousseau tries to do what he considers nearly impossible: to make religion a force for genuine morality in a corrupt society.

As for the problem of knowledge of the natural law, Rousseau argues that "we have an internal guide, much more infallible than all the books" (*Works*, III, p. 42). According to the Savoyard Vicar, conscience, a moral sentiment distinct from reason, is a "Divine instinct, immortal and celestial voice . . . infallible judge of good and bad which makes man like unto God" (*Emile*, p. 290). One must agree with Bertrand de Jouvenel regarding the inherent implausibility of this doctrine.

It is to ignore the whole immense problem of the "erring conscience." . . . It is to suppose the infallibility of moral sentiment. Nothing could be more bold: it is to contradict ancient as well as Christian philosophy, which always attributed to reason—whether alone or with aid—the function of perceiving the good. (1947, p. 77)

The doctrine is all the more implausible in light of what we have seen of Rousseau's views concerning the accessibility of the moral truth. I would suggest, then, that Rousseau's true understanding of the conscience was expressed by the Vicar when describing his "philosophical method":

Let us consult the inner light, it will lead me astray less than [the philosophers] lead me astray; or at least my error will be my own, and I will deprave myself less in following my own illusions than in yielding to their lies. (*Emile*, p. 269)

In other words, Rousseau proclaims the infallibility of individual conscience just as he had that of the General Will; he exaggerates in both cases (although far more regarding conscience) and for the same reason: to prevent the moral and intellectual domination of the people by the intelligentsia (see *Confessions*, p. 567).

Thus, Rousseau's natural law doctrine itself seems to confirm our interpretation of his theory of sovereignty. The purpose of the former turns out to be the same as that of the latter: to oppose the evils of natural law doctrines. (And since it has a very limited efficacy or validity, it is meant to yield to the doctrine of sovereignty wherever the latter can apply.)

A second obstacle to the understanding of

Rousseau arises from the common view summarized in the title of Hendel's work *Jean-Jacques Rousseau: Moralist*. It is obvious that Rousseau is filled with moral outrage at the injustices of society, and it is thought to be equally obvious that in his writings he wants to teach men what justice is and exhort them to follow it. On this view, there is little difference between Rousseau's doctrine of the General Will and a substantive natural law. The General Will embodies Rousseau's sense of justice, as the very similar Categorical Imperative embodies Kant's. All men are equal, and the doctrine of the General Will is Rousseau's somewhat utopian demand that the state recognize this moral fact.

I have been arguing that, on the contrary, the General Will must not be understood as a moral and utopian doctrine but as a political and harshly realistic one. Its very egalitarianism illustrates the realism and even immoralism of the doctrine of sovereignty, for by nature men are *not* equal according to Rousseau. The virulent attacks Rousseau directs at unjust and abusive inequality have tended to obscure that he also thought men very much unequal. He believed in "great men," in heroes and philosophers, in innate force of soul and innate genius. Such men are not merely more talented than others, they are more perfect beings. "Cato seems like a God among mortals" (*Political Economy*, p. 219). Moreover, ordinary men need their help: they are "preceptors of the human race" and "are made to guide the others" (*First Discourse*, p. 63; *Works*, III, p. 72). Emile needs the guidance of Rousseau his tutor, Julie and St. Preux need the godlike Wolmar, and above all a nation needs a legislator. "The legislator's great soul is the true miracle that should prove his mission" (*Social Contract*, p. 70).

Because men are unequal, it obviously does not follow that the superior may exploit the inferior. But it is rational and just that the superior lead the inferior, rather than the reverse. "It is manifestly against the law of nature, in whatever manner it is defined, that a child command an old man [or] an imbecile lead a wise man" (*Second Discourse*, p. 181). It also follows from men's inequality that what is good for the superior few often is not good for the many, and vice versa. For example, Rousseau's critique of popular enlightenment is merely an application of this principle. "I have already said a hundred times that it is good that there are philosophers, provided the people does not meddle in it" (*Works*, III, p. 78). Conversely, there are certain general rules concerning what is good for ordinary men, but "all rare cases are outside the rules" (*Emile*, p. 245).

The General Will, being a principle of equality, ignores this natural inequality among men and is therefore, in certain important respects, harmful or unreasonable. It requires the superior to be ruled by laws made by the inferior majority; it makes the superior fit into the narrow mold of what is good for the inferior. Each may do only what all can do; no one is allowed to be "outside the rules." Such considerations led all classical thinkers to regard strict equality as unjust and to have ultimate misgivings about the rule of law or the principle of "generality."

Rousseau favors the General Will not as the embodiment of justice but as a replacement for it. More realistic than the classics, he claims that true justice is not publicly known or sanctioned, and that what appears in the world as "natural law" is always a tool of exploitation. In the harshness of our condition, we cannot afford to do justice to natural inequality, for only if "the condition is equal for everyone [will] no one [have] an interest in making it burdensome for the others" (*Social Contract*, p. 53). With its strict equality, the General Will or popularly enacted law must be sovereign, not because it is just or moral—it is not —but because it is a realistic, political means— and the only means—of preventing widespread oppression.

In other words, Rousseau takes the same realistic attitude toward equality that Hobbes had taken:

> Whether therefore men be equal by nature, the equality is to be acknowledged; or whether unequal, because they are like to contest for dominion, it is necessary for the obtaining of peace, *that they be esteemed as equal.* (*De Cive,* p. 143, Hobbes's italics; see *Leviathan,* p. 120)

Echoing this statement, Rousseau writes in the *Social Contract:*

> I shall end this chapter and this [first] book with a comment that ought to serve as the basis of the whole social system. It is that rather than destroying natural equality, the fundamental compact on the contrary substitutes a moral and legitimate equality for whatever physical inequality nature may have placed between men, and that although they may be unequal in force or in genius, they all become equal through convention and by right. (p. 58)

Rousseau's demand for equality (and the generality it makes possible) is even stronger than Hobbes's because, more realistic than Hobbes, he sees the need for a return to the classical concern for virtue. And from the doctrine of the natural goodness of man, which traces all vice to dependence and oppression, Rousseau concludes that virtue too requires equality and the absolute rule of law. Thus, the General Will must *replace* natural justice and inequality, for it is the only realistic means to virtue as well as preservation.

Rousseau is a thinker filled with moral passion, yet convinced that morality is the source of most evil in the world. His *First* and *Second Discourses* are one long expose of the harm arising from the "appearance of right." The *Social Contract* must be understood in light of these earlier works and this moral realism. Taken in isolation, it seems to present a utopian moral doctrine directed solely against the dangers of political power. In fact, it is a hardheaded political work directed primarily against the dangers of moral doctrine.

References

Burlamaqui, J.-J. *Principes du droit naturel.* Paris: Guillaume Junior, 1791.

Cobban, A. *Rousseau and the modern state.* London: George Allen & Unwin, 1934.

Crocker, L. The priority of justice or law. *Yale French Studies,* 1961-1962, *28,* 34-42.

Derathé, R. *Jean-Jacques Rousseau et la science politique de son temps.* Paris: Presses Universitaire de France, 1950.

Diderot, D. et al. [*Encyclopedia*] (N. S. Hoyt & T. Cassirer, Trans.) Indianapolis: Bobbs Merrill, 1965.

Goldschmidt, V. *Anthropologie et politique.* Paris: Librarie Philosophique J. Vrin, 1974.

Gough, J. W. *The social contract.* Oxford: Clarendon Press, 1957.

Grotius, H. [*The law of war and peace*] (F. Kelsey, Trans.) Oxford: Clarenton Press, 1925.

Hall, J. C. *Rousseau: an introduction to his political philosophy.* London: Macmillan, 1973.

Haymann, F. La loi naturelle dans la philosophie de J.-J. Rousseau. *Annales,* 1943-1945, *30,* 65-109.

Hendel, C. W. *Jean-Jacques Rousseau: moralist.* Indianapolis: Bobbs Merrill, 1934.

Hobbes, T. *Leviathan.* New York: Collier Books, 1962.

Hobbes, T. *De Cive.* In *Man and citizen.* Garden City, N.Y.: Anchor Books, 1972.

Hubert, R. *Rousseau et l'encyclopédie* Paris: Gamber, 1928.

Jouvenal, B. de Essai sur la politique de Rousseau. In J.-J. Rousseau, *Du contrat social.* Geneva: Éditions du Cheval Ailé, 1947.

Keohane, N. O. *Philosophy and the state in France: the Renaissance to the Enlightenment.* Princeton, N.J.: Princeton University Press, 1980.

Masters, R. *The political philosophy of Rousseau.* Princeton, N.J.: Princeton University Press, 1968.

Plattner, M. F. *Rousseau's state of nature.* DeKalb: Northern Illinois University Press, 1979.

Pufendorf, S. von [*Le droit de la nature et des gens*] (Jean Barbeyrac, Trans.) Amsterdam: Pierre de Coup, 1712.

Rommen, H. A. *The natural law: a study in legal and social history and philosophy.* St. Louis: Herder, 1947.

Rousseau, J.-J. *Oeuvres complètes.* B. Gagnebin & M. Raymond (Eds.). Paris: Bibliothèque de la Pléiade, 1959-1969. (Cited as *Works.*)

Rousseau, J.-J. [Letter to M. d'Alembert]. In A. Bloom (Trans.), *Politics and the arts.* Ithaca, N.Y.: Cornell University Press, 1960.

Rousseau, J.-J. [*The first and second discourses*] (R. D. Masters & J. R. Masters, Trans.) New York: St. Martin's Press, 1964.

Rousseau, J.-J. [*On the social contract, with Geneva manuscript and political economy*] (R. D. Masters, Ed. & J. R. Masters, Trans.) New York: St. Martin's Press, 1978.

Rousseau, J.-J. [*Emile or on education*] (A. Bloom, Trans.) New York: Basic Books, 1979.

Shklar, J. N. *Men and citizens: a study of Rousseau's social theory.* Cambridge: Cambridge University Press, 1969.

Strauss, L. *Natural right and history.* Chicago: University of Chicago Press, 1953.

Vaughan, C. E. *The political writings of Jean-Jacques Rousseau.* Cambridge: Cambridge University Press, 1915.

Vaughan, C. E. *Studies in the history of political philosophy before and after Rousseau.* Manchester: University Press, 1925.

Addenda

p. 633, §2, ll.6–8: –/– ; *OC*1.932–35/*CW*1.211–13; *OC*3.106–107/*CW*2.184–85
   Ibid., §4, ll.10–11: *OC*1.404–405/*CW*5.340
   Ibid., §5, l.8: *OC*3.19/*CW*2.14
p. 634, §1, l.3: *OC*1.934/*CW*1.213
   Ibid., l.5: *OC*3.8/*CW*2.6
   Ibid., §2, l.16: *OC*4.311/*Em*.85
   Ibid., §3, l.6: –/–
   Ibid., §4, ll.19–20: *OC*3.842–43/*CW*9.261
   Ibid., §5, l.7: *OC*4.1019/*CW*9.92
   Ibid., §6, ll.9–10: *OC*4.309/*Em*.84; *OC*3.248/*CW*3.145–46
p. 635, §4, ll.33–34: *OC*3.462/*CW*4.217–18
p. 637, §3, ll.8–9: *OC*3.610–11/*CW*11.62–63
   Ibid., §4, l.6: *OC*3.355/*CW*4.134
   Ibid., §6, ll.4–5: *OC*3.412/*CW*4.180
   Ibid., §9, ll.9–12: *OC*2.968–69/*CW*2.193; *OC*3.174–75/*CW*3.51–52, *OC*3.187–89/*CW*3.62–63;
   *OC*3.251–52/*CW*3.148–49
   Ibid., §10, ll.6–7: –/–
p. 638, §2, l.6: *OC*4.242–43/*Em*.34
   Ibid., §7, ll.7–8: *OC*3.351–55/*CW*4.131–34; *OC*3.178–82/*CW*3.55–58
   Ibid., l.12: *OC*3.355/*CW*4.134
   Ibid.,§8, l.6: *OC*3.154/*CW*3.35
p. 639, §2, l.6: *OC*3.153/*CW*3.35
   Ibid., §4, l.9: *OC*3.125/*CW*3.14
   Ibid., §6, ll.5–6: *OC*3.287/*CW*4.81
   Ibid., §7, l.11: *OC*3.124/*CW*3.13
   Ibid., §11, l.6: *OC*3.284/*CW*4.78
   Ibid., §12, l.3: *OC*3.176/*CW*3.53
   Ibid., §13, ll.8–9: *OC*3.285/*CW*4.79; *OC*3.378/*CW*4.152
   Ibid., §15, l.9: *OC*3.284/*CW*4.78
p. 640, §3, l.5: *OC*3.378/*CW*4.152
   Ibid., §4, l.6: *OC*3.125/*CW*3.14
   Ibid., §10, ll.8–9: *OC*3.316–17/*CW*4.103–104; *OC*3.156–57/*CW*3.37–38, *OC*3.202–203/*CW*3.74–75;
   *OC*3.383/*CW*4.156
   Ibid., §12, ll.4–7: *OC*3.364/*CW*4.141; *OC*3.169–94/*CW*3.47–67; *OC*1.404–405/*CW*5. 340; *OC*3.664–
   65/*CW*11.115; cf. *OC*4.857–58/.473
   Ibid., §13, l.2: *OC*3.329/*CW*4.113
   Ibid., §14, l.6: *OC*3.378/*CW*4.152
p. 641, §4, l.9: *OC*3.380/*CW*4.154
   Ibid., l.14: *OC*3.286–87/*CW*4.80
   Ibid., §5, ll.5–6: –/–
   Ibid., §6, l.4: *OC*4.11/–
   Ibid., l.11: *OC*3.251/*CW*3.148
   Ibid., l.20–21: *OC*3.113/*CW*3.4; *OC*3.385/*CW*4. 158
p. 642, §4, ll.18–19: *OC*3.181/*CW*3.57, *OC*3.192/*CW*3.65
   Ibid., §6, ll.6–7: *OC*3.124/*CW*3.13; *OC*4.569/*Em*.268–69
   Ibid., §8, l.9: *OC*3.36/*CW*2.38
   Ibid., ll.15–16: *OC*2.970/*CW*2.195; *OC*3.28–29/*CW*2.20–21
   Ibid., §9, ll.8–9: *OC*4.967/*CW*9.52; *OC*4.836–37/*Em*.458
p. 643, §1, l.8: *OC*3.194/*CW*3.67, *OC*3.204–205/*CW*3.76–77
   Ibid., §2, ll.15–16: *OC*3.8/*CW*2.6
   Ibid., §5, l.6: *OC*3.554/*CW*4.70
   Ibid., §7, l.7: *OC*4.819/*Em*.446

651a

Ibid., l.23: *OC*4.329/*Em*.97
Ibid., §8, ll.6–7: *OC*4.602/*Em*.291–92; –/–
Ibid., §10, ll.9–10: *OC*4.308–309/*Em*.83–84, *OC*4.816/*Em*.444
Ibid., l.13: *OC*4.819/*Em*.445
p. 644, §1, ll.1–2: *OC*3.176/*CW*3.52
Ibid., §2, l.12: *OC*3.9/*CW*2.7
Ibid., §3, l.4: *OC*3.5/*CW*2.4
Ibid., l.: 8: *OC*3.478/*CW*4.19
Ibid., §4, ll.9–10: *OC*3.475/*CW*4.17; *OC*3.478/*CW*4.19, *OC*3.54/*CW*2.52, *OC*3.610/*CW*11.62;
*OC*3.606/*CW*11.68; *OC*3.518/*CW*4.46; *OC*4.937/*CW*9.28–29, *OC*4.1734–35/–; *OC*4.524–25/*Em*.236
Ibid., §6, l.7: *OC*3.351/*CW*4.131
Ibid., §7, l.8: *OC*3.132/*CW*3.18
Ibid., §10, l.7: *OC*3.177/*CW*3.53–54
Ibid., §11, l.12: *OC*3.284/*CW*4.79
Ibid., l.22: *OC*3.177/*CW*3.54
Ibid., l.27: *OC*3.180/*CW*3.56
Ibid., l.32: *OC*3.187/*CW*3.62
Ibid., §12, l.5: *OC*3.203/*CW*3.75
p. 645, §3, ll.18–19: *OC*3.30/*CW*2.22; *OC*3.380/*CW*4.154
Ibid., l.28: *OC*3.948/*CW*11.162–63
Ibid., l.34–35: *OC*3.474/*CW*4.16–17
Ibid., §4, ll.17–18: *OC*1.405/*CW*5.340; *OC*1.935/*CW*1.213
Ibid., §5, l.19: *OC*3.245/*CW*3.143
p. 646, §1, l.12: *OC*3.360–61/*CW*4.138–39
Ibid., §2, l.4: *OC*3.360–61/*CW*4.138
Ibid., §4, l.4: *OC*3.379/*CW*4.153
Ibid., §6, ll.5–6: *OC*3.246/*CW*3.144; *OC*3.371/*CW*4.147
Ibid., l.12: *OC*3.438/*CW*4.198–99
Ibid., l.19: –/–
Ibid., §7, ll.11–12: *OC*3.440/*CW*4.200
Ibid., §9, l.4: *OC*3.441/*CW*4.201
Ibid., §12, ll.18–19: *OC*3.460–69/*CW*4.216–24
p. 647, §1, l.4: *OC*3.435/*CW*4.197
Ibid., ll.14–15: *OC*3.435–36/*CW*4.197, *OC*3.368–71/*CW*4.145–47, *OC*3.395–400/*CW*4.166–70.
Ibid., §2, l.9: *OC*3.771/*CW*9.201
Ibid., §5, l.5: *OC*3.463 n. 1/*CW*4.218 n.
Ibid., §7, ll.6–7: *OC*3.371/*CW*4.147
Ibid., l.10: *OC*3.557/*CW*4.73
Ibid., §8, ll.14–15: *OC*1.967/*CW*1.238–39; see *OC*1.890, 964–65/*CW*1.178–79, 236–37
p. 648, §1, ll.11–12: *OC*3.505/*CW*4.38; *OC*3.459–60/*CW*4.215–16; *OC*3.317–18/*CW*4.104–05
Ibid., ll.22–23: *OC*3.246/*CW*3.144; *OC*3.12–14/*CW*2.9–11; *OC*3.73n/*CW*1.111 n. 2
Ibid., §3, ll.11–12: *OC*3.516–17/*CW*4.44–45; cf. *OC*3.609–10/*CW*11.61–62
Ibid., §6, l.6: *OC*4.857/*Em*.473
p. 649, §1, l.9: *OC*3.285/*CW*4.79
Ibid., §3, l.4: *OC*3.42/*CW*2.42
Ibid., l.8: *OC*4.600–01/*Em*.290
Ibid., §6, l.5: *OC*4.569/*Em*.269
Ibid., §7, l.7: *OC*1.567/*CW*5.474–75
Ibid., §10, l.15: *OC*3.255/*CW*3.151
Ibid., l.18: *OC*3.29/*CW*2.21; *OC*3.72/*CW*2.111
Ibid., l.23: *OC*3.384/*CW*4.157
Ibid., §11, ll.7–8: *OC*3.194/*CW*3.67
Ibid., l.15: *OC*3.78/*CW*2.115
Ibid., l.18: *OC*4.537/*Em*.245
p. 650, §2, ll.10–11: *OC*3.360–61/*CW*4.138
Ibid., §6, l.10: *OC*3.367/*CW*4.144

Part III
The General Will and Totalitarianism

[5]

THE RELATION OF ROUSSEAU'S SECOND *DISCOURS* AND THE *CONTRAT SOCIAL*

By Lester G. Crocker
GOUCHER COLLEGE

WHILE the *Discours sur l'origine de l'inégalité* and the *Contrat social* apparently stand in polar relationship to each other, there is actually a fundamental theoretical consistency between the two, if we consider them as a movement from one frame of reference to another.[1] Let us consider the main theses, postulates and conclusions of each work in this light.

To ask how inequality came to be is to inquire how society came to be, since inequality inheres in social relationships. Rousseau's cardinal assumption, then, in the *Discours sur l'origine de l'inégalité*, is that society "came to be," as an act of human will, and that it is possible to conceive of a "natural man" living in isolation. On this all the rest stands. If it is not historically true (Rousseau cautiously avoids the commitment to fact, though his reasoning later proceeds as if his hypotheses were factual), it is at least a theoretical truth, necessary to an understanding of the present condition of man.

In the drama of the establishment of civil society, the villain in the piece is property; from it grew the inequalities and moral ills of mankind. But property itself was a rather late institution, that "came to be" as a result of increasing population, the discovery of metallurgy and consequent division of labor. To determine how all this may have developed, Rousseau paints an unforgettable picture of man in the "state of nature," and then describes the steps which led to what might be called a secular version of his "Fall" and expulsion from the "Garden of Eden." While much of Rousseau's anthropology is utterly false, some of it is valid. It little matters, for it is his philosophy that is a constant provocation and challenge.

What is man? What is nature? These are the ultimate questions at stake. Rousseau tries to reconstruct the logic of human development. In so doing, he posits a "man" who lacks qualities we consider necessary to the human status: moral notions, language, thought, the need for others, and a continuing relationship with others. His "original man" is human only by virtue of his feeling of pity, his freedom and his fatal

1. The *Discours* was published in 1755. The *Contrat social* was published in 1762, but a considerable part of it was written as early as the *Discours*.

perfectibility (once again, the transposed myth of the Fall). Historically, this "natural" man is completely artificial. Yet the picture has a strong appeal to our imagination, and upon it Rousseau builds his theory. Its appeal is due, in part at least, to his having grasped the essential fact for an understanding of human nature: man is free and creative; and yet, within the social context, these powers are and must be confined. Thus they become elements of disorder.

It is also possible to consider Rousseau's natural man, although he never so states, as a pseudo-historical transposition of a psychological reality. This is the "original nature" we bring with us at birth, before the awakening of moral responses and the molding process of social patterns. Again it might be objected that "human" beings have never existed and never could exist without others, nor, consequently, without judgments of right and wrong. This was the common eighteenth-century opinion. But Rousseau really escapes this criticism, since the creature he paints is admittedly not human, but pre-human, living "in a state of animality." If we should object further that even this animal is a purely mythical construct, as unreal as a faun or a phoenix, Rousseau again might reply that it is a necessary hypothetical construct for his purpose, leading to valid conclusions.

We must remember that Rousseau is striving to show that man, naturally good, has been corrupted and perverted by society. To demonstrate this, he must obviously find a way of revealing a man who is outside of society, and prior to it. This, then, is his artificial construct of a hypothetical "natural man"—"natural" only in the sense of a nature which is purely metaphysical, abstracted from all empirical existence. The real difficulty in Rousseau's argument is that he cannot stay on this level. To make his point he must consider man in an empirical nature and in a historical order. His "trick" is to make it seem that there is no break, that the historical man is the logical and actual development of the other, the abstract "original" man. In the first situation, man is good, or at least, not evil; in the second he is, inevitably, evil. So the conclusion becomes inescapable: society has corrupted man!   .

Yet is there not a basic truth in all this? Rousseau's logic and anthropology, to be sure, break down. He conceives of social relationships as external to man, as an accidental and unnecessary accretion—as if human nature could be abstracted from these relationships and considered "in itself." He is right, however, in thinking that our human qualities are unfolded by social experience; that we are born with little baggage other than some basic drives, freedom from the fixity of animal instinct, and "perfectibility," or certain faculties which we can develop. He is right again, in a large measure, in attributing to society the development of man as a moral being; a being who is moral not only in the acquisition of a particular code of ethics, but in an even wider and more basic sense, in the experience of spiritual love and the need for power, for security and prestige. In society, man comes to feel the insatiable restlessness of curiosity and increasing needs. In society, he inevitably knows, does and suffers evil—as well as good. In this sense, society corrupts man, and man in society is inevitably evil. But both good and evil were already in him, as vìrtualities; and as he cannot exist or be empirically and historically considered without society, man, we must conclude—despite all Rousseau's refusals to admit it—is necessarily evil, naturally evil. To say that man must inevitably, because of his nature, become evil, is to say that he is naturally evil, even if he is not "originally" so.

Rousseau's own conclusion, however, is precisely a rejection of the doctrine that man is naturally evil. He eludes it, not only by his concept of a pre-social "natural man," but by semantic juggling or trickery. He speaks often of human nature as "naturally good." Actually, even if we take him on his own terms, all he has shown is a picture of a pre-human who is also pre-moral. This pre-human is a stranger to moral goodness, or virtue, which requires moral judgment and self-sacrifice—of which man is capable, precisely, only in society. The germs of what in society will become moral good and moral evil are both present in Rousseau's natural men. They are not morally evil, it is true. While they will not restrain their ego or self-interest in any way, they are free of the compulsive desires, which society develops, to hurt others. When they hurt others, they do so in innocence, knowing no moral judgments. On the other hand, their "goodness" is also a mere biological impulse, one of pity; it will not lead them to help others, much less to risk their own well-being or to make any sacrifice. Consequently, the most Rousseau could logically claim is that society has developed the potential *moral* good, which is naturally in man, far less than the potential *moral* evil which is naturally in him—both of these qualities existing equally, in "natural man," as biological, non-moral sources of action. In other words, the type of statement, "man is naturally good, society has made him wicked" is a semantic trick which creates an utterly false impression. It induces us to overlook the fact that the "goodness" of natural man was not moral goodness, and also the correlative fact that the "wickedness" of social man had its analogue in natural man's self-love (*amour de soi*). While society has perverted the latter into selfishness (*amour-propre*), it has also sublimated the former into virtue.

From Rousseau's point of view, the important thing is that there is not an absolute, ontological identity between the "original nature" and what it becomes. The child does *become* something. Even if evil is a necessary outcome of virtual and latent characteristics, the fact that an intermediate, developmental *process* is involved allows the possibility of intervention—of conditioning—so that a wide latitude of character formation exists. (This is also the basis of modern psycho-analytic theory.)

Building upon his devastating basic assault, Rousseau draws up a more detailed indictment of society. Luxury and property are shown to be evils. The perversion of self-love into selfishness; the substitution of "opinion" (the "look" of others) for self-judgment, culminating in the non-fraternal motives of prestige and power; the flight from the self into a formalized, mechanized, therefore empty existence; the loss of freedom and equality—these are all parts of the dark picture of a competitive society. A competitive society is one whose values are perverted by a false notion of "progress" and "good"; one in which men have every interest in hating each other and in hurting each other.

Rousseau's apparent "primitivism" had a powerful appeal to his contemporaries, as well as to men of later times. Others followed the logic of his *Discours* to its obvious end, dreamed of an equalitarian, communistic society, or even of an anarchistic social state. But Rousseau himself, as he turned to the constructive part of his work and sought a way out of man's dilemma, rejected primitivism. While he urged a simple way of living for the individual and abjured none of his criticism of society, he realized that the simplistic solutions of "abolition" were pure fantasy. Evolution is an irreversible process. The question is: Where can we go from here?

For Rousseau, society is the original sin, but it is also the testing place, as is earthly life in the Christian tradition. The direction man must take is not a "return to nature"—neither the hypothetical, metaphysical nature of "natural man," nor the empirical, historical nature which obtains around us. We must leave all this behind and forge a new destiny, utterly unknown to nature, that is truly man's own. The paths are mapped out in three books, *La Nouvelle Héloïse* (1761), *Emile* (1762) and *Du Contrat social* (1762). To be sure, Rousseau still speaks of "natural" ways of living; but in *Emile* he clearly says, "We must not confuse what is natural to the savage state and what is natural to the civil state." It is the latter he is concerned with now. Montesquieu, he thought, had made this error, overlooking the opposition between the natural order of things and the civil order. In physical nature, man depends on things, which have necessity and stability. In society, man depends on men. Rousseau's hope, expressed in *Emile*, is to give to human laws the necessity and inflexibility of physical laws; in this way, "we would unite in the Republic all the advantages of the natural state to those of the civil state." But in order to accomplish this, we must, precisely, overcome what is "natural" in man—impulses and passion. We must "denature man," change him from an absolute individual to a part of a unified whole, thereby destroying the contradictions existing within him.[2] For the society which history has created (the truly *natural* society, since it developed not rationally, but out of natural determinisms) has—paradoxically—created an "artificial man" who is in constant tension and antagonism with the "natural man" who persists within us. We must, then, overcome this unhappy contradiction by creating an artificial man: a social man, in whom internal and external conflicts will be minimized, because he is in harmony with the artificial context of life which is designed for him, and into which he is molded by education and society.

Du Contrat social opens with a famous first sentence, "Man was born free, and everywhere he is in chains." It would be wrong to take these words as a protest. They are only the statement of a fact, that man in society no longer enjoys the freedom of "natural man."[3] The prime purpose of Rousseau's inquiry will be to determine what conditions justify this civil status; in other words, what are the foundations of a legitimate political society. Here he breaks cleanly with most other thinkers of his time who, like Montesquieu, were seeking to found the body politic on natural laws, or on a rational "Natural Law." Following his view that society is not natural to man, he looks elsewhere, to artificial and deliberate conventions. In this, Hobbes' influence was doubtless great, but the two men reach quite different conclusions. In nature, argues Rousseau, there is only force. In society, men create right, which, though using force, supersedes it. Force under law is quite different from force without law. Right comes into being by the convention of the social compact. Here again, the compact is a symbol: man, by the fact of society, creates right, and also rights. These are "natural" only inasmuch as they are inherent in organized social existence.[4]

Rousseau's version of the social contract theory is brilliantly original. For him, as for Hobbes, it completely terminates the state of nature, with its natural freedom and equality. But a legitimate political society gives men, in their stead, something new and far more precious, political liberty and civil equality. The compact is the one unanimous act

2. See *Emile*, éd. Richard, Garnier, pp. 9–11.

3. The opening sentence has always been incorrectly translated, to read "Man is born free. . . ." The difference is considerable for the implications of Rousseau's thought. The present tense might well indicate a protest, against a constant process of enslavement of free beings by society. By using the past tense, Rousseau clearly refers to men in the "state of nature," and indicates that his freedom was surrendered, once and for all, by his acceptance of the social compact.

4. Rousseau, then, is opposed to Natural Law because it defines man as a naturally moral and social being. According to his own diagnosis, society is an artificial accretion which changes everything in nature and brings the realm of morality and law into being. The liberal, and the humanist, would readily agree with Rousseau, if he took "nature" to mean all that is *outside of man*. The question is whether we can make such a separation, *for man*, between social and natural.

which obviates the need for further unanimity. It creates the obligation
to submit to the will of the majority: legally, since the individual has
agreed to its rule; morally, since he is still obeying his true will, which
is that the general will shall rule. Rousseau shows in detail what is lost
forever on accepting the compact, and the gains which, point by point,
are substituted for the losses. Possession, for instance, a usurpation which
is limited only by strength, becomes property, a right which is both secured and limited by the community. Further, society is assumed, in
Rousseau's theory, to be prior to government. The consequence is revolutionary. The so-called rulers of men have no part in the contract; they
are only the instruments and servants of the people, in whom all sovereignty inalienably resides, and they may be dispossessed by the simple
will of the sovereign people.

This summary points to the two great problems of the *Contrat social*
which have puzzled and exercised the minds of countless commentators.
The first is the expression of the will of the community, which is to be
the determinant of social control and discipline. This involves Rousseau's famous notion of the "general will." The general will is to be as-
certained or formulated by the process of majority vote, that is, by a
process of cancellation, in accordance with what Rousseau considered
to be the workings of the mathematical laws of probability. But we must
not err by confusing the nature of the general will with this positivistic
process of its expression, or, more exactly, its discovery. The "general
will" is essentially a rationalistic notion and involves the same type of
hypothesis as "natural man," the "state of nature," or the "social contract." Rousseau does not deny what we might call "empirical man,"
man as he is, fighting primarily for his own interest. But beyond this
he assumes a rational unity among all men, consisting of what their
reason would desire if all individual passions and desires could be stilled.
This is the "general" will. (He derived its notion, I believe, from Spinoza's *Ethics* and *Tractatus theologico-politicus*.) It is questionable
whether in the cancellation process Rousseau has found a procedure
that would realize it. However, this belief underlies his theory that civil
liberty consists not in doing what we want, but in doing what this hypothetical or metaphysical "general will" wants. Thus, when we suppress
the individual's protest, we merely force him to be free, force him to
do what he *really* wants to do. Once again, Rousseau mingles in one
concept a real, empirical situation and a purely metaphysical postulate.

The second difficult problem is the new relationship of the individual
citizen to the State. Is Rousseau's thought totalitarian or liberal? A remarkable quantity of ink has flowed in the attempt to prove it one or
the other. As in all such situations, elements of both tendencies are
clearly in the book. Rousseau of course was not thinking of political

labels or philosophies that did not exist. He wanted only to secure men's happiness, through the liberty and equality of a legitimate, just political society; and this could not be done without a certain amount of sacrifice and a certain amount of control. If we are to make the transition from a natural state of force to a civil state of right a successful one for mankind, we must think of men as citizens who have become part of a greater whole, and not as independent, self-centered individuals. Society terminated the natural isolation of individuals, but it is necessary also to end the atomism of individual wills. The mutuality of the sacrifice, the respecting of others as we wish them to respect us, and the limitation of the sacrifice as determined by the sovereign people itself —this is the foundation.

What the liberal cannot accept is Rousseau's return to Hobbes, both in his unreserved alienation of the individual will to the collectivity, and in his concomitant rejection of Natural Law as a limit to the political power of the collectivity, as exercised through its governmental organs.[5] Rousseau thought he had remedied Hobbes' great error, when he posited alienation not to an individual (the monarch), but to the "general will," which, by a process of dubious logic, he makes equivalent to the "true" individual will—so that there is no alienation at all, and we are free even when we are frustrated. In this fashion, he believed he had solved the greatest enigma of the eighteenth-century ethical and political thought: the harmonizing of self-interest and the general interest. Unfortunately, his "general will" remains a metaphysical entity (*un être de raison*), and deteriorates, in the empirical realm, into majority rule.

A comparison between two ideas in the works we are discussing emphasizes the problem. In the *Discours,* Rousseau had said, countering the ethics of enlightened self-interest, that more is to be gained by the immediate satisfaction of the private will than by the ultimate benefit accruing from sacrificing it in favor of the general good. How does Rousseau overcome this essentially nihilistic proposition in the *Contrat social?* To begin with, he postulates the existence of a general will in each citizen (*qua* citizen), concomitant to his private will. This is, by definition, that which "always tends to the general welfare" (II, 3), and is what he would prefer if his personal interest could be abstracted from a given situation. Then Rousseau adds that will, for reasons which he explains, is subject to error. Later he again remarks (II, 6), "The general will is always *droite,* but the judgment that guides it is not always en-

5. Clarity and exactness require us to carry Rousseau's analysis one step further. Rights (and right) are indeed developed by human collectivities. They are, however, created in two distinct ways: by the "natural" process of living communally, and by the "artificial" (willful, rational) process of positive legislation. It is the first of these that the liberal will not alienate "totally" to the second. Rousseau does not recognize the distinction.

lightened." This is a perversion, a straying from the mark, a ἁμαρτία that must be prevented. Consequently, "all are in equal need of guides." Just as the private will must be "obliged" to conform to reason, the public will must be taught what will satisfy it. Such a theory of "guidance" (to be furnished apparently by the legislator and the censor) implies that some know the general will in advance, and that they, speaking in the name of all, oblige all. The element of "education," in the strict literal sense of that word, comparable to what today is called "conditioning" or "thought control," thus holds the ultimate key to the enigma. It is a coercive element.

Rousseau's concept of voting procedures, moreover, is "democratic," but not "liberal." The vote is not a way of expressing our wills, but of discovering the general will. When you lose, you are therefore "in error," and must conform to a new way of *thinking*—and not, for instance, try to change the minority to a majority. Rousseau is consistent. The process assumes an abstract general will, other than what individuals wish as individuals. It does not sanctify the majority in the sense of the largest number of private wills, but only as the discoverer of that abstraction which is the general will: what all *should* desire, and what they would desire in the absence of private interest. We have here an absolute, which we again see theoretically pre-exists the vote, and which allows the guide to speak in the name of the general will and to direct the components of the social whole accordingly. Political freedom is submission to the general will, thus discovered, which represents the authentic will of the individual. Rousseau could not foresee what the French Revolution, and later revolutions, were to make all too clear: there is always some individual (or some group) that declares himself (or itself) to be the true and sole voice and expression of the "general will." This individual conceives of himself as the leader, or guide, who denounces errors and deviations which cannot, of course, be tolerated, and who points out the right way.[6]

At bottom, what Rousseau desired most urgently to avoid was a thoroughly competitive society, and to create in its stead a cooperative (or collective) society. We see this in *La Nouvelle Héloïse*, on Wolmar's ideal estate—although competition is preserved there, in a minor way,

6. Further evidence for this interpretation is found in "Economie politique." It is not always necessary, Rousseau affirms, to assemble the nation to discover the general will. On the one hand, "it is not certain that its decision would be the expression of the general will"; on the other hand, "the chiefs know that the general will is always for the decision which is most favorable to the public interest...." (Vaughan, *Political Writings*, I, 247). See also the important passages on coercive "education" and conditioning, carried to ultimate extremes, *ibid.*, pp. 248, 255–58, 277. In a fragment (p. 324), Rousseau speaks of the need to "change the nature of men," to "mutilate . . . their constitution," in order to transform the individual from a self-centered whole to an other-centered "part of a larger whole."

significantly in the form of work incentives. If a society is run by the power-play of various interests and particular wills, the result is war, coercion, fraud, injustice, as each strives to impose itself. We have, for instance, labor against capital, trying to influence voters and representatives, and the general interest suffers, along with the private. The essential thing, then, is to still, to by-pass, or to eliminate this process—to end the war. This is precisely what Marx also desired. And it is in total opposition to the main current of eighteenth-century Physiocratic and pre-capitalistic thought, which envisaged the general welfare as arising, necessarily and *naturally*, from the free clash of *volontés particulières*.

The working of Rousseau's plan is quite consistent. Political parties are excluded. Not only are there no minority rights; there cannot even be minorities—exactly as in Russia there cannot be parties or trade unions, since these would form fragmentized particular wills, contrary to the general will, for which the government speaks. Rousseu tends to confuse liberty with political equality and with sovereignty. Liberty, moreover, though it certainly means, as he holds, obedience to a general will (of some kind), as expressed in the law, must mean more than this. The liberal view, as developed in the eighteenth century and thereafter, rejects, as I have said, Rousseau's concept of a "total alienation" of the individual to the collectivity, with the latter returning to him only what it wishes—even if he does keep an equal voice in the expression of its will. Liberalism fears the tyranny of the majority, even the tyranny of the "whole" which it supposedly expresses. Can a people be called "free" if it freely decides to be slaves? Rousseau, it seems, does not discriminate sufficiently between the promotion of individual good through collective action and the sacrifice of the individual to the collective whole.

Assuredly this is not his intention. If it is true that the majority becomes a total tyranny, the people are their own tyrants and are free to redress any situation they consider wrong. There is no abstractly existing State, separate from the people, even though the State is considered to be a superior "moral person." The situation, we must bear in mind, is one in which the individual citizens are both end and means, sovereign and subjects. We should not forget, too, that Rousseau's concept of the dignity of the individual is not totalitarian. "It is never permissible," he writes in *La Nouvelle Héloïse* (V, 2), "to degrade a human soul for the advantage of others." Doubtless he saw no conflict between this view and the consequences of the surrender in the *Contrat social*.

Still more important, we must not forget the lesson of the *Discours sur l'inégalité*. Historical or social man, because of the very conditions of social living, is inevitably evil—that is, he is impelled to selfish actions that will hurt others. The more civilized the society, the more evil he will be. The development of virtue (as contrasted with natural man's merely instinctive "goodness" or sympathy) is therefore Rousseau's principal consideration.

Here his thought offers an outstanding difference from that of the majority of the *philosophes*. The latter planned to rebuild society and even "morality" by utilizing man's inevitable egoism, and by conditioning it to seek expression in socially approved outlets. Others, especially the Physiocrats, held that egoistic forces, if allowed free play, would work out to a natural harmony. Rousseau would use conditioning processes to overcome egoism itself and to reach moral virtue. Precisely as he had rejected the sensationist reduction of the personality and insisted on the distinctively human, so he felt that such qualities as spontaneous sympathy, fraternal cooperation and moral feeling, which were as real as the motives of pleasure and pain, could become social factors. But this could never come about naturally. Individual rights, as an immutable concept of Natural Law, had to be abandoned, and powerful coercive forces put at the disposal of the collectivity, to be used from earliest childhood onward. Virtue then, can be attained partly through self-control (*Emile, La Nouvelle Héloïse*), partly through social discipline and a political organization that will make evil tendencies harmless. Social man is an artificial man, and social life must not be confused with the state of nature: its rights, its morality, its conditions of interdependence, *man himself*—all are radically different. The free individuality has been surrendered. To live a "natural" life, *in society*, we must, paradoxically, give up natural freedom, the freedom to satisfy one's desires as one wishes. Natural freedom was good in the state of nature, because then men had only natural needs. But where they are exposed to all sorts of artificial needs and urges, individual liberty would lead to luxury, acquisitiveness, power drives and all the other evils of a competitive society which it is precisely Rousseau's intention to eliminate or minimize, as destructive to the true happiness of the individual. We must therefore overcome the natural in man, in order to give human affairs "the necessity and inflexibility" of natural events. We must create a new, artificial man, a "social" man, one who experiences his participation in the collectivity more strongly than his individual egoism. Paradoxically, this will satisfy our natural desires—but those very desires will be transformed.

This is a matter on which we must be clear. On the one hand, it would be strange if Rousseau, after his radical criticism of society for what it has done to man's life and character, did not wish to restore some of the qualities he valued in a "natural" way of life. We know from his writings on the *individual* and his life just what these are: sincerity and mutual understanding in personal communication; simplicity and closeness to nature; independence from what he called *opinion:* reliance on one's own moral judgments, and respect for one's own integrity, rather than conformity in order to win the approval of others. On the other hand, it is obvious, even as we mention these qualities, that at least the first and third of them have no meaning if thought of as "natural," or as referring to Rousseau's concept of our original nature (or, in other words, to man in the state of nature). They exist only in relation to a social life, and are therefore in themselves non-natural, according to Rousseau's own conceptual scheme. But though they are not independent of society, it is obvious that neither are they formal attributes of society. This is merely to say that a social structure is inevitable, as are a set of *social facts* which ensue from it, but they are likely to be harmful. The good society will minimize their ill consequences, and also maximize their advantages (the moral life, self-perfection) which Rousseau gladly admits. The essential point is that we cannot understand Rousseau if we approach him solely from the viewpoint of his ideas on the individual, just as social life cannot be understood or organized on the basis of individual atomism. We must consider the individual *within* the social fact, go *through* the social fact to him. There is only one *right* way. The great contribution of society is to give man a moral dimension. Therefore society must make man a moral being (instead of a being who is instinctively "good," or sincere), make him a being of virtue, a social being. Thus man, starting from independence, will have passed through an unhappy stage of semi-socialization, characterized by competition and rivalry, in order to reach finally a truly social or cooperative life. There is perhaps no clearer confirmation of the validity of this interpretation than the confrontation of Rousseau's two sets of ideas on pride or approbation: his condemnation of that motive in the *Discours,* and his purposeful utilization of it in *La Nouvelle Héloïse, Emile,* and *Du Contrat social.* But again, in order for the individual to become a moral being, society must become a moral society. In this way we may have a truly human (as contrasted with "natural") community; one which, in Cassirer's words, "no longer depends on these motives of power, greed and vanity, but which is entirely based on a law recognized as inwardly binding and necessary."

Here again, it seems difficult to deny that Rousseau, despite his noble ideal, opened the door to collectivism and totalitarianism—if indeed he did not walk through it. Is it not clear that, in view of his theory of human nature and society, Rousseau was bound to fear individual liberty? This re-making of the individualistic personality into a social personality involves both the repression of natural competitive instincts and a process of coercive conditioning through education and law, through thought control by state censorship, a compulsory state religion, and the absolute control exercised by the "general will." Death is the penalty for resistance. Although Rousseau passes lightly over economic activity, his chapter on property is in consonance with the rest. All in all, he would have the individuals in a community be like the organs of our own body. But surely, this is totalitarian. Let us remember that democracy and totalitarianism are not exclusive terms. Democracy is rule by the people. Totalitarianism is the attempt to impose a single pattern upon the thought, feelings and actions of a community. The opposite of totalitarianism is not democracy, but the pluralistic society, in which people are free to differ, and in which complete conformity is not the test of good citizenship. The liberal, then, cannot accept Rousseau's total submergence into a higher unity. He will cry out with Rousseau the *romantic*, "I am I, a sacred I. Thus far do I surrender myself, thus far do I *belong*, but no further." He will not accept censorship which (Rousseau claims) "far from being the arbiter of the people's opinions, is only its voice." He will not accept Rousseau's "people's democracy."

It would be hard to imagine a more dramatic contrast than that between the *Discours sur l'inégalité* and *Du Contrat social*. Little wonder that many critics, in Rousseau's lifetime and in later years, have accused him of inconsistency. Yet there is no basic contradiction between the two works, for their frames of reference, their controlling concepts of nature and man are different. Let us summarize their relationship, taking Rousseau, now, on his own terms. The basic value, man's happiness, remains unchanged. Freedom, in both, is only an instrumental value. The independence of natural man assured his freedom and his happy existence. The imposition of society on this natural man created a situation of conflict, inequality, distorted values and misery. Freedom is still necessary to the happiness of social man; but his interdependence requires the creation of an entirely different "political liberty," based on the civilized—that is, artificial, non-natural notion of right. The good society is one in which men would be made to live according to virtue, "remade" into beings adjusted to that society. Its realization depends on political liberty, equality and control; these in turn must inhere in the organization of a legitimate human polity.

The *Discours sur l'inégalité* tells us what men may have been, in their remote origins, or what they still are in their fundamental substructure, and what has happened to them because of social experience. *Du Contrat social* was written as a theoretical work, not as a practical program. Nevertheless, it indicates a direction. It tells us how we must overcome and transform this "natural man" within us. It tells us what men may become—or rather, what Rousseau thought they must become, if the unique *human* experiment in a *natural* universe is to succeed and to survive.

Addenda **44a**

2. *OC4.248–50/Em.39–40*
6. 11.5–6: *OC3.251/CW3.148*
    1.7: *OC3.251–52/CW3.148–49*, *OC3.259–62/CW3.154–57*, *OC3.1400*, n.261/ –
    1.8: *OC3.313/CW4.101*

(References within the text are to specific chapters in particular works of Rousseau; they are therefore just the same both in the *OC* and in the *CW*.)

[6]

Reflections on Rousseau: Autonomy and Democracy

JOSHUA COHEN

In this essay I discuss several recent studies of Rousseau's political philosophy. These studies cover a broad array of issues, ranging from Rousseau on the nature of the will to Rousseau on direct democracy, and from the intellectual context that shaped Rousseau's ideas to the influence of those ideas on Robespierre and the sans-culottes. I have focused here on problems that are both central to Rousseau's work and of interest in contemporary political philosophy. My discussion emphasizes three central Rousseauean themes: (1) the basic problem in political philosophy is to characterize a form of social order that encourages the autonomy of the members of that order; (2) social institutions play a central role in shaping the motivations and self-understanding of the members of society; and (3) the form of social order that most adequately accommodates both the central value of autonomy and the shaping role of institutions is a system of egalitarian-democratic institutions.[1] The first theme pro-

The following works are discussed in this review essay: Richard Fralin, *Rousseau and Representation* (New York: Columbia University Press, 1978); Hilail Gildin, *Rousseau's Social Contract* (Chicago: University of Chicago Press, 1983); Nannerl Keohane, *Philosophy and the State in France: The Renaissance to the Enlightenment* (Princeton: Princeton University Press, 1980); James Miller, *Rousseau: Dreamer of Democracy* (New Haven: Yale University Press, 1984); Patrick Riley, *Will and Political Legitimacy* (Cambridge, MA: Harvard University Press, 1982); and Judith Shklar, *Men and Citizens: A Study in Rousseau's Social Theory*, 2d ed. (Cambridge: Cambridge University Press, 1985). All references to these books will be included in the text. I should emphasize that the amount of attention devoted to particular works does not reflect a judgment of their relative merits or their likely interest to readers of this journal. Similarly, it is limitations of space and the topics of the essay that preclude discussion of Joel Schwartz's interesting book, *The Sexual Politics of Jean-Jacques Rousseau* (Chicago: University of Chicago Press, 1984).

1. Miller emphasizes the first and third of these themes, and weaves them together with a well-crafted historical account of Rousseau's relations with Geneva and his influence on the French Revolution. The range of Miller's book is impressive, and I find his general line

vides the focus in Part I, the third in Part II; the second plays a role throughout.

I. ROUSSEAU'S CONTRACT THEORY

Rousseau's *Social Contract* defends "principles of political right" and explores the operations of institutions in light of those principles. In his discussion of Rousseau in *Will and Political Legitimacy* (chap. 4), Patrick Riley criticizes the defense of principles. He argues that there are tensions between the "voluntarism" endorsed in Rousseau's contractarian theory of legitimacy and the "morality of the common good" that Rousseau embraces in describing his political ideal, and he maintains that the general will is a failed attempt to overcome these tensions.[2] Riley's own explication of Rousseau's views about the social contract and the general will are vague and unsatisfactory. In order, therefore, to evaluate Riley's criticisms, I first sketch an account of the main elements of Rousseau's view, and then use this sketch to assess the alleged tensions.

Autonomy and Social Interdependence

Rousseau's defense of principles of right in the *Social Contract* assumes conditions of social interdependence.[3] Abstracting from certain matters

---

of interpretation and points of emphasis very congenial. But excessive shifting between different sorts of material and diverse types of argument sometimes obscures the more analytical concerns.

2. Discussions of Rousseau by Hegel and the British Hegelians also suggest such a tension. See G.W.F. Hegel, *The Philosophy of Right*, trans. T. M. Knox (Oxford: Oxford University Press, 1952), paragraphs 29, 258; *Lectures on the History of Philosophy*, volume 3, trans. E. S. Haldane and Frances Simpson (London: Routledge & Kegan Paul, 1892); T. H. Green, *Lectures on the Principles of Political Obligation* (Ann Arbor: University of Michigan Press, 1967), sec. 77; Bernard Bosanquet, *The Philosophical Theory of the State* (London: MacMillan and Company, 1899), pp. 84–102; Brand Blanshard, *Reason and Goodness* (London: Allen and Unwin, 1961), chap. 14, esp. pp. 402–403.

3. Rousseau's works are cited in the text as follows: SC I.6.i: *On the Social Contract*, ed. Roger D. Masters, trans. Judith R. Masters (New York: St. Martin's Press, 1978), Book I, chapter 6, paragraph 1; GM I.2: *Geneva Manuscript*, ed. Roger D. Masters, trans. Judith R. Masters (New York: St. Martin's Press, 1978), Book I, chapter 2; PE: *Political Economy*, ed. Roger D. Masters, trans. Judith R. Masters (New York: St. Martin's Press, 1978); D2: *The Discourse on Inequality* in *The First and Second Discourses*, trans. Roger D. Masters and Judith R. Masters (New York: St. Martin's Press, 1964); E: *Emile*, trans. Allan Bloom (New York: Basic Books, 1979); P: *The Government of Poland*, trans. Willmoore Kendall (Indianapolis: Bobbs-Merrill, 1972); C: *Constitutional Project for Corsica in Rousseau:*

of detail, he supposes in particular that: (1) individuals each have basic needs and interests that they aim to satisfy; (2) the satisfaction of these needs and interests depends on the actions of others. In particular, if each acts solely with the aim of advancing his or her own interests (the "will of all"), all do less well than if their actions are coordinated; (3) agents have the capacity to recognize and do recognize their dependence on the actions of others (that is, they recognize that mutually beneficial coordination is possible); and (4) individuals have views—typically conflicting views—about the claims that they can legitimately make on one another (*SC* I.6.ii, I.7.vi–viii, II.1.i, II.3.ii; IV.1.vi; *GM* I.2; *D2*, pp. 154–59).

The aim of the *Social Contract* is to identify norms of social cooperation that are reasonable in view of conditions (1)–(4) together with two central features of human beings: first, that human beings have an equal capacity for and interest in *freedom*; and second, that we are *motivated by self-love*.4 "The fundamental problem," as he puts it, is to "Find a form of association that [1] *defends and protects the person and goods of each associate* with all the common force, and by means of which [2] *each one, uniting with all, nevertheless obeys only himself and remains as free as before*" (*SC*, I.6.iv, emphases and bracketed numbers are mine). The problem is to characterize a form of social interdependence that permits each to secure the benefits of association—the protection of person and goods, the development and exercise of capacities, the broadening of ideas and feelings (*SC* I.8.i)—without sacrificing the freedom that defines our nature.

This fundamental problem is "solved by the social contract" (*SC* I.6.iv), that is, by answering the question: What kind of association would be rationally agreed to by socially interdependent individuals who are moved by self-love and, above all, by an interest in securing their freedom?

Rousseau's contractual problem has, he believes, a determinate solution (*SC*, I.6.v), namely, a society in which each member "*puts his person*

Political Writings, trans. Frederick Watkins (London: Nelson, 1953); OC III (*LM*): *Lettres écrites de la montagne* in *Oeuvres Complètes*, eds. Bernard Gagnebin and Marcel Raymond, vol. 3 (Paris: Gallimard, Bibliothèque de la Pléiade, 1959–1969); OC III (*PF*): *Fragments Politiques* in ibid.; *LD: Letter to M. D'Alembert on the Theatre*, trans. Allan Bloom (Ithaca: Cornell University Press, 1968).

4. On freedom as an aspect of human nature, see *D2*, pp. 114, 167–68; *SC* I.4.vi; *E*, p. 280. Miller (chap. 7) provides an insightful treatment of this central issue.

and all his power in common under the supreme direction of the general will" (SC I.6.ix).[5] In such a society, authority rests ultimately in a shared understanding of the common good. More exactly, for a general will to provide supreme direction, the social order must satisfy four main conditions.[6] First, members (that is, citizens) have separate, particular interests (*SC* I.7.vii), and take those interests as providing reasons for action (Keohane, p. 445; Shklar, pp. 185–86). Second, citizens *share* and it is *common knowledge* that they share a conception of their common interests (of the "common good") though they may have different beliefs about what will advance those common interests.[7] Although no determinate conception of the common good follows from Rousseau's social contract, it does impose some general constraints on what will count as a genuine conception, including a requirement that the interests of each member (in security of person and goods, and in liberty) be advanced (*SC* II.1.i, II.11, and below p. 293).[8] Third, citizens take the fact that an institution

5. In this formulation of the clauses of the contract, Rousseau does not say that the general will provides *the* direction (or the *sole* direction) of a person and his powers, but the *supreme* direction. Neglect of this distinction leads naturally to the view that Rousseau endorsed a particularly extravagant form of communitarianism on which the general will provides the sole direction. See, for example, Cassirer, *The Question of Jean-Jacques Rousseau*, trans. Peter Gay (Bloomington: Indiana University Press, 1963), p. 52.

6. There are some fifty-five separate passages in the *SC* that at least mention the general will. (I would like to thank Marilyn Webster for help in compiling a list of these passages.) The interpretation here comes from trying to piece them together with one another and with passages in *GM*, *PE*, and elsewhere.

7. Gildin (pp. 54–56) and Keohane (pp. 439–42, 448) correctly emphasize that Rousseau's talk about the common good should be explicated in terms of the interests of the individual members of an association. See *SC* II.i.i. Using the example of a pure public good, Gildin underscores as well that to interpret the common good in terms of the common interests of individuals is not to identify the general will with the will of all. A public good meets a common interest, but it would not be voluntarily provided by individuals acting on their private interests. To put the point very schematically: the general will wills the cooperative solution to a positive-sum game whose noncooperative solution—the will of all—is Pareto suboptimal. For further discussion, see Brian Barry, "The Public Interest," *Proceedings of the Aristotelian Society*, 38 (1964): 9–14; W. G. Runciman and Amartya Sen, "Games, Justice, and the General Will," *Mind* 74 (1965): 554–62; David Braybrooke, "The General Will Demystified," unpublished; and W. T. Jones, "Rousseau's General Will, the Pareto Principle, and the Problem of Consent," Caltech Social Science Working Paper, no. 412 (December 1981).

8. On the requirement that the good of each be advanced, see *PE*, pp. 220–21; *OC* III (*PF*), p. 511; *OC* IV, p. 1126. Because the general will wills the common good, and the common good is understood in nonutilitarian terms, Rousseau holds that the institutional problem is to ensure that deliberations and decisions reflect the general will, not to protect citizens from that will (*SC* I.7.v, II.4).

or law advances common interests as itself providing *a* reason for supporting that institution or law, and recognize that they ought to act on reasons of the common good when they have reasonable assurance that others will so act. Fourth, social institutions generally conform to and citizens have reasonable confidence that the institutions conform to their shared conception of the common good.

Rousseau's argument that the general will is the solution to the social contract is very compressed (*SC* I.6.vi–viii). But it has two main elements, corresponding to the considerations of self-love and freedom that figure in the description of the contract. The fact that the social order ought to advance common interests corresponds to the fact that the contract is a unanimous agreement among rational individuals who are moved by self-love. And the fact that the members of the order share the conception of the common good that the social order ought to advance corresponds to the interest in remaining "as free as before." By sharing the conception, they achieve the autonomy that comes from acting on principles they recognize as their own, from "obedience to the law one has prescribed for oneself" (*SC* I.8.iii). For citizens to have, that is, the general will as a rule is for them to have "their own will as a rule," and so "it [the social contract] leaves them as free as before" (*OC* III [*LM*], p. 807; *SC* I.8.iii, II.4.viii; *E*, p. 461; *OC* III (*PF*), pp. 483–84).

This account of the contract, the general will, and the connections between the two is, of course, only the barest sketch. But it suffices for present purposes insofar as it highlights the role of social interdependence and autonomy, and provides some intuitive content for the main notions in Rousseau's theory. Having thus fixed an interpretation of certain central features of Rousseau's view—what I will refer to as a "social autonomy" interpretation—we can now consider Riley's objections.

Rousseau's Dilemma?

According to Riley, "Rousseau's system is somewhat paradoxical." The source of the paradoxes, he says, is the fact that "the standard to which will must conform—ancient perfection or its equivalent—is itself nonvoluntaristic; therefore, will and the standard to which it must conform are contradictory. The standard that gives will its object is the very negation of voluntarism" (p. 121). This description of the tension between Rousseau's "voluntarism" and his embrace of what Riley calls a "common good morality" resists straightforward construal. At least two importantly different accounts of the alleged tension are supported by Riley's discussion.

The first account of the tensions is that Rousseau shifts between a social and an individualistic *explanation of the acquisition of moral notions*. The social explanation assumes that people live in a society and holds that the acquisition of norms occurs through a process of socialization in which they learn the norms of the society; the individualistic explanation does not make that assumption and holds that acquisition takes place through an initial agreement.

> Despite the fact that he sometimes treats moral notions *as if they simply arose in a developmental process during the course of socialization,* Rousseau often *falls back on a kind of moral a priorism, particularly when speaking of contract and obligation,* in which the wills of free men are taken to be the causes of duties and of legitimate authority. (p. 102, emphases added; see also pp. 16, 123, 202)

It is certainly true that Rousseau offers an account of the acquisition of moral notions "during the course of socialization." And it is true as well that he endorses "a kind of moral a priorism" in his contractual justification of the general will. But it is not correct to say that Rousseau "falls back" from the one to the other, since the theory of socialization and the social contract respond to two different questions. The social contract addresses the question: What are the correct social norms? It is not an account of the acquisition of those norms. The account of socialization addresses the question: How do people develop an understanding of, and motivation to act on, the correct principles of right (that is, acquire a general will)? His response to this question draws on his psychology and theory of institutions. In part his answer is that socialization in a democratic order leads to the formation of a general will. While the social contract shows that autonomy requires a general will, the psychological theory suggests that socialization is the way that a general will, and therefore autonomy, is socially engendered.

Rousseau's views about acquisition and justification are not wholly disconnected. They are linked by the notion of reciprocity which figures in the contractual argument for the general will (*SC* I.6.viii, II.6.ii), in motivation formation (*E*, pp. 213–14), and in the social experience in a democratic order which leads to the formation of a general will. The social contract idealizes, so to speak, what political participation realizes (see below, pp. 293–294). But these connections notwithstanding, the *point* of the contract and of the account of socialization are different whereas Riley seems to confuse them.

The removal of this confusion does not, however, eliminate the problem that Riley is concerned about. It leaves a second construal of the tension between voluntarism and common good morality that does not turn on the putative use of the social contract as an explanation of acquisition. Thus Riley refers to what he calls the "greatest paradox in all of Rousseau: the paradox created by the fact that in the original contractual situation the motives needed by individuals to relinquish particular will and self-interest and to embrace a general will and the common good cannot exist at the time the compact is made but can only be the result of the so-cialization and common morality that society alone can create" (p. 110).

The suggestion is that Rousseau faces a dilemma in his contractual justification of the general will. If the parties to the social contract are *not socialized*, then they will not agree to a social order regulated by a general will. For if they are not socialized, then they are self-interested. And if they are purely self-interested, then they cannot rationally agree to be motivated by non-self-interested reasons. If, however, the parties to the contract *are socialized*, then they already have a "common good morality." But since that morality is "the very negation of voluntarism" (p. 121), if citizens have a common good morality, then they would them-selves reject the voluntarist conception of morality embodied in the social contract. Therefore, the contract either fails to justify the general will or it has no justificatory power at all. There is no single point of view, however, from which both a contractual justification and the common good morality embodied in the general will might consistently be en-dorsed.

This dilemma raises interesting questions about Rousseau's view. But the questions it raises pose genuine difficulties only if we reject the social autonomy interpretation and instead construe Rousseau as endorsing what I will call "self-effacing Hobbesianism."[9] In the discussion that follows, I will first outline this interpretation, then indicate that, while self-effacing Hobbesianism may be coherent, it is not a view that Rous-seau could accept, and finally suggest that Riley's dilemma concerning

9. On self-effacing theories, see Derek Parfit, *Reasons and Persons* (Oxford: Oxford University Press, 1984), secs. 9 and 17.

the consistency of Rousseau's contractual justification and common good morality can be resolved within the social autonomy interpretation.

According to self-effacing Hobbesianism, individuals are initially motivated solely by their own long-term interests in protecting their person and goods (hereafter I will refer to these as their "self-interests"). There comes a point at which they recognize that mutually beneficial coordination is possible, and that it is in their own long-term self-interest to cooperate on mutually beneficial terms if they can rely on the cooperation of others. They recognize as well that there are two obstacles to mutually beneficial coordination. First, there are a variety of mutually beneficial arrangements, none of which provides a focal point for their cooperation. An explicit stipulation of terms of order overcomes the first problem. Second, they need to ensure the stability of the resulting arrangements. But they see that their agreement is not self-enforcing both because there will be temptations to violate the agreement arising from motivations other than long-term self-interests and because they need assurance that others will keep the agreement.

Assessing various solutions to their dilemma, the contractors decide that a Hobbesian sovereign will likely be insufficient to motivate general compliance and to produce a stable order. For even with an absolute sovereign, obedience depends on self-interested calculation, and they judge that calculators are not reliable cooperators (SC I.3.i). The contractors conclude that only a society with a general will can ensure the stable satisfaction of the long-term self-interests, and so agree that they ought to have a general will. Aware, however, that one cannot just *decide* to have a general will, they agree to institutions that they expect will, over time, transform individuals in society from self-interested individualists into citizens whose primary allegiance is to the common good— thus producing a "remarkable change in man, by substituting justice for instinct in his behavior and giving his actions the morality they previously lacked" (SC, I.8.i).

Self-effacing Hobbesianism responds to Riley's dilemma as initially stated, since it shows that self-interested individuals *could* rationally "embrace" a general will, even if their first embrace consists only in the recognition that they ought to have a general will that takes precedence over their particular interests. But there is a variant of the dilemma that is not resolved, as a continuation of the historical story shows.

Once "the remarkable change in man" occurs, the members of society no longer regard themselves as, at bottom, self-interested. While they continue to have separate interests, their chief allegiance is to the common good, and their chief reason for complying with the rules of the association is that those rules advance the common good. Since they continue to have self-interests, some justification for their form of association is provided by the fact that it *would* be rational, in view of those self-interests alone, to bootstrap their way into the general will. But the fact that purely self-interested individuals would agree to the association cannot be their chief reason for complying with it, since they are not such individuals. Thus, if individuals regard self-interested reasons as fundamental, then they can agree that they *ought* to have a supreme general will but they do not *have* one. If they have one, then the self-interested contract does not provide *them* with the basic justification for having it. There is, then, no single point of view which embraces both the contractual justification and the general will.[10]

The absence of such a point of view is not by itself, however, an objection to a theory. A social contract theory could in principle be self-effacing. But I do not think that Rousseau held such a theory. He gives no evidence of believing that a contractual argument cannot provide a justification for having a general will to those with such a will. He appears instead to endorse a non-self-effacing interpretation of the social contract, and in fact to believe that public recognition that the social order would be agreed to contributes to the stability [solidité] of that order (*OC* III [*LM*], pp. 806–807; *SC* II.6.ii). If Rousseau requires that the contractual justification be non-self-effacing, and if the only way to make sense of Rousseau's combination of social contract theory and common good morality is to interpret him as endorsing self-effacing Hobbesianism, then a variant of Riley's dilemma raises a serious problem.

But the self-effacing Hobbesianism interpretation is not correct. While it captures certain strands of Rousseau's view, it rests on a misunderstanding of Rousseau's fundamental problem. That problem is not: What sort of society would rational, asocial, and purely self-interested individuals agree to? And Rousseau's view is not that such individuals would agree that they ought to regulate their actions by non-self-interested reasons. His question is: What form of association would *socially inter-*

---

10. For discussion of problems faced by Hobbesian contractualism when it is understood as a public justification of terms of social cooperation, see David Gauthier, "The Social Contract as Ideology," *Philosophy & Public Affairs* 6, no. 2 (Winter 1977): 130–64.

dependent individuals agree to if they were interested in protecting their person and goods and *in being free*?[11] Rousseauean contractors do have interests in person and goods, and those interests are advanced by a society directed by a general will. But the protection of those interests is not the only or the primary aim of the participants in the social contract, and in particular not the sole source of the "common good morality" that issues from that contract. Its source, as I indicated earlier (p. 279), is also in the freedom that socially interdependent individuals aim to preserve. By contrast with self-effacing Hobbesianism, then, the social autonomy interpretation emphasizes both that social interdependence sets the problem which the social contract addresses, and that there is, so to speak, an anticipation of the general will—something universal—present within the contractual situation itself, and therefore a basis for that will in the nature of human beings.

To see how the social autonomy interpretation meets Riley's dilemma, I want to sketch a version of that dilemma that might be thought to arise even with the rejection of self-effacing Hobbesianism, and then suggest why it in fact does not arise. The dilemma here can again be stated as a conflict between the standpoint of contractor and the standpoint of citizen. As contractors, individuals regard themselves as free. From this standpoint, an allegiance to the common good is simply one possible allegiance among others, and lacks any special authority. Volunteers in service to the common good, persons who regard themselves as contractors cannot have the attachment to the common good that is required on Rousseau's conception of the general will. Thus from the point of view of the contractor, the contract does not justify the general will.

Citizens, on the other hand, identify with the common good. They do not regard themselves most fundamentally as free choosers of ends, but as members of a state, and their choices are always made against the background of an identification with that state. And so the question of what would be chosen when this identity is abstracted from is of no interest from the perspective of the citizen (if the question has any content at all). Trying to answer it, like trying to write a book on *Chess Without*

---

11. Miller's emphasis on freedom (pp. 61–62, chap. 7) is close to the right track here, although he downplays the role of "particular" interests in protection of the person and goods. The problem, as Keohane underscores, is to find a way to combine both aspects of the self in the argument (Keohane, pp. 442–49, 461–63).

the King: Opening Strategies, shows that reflection has gone on holiday.[12] To treat the social contract as providing reasons for having a general will they would have to regard the freedom that figures in the contract as more fundamental than the substantive ends that they have as citizens. So regarding themselves would, however, undermine their allegiance to those ends. For once they recognize their freedom, they would also come to regard their social order as simply one among the many alternative choices they might make about how to live. So here again, there is no single point of view from which both the contractual justification and the common good morality might both be embraced.

This is an important problem, and my brief remarks here are intended to indicate how a more complete response might proceed, and not to provide that response. In these remarks I will assume that the general will *is* the solution to the problem of collective choice presented by Rousseau's social contract (see p. 279 above). This may seem to beg the question presented by this second version of the dilemma. But that appearance is misleading. The question: Why have a general will? cannot be answered simply by showing that people constrained to make a social contract would agree to the general will. For even if they would, one still needs to say what reason there might be for individuals to comply with the terms of an agreement that they would make if they had to reach an agreement.[13]

First, then, consider the dilemma from the perspective of the individual with an interest in freedom but who does not have a general will. In this consideration, recall that Rousseau's defense of the general will premises

12. See Philippa Foot, "Morality as a System of Hypothetical Imperatives," in *Virtues and Vices and Other Essays in Moral Philosophy* (Berkeley: University of California Press, 1978), pp. 157–73; Bernard Williams, "Persons, Character, and Morality," in *Moral Luck* (Cambridge: Cambridge University Press, 1981), pp. 1–19; Michael Sandel, *Liberalism and the Limits of Justice* (Cambridge: Cambridge University Press, 1982); and Michael Walzer, *Spheres of Justice* (New York: Basic Books, 1983).

13. For discussion, see Rawls, *A Theory of Justice* (Cambridge, MA: Harvard University Press, 1971), pp. 257, 565, 570–72. Also, T. M. Scanlon, "Contractualism and Utilitarianism," in *Utilitarianism and Beyond*, eds. Amartya Sen and Bernard Williams (Cambridge: Cambridge University Press, 1982), pp. 116–19; and Bernard Williams, *Ethics and the Limits of Philosophy* (Cambridge, MA: Harvard University Press, 1985), pp. 64–70. I am following Rawls's distinction (p. 257) between construing the problem of the content of freedom as a collective choice problem and construing it as a problem for a "single self," and focusing here on the latter.

the existence of social interdependence. It is not addressed to individuals who are not members of a society, with a view to persuading them that social cooperation is preferable to no cooperation. In assuming that there is social interdependence, he assumes that people have desires that can only be satisfied socially, developed capacities that can only be expressed socially, and ethical views. Nor does Rousseau hold that it is reasonable for a single person to have and to act on a general will under circumstances in which there is no assurance that others will do the same (*SC* II.6.ii; *GM* I.2).

Imagine, then, a person who has reasonable assurance that others will act to advance the common good, who recognizes that existing institutions do advance common interests, and who is aware (as we are now supposing) that the general will would be agreed to by the members of the society. The person is faced with two alternatives. The first is to have and to act on a general will, knowing that that will is the outcome of the social contract; the second is to conform to the requirements of the institutions only instrumentally, that is, only when such conformity advances their particular interests. Is there any reason to choose the former over the latter?

Rousseau supposes that a person who is self-consciously free desires to act in a way that manifests that freedom (to be "as free as they were before"). In view of that desire, the instrumental attitude is not satisfactory. For such a person wants more than an availability of alternatives within a system of laws and institutions that they view as a set of constraints imposed by others on their action. Rather, they want to be able to regard those institutional "constraints" as themselves conforming to their own judgments of what is right. Instead of taking the instrumental attitude which regards the social framework as constraining, the free person wants to affirm the framework of rules itself; they want to "have their own will as a rule" (*OC* III [*LM*], p. 807). But under circumstances in which there is a widely shared general will to which institutions do on the whole conform, to affirm the arrangements—to have one's own will as a rule—is just to have a general will. The relationship between the interest in freedom and the general will is, it should be emphasized, not of the same kind as the relationship between long-term self-interest and the general will suggested by self-effacing Hobbesianism. Having a supreme general will is a *means* for advancing long-term self-interests (even if it can only serve as such a means for someone who does not see it instrumentally). Having a general will is not, by contrast, a means to autonomy; under the conditions described above, it is, Rousseau claims, what autonomy consists in.

This indicates the lines along with a response to the first horn of the dilemma—the problem from the standpoint of the contractor—could be pursued. What of the second? Is it true that actually having a general will or a common good morality precludes regarding oneself at the same time as autonomous—that, as Riley puts it, a common good morality is the "very negation of voluntarism."

Riley's claim can be taken in either of two ways, corresponding to two interpretations of "common good morality." On the first, to endorse a common good morality is to endorse the communitarian relativist *theory* of morality on which there is no distinction between the moral rightness of an action for an agent and that action's advancing the common good of the community to which the agent belongs. This gives force to the claim that a common good morality is the very negation of voluntarism. But the fact that Rousseau endorses a non-self-effacing contractual jus-tification of social norms shows that he did not believe the communitarian relativist theory of morality and did not endorse the view that an iden-tification with the common good must be unreflective.

On the second construal, to have a common good morality is not to endorse a *theory* of morality but to embrace the *substantive moral con-ception* that one ought to act to advance the common good. But having put communitarian relativism to the side, it is no longer clear why a common good morality is inconsistent with the voluntarist theory em-bodied in the social autonomy interpretation of Rousseau's contract. There would be such inconsistency if considerations of autonomy could not support a general will. In the ways that I suggested earlier, however, reasons of autonomy can provide reasons for having a general will. So the second aspect of the dilemma can be handled by responding more fully to the first.

Much more would need to be said to provide such a full response, and to judge, finally, whether the social autonomy interpretation provides the basis for a full answer to Riley's dilemma about voluntarism and a com-mon good morality, or whether it is really true that self-conscious freedom dissolves the general will. In considering that problem here, I have tried to defend Rousseau's views only in the limited sense of emphasizing that they are not straightforwardly *incoherent* in the ways that Riley suggests, and indicating some of the resources that Rousseau has for responding to his problem. Keeping in mind the importance of both autonomy and social interdependence in framing the fundamental problem addressed by the social contract, as well as the structure of the general will, Rousseau's solution to the fundamental problem may seem less an incoherent attempt to found an undifferentiated community on an abstract form of "voluntarism," and more a reasonable attempt to justify a social ideal in terms that might be of interest to those living both inside and outside of that ideal.

II. ROUSSEAU ON DEMOCRACY

While much of the literature on Rousseau's political philosophy focuses on the foundational issues considered in Part 1, much of Rousseau's own political writing addresses more institutional questions. The most striking feature of those institutional views is Rousseau's rejection of representation and endorsement of a system of popular legislative assemblies, a direct democracy.

Democracy?

In an illuminating and detailed study on *Rousseau and Representation*, Richard Fralin argues that Rousseau's commitment to democratic principles and politics is not as strong as it appears on the surface of the *Social Contract*.[14] Fralin indicates three ways that the *Social Contract* can mislead.

First, he points out that the condemnation of representative government is nearly unique to the *Social Contract*. In the *Political Economy*, published seven years before the *Social Contract*, Rousseau argues against direct democracy (*PE*, p. 216). And in the constitutional writings on Poland and Corsica which Rousseau wrote after the *Social Contract*, he defends a representative system with representatives bound by mandates (*C*, pp. 285–86; *P*, pp. 35–37).

Fralin's second claim is that Rousseau's general pronouncements about the locus of legitimate authority are a misleading guide to his views about

14. Fralin argues as well for the "developmental thesis" that Rousseau's political views were much more influenced by eighteenth-century Genevan constitutional conflicts than recent commentators have allowed.

the proper *de facto* distribution of political power in a democratic order. At the more formal level, Rousseau supports a division of political authority between a sovereign people, who directly enact laws in a legislative assembly, and a subordinate government, in which the people vest the authority to apply these laws to particular cases. Fralin contrasts this formal structure with Rousseau's description of the real powers of the popular assembly and the government. He argues that Rousseau defends a regime which concentrates political initiative in the hands of a largely self-sustaining political elite that sets the political agenda, monopolizes all but the final stage of the legislative process, and administers the state (Fralin, p. 6). In support of this thesis, Fralin argues that the *Social Contract*: (1) imposes considerable restrictions on popular *selection* of officials, in effect allowing the government to choose its own successor through its control over nominations; (2) rejects popular legislative *initiative*, placing all such initiative instead in the hands of the government; and (3) bars popular *deliberation* about the legislation introduced by the government (Fralin, chap. 6).

Fralin's third point is that these limits on the power of the assemblies reveal Rousseau's deep ambivalence about the political capacities of ordinary citizens and indicate his underlying conception of the nature of democratic politics and the point of political participation (ibid., pp. 3, 5–8, 72, 221n.22; Shklar, pp. 18–20, 179–86). The people *are* capable of helping to check the temptations of the government to promote its own corporate will at the expense of the general will. To play this role, citizens must be brought to identify with the community. The function of the citizen assemblies (like public festivals) is to bring about that identification, to form the general will. But in this educative role, political participation is basically "passive." Even the most participatory forms of democratic politics are not meant to provide an arena in which citizens can debate, judge, and act on their conception of the public good. Instead, they provide a forum in which they can internalize the conception embodied in existing laws and advanced by the government.

By contrast with Fralin, Hilail Gildin and James Miller argue that there is "more democracy" than is evident on the surface of Rousseau's writing about institutions, though they find the sources of Rousseau's democratic commitments in very different places. Gildin's *Rousseau's Social Contract*, a very helpful commentary, follows Leo Strauss in arguing that

Rousseau draws democratic conclusions from Hobbesian foundations (Gildin, pp. vii, 1, 18–22, 45–46, 165–66). According to Miller's *Rousseau: Dreamer of Democracy*, Rousseau's commitment to democratic politics flows from a commitment to autonomy. He says that Rousseau offers a vision of democratic politics as "the home of whole men, unalienated in their enjoyment of a thoughtful independence, in effective control of their powers, each able to satisfy his wants with self-confidence. In Rousseau, the idea of democracy finally found an able and eloquent advocate, a philosopher dedicated to the ideal of self-development" (pp. 202–203). Here I want to abstract from these important differences, and focus on their disagreements with Fralin on institutional issues, the second of Fralin's three points.

First, then, they argue that there is more democratic *government* in Rousseau than is suggested by his claim that popular sovereignty is compatible with democratic, aristocratic, monarchical, and mixed forms of government. For Rousseau construes the choice of officials as an act of government and defends a basic constitutional requirement that officials be reviewed at the start of each regular meeting of the popular assembly (*SC* III.18.vi–viii). These two points together imply that the assembled people reserve some of the executive power, and therefore that, as Gildin says, the government must have "a strongly democratic component" (Gildin, p. 137, chaps. 4, 5; Miller, pp. 65–73, 107). Second, they underscore that Rousseau endorses the right of the people in assembly to oversee the enforcement of the law and to overturn the government's interpretation of the law (*OC* III [*LM*], pp. 814, 826, 828–29, 847, 849).

Gildin and Miller thus agree with Fralin that the simple picture of a division of political labor between a popular assembly making laws and an institutionally separate executive power enforcing those laws is misleading. But for them it misleads by *understating* the powers of the assembly, not by exaggerating them.

Since Fralin is surely right about the differences between Rousseau's views of representation before and after the *Social Contract*, there are two issues at stake here: (1) what sorts of political institutions did Rousseau actually endorse?; and (2) what do those institutional views show about the aims of Rousseau's theory of democracy in particular and his views about political and property institutions generally? Let us consider these in turn.

Democratic Procedures

Fralin's case on the issue of political procedures is not persuasive, as a brief consideration of the issues of *elections, deliberation,* and *initiative* shows. On the question of elections, Fralin misconstrues Rousseau's claim that elections are an exercise of executive power.[15] Fralin takes this to imply that the government can effectively choose its own successor. But while elections are an exercise of executive *power*, the proper question is what body has the authority to exercise this specific aspect of executive power. As Gildin and Miller argue, it must be exercised by the assembled citizens or their mandated representatives. In the *Letters From the Mountain*, Rousseau in fact describes a system of elections in which the people select officials from a government-provided list as "an empty formality without consistency" (*OC* III [*LM*], pp. 828–29). Fralin argues that this represents a change of view (pp. 159ff.). But once the confusion about the executive power has been eliminated, there is no evidence for the change.

Fralin's discussion of deliberation (pp. 106–107) rests on an ambiguous passage in the *Social Contract* which emphasizes the ceaseless efforts of governments to monopolize political discussion (*SC*, IV.1.vii). But emphasizing is not endorsing (Gildin, pp. 158–59). And in *Letters From the Mountain*, Rousseau explicitly defends the right of legislative assemblies to order their own affairs (*OC* III [*LM*], pp. 814, 824–25, 830). He argues that it is "contrary to reason that the executive regulates the order [police] of the legislative body, that it prescribes to the latter the subjects which it ought to consider, [and] that it prohibits to the legislative body the right of opinion" (ibid., p. 830). He defends as well the right of the Genevan citizenry to "deliberate among itself" outside of their legislative assembly (ibid., pp. 850–53).[16]

---

15. Part of the problem here is that Rousseau uses the term "government" (as he uses the term "sovereign") both (1) normatively, to designate "the legitimate exercise of the executive power," and (2) sociologically, to designate an "intermediate body" with "rights to exercise executive power" (*SC* III.1.v–vii, xx). When Rousseau says that the choice of officials is a "governmental function" (*SC* III.17.iii) he is using the term "government" normatively, and it therefore does not follow that an intermediate body has the right to exercise that power. Even in a system in which there is a government in the sociological sense, the people can reserve some governmental powers, that is, share in government in the normative sense. See Robert Derathé's notes to the *Social Contract* in *OC* III, p. 1474.

16. It is commonly thought that Rousseau was not very enthusiastic about rights of assembly. This comes, I believe, from a misconstrual of his remark that citizens should

Fralin's third piece of evidence is Rousseau's restriction of legislative initiative to the government (*OC* III [*LM*], p. 861; also p. 846). This restriction is important, but there are several reasons for doubting that it is quite as telling as Fralin suggests. While Rousseau permits and even praises the Genevan limitations on popular legislative initiative, he does not say that a broader right of initiative would be *illegitimate*, but that it would be unwise (Gildin, p. 159). Nor does the restriction on legislative initiative bar citizens from proposing new laws to the government; in indicating their opinions on such matters, they do their duty (*OC* III [*LM*], p. 846). He insists only on the wisdom of an arrangement in which the government must endorse new legislation before it can be considered for *final* approval by the assembly (ibid., pp. 846–47). Finally, Rousseau endorses popular "negative initiatives," that is, rights to pursue inquiries into the government's execution and interpretation of the laws without prior approval by the government.

Democratic Principles

There remains, nevertheless, a significant restriction on popular political initiative. This brings us to the second issue: What does this restriction tell us about Rousseau's conception of democratic order? Does it reveal that Rousseau aims effectively to *eliminate* popular political initiative and that he construes popular participation as a form of socialization and public celebration?

In answering this question, we must first bear in mind the *system* of institutions in which the restrictions on legislative initiative are embedded: the people have final legislative authority and the right to oversee the administration and interpretation of the law; they must regularly decide if they want new officials and if they wish to alter the form of government; they control the government's revenues through their exercise of the power to tax (ibid., pp. 820–21); they have rights of assembly outside of their legislative meetings; and they exercise those political powers against the background of a basic equality of both economic resources and power (*SC* I.9.viiin., II.3.iv, II.11.ii; *PE*, p. 221; *LD*, p. 115;

---

deliberate with "no communication among themselves" (*SC* II.3.iii). Rousseau's concern here is not with assembly and discussion as such, but with the division of the population into organized factions. He endorses both a society without factions and a society with many relatively equal factions. But he never proposes a bar on rights of assembly. See *OC* III (*LM*), pp. 850–53, and notes by Jean-Daniel Candaux, pp. 1698–1700.

OC III [*LM*], p. 890). These conditions together do not, of course, constitute a right of legislative initiative. They do, however, impose costs on a government that resists the legislative ambitions of the sovereign people. Why, then, propose the restrictions at all?

The rationale for the restriction on legislative initiative is best understood as one component—a cognitive element—in a broader system of considerations that Rousseau deploys in assessing social institutions in terms of the general will. A proper response to Fralin's view requires mention of these different considerations, each of which reflects an aspect of the general will and social interdependence.

First, there are arguments of *principle*. Arguments of principle are intended to support basic rights and the institutional consequences that follow from those rights. In a society in which there is a general will, there are certain interests that ought to be respected and that people recognize that they ought to respect. Construing rights as based on interests that ought to be respected, then, the existence of a general will implies the existence of fundamental rights. For example, citizens have rights to the basic goods of security and liberty that are components of the common good, in that they have an interest in these goods and the existence of a general will implies a public recognition that the interests of each ought to be advanced.[17] They also have rights of political participation (though not to a particular form of participation) deriving from the requirement of public confidence that institutions advance the common good, rights Rousseau underscores in arguing for the inalienability of popular sovereignty (*SC* II.1). But certain suggestions by Rousseau notwithstanding, arguments of principle are not sufficient to give specific institutional shape to these rights. They are, as Fralin argues, not sufficient to support direct democracy.

The second strategy of argument concerns the *formation* of a general will. In part, this is a problem of explaining how a general will is maintained once such a will exists. Maintaining this will requires that citizens develop a capacity to recognize common interests and that they be mo-

---

17. Rousseau affirms a right to religious liberty, within the limits set by the dogmas of civil religion: that God exists, that there is an afterlife, that the soul is immortal, that the just are rewarded and the wicked punished, that the social contract and the laws are sacred, and that there is to be no toleration for the intolerant (*SC* IV.8.xxxiii). While the content of the dogmas is religious, their defense is secular (*SC* IV.8.xxxi–xxxii; *OC* III [*LM*], Letters 1 and 2). On the liberty of the person, see *SC* II.4.x, and the discussion of punishment at the end of Letter 8 in *OC* III (*LM*), pp. 864–66.

tivated to advance those interests. But neither the capacity nor the motivation are at all automatic, and so the preservation of a general will needs to be addressed institutionally. Rousseau's conception of the role of reciprocity in motivation formation provides the psychological background for addressing it: "What transforms instinct into sentiment, attachment into love, aversion into hate, is the intention manifested to harm us or to be useful to us. . . . [F]rom those from whom one expects good or ill by their inner disposition, by their will—*those who we see acting freely for us or against us*—inspire in us *sentiments similar to those they manifest toward us*" (*E*, p. 213, emphasis added). Thus a willingness to advance the interests of others develops together with the recognition that others aim to advance our interests. Since a general will involves a willingness to act in ways that advance the interests of all others, if the reciprocity mechanism is carried to its limit—that is, to include all members of society—it results in a general will. The institutional problem is to characterize circumstances in which the mechanism operates.

The particularly "participatory" forms of political rights that Rousseau endorses—that is, direct democratic forms—have their place here. In popular assemblies that operate in circumstances in which citizens have a general will, members recognize that others take their interests into account. Since members do "see [others] acting freely for [them]" they reciprocate, and thus form similar sentiments. That is, they form a general will. The experience of being treated as an equal in public arenas, then, leads to the formation of a motivation that expresses this equality. This provides a rationale for a direct democracy, though as Rousseau perhaps recognized in the later constitutional writings, there are other political and social institutions that might engender a general will.

Third, engendering a general will is not sufficient to ensure its regulative role. Since citizens also have particular interests, they can *have* a general will, but not *act* on it because that will is "subordinate to others that prevail over it" (*SC* IV.1.vi; *PE*, pp. 212–13). The problem of avoiding subordination has two aspects: to avoid arrangements that *tempt* people to subordinate their general will to their private advantage, and to *assure* those who are not tempted that their cooperation will not be abused (Gildin, pp. 5–6; Miller, p. 106). Institutionally, the problem is to prevent individuals and groups from being in positions in which they are able to design or advance policies which have predictable benefits for themselves alone or which are especially onerous for others, and thus to "reconcile

Reflections on Rousseau

... what right permits with what interest prescribes, so that justice and utility are not at variance" (SC I.i).[18]

Several institutional arguments fit this strategy, including those in support of the rule of law and limits on inequalities of resources and power. Considerations of temptation and assurance are also deployed against a significant popular role in the administration of the laws and in favor of popular supervision of the government: because they do not apply the law to individual cases where the costs and benefits are clear, the people are less tempted to invert the proper order of wills (SC III.4.ii); by supervising the work of the government that does apply the rules, they increase the costs to it of subordinating the general will to a particular will, and thus reduce its temptation to do so (SC III.1.viii–xiv).

The fourth strategy of argument concerns the cognitive aspect of the general will. Suppose that citizens have *beliefs* about what advances the common good—and not just preferences for policies—and are prepared to act on those beliefs (SC IV.2.viii). With faulty beliefs or badly designed decision rules, collective decisions can still fail to achieve the shared aim of promoting the common good (SC II.3.i, II.10.vi). The institutional issue is to increase the likelihood that the common good will be advanced if collective decisions are made by individuals who express their different opinions about what will promote common interests. This problem of sound collective judgment naturally divides into two: improving individual judgments about what advances the common good and designing decision rules such that collective judgments are more likely to be right than individual judgments. Rousseau's concerns about information (SC II.3.ii) illustrate the first aspect, and his views about the virtues of simple and qualified majorities (SC IV.2.x–xi) illustrate the second.[19]

The restriction on initiative plays a role here as well. It can plausibly be construed as designed to enhance popular judgment about the conduciveness of new legislative proposals to the common good. In states in which people do not devote all their time, or even most of their time to politics—and this is what Rousseau knew to be true about Geneva (*OC* III [*LM*], pp. 881, 888) and thought would be true of any society without slaves (SC III.15.ix-x)—*some* sort of initial review of the merits of leg-

---

18. On institutional solutions to problems of temptation, see Jon Elster, *Ulysses and the Sirens: Studies in Rationality and Irrationality*, rev. ed. (Cambridge: Cambridge University Press, 1984), pp. 87–103.

19. See Brian Barry, "The Public Interest," p. 13.

islative proposals is needed. Rousseau supposes that the review should be carried out by an executive, subject to the system of constraints I have indicated. If the government refuses to propose laws that are desired, then the people can get rid of it. This is, in effect, a roundabout and potentially costly way to initiate legislative changes. But perhaps Rousseau thought that this more indirect method would be more deliberate— that it would induce reflection on the reasonableness of the changes, and that this further reflection would improve popular judgments about legislative changes, and thereby help to sort good proposals from bad.

Taking into account the full system of institutions and strategies of argument, then, it seems unwarranted to construe the restriction on initiative as betraying a desire to promote a monopoly on independent political action by a self-sustaining political elite. And it seems unwarranted as well to treat that restriction as evidence for the more general understanding of political participation as a form of passive moral education aimed at securing the internalization and celebration of the public values articulated by a political elite.

Strategies of Criticism

Underlying the attention in Part II to Rousseau's institutional views is a more general point about social criticism generally and Rousseau's social criticism in particular.[20] While limitations of space preclude any defense of this perspective on Rousseau, it seems appropriate to note it by way of conclusion.

20. Shklar offers an important alternative to the view I suggest here. On her view, Rousseau presents utopias with a view to condemning existing arrangements. His utopias "stand as reproaches to actuality" (p. xiii) whose problems he believed to be "as irreparable as they were unnecessary" (p. 7). Because the problems are irreparable, the proper practical attitude is "resignation and prudence" (p. 214). In the course of defending this reading, Shklar says much that is illuminating about Rousseau's psychological views, and about the second of the three themes I mentioned at the outset of the review. But I do not find this interpretation plausible overall, and it strikes me as a particularly strained way of making sense of Rousseau's institutional writings. I do agree, with Shklar, however, that "Rousseau is one of those authors who says something personal to every reader, and that it is both vain and illiberal to insist that one's own reading is the right one" (p. vii). And so I won't insist.

I would like to thank Paul Horwich, Andrew Levine, Charles Sabel, and the Editors of *Philosophy & Public Affairs* for suggestions on an earlier draft of this essay. I would particularly like to thank John Rawls for helping to bring the main points of the essay into sharper focus. Work on this article was supported by a grant from the National Endowment for the Humanities.

There are several different sorts of criticism of social practices. *Moral criticism* explores the disparity between moral principles and social practices; *unmasking criticism* emphasizes the disparity between the interests that actually motivate action and the norms that individuals themselves appeal to in justifying their action. Moral and unmasking criticism can be used in the service of very different practical attitudes, including religious condemnation of the world, moralizing disapproval of current social practice, and general cynicism about humanity. Perhaps cynicism or moralizing disapproval or religious condemnation is the most reasonable practical attitude. They should not, however, be confused—as they commonly are—with the perspective of *political criticism*.

Political criticism has its own aims and standards. Political critics believe that existing institutions are fundamentally flawed because they are incapable of satisfying principles that could be satisfied, taking human beings as they are and institutions as they can be. While moral and unmasking criticism serve in the exploration of those flaws and in assessing the obstacles to surmounting them, these play a subordinate role in political criticism. Believing-that the principles they use in criticism could be satisfied by an alternative form of social cooperation, political critics must indicate the political arrangements that their criticism aims to advance—what alternatives there are and how they might work as a stable set of institutions. The force of their criticism of current institutions ultimately depends on the power and plausibility of those alternatives.

It is tempting to locate the force of Rousseau's social criticism in his endless unmasking of vice or in his repeated insistence that politics consists, or anyway can consist, of something more than a mask for the promotion of interests and the exercise of force. Neither of these by itself, however, captures Rousseau's power as a political critic. For this, one must look to the institutional ideal that realizes autonomy under conditions of interdependence. There is plainly much that is wrong with Rousseau's account of that ideal. But in the face of widespread skepticism among political critics about the guarantees that history will produce an ideal, and broad recognition that the absence of such guarantees makes the elaboration of political ideals an important enterprise, Rousseau's work as a theorist of institutions remains a paradigm of, and reasonable point of departure for, egalitarian political criticism.

Addenda 297a

References within the text:

p. 277, §1, ll.10–11: *OC*3.360/*CW*4.138, *OC*3.363–64/*CW*4.140–41, *OC*3.368/*CW*4.145,
   *OC*3.371/*CW*4.147; *OC*3.438/*CW*4.199; *OC*3.281–89/*CW*4.76–82; *OC*3.173–77/*CW*3.50–54
   Ibid., §2, l.9: *OC*3.360/*CW*4.138
   Ibid., l.13: *OC*3.364/*CW*4.141
   Ibid., §3, l.1: *OC*3.360/*CW*4.138
   Ibid., §4, l.2: *OC*3.360/*CW*4.138
p. 278, l.2: *OC*3.361/*CW*4.139
   Ibid., l.6: *OC*3.363/*CW*4.140–41
   Ibid., ll.14–15: *OC*3.368/*CW*4.145, *OC*3.391–93/*CW*4.162–64
p. 279, §2, l.2: *OC*3.360–61/*CW*4.138–39
   Ibid., l.12: *OC*3.365/*CW*4.142
   Ibid., ll.14–15: *OC*3.807/*CW*9.231–32; *OC*3.365/*CW*4.142, *OC*3.374–75/*CW*4.149–50;
   *OC*4.841/*Em.*461; *OC*3.483–84/*CW*4.22–23
p. 280, §5, l.3: *OC*3.361/*CW*4.139, *OC*3.378/*CW*4.152
   Ibid., l.4: *OC*4.492–94/*Em.*213–14
p. 282, §3, l.5: *OC*3.354/*CW*4.133
   Ibid., l.14: *OC*3.364/*CW*4.141
p. 283, §2, ll.8–9: *OC*3.806–807/*CW*9.230–32; *OC*3.378/*CW*4.152
p. 286, §1, ll.8–9: *OC*3.378/*CW*4.152; *OC*3.281–89/*CW*4.76–82
   Ibid., §3, l.11: *OC*3.807/*CW*9.231–32
p. 288, §4, l.4: *OC*3.250–51/*CW*3.147–48
   Ibid., l.7: *OC*3.907–08/*CW*11.128–29; *OC*3.978–80/*CW*11.189–91
p. 290, §2, l.7: *OC*3.435–36/*CW*4.197
   Ibid., ll.13–14: *OC*3.814/*CW*9.237–38, *OC*3.826/*CW*9.247–48, *OC*3.828–29/*CW*9.249–50,
   *OC*3.847/*CW*9.265, *OC*3.849/*CW*9.266–67
p. 291, §1, l.12: *OC*3.828–29/*CW*9.249–50
   Ibid., §2, l.3: *OC*3.438–39/*CW*4.199
   Ibid., l.6: *OC*3.814/*CW*9.237–38, *OC*3.824–25/*CW*9.246–47, *OC*3.830/*CW*9.250–51
   Ibid., l.10: *OC*3.830/*CW*9.251
   Ibid., l.12: *OC*3.850–53/*CW*9.267–70
p. 292, §1, l.2: *OC*3.861/*CW*9.276–77; *OC*3.846/*CW*9.264
   Ibid., ll.9–10: *OC*3.846/*CW*9.264
   Ibid., l. 12: *OC*3.846–47/*CW*9.264–64
   Ibid., §3, l.7: *OC*3.820–21/*CW*9.242–44
   Ibid., l.10: *OC*3.367n/*CW*4.144n, *OC*3.372/*CW*4.147–48, *OC*3.391–92/*CW*4.162–62; *OC*3.258/*CW*3.
   153–54; *OC*5.105/*CW*10.336
p. 293, §1, l.1: *OC*3.890/*CW*9.300
   Ibid., §3, l.15: *OC*3.368–69/*CW*4.145
p. 294, §1, l.10: *OC*4.492/*Em.*213
   Ibid., §3, l.4: *OC*3.438/*CW*4.199; *OC*3.245–46/*CW*3.143–44
p. 295, §1, l.2: *OC*3.351/*CW*4.131
   Ibid., §2, l.7: *OC*3.404/*CW*4.173
   Ibid., l.10: *OC*3.396–98/*CW*4.167–68
   Ibid., §3, l.4: *OC*3.440–41/*CW*4.200–201
   Ibid., l.6: *OC*3.371/*CW*4.147, *OC*3.391/*CW*4.162
   Ibid., ll.13–14: *OC*3.371/*CW*4.147
   Ibid., l.15: *OC*3.441/*CW*4.201
   Ibid., §4, ll.5–6: *OC*3.881/*CW*9.293, *OC*3.888/*CW*9.298–99
   Ibid., l.7: *OC*3.430–31/*CW*4.193–94

297b

Endnotes:

4. *OC*3.141–42/*CW*3.26, *OC*3.183–84/*CW*3.58–59; *OC*3.356/*CW*4.135; *OC*4.585–86/*Em*.280
7. l.3: *OC*3.368/*CW*4.145
8. ll.1–2: *OC*3.256–58/*CW*3.152–54; *OC*3.511/*CW*4.41–42; *OC*4.1126/–
   l.5: *OC*3.363/*CW*4.140
15. l.4: *OC*3.396/*CW*4.166–67, *OC*3.399/*CW*4.169
   l.5: *OC*3.433/*CW*4.195
   l.9: *OC*3.1474/–
16. l.3: *OC*3.371/*CW*4.147
   ll.6–7: *OC*3.850–53/*CW*9.267–70; *OC*3.1698–1700/–
17. l.4: *OC*3.469/*CW*4.223
   ll.5–6: *OC*3.468–69/*CW*4.222–23; *OC*3.687–726/*CW*3.134–52
   l.6: *OC*3.375/*CW*4.150
   l.7: *OC*3.864–66/*CW*9.279–81

[7]

Rousseau's General Will and the Problem of Consent

W. T. JONES

THERE ARE ALMOST as many views of Rousseau's general will as there are writers on Rousseau. Some hold that what he says about the general will is either a truism or else false.[1] Others equate the general will with natural law.[2] Others again find in the general will anticipations of Hegel.[3] More, perhaps, agree with a recent student of the subject who, holding that Rousseau "formulated the question badly," concludes that he "appears genuinely unable to make up his mind about what constitutes the general will and how it comes to be."[4] Thus, despite radical differences in interpretation, the nearly unanimous verdict—one might almost say, the general will—on the general will is unfavorable. I believe that Rousseau's critics are themselves partly to blame. For the most part they have anachronistically[5] assumed him to be interested in problems that interest them and have not asked themselves what problem concerned him. No wonder, then, that he appears to them to be confused.

The problem that concerned Rousseau was a moral problem—the problem of demonstrating that political organizations can have a moral foundation.

I am much indebted to Brian Barry, John Benton, Bruce E. Cain, Gary Cox, Alan Donagan, Edward Green, Morgan Kousser, Lee C. McDonald, J. Donald Moon, Roger Noll, Charles R. Plott, Alan Schwartz, and Charles Young for commenting helpfully on an earlier draft of this paper.

[1] For instance, John Plamenatz in *Man and Society*, 2. vols. (New York: McGraw-Hill, 1963), 1: 394.

[2] For instance, Franz Haymann in "La loi naturelle dans la philosophie politique de J.- J. Rousseau" in *Annales de la Societé Jean-Jacque Rousseau* 30 (1943–45): 96–97.

[3] Among them—alas!—at one time the author of this paper, for instance in his *Masters of Political Thought* (Boston: Houghton Mifflin, 1947), 2: 265.

[4] Richard Fralin, *Rousseau and Representation* (New York, 1978), 79, 86–87.

[5] For an illuminating discussion of the anachronistic tendencies of many twentieth-century historians of philosophy see *Philosophy in History*, edited by Richard Rorty, J. B. Schneewind, and Quentin Skinner (New York: Cambridge University Press, 1984), 11–14.

Rousseau understood that some compulsion is necessary, and he was well aware that most states have actually been founded on, and maintained by, force. The only question was whether compulsion is compatible with morality: was it possible to design a political organization in which "a man can be free and forced to conform to wills that are not his own" (IV, 2: 101; 440)?[6]

If freedom and compulsion cannot be reconciled the notion of a moral political organization is only a "vain and chimerical illusion." The phrase is Kant's, not Rousseau's, and Kant of course was discussing the problem of reconciling freedom of the will with Newtonian physics. But the phrase, and even more the thought, would have been congenial to Rousseau. However, whereas Kant's reconciliation of personal morality and physical determinism depends on the obscure metaphysical notion of noumenal causality, Rousseau's reconciliation of political morality and political compulsion depends on the notion of a general will, and that, as I shall argue, is an empirical concept. If political organizations have such-and-such an organizational structure—this is Rousseau's claim—a general will among the citizens emerges, and they will consent to be compelled.

In a word, political morality depends on the consent of the citizens, and the consent of the citizens depends on there being a general will. That is a necessary condition for the existence of political morality. Thus, though the focus of this paper is narrow, the topic is of central importance to Rousseau—and not only to Rousseau. It is of central importance to all those who agree with him that the morality of any political order depends on the consent of those subject to it.

But does his concept of a general will solve the problem of consent? In this paper I shall argue that Rousseau's claim is largely, though not entirely, warranted. I believe that a careful reading of *The Social Contract* shows that the concept of the general will is neither muddled nor paradoxical nor utopian. On the contrary, it is possible that there can actually be, in the very small homogeneous state Rousseau envisaged, a general will.

I shall begin, in Section 1, by setting out what Rousseau actually says about the general will. Here my account will focus on the procedures Rousseau specified for conducting meetings of assemblies at which he thought the general will is expressed. I concentrate on these procedures because they have usually been neglected by critics of Rousseau and because, inasmuch as Rousseau believed the general will of a group emerges if, and only if, these rules are followed, they should be clues to understanding what he conceived

---

[6] The first page reference is to the English translation by Charles M. Sherover (New York: Harper and Row, 1984); the second page reference is to the French text in *Jean-Jacques Rousseau Oeuvres Complètes*, ed. by B. Gagnebin and M. Raymond (Paris: Gallimard, 1959 ff), vol. 3.

the general will to be. In Section 2 I propose that Rousseau believed that a general will exists in a group when every member of that group takes into account not only his own interests—his own gains and losses—but those of every other member of the group. Since Rousseau did not formulate this view explicitly, my evidence must be indirect: on the assumption that this was his view, what he actually says make much more sense than it otherwise would; scattered passages and seemingly random remarks fall into place as interconnected parts of a persuasive argument. Next, in Section 3, I shall explain why, if this is Rousseau's view of the general will, it has been so frequently misunderstood. Finally, in Section 4, I will show that the concept of the general will, so understood, is viable.

1.

I have said that the procedures Rousseau laid down for decision-making by the citizens meeting together in an assembly are important clues to understanding his concept of the general will. To understand these procedures in their turn it is necessary to bear in mind the distinctions he drew between governments and sovereigns. A government is an administration which has been established by law, i.e., by the decision of a sovereign. A sovereign is any assembly of people who have a common interest and who have a good idea what that common interest is.

Governments can be of many kinds—monarchies, aristocracies, oligarchies, republics, democracies, or some mixture of these—depending on the decision of the assembly. Every type of government has its own characteristic procedures both for reaching agreement on the form and substance of the decrees it enacts and also for enforcing them. It is necessary to mention these activities only to exclude them from consideration, for it is in the actions of sovereigns, not of governments, that a general will is manifest, if indeed it is ever manifest.

Because the sovereign assembly is the locus of the general will, Rousseau not only assigns it the legislative function but also a review function—the function, that is, of vetting the conduct of the government since the last meeting of the assembly.

First, as regards the legislative function: Rousseau held it essential for the sovereign to resist getting itself involved in implementing the legislation it has enacted. It should concern itself only with "the subjects in a body" and with "actions in the abstract." Thus it "may set up several classes of citizens, and even lay down the qualifications for membership in these classes, but it cannot nominate such and such persons as belonging to them" (II, 6: 34–35; 379). It may, in times of crisis, suspend the government and install a dictatorship (IV, 6); it may create a "tribunate" as "a liaison or a middle term, either between the Prince and the People, or between the Prince and the Sovereign" (IV, 5: 116; 454); it may "settle the articles" of a "purely civil profession of faith . . . not precisely as dogmas of religion, but as sentiments of sociability, without which it is impossible to be a good Citizen or faithful subject" (IV, 8: 133; 468). On the other hand, it may not declare war or make peace (II, 2).

Beyond these remarks Rousseau has little to say about the legislative function of the sovereign assembly, and for two reasons. First, *The Social Contract* is concerned with the problem of consent, not with the art of legislation. Lawmaking, he thought, will more or less take care of itself if a general will exists in the assembly, for then the citizens will know what laws are desirable in the particular circumstances of their own community. Second, laws which the assembly has enacted in the public interest can all too easily be perverted by the government if its operations are not periodically reviewed by the assembly. Accordingly, Rousseau formulates two propositions that are to be discussed without fail—they "cannot be suppressed"—at the opening of each meeting of the assembly and that are to be "voted on separately": (1) "Whether it pleases the Sovereign to preserve the present form of Government." (2) "Whether it please the People to leave the administration to those presently charged with it" (III, 18: 97; 436).

Having thus specified the functions of a sovereign assembly we have next to ask whether the members of such an assembly are likely to have a common interest and, if so, whether they are likely to vote in accordance with it, instead of in their own private interest or that of some party or faction? These are the questions with which *The Social Contract* deals. Rousseau believed that though it is theoretically possible that any society, large or small, have a common (public) interest, the larger the group and more diverse its members, the less likely it is that a common interest exists. In contrast, members of small homogeneous groups are likely both to have a common interest and also to know what that common interest is. The only problem with respect to such groups is to design a political structure that both makes it possible for the members of the group to recognize their common interest and that also encourages them to act in accordance with it. In *The Social Contract* Rousseau describes the structure that, he believes, accomplishes these two ends.

Because a large group may not have a common interest, and because, even if it does have a common interest, that interest is not likely to be plainly evident to all of the group's members, small, relatively homogeneous subgroups are likely to form within any large, heterogeneous group—a subgroup of the wealthy as opposed to a subgroup of the poor, a subgroup of farmers as opposed to a subgroup of industrial workers, a subgroup of suburbanites as opposed to a subgroup of central-city dwellers and so on. Such subgroups, or factions, form precisely because the members have recognized that they do have a common interest; each such subgroup is constituted by, and limited to, people who believe—whether rightly or wrongly is for the moment irrelevant—that the existence of this subgroup will promote that common interest. The cohesion of each such subgroup is sustained by its opposition to the other subgroups. "Unless there were different interests, the common interest would scarcely be felt and would never meet with any obstacles; everything would go of itself, and politics would cease to be an art" (II, 3: 26; 371).

In his studies of Poland and Corsica, Rousseau was much concerned with the art of politics—the art, that is, of balancing and equilibrating the divergent common interests of the various subgroups that together constitute a large state, and with finding ways to lessen the divergencies (by means of a national educational system, for instance). But in *The Social Contract* Rousseau is less concerned with such problems—the "art" of practical politics—than with what he held to be the *conditio sine qua non* for the existence of any moral community whatever—the generation of a consent to be compelled. This is why, in that work, he concentrates on small homogeneous groups, for he believed that men can be free and yet subject to laws they oppose only to the extent that (1) they have a common interest and (2) know what that common interest is.

But it is not enough, of course, that group members merely recognize that they have a common interest. It is essential that this common interest guide the decisions the group makes. In very small and very homogeneous groups, where everybody participates in all decisions, this will take care of itself; every group member knows what the common interest is and acts in accordance with it. "When one sees among the happiest people in the world groups of peasants regulating the affairs of State under an oak tree and always conducting themselves wisely," this is the case because in such groups "the common good is clearly apparent everywhere and only good sense is needed to perceive it" (IV, 1: 98; 437).

But in groups too large for everybody to participate in all decisions, some decisions must be delegated. In such groups—groups large enough to require an administration, even if only a rudimentary one—the common interest may not be "everywhere clearly apparent." How can matters be so arranged that decisions taken by an assembly of all the group members will reflect the common interest of all those members, rather than their individual interests? That is the structural problem Rousseau tackles in *The Social Contract*. His solution is that the common interest of the group will emerge if five procedural rules are followed:

1.   Assemble all members of the group together. (The group must be small enough for this to be possible.)
2.   Put all questions on which the assembly is to reach a decision in a special form: never, "Are you in favor of such-and-such?" but always, "Do you believe such-and-such is consistent with the common interest?"
3.   Put only general issues before the assembly, never specific ones. Never, for instance, ask whether so-and-so should be king (or president). Ask only whether the public interest is served by a monarchical (or republican) form of government.
4.   When the members of the assembly, having been "adequately informed," are deliberating over some issue, there should be "no communication among them" and "each Citizen should speak only his own opinions" (II, 3: 26; 371).
5.   Count the votes, seeing to it that every vote is counted (II, 2).

Rousseau was realistic enough to recognize that these procedures are not infallible—that no procedures are infallible: it is always possible, he pointed out, that factions may emerge and influence the result or, alternatively, that the administration may be able to manipulate the voting (III, 18). But he did hold that these five procedures are more likely than any others to permit the general will of the assembly to emerge. Why? What was his reasoning? Answers to these questions will reveal what he understood the general will to be. I shall therefore take up the procedures one by one.

1. *Assemble all members.* This is the easiest way—in Rousseau's time perhaps the only way—to assure that all members of the group vote and that all the votes are counted, and these are essential conditions for any expression of the general will of the whole group instead of the general will of some subgroup or other.

2. *Put the question in a special form.* The form prescribed reduces the possibility that the personal interests of individual members will affect their votes. For voters are asked a *factual* question—Is the proposal consistent with the public interest?—a matter about which most of the members of a small homogeneous group can be presumed to have reasonably reliable opinions. Unfortunately, there is nothing to prevent some of the members from answering a different question from the question they have been asked—"instead of saying by [their] vote, 'It is advantageous to the State' [these members may in effect say] 'It is advantageous to a certain man or a certain party that such or such a motion passes' " (IV, 1: 99, 438).

Rousseau's recognition of this possibility is one of the reasons why he did not think that assemblies of the people *guarantee* that the general will is expressed. It is nevertheless important for two reasons that the question be posed in the form prescribed. First, many, perhaps most, people will answer the question asked, rather than some other question. Second, the varied opinions of those who answer a different question will to some extent cancel each other out, whereas the answers of those who reply to the question asked will cluster around one point since everybody has a good idea of what the public interest is: "There is often a great difference between the will of all and the general will; the latter regards only the common interest, the other regards private interests and is only the sum of particular wills: but remove from these wills the pluses and minuses which cancel each other out and the general will remains as the sum of the differences" (II, 3: 26; 371).

3. *Put only general issues.* This rule, like Rule 2, is intended to reduce the chance that the vote of the assembly will reflect some combination of private interests rather than the public interest. And it is even more effective than Rule 2, for whereas Rule 2 merely tends to direct attention away from private interests by the form in which the questions are posed, Rule 3, by restricting questions to general issues, tends to eliminate the possibility of private interests having a seriously distorting effect.

It is true that the veil envisaged by Rousseau is not opaque; his citizens are not in an original position.[7] Unlike Rawls, Rousseau was not working out a general theory of justice; he was focusing on a structural, or practical, problem: how to arrange matters so that citizens will not take too narrow, or too immediate, a view of their own self-interest. Obviously, citizens cannot decide whether a proposal put before the assembly is, or is not, consistent with the public interest unless they understand what is involved—that is why the veil was not opaque; the citizens had to be "adequately informed." But they can be adequately informed about the overall advantages and disadvantages of, say, a monarchical (alternatively, republican) form of government without it being spelled out for them how their own personal interests are affected. Doubtless some citizens may be able to calculate where their personal interests probably lie, and these may vote those interests, without regard to the common good. Since many voters will be unable to make this calculation or, making it, will be too uncertain of the results to want to take it into account, this procedure makes it more difficult for the average voter to know how the proposal put before the assembly affects his private interests and so increases the likelihood that a majority will vote for the public good.

4. *Do not allow "communication."* Since the citizens have been adequately informed regarding the issue posed, and since deliberation is a matter of each speaking his own opinions, communication could only be an attempt to arrange side-deals. So far from enlightening the citizens it would only invite

---

[7] See below, 123 and note 19.

the formation of factions which would vote the different common interests of those factions, rather than the public good, i.e., the common good of all the citizens.

5. *Count all the votes.* If some citizens do not vote (or if some votes are not counted), sampling errors will be introduced. The result might be a badly skewed distribution that did not represent the general will at all. To put this differently, since Rules 2 and 3 do not eliminate, but only reduce, the expression of private interests, the best way to obtain a distribution with a strong central tendency that represents the public interest is to count all votes, in the hope that the expressions of deviant opinions "cancel one another."

2.

From this discussion of why Rousseau introduced these five rules for ascertaining the general will, what can be inferred about his view of what the public interest is? We know that the rules were designed to produce an expression of the general will in contrast to the will of all. The general will does not differ from the will of all in being a group will; it is no more a supra-individual will than is the will of all. Like the will of all, the general will is the aggregated expression of a number of distinct, individual decisions. How, then, do the two wills differ?

When each voter's decision is determined by no other consideration than that voter's estimate of his own private interest, the result is an expression of the will of all. When each voter, whether he be voting on a particular piece of legislation or on the two review questions,[8] takes into account the interests of his fellow citizens the result is an expression of the general will.

Each citizen who thinks that he will be adversely affected by the proposed legislation or that his interests have suffered in the interval since the last meeting of the assembly (who estimates himself to be worse off now than he was then) will naturally vote against the proposed law or against the government, as the case may be. So far, one cannot tell whether what is expressed is the general will or merely the will of all. The test is whether the citizens are thinking only of themselves or also of others. One can be confident that a general will exists if citizens who do not believe a proposed piece of legislation will harm them nonetheless vote against it because they believe it will harm some of their fellow citizens or if they vote for the legislation believing it will help others but not themselves. Similarly, regarding the review function, if citizens who do not believe their own lot has been worsened by actions of the government nonetheless vote against it because they believe

---

[8] See above, 107.

some of their fellow citizens are now worse off or if, even though their own lot remains unchanged, they vote for the government because they believe the lot of some of their fellow citizens has been improved since the last meeting of the assembly, then, once again, the general will, not merely the will of all, is being expressed. This is the case because the citizens are now taking into account not merely their own private interests, but also the interests of the other citizens as well, that is, the public interest.

The procedural rules are best understood, then, as devices to make it difficult for people to focus too exclusively on their own private interests, thereby making it more likely that they will take into account as well the interests of the other citizens.

It is now possible to understand why Rousseau insisted that the state be small and homogeneous. In the first place, in large and heterogeneous states optimality is achieved at a very low level of satisfaction. In such states it will be very difficult to design legislation that effects an improvement for some that does not entail losses for others. In small homogeneous states, in contrast, any improvement for some is likely also to be an improvement for many, if not most, citizens and—perhaps more to the point—any change that entails a loss for some is likely to entail a loss for many.

In the second place, members of small homogeneous groups are likely to empathize with one another—not merely to know (in the cognitive sense)[9] whether some of their fellow citizens will be made worse off by a proposed law, or by the government's past policies, but to feel the losses of those other citizens almost as they would feel losses of their own. These empathizing sentiments are likely to develop naturally in the kind of community Rousseau envisages—stable families living on the land, interacting constantly, intermarrying frequently, understanding each other's ways because they share them.

But Rousseau was well aware that empathizing sentiments can also be deliberately cultivated and reenforced by education. The educational practices he proposed for his Emile and Sophie were by no means intended to stifle a child's self-love (to stifle it would be both impossible and undesirable), but rather to strengthen his "love of those about him," a love which is as natural as his self-love and, as a matter of fact, "derived from it."[10] *Emile* and *The Social Contract* were published in the same year (1762), and we may take it that the educational program put forward in the former was intended to support the political program put forward in the latter: the education de-

---

[9] "To see without feeling is not knowledge." (Jean-Jacques Rousseau, *Emile* (London: Dent, 1911), 183.

[10] Ibid., 174.

scribed in *Emile* was intended to generate the kind of social context in which the procedural rules described in *The Social Contract* would produce an expression of the general will.

It is therefore important to bear the educational program of *Emile* in mind in connection with the distinction Rousseau draws in *The Social Contract* between what he calls an "aggregation" and what he calls an "association." An aggregation is any merely haphazard collection of "scattered men" who live under some rule (for instance, "a multitude . . . subjected successively to a single person" (I, 5: 12; 359).[11] If this one man were by some improbable chance a beneficient ruler he would aim at maximizing the total amount of satisfaction in the aggregation as a whole, without regard to the satisfactions allocated to the individual components of that aggregation. Similarly, because the individual components of the aggregation are "scattered," each naturally aims only at maximizing his own interest. In contrast, an association is a collection of people who share memories, sentiments and a way of life. Because they share memories, sentiments and a way of life, they have a common interest. That is to say, their private interests are mediated by the sentiments and memories they share.

This is why Rousseau thought those members of an association who would gain by a proposed law would nonetheless oppose it if they thought others would lose by it, and why he thought those whose lot the government has improved would vote against it when the review questions were posed if at the same time it had caused certain other members of the association to suffer losses. And this is why they would vote in favor of an administration that had improved the lot of certain other members of the group, even though it has not improved their own lot. But while fellow-feeling—resulting from the natural homogeneity of the group and inculcated by an Emile-like education—would moderate a narrow selfishness, Rousseau did not desire or expect that fellow feeling would ever be strong enough to lead anyone to vote in favor of an administration that has caused him to suffer net losses, however much it has caused net gains for others.

For each citizen's interests, however much they may be mediated by memories and sentiments he shares with the other citizens, remain incorrigibly his own. That is, though members of an association have a broader view of their interests than the scattered components of an aggregation can have, no one who enters an association intends to "harm his own interests" or "neglect the care he owes to himself." The common good of an association

---

[11] Had Rousseau been acquainted with the conditions of life in twentieth-century states he would have held all of them to be mere aggregations, those that call themselves "democracies" as much as those ruled by one man.

therefore is not simply maximization of the total amount of satisfaction; it is maximization subject to the restriction that no one loses any part of what he had when the association was set up. Apart from that restriction, the common good is not concerned with "justice," that is, with how the improvements, if any, are distributed. To repeat, it is not in the common interest of an association that anyone should lose, no matter how much the total quantity of satisfaction might thereby be increased.

In a word, it is obviously in the common interest of an association that all should gain. But if all cannot gain, it is in the common interest that at least some, it matters not who, should gain, providing that no one loses. To say that the general will has been expressed in an assembly is simply to say that the citizens have voted for the common interest, thus defined.

3.

If this is what Rousseau meant by the expression "general will," why has his view so often been misunderstood? It must be allowed that Rousseau is partly responsible for the misunderstandings. As we have seen, nowhere in *The Social Contract* is there a systematic exposition of his view of the general will; it has to be collected from a number of what look almost like *obiter dicta* scattered through the work. In particular, the procedural rules for ascertaining the general will, so far from having been grouped together and discussed systematically, have been inserted in the text haphazardly, appearing often as appendages to other topics—thus Rule 3 turns up as in connection with Rousseau's contention that the general will is indestructible (IV, 1). The result is to obscure the means—end structure that would, were it set out, explain the rules by showing what was to be gained by following them. Thus it is all too easy for a reader to miss the light the rules throw on the nature of the general will as Rousseau understood it.

Further, and despite Rousseau's explicitly expressed hostility to "metaphysical ideas" (for instance, II, 6: 34; 378), his general will vocabulary has misleading metaphysical connotations for many post-Hegelian readers. Consider, for instance, the much quoted remark, "whoever refuses to obey the general will . . . shall be forced to be free" (I, 7: 17–18; 364). Taken out of context and read as if Rousseau were a nineteenth-century writer, instead of the eighteenth-century writer he was, Rousseau seems to be anticipating Hegelian notions. But if the context is taken into consideration, it will be seen that Rousseau is simply saying that anybody who refuses to conform to the outcome of the voting in the assembly can be forced to conform, inasmuch as he has agreed in advance to do so.[12]

---

[12] See below, 128.

Sherover's translation, like Cole's and Masters' and Kendall's, sometimes reinforces a Hegelian misreading. Thus when they all cause Rousseau to declare that the state is a "moral person whose life consists in the union of its members," thought of Hegel is almost inevitable, but in this context the French expression "personne morale"[3] is better rendered as "artificial person," as Watkins translates. For the state is a moral person in the same sense, no more and no less, as any corporation or "collective." And when in the next paragraph Rousseau writes that "besides the public person we have to consider the private persons who compose it," "compose" is the operative word. If it is true that "the Sovereign is sole judge" of the line "between the respective rights of the Citizens and of the Sovereign," it is also true that Rousseau's sovereign is the citizens assembled together and voting in accordance with the prescribed rules (II, 4: 27–28; 372–73).

Thus, too, the assertion that "the general will is always upright" has a metaphysical ring if it stands alone, but the context qualifies it, for the sentence goes on: "and tends to the public utility" (II, 3: 26; 371). In a word, so far from making a metaphysical claim, Rousseau is making an empirical claim, viz. that what the assembled people, guided by the prescribed procedures, believe is the common good is likely in fact to be the common good.

Again, to say that the members of the assembly have "only one will" also sounds metaphysical, but Rousseau's intention, as the context again shows, is not to say that the will is single but that if an assembly follows the prescribed procedures all of its members will be aiming at the same object, namely their "common preservation and general well-being" (IV, 1: 98; 437). That is to say, it is not the will, but the object aimed at, that is "one." And later in the same chapter, assertions to the effect that the general will is never "annihilated," never "corrupted," but always "constant, unalterable, and pure," sound as if Rousseau's general will is a timeless, transcendental entity in which the various empirical wills are *aufgehoben*. But the context shows once again that Rousseau is not making a metaphysical claim; he is saying only that in small, homogeneous groups there is in fact some state of affairs that is, and is known by the assembly members to be, in the public interest. Even when some member of the assembly lies about what he thinks is the public

---

[3] The Dictionary of the French Academy defines *personne morale* as "Groupment de personnes ou de biens qui constitue un être morale, qui possède, en raison de ses droits actifs ou passifs, une existence civile." And the corresponding, and longer, sentence in the first version of *The Social Contract*, explicates this usage: "Par ou l'on voit que le souverain n'est par sa nature q'une personne morale, qu'il n'a qu'une existence abstraite et collective, et que l'ideée qu'on attache a ce mot ne peut être unie a celle d'un simple individu" (*The Political Writings of Jean-Jacques Rousseau*, ed. by C. E. Vaughan [Cambridge: The University Press, 1915] 1: 460). I am indebted to John F. Benton for calling my attention to this meaning of "personne morale."

interest (e.g., even when he sells his vote), he knows perfectly well what the public interest is; it is simply the case that on this occasion the public interest "seems to him negligible beside the exclusive good he aims at making his own." Thus, to say that the common interest is "unalterable" does not mean that it never changes, for in different circumstances the common interest of the assembly may well be different. Rather, it means that the common interest of this assembly in these particular circumstances is not affected—not "corrupted"—by the venality of this or that member of the assembly.

To round off this discussion of the differences between Rousseauean and Hegel-like conceptions of the general will and the common interest, I should add that there is no sign in Rousseau's text of what might be called an empirical version of Hegelianism—that is, a Hegelianism removed from its metaphysical setting but preserving the complex, yet unified, structures of the Hegelian state. Rousseau's "civil state," so far from being similar in organization and in aim to such a Hegelian state, is pretty much what Hegel called a "civil society," which for Hegel, of course, was only a transitional stage en route from a primitive to a fully formed social organization. For Rousseau, in contrast, though "passage from the state of nature to the civil state produces in man a remarkable change," this change is chiefly a matter of personal growth: man's "faculties are exercised and developed; his ideas are expanded; his feelings are ennobled; his whole soul is exalted" (I, 8: 18; 364). These are the advantages of what Rousseau called "civil liberty," and they are advantages that each citizen can realize for himself, if he chooses; their realization is not dependent on special institutions that the state sets up on behalf of the citizens.

Again, in the civil state man "gains the ownership of all he possesses." That is to say, in the Rousseauean state "possession," which in the state of nature "is only the result of force or the right of the first occupant," is replaced by "ownership, which can be based only on a positive title." But the Rousseauean conception of property is of individual, not of state, ownership.[14]

To sum up my comments on Hegelian misreadings (as I take them to be) of Rousseau: the state, as Rousseau envisaged it, is still the state envisaged by the *philosophes* of the Enlightenment. In Rousseau's civil state as in his state of nature, individuals are animated by self-interest, and though, in the new civil environment, self-interest has become enlightened, it has not been

---

[14] Given the powers that Rousseau assigns to the sovereign, there is nothing to prevent an assembly of the people from voting to abolish private property and to introduce state ownership. But this is a theoretical possibility that Rousseau does not consider, and the fact that he does not mention it shows how far it is from his thought.

transformed, as with Hegel, into something other than self-interest. Civil liberty, that is to say, makes "a stupid and ignorant animal" with narrow horizons into "an intelligent being and a man" with broader horizons, who is "truly master of himself." But each individual remains the center, as it were, of his now broader horizons and his new "moral freedom" (I, 8: 19; 365).

Another type of misinterpretation results from a disposition to read Rousseau as anticipating one or another currently fashionable contemporary view. Many writers detect a relationship between Rousseau's general will and utilitarianism. Thus Glenn O. Allen,[15] after correctly stating that "the general will wills the public advantage," assumes that this is "the greatest good of all, the greatest good of the greatest number"—as if it is self-evident that Rousseau was just another Benthamite. Given this assumption, Allen complains that Rousseau "neglects to work out clearly the means whereby the formal principle of the general will acquires content."

Now it is certainly true that in *The Social Contract* Rousseau was not concerned with the criteria which citizens should use in deciding whether policy A (e.g., lowering the marginal income tax rate and eliminating certain exemptions) or policy B (e.g., raising the marginal rate and increasing certain exemptions) will increase the general good. But why describe Rousseau's unconcern as "neglect"? Allen's account, like many twentieth-century studies of *The Social Contract*, first mistakenly supposes that Rousseau was concerned with the criteria by which a rational choice can be made amongst various alternative economic and social policies and then complains, unreasonably, that he failed to deliver. This is not to suggest that the problem with which Allen and like-minded writers want Rousseau to be concerned is unimportant. Of course, it is important, but no writer can deal with all the important problems, and the problem Rousseau was tackling in *The Social Contract* was the moral problem of consent, not the economic problem of maximization. In a word, Rousseau was not a rational-choice theorist, and it is a mistake to read him as if he were.

A number of other writers have detected similarities between Rousseau's general will and the Pareto principle. There certainly are similarities—for instance, both Rousseau and Pareto disallowed improvements for some members of the group unless none is made worse off—but such readings of *The Social Contract* go astray if they also read Rousseau as a rational-choice theorist. Thus, Runciman and Sen[16] argue that "useful sense may be given

    [15] Glenn O. Allen, "Le Volunteé de tous and le voluntee générale: a distinction and its significance," *Ethics* 70–71 (1959–61): 263–75.

    [16] W. G. Runciman and Amartya K. Sen, "Games, Justice and the General Will," *Mind* 74 (1965): 554–62.

to the 'General Will' and the 'Common Good' by reference to the theory of non-zero-sum, non-cooperative games." They take the so-called prisoners' dilemma as paradigmatic of the general will problem, the difficulty being that "the self-seeking of each prisoner will lead them both to confess, whereas they would both be better off if neither confesses." The solution, as Runciman and Sen see it, is to "enforce" the "collusion" of the prisoners. When collusion has been successfully enforced, Runciman and Sen believe that a general will exists.

I agree that "enforced collusion" and Rousseau's general will both achieve optimality, but that is the only similarity between Rousseau's view and Runciman and Sen's. Enforced collusion would never result in a general will. Runciman and Sen see that for there to be an enforceable contract between the prisoners (alternatively, among citizens) a sanction is required; they also see that this depends on there being an external and independent sovereign—a third person, who is not a prisoner, i.e., not a citizen. But of course on Rousseau's view, the sovereign is not an outsider but the citizens themselves meeting together in assembly, and given the conditions stipulated by Runciman and Sen in the prisoners' dilemma case, the prisoners/citizens will never manage to cooperate. It follows that Rousseau must have in mind something different from a non-zero sum, non-cooperative game.

Runciman and Sen assume that Rousseau was interested, as they are, in a general theory about how to bring it about that "good" decisions are made at choice points. Though I do not think Rousseau was interested in any kind of general theory—he was allergic to abstract generality wherever he encountered it—he was of course much interested in the practical question of how to encourage good decision-making, or rather, how to encourage the decision-making he more or less uncritically assumed to be good. That is the topic of the *Emile*, for instance. But in *The Social Contract* the emphasis is different. It is not on how to cultivate good decision-making in the citizens, but on how to bring it about that the citizens consent to being compelled. And their consent will not be generated—this is Rousseau's thesis—unless their political decisions are made within the context of a political structure of the kind he has outlined.

For the rest, in Rousseau's view it is governments, not sovereigns, that introduce sanctions. They do so for reasons like those Runciman and Sen discuss; and he would, I think, have much appreciated Runciman and Sen's discussion of the prisoners' dilemma: he would have seen it, as they do, as demonstrating the need for enforceable contracts. After all, he held that people enter into a social contract and set up a government precisely because they believe they will be better off if there are contracts of the kinds that only governments can introduce and maintain. But Rousseau focused his attention on the fact that governments, once set up, may enforce contracts that disadvantage some people even while advantaging others. How to prevent that from happening was the problem which occupied his attention, not the problem that concerns Runciman and Sen. That is to say, not the problem of seeing to it that a system of enforceable contracts exists, but the problem of seeing to it that no one's lot is worsened as a result of his agreement to enter into a system of enforceable contracts.

4.

So much, then, for the reasons why Rousseau's view of the general will has been misunderstood. The last question to be examined is whether the view of the general will I have attributed to Rousseau solves the problem of consent. Since the analysis applies *mutatis mutandis* to those occasions on which the assembly is voting on a proposed law and to those occasions on which it is voting on the two review questions, I shall limit the discussion to the latter kind of occasion and so avoid unnecessary repetition. Even so, the exposition will be complex, for it breaks down into three subquestions. (1) Inasmuch as this view asserts that all the members of an assembly (i.e., of a small, homogeneous group) will know whether, since the last meeting of the assembly, the government has improved the lot of some citizens at the cost of other citizens, I shall ask whether it is likely they will have this information. (2) Inasmuch as, on this view, most citizens will answer truthfully when they are asked whether the government has acted in this prejudicial manner, I shall ask whether this claim is plausible. (3) Finally, and assuming that (1) and (2) have been answered satisfactorily, I shall ask whether the problem of consent is solved.

(1) I shall begin by reviewing the kind of information the citizens must have and act on. It is not necessary that citizens be able to assess the specific effect of such-and-such decrees that the government has introduced since the assembly last met. It is necessary only that they be able to make an overall estimate of the results achieved by the government in the interval since the last periodical assembly. During that interval the government (whether it be monarchical, republican, or whatever) will have issued a number of decrees, each of which will have had effects, some favorable, some unfavorable, on the citizens. The effects, favorable and unfavorable, of these decrees will be differentially distributed among the citizens, and it is only required that each citizen be able to make a reliable estimate of the net effect—on balance favorable or on balance unfavorable—of these decrees on himself and on the other citizens. If the citizens can make this estimate they will have all the information they need in order to be able to vote

intelligently on the two review questions. But will they have the requisite information? And if they have it, will they vote in accordance with it?

If the members of a small, homogeneous group do not know whether the government they have been living under has disadvantaged some members while advantaging others, who would know? It is surely arguable that an assembly of the Hopi has a clearer view of Hopi interests than some bureaucrat or politician in Washington, that the opinions of slum dwellers (if collected in accordance with Rousseau's procedures) are more reliable than those of a social worker with an MA from Columbia or City College who commutes from the suburbs to spend an eight-hour day in an office in City Hall, that the members of a primitive tribe in some third-world state know better what their interests are than a development economist imported from abroad to advise the government.

Recall that long-range future interests are not at issue here. Any assembly—whether of Rousseauean farmers, Hopis and/or modern slum dwellers—might not be able to reach a consensus regarding the effects on their lives of future possible, but as yet unknown, policy decisions by the government. But the members of the assembly are asked only how policies already operating have affected their lives. It is surely not implausible to argue, as Rousseau did, that they will know this better than any outsider, even the most beneficent and intelligent of outsiders, could. This explains why he was so insistent that the state be small enough for all the citizens to sit together and vote together.[17]

(2) Allowing, then, that it is at least plausible to argue that the members of an assembly are better informed than any outsider regarding the common interest of those assembly members, the next question is whether it is also plausible to hold that the members will vote in favor of that common interest. Are they not more likely to vote, each of them, for their own private interests?

Before trying to answer this question it is necessary to spell out exactly what Rousseau's scheme requires of the citizens in the way of sacrificing their private interests for the public good. First, citizens who believe that the government's policies have affected them adversely and who vote against it for that reason are not voting against the public interest, inasmuch as·any change that affects anyone adversely is against the public interest. Secondly,

---

[17] The situation is different, of course, when the state is too large for all the citizens to participate directly. Then, though representation interposes an unfortunate, complicating step between the citizens and their government, it may be better than any alternative, and Rousseau was prepared, when he was asked to design a new constitution for Poland, to recommend reform of the Sejm, rather than its abolition.

citizens who believe that the government's policies have affected them favorably and who vote for it are not voting against the public interest, providing they believe that those policies have not affected other citizens adversely. What has to be guarded against is, first, the possibility that individuals will vote for the government if its policies have affected them favorably, even though they believe that its policies have affected others adversely, and second, the possibility that they will vote against the government because it has not improved their own lot, even though they believe it has affected others favorably.

Is it plausible to hold, with Rousseau, that at most only a minority of citizens is likely to vote in this way—that a majority is likely to vote for the public interest even when it conflicts with their own private interest? But that, from Rousseau's point of view, is a very confused way of posing the question. It is not a matter of expecting people ever to vote against their own private interests, and they never do so vote. This follows from "man's nature": "his first law is to attend to his own preservation" (I, 2: 5; 352). On the other hand, however, every man's private interest is a part of the common good. Accordingly, since the common interest is the sum of private interests, if one chooses the common interest "one cannot work for others without working for oneself. . . . No one appropriates this word *each* to himself without thinking of himself as voting on behalf of all" (II, 4: 28; 373). Thus it is not a matter of selfishness vs. altruism, but of what may be called unmediated vs. mediated selfishness, i.e., selfishness modulated by sympathy and fellow-feeling. It is not a matter of expecting anybody to be altruistic, if that means handing over to someone else a good that one now possesses; it is only a matter of expecting people to be willing to forego *additional* goods that they might acquire, if acquisition of those additional goods were to cause someone else—someone who is no mere anonymous "other," but a neighbor—to lose a good he now possesses.

So much, then, for Rousseau's reasons for thinking that in small homogeneous societies fellow-feeling will reduce people's tendency to ignore the losses of others. But there is a possibility that a majority, or a large minority, might vote against the government, not because anyone has suffered losses, but merely because they themselves have not gained as much as some others have gained. In other words, envy may prevent a general will from emerging and being effective.

If the will is truly general the citizens will ignore the matter of the distribution of improvements, if any. That is to say, it is the general will that the government be retained if an improvement has occurred, regardless of how that improvement has been distributed among the citizens. The question is, will voting in the assembly reflect the general will?

I believe the answer to be probably "yes" if fellow-feeling is strong and if differences in distribution are not great, but probably "no" if the distribution has been very skewed, though it is possible to think of circumstances in which even a very skewed distribution might be accepted by an assembly, with the result that its vote would conform to the principle and, hence, to the general will.

Suppose, for instance, that the crown gives £100,000 to a victorious admiral (Nelson) or a victorious general (Wellington) without reducing the material well-being of any citizen (i.e., without a tax assessment).[18] Would this advantaging of a very few have been acceptable to the British public in 1805 or 1815? That surely depends on how much the hero was "appreciated," that is, on whether what might be described as "normal" envy was suppressed by patriotism and gratitude.

Thus a skewed distribution that is acceptable at one time may be unacceptable at another. Suppose, for instance, that a college receives an unrestricted gift of $1,000,000 and the administration uses it to reduce tuition payments, reducing the tuition of minority students by $1,000 and the tuition of others by only $50. It is my guess that whereas in the climate of opinion of the sixties an assembly of students, asked to approve or disapprove this action, would probably have voted to sustain the administration, in today's climate of opinion it might vote to throw the administration out.

Though these examples suggest that envy can sometimes be moderated enough to obtain a majority in the assembly that conforms to the general will, they nonetheless have only a limited relevance to the kind of society Rousseau envisaged. One should not think, as one is prone to do when estimating the likely reactions of public opinion to government performance, of dynamic modern societies with their built-in expectations for steady increases in the standard of living. In Rousseau's day Europe was only just breaking out of a largely static, largely agrarian pattern where the emphasis was less on growth than on not letting things deteriorate. Thus it is not surprising that for Rousseau the operative words were "defends and protects . . . the person and goods of every associate" (I, 6: 14; 360).[19] Expec-

---

[18] A careful government, acting on Rousseauean principles, would not ask the assembly to approve awards it had already made to Nelson and Wellington. It would request, *ex ante*, authority to make awards to unnamed, unspecified heroes.

[19] It is important to distinguish between Rawls' original position and what I will call Rousseau's initial position. The initial position is just whatever set of distributions happens to exist at the time the contract comes into effect. Rousseau was not at all concerned with a theory of justice that would tell us what an equitable distribution, in some ideal sense, would be. No one, he thought, would enter into the contract if he thought he would lose as a result of some subsequent distribution; the initial condition was a optimum against which any proposed redistribution had to be measured.

tations for improvement were still relatively low; a government would get good marks for maintaining whatever status quo happened to exist. In such economic and social conditions envy was not likely to be a powerful force even in large states—still less, obviously, in small homogeneous societies.

Before concluding this discussion of the likelihood that the votes of a majority of assembly members will correspond to the general will, I must revert briefly to· the importance Rousseau attached to the rules for voting. Even if fellow-feeling and an Emile-like education did not have a powerful moderating influence on selfishness and envy in the ordinary affairs of everyday life they might nonetheless have an ameliorating effect in the special circumstances of a meeting of the assembly. And it is on such occasions, when a government is being sustained or removed, and not in the daily round, that the suppression of envy is especially important.

Rule 3 is intended to give moderate selfishness a relatively greater influence, as compared with intense selfishness, by distancing voters from the kinds of calculations that intense selfishness would want, and need, to make. Suppose that a monarchical government is in the public interest and that the voters know this to be the case. They are more likely to vote in favor of monarchy, and so in favor of the public interest, if the question is put "in the abstract," rather by naming "a particular person" as the proposed king (II, 6). They are more likely, that is, to vote what they know to be the common good, if that is all they know, than if they also know who the king is to be and so can calculate whether he is likely to favor them personally or disfavor them. As for Rule 2, Rousseau, so far as I am aware, is one of the first thinkers to recognize—what is now a sociological truism—the extent to which the form in which a question is asked influences the answer given.

Taken together, then, Rules 2 and 3 do indeed have a tendency to moderate intense selfishness, and Rule 4 tends to reduce the influence of faction. But will the combined effect of these rules be enough to produce the result Rousseau hoped for? That depends on what his hopes were, and his hopes seem to have been on the whole modest. He certainly never expected *all* members of any assembly to vote against changes that were not improvements. The most he hoped was that enough members would vote in this way for there to be a reasonable chance that the common good would stand revealed as the central tendency of the distribution of all votes.

For my part, I confess to being a good deal less sanguine than Rousseau about the likelihood of the general will being revealed as the central tendency of the distribution of votes. I think it would be difficult to distinguish between a central tendency that results from manipulations by a cynical administration (or from maneuverings by a combination of factions) and a central tendency that results from the fact that a majority of voters has voted for what those voters believe to be the common good. (I suspect that lurking somewhere in the background of Rousseau's thought is an outside expert—himself!—who knows how to distinguish "good" central tendencies from "bad" ones.) Nevertheless I believe it would be difficult to claim that his rules would *never* work, especially in the small, homogeneous groups for which they were intended.

(3) That being the case, let us ask whether on those occasions—few or many—when the procedural rules actually work and the majority's vote reveals the general will, the problem of consent is solved, as Rousseau claimed. The prima facie difficulty is obvious: what the majority has voted for has been put into effect. The minority, until the next meeting of the assembly when another vote will be taken, are certainly subject to "laws they have not agreed to," for they have voted against these laws and against the government that imposed them. Nevertheless, Rousseau claimed, they are also "free." How can this be? On the one hand, compulsion is an essential element in every social organization, even the smallest and most homogeneous. On the other hand, unless men and women consent to be subjects, compulsion is immoral and so unjustified. Here then, we have reached the heart of *The Social Contract*.

It is possible to reconstruct[20] Rousseau's thinking in the following way: the central tendency of the pattern of voting in an assembly discloses the general will of that assembly, i.e., the public interest, inasmuch as most members of the assembly have a good idea of what the public interest is and they have been asked a purely factual question, for instance, "Has the administration acted in the public interest since the last meeting of this assembly?" Members whose votes deviate from this central tendency will be subject to laws which they opposed, but they will also be free because—the majority being assumed to be correct—the fact that they are in a minority shows them that their votes were mistaken.

To evaluate and at the same time flesh out this argument it will be convenient to distinguish between two kinds of minorities: (1) those who voted for a government which the majority rejected, and (2) those who voted against a government which the majority approved. Let us consider first affirmative minorities. These deviant voters may be further divided into two sub-categories: (i) those who (mistakenly) believed that the present administration had acted in the public interest, and (ii) those who knew that the

---

[20] Perhaps "construct" would be more correct here, for I do not claim that Rousseau himself worked his way through the detailed argument I propose on pp. 125–127. That is not the way his mind worked. He did not reason things out; rather, he simply "saw a truth." Granted that his truths were often muddled and sometimes not truths at all, it is still remarkable how often an *ex post* case can be made for one or another of his insights.

administration had not acted in the public interest but who nonetheless voted for it because they believed it to be in their own private interest.

The problem of consent is solved for both subsets of deviants, but in different ways. (i) Like the majority—indeed, just as much as the majority—the members of the first subset voted for, and wanted, the public interest. They differ from the majority only in that they made a simple factual mistake about what the public interest is. Though they voted to retain the administration and so are now subject to an administration they opposed, they voted for the public interest and so are also free. In Aristotelian terms,[21] they and the majority agreed on the major premise of the practical syllogism and differed only on the minor premise. They agreed with the majority—to use one of Aristotle's own examples—that "Poison is bad"; they differed from the majority in believing that "This is poison" is not true of the liquid in the bottle in question. Now that the voting has shown that "This is poison" is true, they should gladly turn away from the liquid they were about to drink; in abstaining from drinking they would be doing what they really wanted, in distinction from what they erroneously thought they wanted. If they persist in their mistake they can be "forced to be free" (I, 7: 18; 364), that is, forcibly restrained from drinking the liquid.[22] For this first subset of deviant members of the assembly, then, the problem of consent is solved.

(ii) Those who deliberately voted their private interest, instead of what they knew to be the public interest, are in an altogether different situation: they will now be living under an administration which they do not in any sense want, for they rejected the major premise of the Aristotelian syllogism which both the majority and the first subset of deviants accepted. But the members of this second subset of deviants—by voting their private interests, instead of the public interest—have in effect taken themselves out of the community. They are—at least for the present—in the position of those who, at the original foundation of the state, voted against establishing it. It would be sensible for them to emigrate and join some other group with whom they share a common interest; if they do not they are in effect only "resident foreigners." They are subject to laws which are not of their own choosing, but inasmuch as they could leave if they chose, they too are consenting by

---

[21] For instance, *Eth. Nic.*, 1147 a 1–1147 b 5. Robert Paul Wolff has used a somewhat similar argument in his discussion of Rousseau in *In Defense of Anarchism* (New York, 1976), 51–52.

[22] Even Mill, that most libertarian of political philosophers, allowed that "since liberty consists in doing what one desires" and since one "desires not to fall into the river," a person who is about to cross a stream on a bridge he does not know to be unsafe may be turned back, "without any real infringement of his liberty" (*On Liberty* [London: J. M. Dent, 1910], Chap. 5, 151–52).

remaining instead of leaving. Theirs is a possibly grudging and doubtlessly only *ex post* consent, but it is nevertheless genuine consent (IV, 2).[23]

At the next meeting of the assembly these deviants will have an opportunity to remain resident foreigners or to rejoin the community by voting, this time, for the public interest, rather than for their varied private interests. This is still another reason why, in Rousseau's view, the regular convocation of "periodical assemblies" of the citizens is so important (III, 18). Giving the citizens frequent opportunities to approve or disapprove their provisional government (all governments without exception are of course "provisional") not only reduces the danger of usurpation; it also preserves the moral foundation of the state, for if the citizens do not reject the provisional government and replace it by another, they thereby consent to it, and so approve (at least until the next session) all the decrees to which, in the interval since the last assembly, it has subjected them.[24]

So much for minorities that favor an administration that the majority rejects. In the case of minorities that oppose an administration that the majority favors, a different analysis is required, chiefly because it is easier to understand how someone can be mistaken in thinking no one has been harmed than to understand how someone can be mistaken in thinking that someone has been harmed. Yet that is what must be the case, if Rousseau has solved the problem of consent across the whole spectrum of cases in which consent can be an issue. Since his basic assumption is that majorities are correct, these deviants must be wrong in saying that someone is worse off. Here again two sub-categories are to be distinguished: (i) deviants who genuinely believe that someone is worse off, and (ii) deviants who know that no one is worse off, but who voted against the administration because of defeated expectations, i.e., because they had not been made better off than they were, or out of envy, i.e., because others have been made better off.

As regards (i), this will be a small group, though we may suppose that well intentioned people may sometimes be misled by the envious and the disgruntled into believing that the administration has acted contrary to the public good. These people, like the majority, were really aiming at the public good. As regards (ii), these deviants voted against the administration, despite knowing that it had not acted against the public good. Thereby they have taken themselves, at least temporarily, out of the community.

---

[23] Rousseau pointed out that this applies only in "a free State." In states where "family, goods, lack of a refuge, necessity or violence may detain a man against his will" continuing to dwell there does not imply consent.

[24] "The law of yesterday does not obligate today, but tacit consent is presumed from silence, and the sovereign is deemed to confirm continually the laws which it does not abrogate while being able to do so" (III, 11: 85; p. 425).

To sum up this long analysis: the general will, understood as the verdict of an assembly in which a majority has voted for what it takes to be the public good, "reconciles obedience and liberty" in the following way. First, every member of the assembly has freely consented to the original compact to establish this society.[25] Second the original compact "tacitly includes the undertaking" to accept the verdict of the majority whenever the assembly has voted in accordance with the five rules laid down (I, 7). It follows that, if the majority and the minority (whether a pro-government minority or an anti-government minority) have both voted in accordance with what they take to be the public good, the majority is justified in forcing the minority to be free, for (1) everyone alike is aiming at the public good, and (2) everyone has agreed in advance to accept the verdict of the majority regarding the results. As for any minority that has deliberately voted contrary to the public good, it is outside the contract.

As I have already said, this whole analysis presupposes that the majority is correct, and as I have argued (and as Rousseau himself allowed), there are good grounds for holding that this is by no means always the case. If the majority is indeed mistaken—still more, if it acts deliberately against the public interest—then the contract which brought this state into existence has been abrogated, the association has degenerated into an aggregation, and compulsion of the minority is immoral.

But the fact that minorities, instead of being forced to be free, are actually all too often forced into slavery, does not invalidate the logic of the argument. Rousseau was too much of a realist—too knowledgeable about human nature—not to recognize that, whereas ideally "the particular or individual will ought to be null," as compared with the will to aim at the general good, in point of fact "the general will is always the weakest . . . and the private will is first of all, . . . a gradation directly opposed to what the social order requires" (III, 2: 58–59; 401).[26] It is true, of course, that Rousseau believed that the procedures he recommended would mitigate, but he certainly did not hope that they could completely overcome, this "natural and inevitable inclination of the best-constituted Governments. If Sparta and Rome have perished, what State can hope to last forever? If we wish to form a durable establishment, let us then not seek to make it eternal. In order to succeed, one should neither attempt the impossible, nor flatter oneself with

---

[25] "There is only one single law which by its nature requires unanimous consent. It is the social pact . . . no one can, under any pretext whatsoever, subjugate [any man] without his consent" (IV, 2: 101; p. 440).

[26] Rousseau is discussing the motivations of magistrates (i.e., government officials) here, but what he says applies equally to the motivations of ordinary citizens: he is making a point about human, not about bureaucratic, nature.

giving to the work of men a solidity that human things do not admit of" (III, 11: 84; 424). Thus *The Social Contract* was not a cookbook guaranteeing that, if its recipes were followed, states would treat minorities morally; it was rather an exposition of the special conditions under which alone the compulsion of minorities is morally justified.

Rousseau must have seen that these conditions are so special that only very small states can have a moral foundation and he must have known that the day of the very small state—if there had ever been a day of the very small state—was over. Hence, if any modern state were to have a moral foundation, it was essential to find ways of generating a sense of—a passion for—the common good in groups so large and so diverse that the common good is not immediately evident to all the members of those groups.

Hence, again, his emphasis in the *Emile* on "moral" education, i.e., an education of the sentiments. Hence his recommendations in the essays on Poland and Corsica for a systematic cultivation of "patriotic zeal." What he proposed specifically for Poland would apply *mutatis mutandis* to any large nation-state: Develop distinctive national institutions that give form to the character, tastes, and customs of the Polish people; introduce distinctive Polish dress; revive or introduce public games distinctive to Poland; create a truly national educational system with only Poles for teachers and in which the children learn to read by reading Polish literature. The customs thus revived or newly introduced "may be good or bad; that is not the point: even if bad they will endear Poland to its citizens" and so foster a sense of communality that will override the multitudinous private interests of the diverse groups that make up modern Poland.[27]

That strong, even if only temporary, consensuses can be produced in large states is well-known—one might say, painfully well-known. Italy under Mussolini in the heyday of his success, Germany under Hitler before things began to go sour, England in the desperate days of Dunkerque are examples. Though Rousseau had no idea, naturally, of the power of modern techniques of persuasion, he was by no means unaware of the other face of "patriotic zeal." He recognized that by utilizing such means as those he recommended for Poland, "the Prince draws a great advantage in preserving its power despite the people" (III, 18: 96; 435).

How to prevent misuse of this power is a central problem of practical politics, but there is a theoretical problem as well. Rousseau was aware that in very large and very heterogenous groups there is no immediately recognizable common good; he seems to have overlooked the fact that in such groups there may actually be no common good at all. That is, in such groups

---

[27] *Government of Poland*, Chapters 3 and 4.

there may literally be no way of improving the lot of some people without affecting others adversely. If that is the case, if no common good already exists, patriotic zeal cannot generate one; at most it will produce only a fictive, or pseudo, common good. Unlike the veil of ignorance that Rule 3 is intended to cast over the private interests that might otherwise prevent citizens from concentrating on the public interest, patriotic zeal may be a veil obscuring the hard truth that no public interest exists. It would seem, then, that either some new definition of the public interest has to be formulated or that no modern state has a moral basis. That Rousseau put this dilemma so forcefully is a major contribution to political theory.

California Institute of Technology

Addenda

References within the text:

p. 106, §1, 1.5: *OC*3.440/*CW*4.200
p. 107, §5, 1.6–7: *OC*3.379/*CW*4.153
p. 108, §1, 1.2: *OC*3.454/*CW*4.211
  Ibid., 1.5: *OC*3.468/*CW*4.222
  Ibid., §2, 1.14: *OC*3.436/*CW*4.197
p. 109, §1, 1.10: *OC*3.371n/*CW*4.147n
  Ibid., §3, 1.10: *OC*3.437/*CW*4.198
p. 110, §4, 1.4: *OC*3.371/*CW*4.147–48
  Ibid., §8, 1.10: *OC*3.438/*CW*4.199
p. 111, §1, 1.10: *OC*3.371/*CW*4.147
p. 113, n.9: *OC*4.504/*Em*.222
  Ibid., n.10: *OC*4.492/*Em*.213
p. 114, §2, 1.6: *OC*3.359/*CW*4.137
p. 115, §4, 1.2: *OC*3.378/*CW*4.152
  Ibid., 1.5: *OC*3.364/*CW*4.141
p. 116, §1, 1.13: *OC*3.372–73/*CW*4.148
  Ibid., §2, 1.3: *OC*3.371/*CW*4.147
  Ibid., §3, 1.5: *OC*3.437/*CW*4.198
p. 117, §2, 1.13–14: *OC*3.364/*CW*4.141
p. 118, §1, 1.5: *OC*3.365/*CW*4.141–42
p. 122, §2, 1.7: *OC*3.352/*CW*4.132
  Ibid., 1.12: *OC*3.373/*CW*4.148–49
p. 123, §4, 1.11: *OC*3.360/*CW*4.138
p. 126, §2, 1.16–17: *OC*3.364/*CW*4.141
p. 128, §3, 1.8: *OC*3.401/*CW*4.170–71
p. 129, §1, 1.2: *OC*3.424/*CW*4.188
  Ibid., §4, 1.9: *OC*3.435/*CW*4.196

Endnotes:

13. *OC*3.294–95/*CW*4.87
24. *OC*3.425/*CW*4.188–89
25. *OC*3.440/*CW*4.200

[8]

Rousseau's Two Concepts of Liberty

Robert Wokler

I

It is the misfortune of extraordinary doctrines that they suffer a remarkably common fate in the hands of their interpreters, and at first glance there may appear to be nothing very special about the prevalent distortions of the political thought of Rousseau. His ideas, like those of other great thinkers, have been widely embraced or denounced with almost equal abandon, in fierce and recurrent controversies which merely reflect the striking impact his philosophy has had upon his followers from the French Revolution to the present day. It is not particularly odd that professed disciples should have obscured his meaning as much as his detractors have done, nor even that we have come to judge the significance of his claims in the light of the activities of others who sought to realise them in practice. What is peculiar about Rousseau's reputation among pre-eminent political theorists, however, is the extent to which his critics are agreed that he could not have been committed to the philosophy he actually set forth.

In the history of political thought there is no more outspoken defender of freedom than Rousseau, no one who expressed a deeper regret over the liberty we have lost or a more profound longing for the liberty we should seek, and yet the main charge levelled against him by his opponents has consistently been that the manipulative powers entrusted in his works to sovereign assemblies, legislators, and tutors alike deprive persons of the very liberty he claims they should enjoy. Of all thinkers decried as collectivist or totalitarian, of all those vilified for sacrificing liberty upon the altars of state control and social indoctrination, none professed a greater love of freedom, nor a more resolute determination to maintain the independence of a free man. My remarks here are inspired by just this puzzling antinomy, as if what Rousseau really stands for is the opposite of what he stood for in his life and thought. The objection to his doctrine which I wish to consider, therefore, is not the reproach so commonly made against political and social thinkers that their pursuit of one great goal conflicts with others of at least equal value. It is, rather, that the very concept acknowledged to lie at the heart of his philosophy in fact means the opposite of what he claims on its behalf – in effect, that his defence of liberty is illiberal.

That charge of illiberalism is of course generally premised on the claim that Rousseau defined liberty falsely, and that the institutions he prescribed for its fulfilment in fact thwart or destroy it. At least when Bertrand Russell spoke of Hitler as 'an outcome of Rousseau', or when T. D. Weldon remarked that men can be forced to be free in Rousseau's sense when they are incarcerated in Wormwood Scrubs or Broadmoor,[1] I take it that something like this complaint is what they had in mind. To be sure, the alternative view of liberty presupposed by such criticism is all too seldom explained, and it may seem difficult to identify such darkly sinister portraits as are commonly drawn of Rousseau's thought against an allegedly contrasting background that is itself so dimly lit. Yet just that lack of definition, I believe, forms an essential ingredient of the concept of freedom which Rousseau is accused by his liberal critics of having ignored. For while he is said to have prescribed and delimited the nature of human freedom by confining it in a political strait-jacket that requires all men to act together, his opponents hold dear a principle which has no determinant content, and whose attainment is marked by the lack of interference of other persons in the pursuit of what each of us may choose to do. Rousseau's imputed circumscription of an imprescribable concept is crucial to the liberal case against him, for from a truly liberal perspective individuals are free only when they are unhindered in their actions, when they have no duty opposed to their will, and not, as it is suggested he would have us believe, when they have no will but to perform their duty.[2] Now at least since the late eighteenth and early nineteenth century, liberalism has come to be associated above all with the idea and exercise of personal freedom safeguarded from public control, but this element of its theory is generally acknowledged to stem largely from the definition of liberty as 'the absence of external impediments' which was first provided by Hobbes, and the same theme also lies at the heart of the concept which Isaiah Berlin has rightly termed 'negative liberty'.[3] Freedom in that sense is properly defined by the non-existence of forces that might confine it, by the absence of any restrictions against it and not the presence of prescribed ends towards which it should be aimed. Those to whom it is attributed are directed nowhere in particular; quite the contrary, others are enjoined not to harm them or stand in their way.

It is true that for nearly all liberal thinkers a rule of law is acknowledged to be indispensable to the enjoyment of such freedom, in that it establishes where the frontiers of individual liberty lie and protects each person's freedom from infringement by everyone else. But in its enforcement, the rule of law can only preserve liberty and does not itself create or promote it. Since by their very nature laws set limits to the enjoyment of freedom, men in society are most free, as Hobbes imagined, when the rule of law is most effective but the laws themselves remain most reticent about what men may do. Because he defined liberty in terms of the outspoken making of laws rather than in the context of their general silence – because he thought it prevailed under the very constraints imposed by a legal system – Rousseau, it is claimed, did not hold to this conception of freedom.

His alleged failure to safeguard personal rights and interests from state interference has also not endeared him to most liberals. It is precisely on account of their fundamental concern with the demarcations between us rather than with the activities we pursue within those bounds that liberals are so anxious to preserve the distinction between our private and public domains which Rousseau's political doctrine is seen to have undermined. Here again Hobbes laid the foundation for this principle of liberalism, above all, perhaps, in his contention that the ancient Greeks and Romans and their followers had adopted a confusing concept of liberty in associating it with the commonwealth as a whole rather than with the relations between particular men within it.[4] Under the classical liberal formulations of such thinkers as von Humboldt, Constant and John Stuart Mill, the liberty of particular men has come to require the protection of their individual affairs and aspirations from state or social control. But in extolling the merits of so-called civil liberty under the rule of an absolute sovereign, Rousseau, it is so often alleged, sought to submerge all that makes us different from one another under a fictitious liberty of the commonwealth which true liberals decry. More than any other complaint, this anxiety underlies most liberals' mistrust of his doctrine. Committed as they are to the liberties of separate individuals pursuing diverse personal initiatives, they show little sympathy for Rousseau's apparent confusion of liberty with public engagement and social solidarity.

64   *Rousseau's Two Concepts of Liberty*

Even under regimes of popular self-rule of the kind he prescribed, it is not the liberty of particular men that prevails but the illiberal rule of each person by all the rest. Never mind Rousseau's contention that in our political institutions we have already fabricated such a world; according to his liberal critics, this is what his doctrine entails.

Of course such misgivings about Rousseau's doctrine are not shared by all liberal interpreters of his political thought. Robert Derathé, the most distinguished of contemporary commentators, has stressed the importance of the safeguards for individual liberty against the exercise of sovereign power that Rousseau introduced in his writings,[5] and which have been overlooked by so many of his critics, while other scholars have even attempted to restore Rousseau to his rightful place near the pinnacle of classical liberal thought, from whose principles some modern pretenders have been seen to renege.[6] If only for the good reason that I believe they generally provide more accurate readings of Rousseau's works than do the denigrators of his totalitarianism, I do not intend to challenge these perspectives here, except perhaps for such oversights as stem from the company in which they have thought fit to re-introduce Rousseau, now that their interpretations show him to have really been on his best behaviour. In attempting to dissociate his remarks about liberty from the history of liberalism, I mean to show that liberal adumbrations of his ideas have as a rule departed from their actual meanings, and indeed that Rousseau may be portrayed as hostile to freedom only against a canvas from which the widely shared conceptions of liberty he inherited, employed, and refined before the advent of liberalism, have been wiped out.

Hobbes, I believe, was quite right to remark upon the absence of his own idea of liberty from both ancient and modern political thought. But to accept the originality of his perspective on this subject is tantamount to admitting that other uses of the term which he and his followers have rejected may be more orthodox than the meanings they have stipulated and prefer. Liberals have shown themselves to be remarkably tolerant about most matters apart from the definition of liberty, and yet before Hobbes, and in his own day, and with Rousseau later, liberty was conceived as having a quite different sense from 'the absence of external impediments' and 'the silence of the law' as applied to particular men rather than to commonwealths as a whole.

Contemporary scholars have come to agree with Hobbes that the ancient Greeks did not share the definition of liberty which he supposed to be uniquely correct. Herodotus showed no hesitation in ascribing the term *eleutheroi* – free men – to the Greeks in general, whose liberty he contrasted with the tyranny of Persian government; nor did Thucydides doubt that Athenians owed their greatness over Sparta to the liberty of their *polis* as a whole. Even when Plato and Aristotle condemned the excesses and abuses of individual liberty, they perceived it as engendered under democratic constitutions and not just as a matter of the unfettered relations of particular men. For Hobbes the idea of a free state meant no more than its lack of subjection to alien rule; for the Greeks it had everything to do with the quality of life of politically autonomous citizens. Whereas for liberals the idea of freedom has come to be divorced from that of democracy, the Greeks had no conception of liberty without it; while for liberals we are free when left by the state to ourselves, for the Greeks we were most free when as political agents we took common part in the deliberations of public affairs.

If for the ancient Greeks liberty meant democratic self-rule above all, for the Romans the idea was connected more closely still with the obligations of law. *Libertas est potestas faciendi quod jure liceat* was a commonplace of the Roman Republic, as Maurice Cranston has observed.[7] To be *liber* – free from paternal control – was at the same time to be *civis* – civilised for political life, so that the acquisition of citizenship and liberty went hand in hand. Hobbes was later to oppose liberty and law, but lawlessness was defined by the Romans not as *libertas* but *licentia*, a distinction appropriated by Locke in his own conception of natural liberty, so different in turn from that of Hobbes.

Machiavelli of course drew most of his account of liberty from Roman Republican sources, specially emphasising the need for a patriotic spirit and the public devotion of a free people bearing its own arms. Such was enough to try the patience of Hobbes yet again, who dismissed Machiavelli with the same stroke as had swept away the ancient Greeks and Romans, for neglecting the liberty of particular men.[8] Among Hobbes's contemporaries, moreover, perhaps the most systematic political philosopher was Spinoza, who defined true liberty as the guidance of reason which overcame our enslavement to passion. This was hardly an original notion, since it had been central to ancient Greek, Roman and Christian accounts of the human will and the nature of self-determination, which Rousseau was also to recapitulate in a wholly familiar terminology

in the next century. But the idea of freedom of the will, so crucial to that tradition, was similarly rejected by Hobbes, for whom
the postulate of slavery to one's passions, that is, subjection to
internal impediments, was nonsense. Hobbes may have been right
on every point that he raised against both ancient and modern
thinkers, but his Procrustean disposal of Western political thought
hardly left a single unmutilated bedfellow with whom he might share
his concept, and it is therefore at least odd that liberals should have
adopted his definition of liberty as if it were central to all meanings
of the term.

I leave aside Marxist, so-called New Liberal, and other more
recent conceptions of liberty which have been similarly judged an
abuse of language, but before I move on to those elements of
Rousseau's account of freedom which are most strikingly his own, I
think it is worth noting that his doctrine, unlike that of Hobbes,
contains so many commonplace and familiar features. Rousseau's
reflections on liberty in the light of autonomy, democracy, political
engagement, citizenship, patriotism, the rule of law, the bearing of
arms, and subjection to reason, were the stock-in-trade of most
definitions of liberty, apart from those stipulated by Hobbes, up to
his own day. Why, then, has his conception of liberty been judged
so illiberal?

One historical reason above all others, I believe, underlies this
charge against him – and that is the influence which his ideas allegedly
exercised upon the French Revolution. Liberalism as a political
doctrine has been traced to a variety of sources, including Greek
democracy, the Protestant Reformation, modern constitutionalism
and *laissez-faire* political economy, as against Oriental or Papal
despotism, royal or mercantilist absolutism, and much else besides. I
have here instead stressed the contribution of Hobbes, simply
because I believe that his philosophy enunciates the theoretical
foundations of liberalism in the framework which has most
characteristically shaped its language since the turn of the nineteenth
century. It may appear strange that Hobbes – the pre-eminent
theorist of absolute sovereignty – should have played as crucial a
part in the conception of liberalism as Rousseau – the foremost
theorist of liberty – has played in its apparent betrayal; but it seems
to me that both figures, of whom neither was a liberal, have had a
decisive impact upon the course of its history, the one by way of
originally articulating its central ideas, the other by bearing its
severest censure.

As a political ideology liberalism is of course as absent from the periods in which Hobbes and Rousseau lived as it is alien to their writings. Not only did the words 'liberal' and 'liberalism' first appear in European political discourse around the beginning of the nineteenth century, but the peculiar terminology of liberal doctrines which we have come to inherit from von Humboldt, Constant, and later John Stuart Mill, as well as others, may be distinguished from earlier languages of liberty along just those lines that Hobbes had stipulated as uniquely correct. Hobbes's contention that the Greeks and Romans and their modern disciples had failed to address themselves to the liberty of particular men was recapitulated by liberal thinkers of the early nineteenth century in their focus upon the private liberty of individuals as against the allegedly false doctrine that freedom could be achieved through our shared subjection to the community. For Constant, no less than for Hobbes, this plain contrast marked the difference between what he termed 'ancient liberty' and 'modern liberty'. On his interpretation, any idea of collective liberty as realised through democracy, political legislation, or the institution of popular sovereignty, at least in the context of modern society, was a dangerous sham.[9]

Just such a confusion of real liberty with despotism was unearthed by Constant as an implication of Rousseau's thought, which in Constant's own lifetime had given rise to the worst excesses of Jacobin tyranny, upheld in the name of the people's freedom. It has today become fashionable to follow Jacob Talmon in attributing to Rousseau the first principles of totalitarian democracy,[10] but we too often forget that much the same charge had already been made against Rousseau in the course of the French Revolution, once the Jacobins had been deposed. Of course this imputed influence of Rousseau upon the Revolution by early liberals is hardly surprising, both in the light of the immense intellectual debt which the Jacobins and other revolutionaries professed to owe to him, and on account of the fact that for most major nineteenth-century thinkers – Hegel, Marx and Proudhon, for instance, as well as Constant – the authentic voice of Rousseau was actually that of Rousseauism, with his meaning thus in effect distilled from his interpreters' assessments of a revolution which, it was taken for granted, he had inspired.

This is not the place to pursue the details of that strange saga in the history of political theory and practice, and I shall not even attempt to disengage what I take to be Rousseau's meaning from his revolutionary influence, however much it should be stressed that he in fact recoiled from any actual revolution he anticipated, and claimed that the liberty of the whole of humanity could not justify shedding the blood of a single man.[11] My point here is rather to emphasise that the modern political doctrine of liberalism first took shape around the perceived judgement, confirmed by Jacobin despotism, that Rousseau had defined freedom wrongly.[12] The Revolution had shown that liberty and popular sovereignty could not go hand in hand. Thereafter, no defence of liberty other than in terms of the private life of unregulated individuals could be acknowledged as truly liberal. Rousseau has become the enemy of freedom just because the triumph of his ideas in practice was held to have destroyed the only form of liberty which liberals judge worthy of the name.

II

Such misconceptions have strayed from Rousseau's political doctrine almost as far as it is possible to go. Perhaps the most remarkable feature of the critique of his illiberalism has been its utter neglect of the central theme of all his writings – that is, his constant lament that while Nature has made us happy and good, in society we have made ourselves miserable and depraved. This continual refrain, this guiding principle which he tells us informed all his major works,[13] has been wholly ignored by those who have instead resolved on his behalf to fix his gaze upon a vision of mankind's liberated future which they then judge unsatisfactory. In his own lifetime and before the Revolution it was Rousseau's philosophy of history, his bitter attack upon the trappings of civilisation and culture, which at once excited most of his radical admirers and at the same time estranged him from both the *philosophes* and the religious and political establishments of his day. Only in the Revolution and afterwards did the attention of disciples and critics alike come to be focused instead upon his theory of our political redemption, in which our liberty might be achieved through membership of a sovereign assembly. The significance of this oversight by his detractors can scarcely be exaggerated, since the idea of liberty allied most closely to his principal doctrine is in fact not that which persons might somehow gain or regain in political life but rather the liberty they have lost in becoming subject to the laws.

In his *Discourse on the Arts and Sciences*, with which he effectively burst upon the literary world of the Enlightenment, Rousseau charged that civilisation had been the bane of humanity and that men in society had forsaken, as he put it, 'that original liberty for which they seem to have been born' (*OC*, III:7). It is this deprivation of the freedom for which we had been born that in Rousseau's philosophy marked our passage from nature to culture and our enslavement in the stultifying social world we had constructed. In his *Discourse on Inequality* he developed that proposition largely in terms of the subjugation of our freedom attributable to private property and all the morally pernicious institutions and forms of government built upon such a miserable base. Liberty, he exclaimed there, was an essential gift of Nature, which men possessed by virtue of their humanity alone (*OC*, III:184) – an attribute which thus could only be impaired and not fulfilled through our civil and political undertakings. In his *Essay on the Origin of Languages* he put forward much the same thesis in terms of the corruption of our speech that had occurred in the course of our social history, as modern languages, increasingly devoid of their original musical inflexion, had rendered those who spoke them progressively more passive, servile and unfree. These themes recur throughout Rousseau's works and lie very near the heart of most of them. However sharp was the contrast between his own account of the state of nature and that of Hobbes, he certainly agreed with Hobbes that our fundamental liberty was to be found there, and not under the political hegemony of any sovereign's rule.

As distinct from Hobbes, however, Rousseau is alleged by his liberal critics to have believed in an illusory form of freedom which was realised when men were bound by civil laws or 'artificial chains', as Hobbes described them. That illusion of freedom can indeed be found in Rousseau's doctrine, but only because it is explicit in his argument, in his claim that civil society was fabricated from it. In the course of our history, he contended, we have made ourselves slaves just because we have been credulous, running 'headlong into our chains', he remarked, 'supposing that we had ensured our freedom' (*Discours sur l'inégalité*, *OC*, III:177). How else could we have accepted the yoke of despotism but because it had been wrapped around us like a mantle of justice? In a passage of an essay entitled 'On the State of War', devoted largely to an attack upon what he termed 'the horrible system of Hobbes', Rousseau developed this theme most emphatically. 'I open books of law and morality', he wrote:

I listen to wise men and jurists and, moved by their penetrating
words, I deplore the miseries of nature, I admire the peace and
justice established by the civil order, I bless the wisdom of public
institutions and take comfort that I am a man in seeing myself a
citizen. Well instructed in my duties and my happiness, I shut the
book, leave the class, and what do I see outside? I see unfortunate
people trembling under an iron yoke, the whole of humanity
crushed by a handful of oppressors, a starving multitude racked
by pain and hunger, of whom the rich peacefully lap up the blood
and tears, and throughout the world nothing but the strong
holding sway over the weak, armed with the redoubtable strength
of the laws.   (*OC*, III:608–9, 610)

Such lines, so characteristic of Rousseau's conception of the liberty
we have lost, do not figure prominently in the canon of his
illiberalism. Yet, in his view, it was only because men thought their
artifical chains had made them free that these self-inflicted shackles
kept them in their place.

More than any other thinker before, and certainly more than any
liberal philosopher after him, Rousseau developed his account of
our illusory freedom across the whole spectrum of social and cultural
life. His conception of private property as the crucial institution
marking our long passage from the natural to the civil state of course
raised an economic dimension of striking significance in his political
thought, addressed as it was to the class origins of different
constitutions and the perpetual conflict, at least of interest, between
rich and poor. So strong was the link he perceived between
inequalities of wealth and deprivations of freedom (in effect between
poverty and slavery) that we might even with some justice ascribe to
Rousseau an economic theory of history, indeed a theory of
economic determinism, according to which our political systems
were shaped by forces of a still more fundamental kind.[14] But we
must bear in mind that even in his account of private property
Rousseau placed greatest emphasis upon the cunning eloquence of
those who claimed that right, and on the foolishness of persons so
readily beguiled. Rhetoric, persuasion and deception were as central
to his account of how we had ensnared ourselves as was the
institution of private property, established through the manipulation
and abuse of language. In a sense, language – the medium of our
conjugation – was for Rousseau the main instrument of our
subjugation as well, since from the linguistic base of our specification

of terms stemmed the moral emblems of our specialisation of roles, and ultimately the fixation of social man in an abstract world of his own making.

Rousseau's whole theory of culture, moreover, reinforces, elaborates and embellishes this conception of the illusory bonds under which political slavery masquerades as freedom. Our arts, letters and sciences, he remarked in his first *Discourse*, are but 'garlands of flowers round the iron chains by which men are weighed down' (*OC*, III:7). Contemporary theatre, he complained in his *Letter to d'Alembert*, not only made an adornment of the most terrible vices but also promoted and increased the inequality of fortunes, which is incompatible with the preservation of liberty.[15] Music, displaced from its springs of poetry and melody, he lamented in his *Essay on the Origin of Languages*, has become a collection of artificial scales and listless harmonies, echoed in speech by the prosaic rhetoric of mountebank kings and charlatan priests.[16] Just as in society we have come to be enmeshed within hierarchical moral relations, so in music we have become enthralled by the calculation of harmonic intervals, each measuring the loss of our independence under artificial chains more insidious than any imagined by Hobbes, each a proof of the strength of our illusions and the captivating power of the instruments of our captivity. When liberals decry Rousseau's commitment to an uplifting form of positive liberty that threatens our true freedom, they forget how profoundly negative was his philosophy of history, according to which our liberty had been lost already. Others might suppose that individuals gained their freedom as society developed and its arts and sciences were perfected. For Rousseau every stride in the apparent advance of civilisation had in reality been a step towards the decrepitude of our species and the alienation of our fundamental liberty (*Discours sur l'inégalité*, *OC*, III:171).

Of course, it must be remembered that his idea of natural liberty was in an important sense illusory as well, in so far as mankind never actually inhabited the innocent pristine state in which such liberty could be enjoyed. According to Rousseau's philosophy, in order to get at the truth it was often necessary to lay the facts aside, as he remarked himself, and even though we must not exaggerate this distinction, since he drew much of the evidence for his portrait of primitive man from the available historical record of our origins, it remains the case that the state of nature he conceived was a fiction. There could therefore be no point in our attempting to return to it, he noted in a long discussion on the subject in his *Discourse on Inequality* (n. 9, *OC*, III:202–8); there was no sense in our trying to recover the merely hypothetical freedom he had ascribed to mankind in that state. Critics, who believe that in his political doctrine Rousseau sought to re-establish the independence from one another which we had lost, rather neglect this feature of his thought, and they also overlook his repeated claims that in political society man's nature is transformed.[17] With duty substituted for instinct as our guide, Rousseau observed, our constitution is altered, and our lives are reshaped. Good social institutions do not fulfil human nature but instead *denature* man, depriving him of the wholeness of his physical existence in exchange for a moral existence that is relative and partial.[18] For these very reasons Rousseau's liberal critics have been wrong to locate his fundamental account of freedom in the state. The liberty that was most expressive of human nature in his philosophy could not be gained or restored in a new form under the institutions he described in the *Social Contract*. Nowhere did he map out a programme for the political redemption of our freedom, made progressively more remote from our grasp as civilisation and society advanced relentlessly towards our subjection.

Indeed, it is almost everywhere else apart from in his political writings that we find Rousseau longing for and attempting to preserve that fragile independence of the human spirit that in the modern world was at least akin to natural liberty. A passionate desire to find freedom informed his botanical communion with Nature in his later years, when the company of other men had become so burdensome to him. Earlier it had inspired his disenchantment with much of the Enlightenment establishment, from whose dark and oppressive influence he had sought refuge in his escape from Paris. Rousseau's uncompromising (if eventually unsuccessful) determination to refuse the pensions that were offered to him, his contempt for urban artifice and culture and his love of the open sky outside the closed city – indeed, the whole of his life, and most of its crises – were inspired by the profoundest expression of the human craving for freedom recorded in Western literature. It is true that many of his works were also emblazoned with the signature 'Citizen of Geneva', and I shall presently return to this proclamation and to its place in his account of liberty. But let us not forget that Rousseau's republican identity was of briefer duration, and brought him less untramelled joy, than this essentially solitary dreamer's life-long rapture in ecstatic love of Nature. 'I was never really fit for civil society', he wrote with weary resignation in his *Reveries*, his last major work.

> My natural independence always left me incapable of the thraldom necessary for anyone who wishes to live among men . . . As soon as I feel the yoke, either of necessity or of men . . . I am nothing . . . I had never thought that the liberty of man consists in doing what he wishes, but rather in not doing that which he does not wish. (*Les Rêveries du promeneur solitaire*, Sixième promenade, *OC*, I:1059)

Critics who find Rousseau so hostile to real freedom are too inattentive to these features of his life and thought. And yet they herald much of the spirit of a dawning age of Romanticism, from which modern liberals have in fact borrowed more of their vocabulary of personal negative liberty than they nowadays admit, even while contrasting its language with that pernicious conception of liberty they instead impute to him.

If there is one work which more than any other expresses Rousseau's fullest account of negative liberty, it must surely be *Emile*. 'The first of all goods', Rousseau remarked there, 'is not authority but freedom' (*Emile*, Livre II [*OC*, IV:309]). It is in vain that we seek to find liberty associated with the laws, he continued, since 'liberty does not exist under any form of government [but] only in the heart of the free man' (Livre v [*OC*, IV:857]). The whole purpose of the tutor's education of the child in that text was to subvert and retard, as far as possible, the development of those relations of mutual dependence which in society have rendered us unfree, for such reasons as Rousseau had already explained in his *Discourse on Inequality*. 'There are two kinds of dependence', he now argued, in one of the work's more celebrated passages,

> Dependence on things, which is natural, [and] that on men, which is due to society. Dependence on things, having no morality, does no harm to liberty and engenders no vices. Dependence on men, being disordered, engenders them all, and it is because of them that master and slave mutually deprave one another. . . . Keep the child in dependence on things alone; you will have followed the order of nature in the course of its education.[19]

The child, born free like savage man, must be protected from the

social bonds that ineluctably debase the savage's nature and destroy
his freedom. Unlike our primitive forebears, who were enticed to
plunge headlong into their chains, Emile is encouraged to improve
his robust faculties spontaneously and without the contamination of
others, until he has gained sufficient strength, with the late
blossoming of his reason, to confront the tribulations of life in
society. If the *Social Contract* recounts the terms required for savage
man's political metamorphosis into a citizen, *Emile* offers instead an
education according to nature, in which the original passions and
attributes of the child – not least its sexuality – are brought to
fruition, each in his good time. To control their nature, as citizens
are required to do, is to reform the work of God, to undo, as
Rousseau put it in *Emile*, what God had inscribed at the bottom of
each person's heart (Livre iv [*OC*, iv:491]). The fundamental task of
Emile's tutor, then, is to avert society's reformation of God's work.
He must, wrote Rousseau, provide his pupil with an education that
is at first 'purely negative' (Livre ii [*OC*, iv:323]), rather along the
isolationist lines of Defoe's *Robinson Crusoe* than the consolidating
paths of Plato's *Republic*.[20]

Critics[21] have of course not been slow to observe that in undoing
the oppressive handiwork of society, Emile's tutor often appears to
exercise God's powers himself, and there are certainly some
extraordinary passages in the text in which Rousseau speaks of the
subjection of Emile to his tutor, in that while acting under the belief
that he is master of his will, he yet finds that all his wishes coincide
with those of his tutor on his behalf.[22] How the tutor's manipulation
of Emile's world establishes his dependence upon things and not
upon man is a problem to which I believe Rousseau provides an
inadequate answer. But if we are persuaded that herein lies the
seeds of his programme of totalitarian indoctrination, we might
pause for a moment to consider how inept must be a social system
built upon that programme, according to which each child must be
kept away from all others by a single tutor who devotes much of his
own life to the task, only to find, in due course, that his charge is
unfit for both political and domestic responsibilities, and, following
the infidelity of his wife, becomes a vagabond, and then a slave to
pirates, perhaps even ending his days on a desert island.[23]
Notwithstanding all the numerous claims about Rousseau's insidious
influence, *Emile* hardly offers the stuff of which Hitler might have
been a proud follower.

In their neglect of his philosophy of history, perhaps the most striking of his critics' omissions is the very definition of our fundamental liberty which Rousseau put forward. For the freedom we had suppressed, he believed, was no uplifting principle of public virtue but only a faint distinction between savage man and beast. All other creatures, he remarked in the *Discourse on Inequality*, behaved as their instincts impelled them to do, while we alone, even in our original state, must have been the authors of our actions, as we came to terms with each situation in a manner free from Nature's control. It was therefore because we lacked a set of prescribed responses to our natural drives rather than because we were endowed with any positive traits unique to our species that, according to Rousseau, we must always have enjoyed a prospect of development – in due course out of the state of nature and into another of our own making – which animals did not share.[24]

This idea of liberty as a merely inchoate trait distinguishing man from beast is perhaps the most remarkably negative conception of freedom in Western social and political thought.[25] In Rousseau's philosophy it was linked to no substantive goal or desirable end of any sort, being without a determinant moral content such as critics have judged to be the principal illiberal characteristic of his doctrine in general. Quite the contrary, Rousseau's conception of our natural liberty was at least partly designed to show how other accounts of freedom were inadequate just because they were not negative enough, a thesis which he developed above all, once again, in reply to Hobbes, whose reflections on this subject he found wanting for two reasons.

First, Hobbes had failed to grasp the fact, so central to our plight, as Rousseau understood it, that men may render themselves subject to internal impediments, which, in their operation upon the human spirit, were no less a constraint upon their freedom than shackles round their wrists or threats to box their ears. Any suggestion that we might be or become slaves to our passions was as absurd for Hobbes as the correlative idea of a disembodied freedom of the will, but freedom of the will and the absence of human slavery to innate passions were for Rousseau crucial to that otherwise scarcely perceptible *differentia* between man and beast. If we were not at least capable of being the agents of what we did, if it was only our appetites and aversions that moved us, then our lives were just a succession of events that happened to us, lacking all merit, vice or perfectibility, with each member of our species trapped in the same changeless world as all the others. Without free will, he supposed, both morality and human history were impossible. In his opposition to Hobbes on this point, Rousseau's view that our distinctive qualities were not wholly explicable with reference to natural causes or impulsions comes to much the same verdict as Isaiah Berlin's contention in 'Historical Inevitability' that if determinism were true then we would not be free to act in a morally responsible way.[26] No less than for Berlin in his understanding of moral agency, for Rousseau the language of free will lay at the heart of our ordinary perception of social relations – with this difference, of course, that according to Rousseau our history bore witness to our becoming slaves to new passions, that is, to the fundamental and ever worsening abuse of our liberty, rather than, as for Berlin, to diverse cases of its exercise for better or worse.

Less controversial, perhaps, is what I take to be Rousseau's second reason for regarding Hobbes's conception of liberty as insufficiently negative, and this was that Hobbes had drawn too complex a picture of human nature in support of his belief that the freedom of each person was imperilled by that of all his neighbours. In ascribing certain socially developed characteristics of our lives, such as the pursuit of power and glory, to humanity in general, Hobbes had wrongly supposed that masterless men were naturally in need of a commonwealth for protection. This is to say that he found fault with human nature mainly because, in Rousseau's terminology, he mistook *amour propre* for *amour de soi*, imagining that we cared for ourselves at the expense of others rather than without regard to them. Much the same error, moreover, was held by Rousseau to be a common failing of most philosophies of natural law and the social contract, including those of Grotius, Locke and Pufendorf, who attributed rather more benign qualities or principles, such as a sense of justice or a right of property, to mankind in the state of nature. All such thinkers had failed to strip away our social traits from their postulates about the essence of the human race as a whole; according to Rousseau, they had confused our acquired attributes with what was fundamental to our constitution.

Yet in their focus upon his unduly collectivist conception of liberty, critics of Rousseau's illiberalism (I must stress once more) forget that he claimed time and again that it was just because we had already made ourselves social that we had forsaken our freedom. While savage man lives within himself, Rousseau remarked, 'sociable man, always outside himself, only knows how to live in the opinions of others'.[27] Our natural integrity, and with it our freedom from one another, had been lost just because we had come to value ourselves in the light of qualities we imagined that others judged worthy of esteem. Rousseau agreed with Hobbes that the natural life of man must have been solitary, but it could only have become poor, nasty, brutish and short when subject to the fears and aspirations of a social world we did not at first inhabit. The more negative our approach to an understanding of human nature, the less negative, or at any rate, the less defective, appears the state of nature we uncover.

As is well known, Rousseau believed that civil society must originally have been founded when men, already socialised by vice, attempted to obtain Locke's political warrant for the morally pernicious institution of private property, which in turn must have occasioned Hobbes's vile state of war, fought over the distribution of property. Rather like the debauched protagonists of the Marquis de Sade's *The New Justine*, the so-called natural men portrayed first by Locke and then Hobbes might well have said of themselves, 'No sooner did we commit a horror than we sought to legitimate it'.[28] These two thinkers and others had inadvertently drawn an accurate picture of the state of civil society, supposing it to be a description of the state of nature, for the vices in need of remedy which they depicted were not those of our original constitution but rather those that stemmed from the very social systems they commended to us. According to Rousseau, in short, Hobbes and Locke had conceived their ideas as solutions to some problems of which those solutions were in fact the cause.[29]

Liberal thinkers since the end of the eighteenth century have largely inherited Hobbes's and Locke's concern with inviolable frontiers, safeguards and barriers between persons; but that is because their philosophies continue to be imbued with many of the assumptions about our essential motives, fears and desires that Rousseau believed his social contract precursors had confused for natural traits. To that extent their views of human nature are overburdened with the weight of attributes they believe universally characteristic of mankind; and, tied to these encumbrances, they stand apart from Rousseau's emptier, more formal, more strictly negative conception of our distinguishing behavioural traits – unique only because, in his view, they are uncontrolled by instincts. Paradoxically, again, it is at least some of the doctrines of negative liberty so often contrasted with his allegedly positive idea which in contemporary political thought constitute the prevailing forms of

78   *Rousseau's Two Concepts of Liberty*

'the retreat to the inner citadel', as Berlin has termed it. In the light
of the argument Rousseau himself presents, we could only retreat to
citadels we had already taken the trouble to construct, and we were
only prompted to seek sanctuary there because we had contrived to
make enemies outside.

                                    III

I suspect that few of these comments about Rousseau's conception
of negative liberty will be thought pertinent by those who deplore
his philosophy of illiberalism and who may be impatient for me to
get to the real point, which is the place of liberty in his specifically
political doctrine. It might at first appear that his prescriptive
writings must be ill-suited to a philosophy of history which charts the
course of human corruption, or at least that his vision of our
transformation into free citizens can have little in common with his
account of our lost natural liberty. Yet Rousseau's political writings
are of crucial significance to his reflections on the human condition
in general, inspired as they all are by the proposition he enunciated
in his *Confessions* and elsewhere, that everything depends ultimately
upon politics and that the character of a people is invariably shaped
by its government.[30] That claim about the central determinant of the
ways we live underlies Rousseau's account of virtue as well as of
vice, and it is scarcely possible for an interpretation of his ethics to
stray far from it. Just the same, it is important that we recognise the
fact that so many themes of Rousseau's political theory of freedom
have a more settled place in the familiar galaxy of great doctrines
than do his philosophies of nature and history.

I have already noted the marked differences between Rousseau's
programme of natural education in *Emile* and Plato's scheme of
public instruction in the *Republic*; and yet perhaps no work by a
major modern political theorist more closely follows the *Republic*
than Rousseau's *Considerations on the Government of Poland*. Here
Rousseau speaks of the solitary individual as nothing, and of the
love of his country as forming the whole existence of the citizen
(*OC*, iii:966). How is it possible, asked Rousseau, to stir the hearts
of a free people and to make them love their fatherland and its
laws? 'Dare I say it?', he replied. 'Through children's games' (*OC*,
iii:955): through a national system of public education, appropriate
only to free men, binding them to a common existence under the

law.[31] I doubt if any other text of Rousseau, moreover, bears the imprint of Machiavelli's influence more conspicuously than does his *Discourse on Political Economy*. 'The fatherland cannot exist without liberty', he wrote there, 'nor liberty without virtue, nor virtue without citizens'.

> Without them you will have nothing but degraded slaves, beginning with the rulers of the state . . . If men could be accustomed early to regard their individuality . . . just as a part of the state, they could at length come to identify themselves . . . with this greater whole, to feel themselves members of the country, and to love it with that exquisite feeling which men in isolation have only for themselves. (*OC*, iii:259)

It would be difficult, furthermore, to find in any pre-eminent political treatise an idea of liberty more conspicuously indebted to that of Montesquieu than this passage from Rousseau's *Social Contract*: 'Liberty', Rousseau remarked, 'is not the fruit of all climates, nor within the grasp of all peoples.' The difference between free states and monarchies lies in the fact that in the one all are devoted to the common good, while in the other subjects are made miserable in order for despotism to reign (iii, viii [*OC*, iii:414, 415]). In each of these statements, and many others like them, Rousseau appears to have set aside what Hobbes termed the liberty of particular men and to have addressed himself instead to the liberty of the commonwealth as a whole. But while his concern with citizenship, obedience to the laws, and the public domain in general shows how he identified freedom differently from most liberals, these features of his doctrine nevertheless stand him in good company among many illustrious predecessors of other persuasions. They form a part, but not a peculiarly original part, of the tradition of positive liberty which liberals decry.

Of course Rousseau seems sometimes to have invited special criticism for his pains, when, as for instance in the *Social Contract* once more, he contrasted lowly natural liberty with ennobling civil and moral liberty: the one now identified, in apparent contradiction with the *Discourse on Inequality*, as mere slavery to one's passions; the others as intelligent self-mastery, limited by the general will.[32] 'People have vainly attempted to confuse liberty with independence', he added in his *Letters from the Mountain*, but

> These two things are so different that they exclude one another.
> When everyone does what he pleases he often does what displeases
> others, and that cannot be called a free state . . . In the common
> liberty no one has the right to do what the liberty of
> another forbids him . . . Liberty without justice is a veritable
> contradiction.   (Huitième Lettre, *OC*, III:841–2)

Passages such as these have prompted Rousseau's liberal critics to
observe that his political philosophy betrays the faith in freedom he
so disingenuously proclaimed. Lester Crocker, the most distinguished,
learned and prolific of Rousseau's modern detractors has no doubt
that real liberty is 'swallowed up' by his 'collective monolith', the
'all-devouring general will'. Throughout his writings, suggests
Crocker, we find Rousseau promoting the 'destruction of privacy'
under systems of 'control and manipulation'.[33] In his doctrine of civil
and moral liberty, therefore, according to which men are denatured
and *made* free, lies the germ of what is perceived by liberals to be
the repressive rule of totalitarian politics. But what is it about that
doctrine which distinguishes Rousseau from other collectivists, so
that only he incurs such wrath?

I have already suggested that the main reason for this has to do
with his assimilation of liberty to popular sovereignty, a link
discredited in both theory and practice under the Jacobin dictatorship
of the French Revolution. That point bears re-emphasis, and its
significance requires further attention, since the conjunction of
liberty with sovereignty forms an original theme in his writings
(indeed, a major innovation in the history of political thought)
which sets Rousseau apart even from Plato, Machiavelli, Montesquieu
and others, who like him were concerned with political and not just
personal liberty. Prior to its use in his philosophy, the concept of
sovereignty had been connected by its interpreters with the idea of
force, power or empire, and it generally pertained to the dominion
of kings or other governors over their subjects rather than to
citizens' freedom. For both Bodin and – yet again – Hobbes, in
particular (the best-known advocates of absolute sovereignty before
Rousseau) the terms 'souveraineté' or 'sovereignty' were derived
from the Latin *summam potestatem* or *summum imperium*, which
defined the prevailing, that is to say, unequalled, power of the ruler.
For Rousseau, by contrast, the idea of sovereignty was essentially a
principle of equality, which identified the ruled element, or the
subjects themselves, as the supreme authority, and it was connected

with the concepts of will or right rather than force or power: it expressed 'le moral' of politics and not 'le physique', a most fundamental distinction in his philosophy, on which I shall comment presently. But I believe it is just because of his innovative association of an altogether unlikely pair of terms –'liberty', as drawn from an ancient republican tradition with emphasis on self-rule, and 'sovereignty', from a modern absolutist ideology addressed to the need for predominating power – which prompts liberal critics to judge his doctrine to be more sinister than any other collectivist conception of freedom. How can absolute force and perfect liberty possibly go hand in hand? To be 'forced to be free', to achieve one's liberty under the constraint of the whole body politic, as Rousseau stipulated in one of the most famous passages of the *Social Contract* (I, Ch. vii [*OC*, III:364]), seems the vilest deception imaginable from a man pretending to be liberty's truest friend. Small wonder, then, that Rousseau perceived as so splendid and just the inscription of the word '*Libertas*' on the prisons and fetters of the galleys of the city of Genoa. 'It is only evil-doers of all states', he observed in a footnote of his *Social Contract* (IV, ii [*OC*, IV:440]), 'who prevent the citizen from being free. In a country where all such men were in the galleys, one would enjoy the most perfect liberty.' As Hobbes had already remarked, 'It is an easy thing, for men to be deceived, by the specious name of liberty' (*Leviathan*, XXI, p. 140), evidenced, in his case, by the meaningless inscription of the word '*Libertas*' on the turrets of the city of Lucca.

Against this hostile construction of Rousseau's doctrine, many of his sympathetic readers have in recent years adopted a point of view, best developed by Robert Derathé, to the effect that the absolute power he attributed to the sovereign was none the less circumscribed by natural law. Several notable passages in his writings confirm that he did indeed conceive the sovereign to be subject to a higher moral principle;[34] but it is not clear how Rousseau's invocation of natural law was designed to protect the freedom of individuals from absolute rule, and, as Maurice Cranston has noted,[35] there seems to be no hint of this constraint in the *Social Contract* itself, whose account of popular sovereignty has been the focus of most objections to his political thought.

What his liberal critics have all too commonly failed to grasp, in my view, is not so much an overriding theory of natural law but rather the very concept of absolute sovereignty they deem a threat to the exercise of our real freedom. For Rousseau defined popular sovereignty in such a way as to exclude precisely the infliction of that harm to persons which his theory is alleged to justify. The absolute authority of the sovereign, he wrote, must both come from all and apply to all (*Contrat social*, ii, iv [*OC*, iii:373]). The voice of the general will which it enacts cannot pronounce on individuals without forfeiting its own legitimacy, since it articulates in laws the common interest of every citizen, whereas the exercise of force over disparate persons is reserved exclusively for a nation's government. Rousseau's sovereign never implements its own laws and never punishes transgressors against it (see the *Contrat social*, ii, v and iii, i [*OC*, iii:377 and 397]) nor indeed forces anyone to be free. In a richly perceptive reading of the remark about enforced freedom, John Plamenatz has suggested that it is inspired by Rousseau's understanding of how men come to discipline themselves and feel at once thwarted and liberated in their performance of duty.[36] Yet even if we allow that Rousseau actually speaks of the force over a person which may be exercised on behalf of the whole body politic and not just a compulsion an individual places over himself, it still does not follow that this force is wielded on command of the sovereign.

More than any other major political theorist before or after him Rousseau distinguished 'right' from 'power', the formulation of principle from its application (in this context the moral will which determines laws from the physical force that implements them) by placing each in different hands, here respectively, the legislative power and the executive power. I shall return to that theme about moral will and physical force, and to its overall bearing on Rousseau's conception of liberty, in my final section; but it is worth stressing just now how much we owe our appreciation of the fundamental contrast between force and freedom in human affairs to the writings of Rousseau himself, and not just to Hobbes and liberal thinkers. As well as because of the fact that sovereignty and liberty had been generally opposed by earlier commentators, it is also because Rousseau so sharply discriminated force from freedom on most occasions, that the conjunction of these terms in the *Social Contract* seems odd. In a later passage of the same text he even added that 'it is only the force of the state which ensures the liberty of its members' (*Contrat social*, ii, xii [*OC*, iii:394]). But critics wholly misread Rousseau's meaning in those passages – indeed, they ignore what he says – when they ascribe to him the view that the punishment we suffer for flouting the law renders us truly free. For such force as governments exercise against recalcitrants, Rousseau contended, was designed to protect them from personal dependence (which invariably *does* deprive them of their freedom), and to legitimate their own civil undertakings, without which the social contract would otherwise be 'absurd, tyrannical and liable to the gravest abuse' (i, vii [*OC*, iii:364]). Rousseau believed that according to the terms of their association, all subjects undertook to obey the laws and that without exception all were then required to take part in the laws' formulation as members of their state's sovereign assembly. His point about force and freedom means scarcely more than that citizens must always be bound by their own agreements, even if they are occasionally inclined to break or overlook them. No force is exercised except over persons who have reneged on their decision to abide by laws they enact themselves, and no force is exercised at all by the sovereign.

The tyrannical abuse of powers which liberal critics impute to Rousseau's sovereign was actually perceived by him to be a misappropriation of the powers of government, against which the absolute sovereignty of citizens was the only real safeguard. In their periodic election of parliamentary representatives the people of England perversely entrusted their legislative authority to what should have been merely an executive power, and thereby showed themselves unfit for the liberty it was their duty to exercise directly themselves (see the *Contrat social*, iii, xv [*OC*, iii:430]). In Geneva, somewhat differently, the executive power (effectively the Petit Conseil) had made itself progressively more dominant by arrogating responsibilities that properly belonged to the assembly of citizens (the Conseil Général), even obstructing that sovereign body from meeting. With the executive force of Rousseau's native state substituted for its popular will, absolute right was corrupted into unfettered power.[37] 'Where force alone reigns', Rousseau remarked in his *Letters from the Mountain*, 'the state is dissolved. That . . . is how all democratic states finally perish' (Septième Lettre, *OC*, iii:815).

Having regard to such claims it is worth bearing in mind that Rousseau's conception of civil liberty in the *Social Contract* was drawn as much from an idealised model of Geneva as from Spartan and Roman sources, and that his political self-identification as 'Citizen of Geneva' thus referred to a republic whose constitutional liberties, in his view, had already been undermined. The modern citizens of Geneva, no less than our primitive forebears portrayed in the *Discourse on Inequality*, had been deprived of their liberty, but in the case of his compatriots that was because they had allowed their sovereign will to be stilled and the executive power of government to rise up despotically in its stead.[38] Paradoxically, it appears, Rousseau's conception of an absolute sovereign ensured civil liberty not so much by virtue of an overarching natural law as on account of an infrastructural separation of powers. Once again, Hobbes, for whom absolute sovereignty entailed the undivided concentration of all powers, appears in this matter as his foremost adversary. Rousseau, no less than Locke, was determined that governments must not exercise 'force beyond right'. Unlike Locke, however, he found protection from such despotism only in a vigilant sovereign of the whole people. Liberty was thus made secure, in his view, by the very institution which, his liberal critics have since alleged, can only destroy it. So long as the general will of a community remained general, citizens kept their freedom under the rule of its laws.

I take this novel association of the ideas of sovereignty and freedom to have informed the meaning of what Rousseau termed 'civil liberty'; but it must be remembered that the *Social Contract* also introduces a second positive concept of freedom, which Rousseau called 'moral liberty', or 'obedience to the law we prescribed to ourselves' (I, viii [*OC*, III:365]). Defined in that way, the concept seems to mean little more than the ancient Greek notion of autonomy, although in Rousseau's nomenclature, especially in its affinities with his idea of the general will, it has distinctive connotations somewhat different from the sense of autonomy as political self-rule or independence. Both in his definition of moral liberty and in his novel use of the expression 'general will', Rousseau articulated classical principles of freedom in a modern vocabulary which may, at first glance, seem as alien to those principles as his invocation of ancient liberty in justification of modern sovereignty. Indeed, some of Rousseau's most striking images derive their force from just such attempts to illuminate the values of old cultures in a new language commonly thought to have dispensed with them, and much may be learnt about his meaning if we regard him, to use his own words (although not about himself) as one of those 'moderns who had an ancient soul'.[39]

A distinctive feature of his concept of moral liberty is its peculiarly reflexive element of self-prescription. For Rousseau, every morally free agent was required to determine the rules that would guide him by looking inward into the depths of his own conscience in a self-reliant manner, free from the influence of all other persons. The most absolute authority, he observed in his *Discourse on Political Economy* (*OC*, III:251), 'is that which penetrates into man's innermost being', incorporating him in the common identity of the state, as he put it in the *Social Contract* (I, vi [*OC*, III:361]). Liberal critics recoil in horror from these claims, in so far as they take them to imply the complete submergence of our separate wills under the collective (even organic) will of the body politic which envelops and moulds us. Yet what Rousseau meant by his conjunction of moral liberty with the general will has no such significance, and it was designed to avert rather than achieve the social indoctrination of individuals. Not only did he insist upon the fact that a nation's general will could only be realised through opposition to the particular wills of each of its members, with the constant tension between two kinds of will or interest – instead of the suppression of one by the other – indispensable to the achievement of the common good (see the *Contrat social*, II, iii, note [*OC*, III:371]). He also stressed that the same opposition was present in the minds of all citizens, so that every person was motivated by both a particular will and a general will, dividing his judgement of what was beneficial to himself from what was right for the community (see the *Contrat social*, I, vii [*OC*, III:363]). Especially in the modern world, Rousseau believed, our general will was much weaker than our particular will, and it was to be strengthened and animated not by our imbibing the collective opinions of our neighbours in a public assembly, but just the reverse – by all men expressing their own opinions alone, 'having no communication amongst themselves', which might render their separate judgements partial to this or that group interest (II, iii [*OC*, III:371]). To ensure that in the assembly there were as many votes as individuals, every member must act without regard to the rest, consulting his own general will as a citizen, thereby still obeying himself alone. Our personal identity was only lost when in legislation we echoed the opinions of an unreflective, undiscriminating multitude. For Rousseau, the more perfect our independence from others (the more profoundly we turned into ourselves for guidance) the more likely were our deliberations to yield the common good.

In the social contract state which he envisaged, deep introspection was therefore the corollary of the outward pursuit of that common good or public interest. The idea of 'will', in this context, as has been noted before, expresses the voluntarist, contractarian strain of

86   *Rousseau's Two Concepts of Liberty*

modern political thought, whereas what is general encapsulates the ancient idea of a public good towards which each person's will should be aimed. It follows that according to Rousseau's philosophy, in order to be a citizen of a *res publica* one must look deep within oneself for a personal commitment to a collective goal. Of course, in promoting the general will, it is our dedication to the shared good of all which renders our moral liberty, as he conceived it, so much grander and more noble than the natural freedom he claimed men forfeit when they enter into civil society. But that belief in an uplifting form of liberty, so often decried by his liberal critics, requires for its fulfilment no great leap forward into the modern world of Hitler and Broadmoor. It is, yet again, an expression of the ancient idea of liberty that Hobbes and Constant, in their different ways, found unacceptable by contrast with the modern concept of personal freedom.

We have only to turn to Rousseau's *Considerations on the Government of Poland* to note how passionate was his commitment to ancient political liberty as against this alternative, individualist notion. In a chapter of that work entitled 'The Spirit of Ancient Institutions' Rousseau grieved over the civil and moral liberty we had lost in passing from antiquity into the modern world, much as in other contexts he lamented our forsaken natural liberty, destroyed in the abandonment of our primeval state. 'Modern men', he wrote, 'no longer find in themselves any of that spiritual vigour which inspired the ancients in everything that they did' (*OC*, III:959).[40] Ancient legislators sought to forge links that would attach citizens to their fatherland and to one another, in religious ceremonies, games and spectacles. The laws that rule modern men, by contrast, are solely designed to teach them to obey their masters (see *OC*, III:958). In his *Letter to d'Alembert* on the theatre he pursued a similar theme (p. 137), complaining that we have lost all the strength of the men of antiquity. In Sparta, especially, the citizens, in continual assembly, consecrated the whole of their lives to amusements which were great matters of state (p. 179). Why should it not be so in modern republics as well?, he exclaimed, above all in Geneva, where the people ought to be 'forever united' through festivals held 'in the open air, under the sky' (p. 168). Yet what do we find instead? 'Private meetings [*les tête-à-tête*] . . . taking the place of public assemblies', the people hiding themselves, as if guilty of a vice that they dare not reveal except in shadows (pp. 172–3). It thus appears that for Rousseau ancient liberty had been lost, largely because of its displacement from the public arena into the world of private affairs. Where today, he asked, is 'the concord of citizens'? 'Where is public fraternity? . . . Where is peace, liberty, equity, innocence?' (pp. 178–9). The term 'fraternity' cited here in conjunction with liberty does not figure often in Rousseau's works, however much its meaning seems so obviously infused in his conception of the general will and indeed resonates throughout his political writings as a whole. But it is employed as well, once again, in his *Considerations on the Government of Poland*, where he proclaimed the need for Polish youth to become accustomed to 'equality' and 'fraternity', 'living under the eyes of their compatriots, seeking public approbation' (*OC*, iii:968).

By so linking the ideas of liberty, equality and fraternity, Rousseau – in this as in so much else – heralded an incoming French Revolution with his gaze fixed upon a bygone ancient world. Without equality, he observed in the *Social Contract*, 'freedom cannot subsist', for between the estate of the rich man and the beggar, public liberty is always traded; the one buys, and the other sells. 'Each is equally fatal to the common good' (ii, xi [*OC*, iii:391–2]). For that common good to be promoted, he added in his *Project for a Constitution for Corsica*, it was necessary that 'no one should enrich himself' (*OC*, iii:924). In the feast of the grape pickers which he portrayed in his *New Eloise*, moreover, all three principles were drawn together. 'Everyone lives under the most intimate familiarity', he wrote; 'all the world is equal' (*La Nouvelle Héloïse*, Cinquième Partie, lettre vii [*OC*, ii:607]). At dinner each gaily joins with all the rest, in 'sweet equality' but without luxury, in the enjoyment of liberty limited only by perfect candour (pp 608–9). The exultant feast in which all partake freely, equally and fraternally was of course purely imaginary; and no doubt similarly fanciful was Rousseau's belief that it reflected (indeed surpassed in joy) the saturnalian banquets of the ancient Romans (see p. 608). But there is no doubting the fact that the concept of liberty which Rousseau's image evokes is altogether different from the ideas of personal liberty set forth by Hobbes and Constant. For in the modern world, as he perceived it, liberty had come to be shorn of its associations with equality and fraternity. Rousseau complained in his *Essay on the Origin of Languages* that whereas our ancestors had once sung 'Aimez-moi' and cried out 'Aidez-moi' to one another, we now only mutter 'Donnez de l'argent' (see the *Essai sur l'origine des langues*, Chs. x and xx, pp. 131 and 197–9). The same expression, repeated in the *Social Contract*, is described there as the harbinger of a society in chains, ruled by the slavish institution of finance, unknown to the men of antiquity.[41] We moderns have been transformed into mute auditors of declamations from the pulpit and proclamations from the throne, our collective voice stilled. While once our interests were openly shared and inscribed in our hearts, now they are in conflict, secreted away in the linings of our purses. Have we forgotten that once we aspire to serve the state with our purses rather than our person, it is on the edge of ruin? Have we forgotten that 'in a well-ordered city everyone flies to the assemblies'? (*Contrat social*, III, xv [*OC*, III:428–9]). Modern liberty, stripped of fraternity, on the one side, and equality, on the other, stands exposed as nothing more than private gain. But so far from it embracing the only proper use of the term 'liberty', the contemporary ethos of private gain was for Rousseau just ancient slavery in a modern form, all the more psychologically insidious for our pursuing it as if it were real freedom. Turned inward on himself and outward against his neighbours, modern man in fact, like primeval man in fiction, had run headlong into chains which he supposed had made him free.

IV

If natural liberty may be regarded as Rousseau's negative idea of freedom, and civil and moral liberty his positive idea, how are these two concepts related? Why did he employ the same term to embrace our personal liberty, on the one hand, and our political liberty, on the other, particularly since he considered the two notions mutually exclusive? To that extent, of course, he would actually have agreed with Hobbes and Constant that different ideas have been implied by a single word, although unlike them he judged both uses correct and still appropriate, each in its proper place. His reason for invoking one expression in two distinct ways, I think, is quite simply that he found them to share at least a certain range of meanings, in the light of which their differences may be seen to be in direct opposition and conflict.

For one thing, each concept meant for Rousseau the absence of personal dependence or domination. When he remarked, for instance, in his *Project for a Constitution for Corsica*, that 'Whoever depends upon others . . . could not be free' (*OC*, III:903), he ascribed to that term a sense which embraced both his negative and positive concepts, since our lack of subjection, either to the will of other individuals, or to our own passions in society, was a central feature of each perspective. So too is his claim, with regard to both concepts, that poverty enslaves us. Our passage from antiquity into modernity, no less than from the state of nature into society, had each been marked by our loss of independence, on account of the unequal distribution of private property that made both rich and poor beholden to one another. Most important of all, perhaps – though it is least often noticed – is the fact that both concepts were for Rousseau indeterminate in their exercise and undirected towards any particular goal. There could be no proper aim of human endeavour that was prescribed in advance with regard to either our natural freedom or our civil and moral liberty. However perfectible men might be, he supposed in his *Discourse on Inequality*, as free agents they had done almost everything possible to make themselves worse than animals. Whatever equality was indispensable to the freedom he proclaimed in the *Social Contract*, moreover, he set out no socialist programme to achieve it, for that would have merely shifted responsibility for our subjection from the rich to the state, thereby bringing the principle of equality into conflict with that of liberty. According to his social doctrine, the abolition of slavery did not entail the abolition of property as well. Liberal critics who complain of the totalitarian nature of Rousseau's absolute sovereign ignore the fact that he prescribed no policies that the sovereign must promote, nor could he have done so, except by legislating what he supposed to be right on behalf of the people, thus again depriving them of their freedom of choice.

These and other similarities between Rousseau's two concepts of liberty are not insignificant, and a proper elaboration of their place in his philosophy might well require a whole essay in itself. I concentrate here upon the differences, however, for two reasons: firstly, because I believe that for Rousseau they were of greater importance than the common frame of reference which warranted his use of the same term 'liberty' in both cases; and, secondly, because my principal aim throughout has been to elucidate those distinctions against the background of liberal critiques of his doctrine and the charge that neither of the two concepts of liberty he employed (if, that is, their difference was even noted) really mean what we understand by freedom. For Rousseau, there were indeed two concepts, and not one. In their failure to recognise this fact, Hobbes and his followers have stipulated a unique alternative definition, but only – it would appear in the light of his doctrine – by abusing its meaning and impoverishing our political discourse.

How could this be so? Let me attempt to explain it. Until recently, it was fashionable in the history of philosophy (albeit quite wrong) to contrast seventeenth-century and eighteenth-century British empiricism with Continental rationalism in the same period. For those who find it useful to take stock of particular doctrines in bulk, I would suggest that a dichotomy between British monism, stemming mainly from Hobbes and Hume, as opposed to Continental dualism, embracing above all Descartes and Kant, might be a slightly more apt wholesale description of the most pertinent difference between two great traditions of thought in and around the Enlightenment. With regard to the concept of liberty, it is at any rate odd that by and large each of the major Continental European languages possesses one term, to which many native philosophers have ascribed two contrary meanings, whereas in English we have two terms, which our leading philosophers have deemed must share the same sense.[42] In most European languages, that is, the idea of liberty has been derived lexically from either the Latin *'liber'* or the Germanic *'fréo'*, whereas in English, with our common inheritance, we employ the terms liberty and freedom more or less interchangeably. It is true that there are certain locutions and contexts in which this is not the case, but these give rise to no profound philosophical differences, and throughout my remarks here I have used both words as if each did indeed serve equally as a translation of Rousseau's term *'liberté'*. Yet notwithstanding the stipulations of Hobbes, *'liberté'*, *'Freiheit'* and their cognates have throughout their etymological history been employed by philosophers in two distinct senses, whose opposed meanings at once informed and reflected dual interpretations of our nature. Whether couched in the vocabulary of reason's opposition to appetite, or of the conflict of mind and body, or the tensions between an inner and outer or higher and lower self, two contrasting concepts of liberty or freedom have been invoked by almost countless European thinkers before Rousseau and after him – for a time, especially in the late nineteenth and early twentieth century, by a fair number of British philosophers who were themselves dualists, in some cases even followers of his doctrine.[43]

The distinction which Rousseau drew between natural liberty, on the one hand, and civil and moral liberty, on the other, derived its terminology largely from that form of dualism which first arose under the influence of Descartes and Malebranche in the seventeenth century, according to which 'l'homme physique' and 'l'homme moral' were marked by different attributes and properties. This dichotomy between 'le physique' and 'le moral' proved almost a commonplace of Enlightenment speculation in a whole variety of disciplines, and it was perhaps most prevalent in French philosophical biology in the late eighteenth century, in the period culminating with the publication, in 1802, of the *Rapports du physique et du moral de l'homme* by Cabanis.[44] Like Buffon and others among his contemporaries, Rousseau adopted that terminology and indeed developed some of the central ideas of his philosophy around it. The contrast of 'le physique' and 'le moral' appears on the opening page of his *Discourse on Inequality* (see *OC*, III:131), where it announces the work's main theme – in effect that our moral distinctions cannot be ascribed to the physical or natural differences between us. Nothing could be more plain to Rousseau's readers than the fact that he was determined to disengage two kinds of inequality, and one critic, Louis Bertrand Castel, even entitled his reply to the second *Discourse, L'Homme moral opposé à l'homme physique*. According to Rousseau, moreover, as he explained in so many of his writings, the same dichotomy set apart love from sex, authority from power, right from force – even legislation from government, he remarked in the *Social Contract*: 'Every free action', he wrote there,

> is produced by the concurrence of two causes, one moral, that is, the will which determines the act, the other physical, that is, the power which executes it . . . The body politic has the same impetus . . . force and will . . . the latter . . . the *legislative power*, the former, the *executive power*.[45]

No political thinker ever drew a sharper divide than Rousseau between what was natural or physical in our constitution and what was moral or political in our social arrangements. If only his biographers had borne that in mind, we might have been spared volumes of misguided analyses of his life, whose authors have thought fit to infer his political principles from his urinary complaint or sexual repressions. It is a particular virtue of Maurice Cranston's recent biography[46] that it keeps intact this fundamental distinction between 'le physique' and 'le moral' and does not, as so many others have done, trace the main promptings of Rousseau's philosophy to the region of his genitals. With regard to his philosophy, it is of

92   *Rousseau's Two Concepts of Liberty*

course that same distinction which marks the contrast between
natural liberty as against civil and moral liberty – the achievement of
the one, as Rousseau put it in the *Social Contract* (i, viii [*OC*,
III:364–5), requiring the alienation of the other. 'What man loses by
the social contract', let us recall,

> is his natural liberty and an unlimited right to everything that he
> attempts to get . . . what he gains is civil liberty and the
> proprietorship of all he possesses . . . Beyond this [he also
> acquires] moral liberty, which alone renders man truly master of
> himself.

In civil society we do not make our natural liberty secure, but
renounce it in exchange for liberty of another sort. 'Give man
entirely to the state or leave him entirely to himself', Rousseau
concluded in a fragment 'On Public Happiness' (*OC*, III:510), for the
contradiction between our desires and our duties renders our
condition miserable. Men could not possibly enjoy both forms of
liberty together.

Neither form of liberty, it is as well to remember, had ever been
enjoyed by men at all. In contrast with Hobbes, who supposed the
misconceived idea of ancient liberty had been corrected by his own
modern notion, Rousseau identified both his positive and negative
concepts with the past – one ancient, and the other antediluvian –
each construed as must have been the case, though the facts did not
always confirm it. His intensely drawn portrait of modern man as
subjugated victim of the illusion of his freedom still speaks eloquently
to our age, perhaps even more poignantly than it addressed his own;
to my mind, it comprises the most remarkable moral indictment
ever conceived of a social and political world which, not long after
his death, was to adopt liberalism as its main philosophy. But his
glorious description of the world of antiquity must carry less
conviction, from whatever perspective we approach it, if only
because – as Rousseau himself admitted in the *Social Contract* (III,
xv [*OC*, III:431]) – the Greeks maintained their freedom because
of their possession of slaves, which is to say that the splendid liberty
of some men had been achieved by cutting it off from others.
Rousseau's contrast between two kinds of liberty was surely not
intended mainly to distinguish classes or to justify slavery: the very
antithesis of liberty in both senses of his term. His intoxicating
images of Sparta and Rome, like his picture of the state of nature,

owed as much to his contempt for the institutions of the present world as to his love of antiquity, and many of their most vivid colours may be seen to emerge only as the sombre canvas of modern institutions is wiped clean. Just because of this, it is difficult to conceive the civil and moral liberty which Rousseau prescribed in the *Social Contract* as any less fictitious than the natural liberty he claimed we had lost as well. Yet if both of his concepts of liberty were drawn from imaginary lost worlds; and if in his day the only states in which men might still be capable of achieving true political freedom were Corsica and, perhaps, Poland; and if, even there, freedom once lost could never be acquired again; what is it about his peculiar vision of liberty that could have inspired the hostility of his liberal critics and occasioned, from some of them, the charge that it lays the foundation of modern totalitarianism? Judging, at any rate, from the experience of Corsica, which was invaded, and Poland, which was partitioned (each soon after Rousseau drafted constitutions for them) the impact of his ideas upon those few specific political causes he advanced ought to have been more a matter for concern to his friends than alarm to his enemies.

But it is not, I believe, because of any of his particular programmes that Rousseau has won the hearts of so many of his readers, and just for that reason has excited the deep enmity and distrust of others. On the contrary, it is on account of the very generality of his doctrines, and the prodigious force of the imagery through which he conveyed them. In discriminating public liberty from private despotism, he has inspired generations of his followers to perceive the malignancies of their world in the light of blissful ideals to which they might aspire. Yet more captivating even than his portraits of ancient virtue and modern vice has been his remarkable vision of our metamorphosis. As he conceived them, our contemporary institutions had betrayed the fundamental principles from which they sprang. 'Nothing is more free than your legitimate state', he addressed his compatriots in his *Letters from the Mountain* (Septième Lettre, *OC*, iii:813); 'nothing more servile than your actual state'. Because our corruption in society had been due to human endeavour, it was possible to conceive how we might correct the abuse of our liberty, how we might turn our will instead in the direction of personal fulfilment and political regeneration. 'The limits of possibility in moral affairs are less sharply circumscribed than we suppose,' he commented in the *Social Contract* (iii, xii [*OC*, iii:425]), and 'we may judge what still can be done by what has been done already'. If, to his critics, his ideas were only chimeras, his reply, in *Emile* (*OC*, iv:549), was that theirs were just prejudice.

Of course Rousseau proposed no revolutionary transformations of corrupt society into new republics of virtue, and it cannot be stressed too strongly that he wished to avert rather than promote revolution and spurned the idea of overthrow, through violence, of any of the governments of his day. The uplifting enhancement of our social relations which he envisaged was all entirely in his dreams and reveries, but it was through those dreams – through what in his *Moral Letters* he called the 'devouring strength' and 'noble distraction' of 'sublime delirium' (Lettre iv [*OC*, iv:1101]) – that he has illuminated the prospect of a wholly changed universe of social relations and thus aroused the profound enthusiasm of his disciples and admirers. While 'the world of reality has its limits', he exclaimed, 'the world of imagination is infinite' (*Emile*, Livre ii [*OC*, iv:305]). There, like his own fictitious pupil Emile, Rousseau could drink from the waters of oblivion, the past effacing itself from his memory, with a new horizon opening up before him (see *Emile et Sophie*, Lettre Deuxième [*OC*, iv:912]). There, in savouring the solitary enjoyment of undisturbed natural liberty, he could contemplate a social world of perfect civil and moral liberty as well.

It is such flights of fancy which, to my mind, offend Rousseau's liberal critics most of all. His idea of 'perfectibility' (a term which, we should recall, he invented in his *Discourse on Inequality*) has raised, as they see it, the nightmare prospect of reshaping human nature in accordance with ideals that violate their sense of personal freedom. Worse still, his claim to the effect that men are always what their governments make of them has for liberals a particularly sinister ring, when it is attached as much to the manufacture of virtue as of vice – especially in the light of Rousseau's belief, as expressed, for instance in his *Discourse on Political Economy* (*OC*, iii:251), that, however good it is to deal with men as they are, 'it is better to make them what they must be'. Does this not suggest, his opponents fear, the complete indoctrination of our minds under governments more despotic than any ever previously experienced? As they read Rousseau, worst of all are his accounts of our need for legislators, that is, persons who occupy an extraordinary position in the state, attempting to 'change . . . human nature', as he put it, and 'transform each individual' from a solitary being into part of a greater whole (*Contrat social*, ii, vii [*OC*, iii:381–2]). Do not such claims anticipate the most insidious feature of totalitarianism in the modern world, in which Hitler has shown us only too well how the monstrous ideal of the legislator may be given real substance?

In reply to his detractors, it is perhaps pointless to recollect Rousseau's insistence that the legislator or lawgiver was the father of a nation and not its ruler, that he had no subjects but instead inspired individuals to form their own new state, and that, if he miraculously succeeded in transforming human nature, this was because his divine eloquence had persuaded others to establish a sovereign for themselves. Never mind the fact that Rousseau's legislators – principally Moses, Lycurgus and Numa – were for the most part ancient prophets and guides who had pointed the way to men's achievement of civil and moral liberty such as had been unknown to them before.[47] In probing the metamorphoses of human nature which Rousseau conceived in his dreams on the model of ancient myths, his liberal critics resolutely uncover a vision of an alternative world that they judge dangerously abhorrent. Yet where else but in his dreams could Rousseau find escape from the social and political tyrannies under which liberals believe their true freedom is enjoyed already? Where else but in reverie could Rousseau's imagination have come to legislate for all mankind? Why is it that his liberal critics find his fanciful ideals more intolerable than all the weight of the social systems of the world that he described and they inhabit? So long as liberal principles prevail, individuals in society who are anxious to learn why their liberty seems so oppressive will find in Rousseau's works the resonant voice of a solitary prophet of the brotherhood of man.[48]

NOTES

1. See Bertrand Russell, *History of Western Philosophy* (London, 1946) p. 711; and T. D. Weldon, 'Political Principles', in Peter Laslett (ed.), *Philosophy, Politics and Society*, First Series (Oxford, 1956) p. 32.
2. See Bertrand de Jouvenel, 'Essai sur la politique de Rousseau', in his edition of the *Contrat social* (Geneva, 1947) p. 95.
3. See Isaiah Berlin, 'Two Concepts of Liberty', in his *Four Essays on Liberty* (Oxford, 1969) pp. 118–72. This immensely influential essay has been the subject of widespread debate in British and American political thought since its first publication in 1958. Much of the criticism to which it has been subjected comes from scholars who contend that there is and has always been only one fundamental concept of (negative) liberty, and not two. I share some critics' misgivings about certain aspects of Berlin's argument, but I am as convinced as ever that there

96   *Rousseau's Two Concepts of Liberty*

are two concepts, and two main traditions of thought, at issue, and I have no hesitation here in adopting Berlin's general distinction as my own, and hence in my choice of title. I am particularly persuaded by his claim that the doctrine of negative liberty is comparatively modern and that Constant prized it most of all (see Berlin's Introduction, p. xlvi). The concept of negative liberty that I associate here with Rousseau, however, does not really form part of the tradition of thought which Berlin has embraced under that concept, for the reasons explained in this section of my essay. I have also treated the subject before, in a different context, in my 'Rousseau's Perfectibilian Libertarianism', in Alan Ryan (ed.), *The Idea of Freedom: Essays in Honour of Isaiah Berlin* (Oxford, 1979) pp. 233–52.

4. See Hobbes, *Leviathan*, Ch. xxi (Oxford, 1960) p. 140.
5. See Robert Derathé, *Jean-Jacques Rousseau et la science politique de son temps* (Paris, 1950).
6. See, for instance, Carole Pateman, *Participation and Democratic Theory* (Cambridge, 1970). It should be acknowledged, however, that Pateman focuses her attention upon Rousseau's status as the foremost theorist of democratic participation and remarks upon his idea of liberty more briefly.
7. See 'Some Aspects of the History of Freedom', in Cranston's *The Mask of Politics* (London, 1973) p. 32.
8. In the passage of the *Leviathan* already cited (see n. 4 above), Hobbes must surely have had Machiavelli uppermost in his mind when disposing of the 'discourse of those that [from the histories and philosophy of the ancient Greeks and Romans] had received all their learning in the politics'. Quentin Skinner, from whom I have drawn the greatest inspiration both here and in general, takes a wholly different view of Machiavelli's conception of liberty, identifying it in what he takes to be its ordinary negative sense of independence from constraints, which, for Machiavelli, however, required the exercise of positive liberty for its attainment. See Skinner's 'Machiavelli on the Maintenance of Liberty', *Politics*, xviii (1983) pp. 3–15, and 'The idea of negative liberty', in Richard Rorty, J. B. Schneewind, and Quentin Skinner (eds), *Philosophy in History* (Cambridge, 1984) pp. 193–221.
9. Constant's famous discourse, *De la liberté des anciens comparée à celle des modernes*, dates from 1819.
10. See J. L. Talmon, *The Origins of Totalitarian Democracy* (London, 1955) pp. 38–50.
11. See especially the 'Préface de *Narcisse*', the 'Dernière réponse [à Bordes]' and *Emile*, Livre iii, in Rousseau's *Oeuvres complètes* (hereafter *OC*), ed. Bernard Gagnebin and Marcel Raymond *et al.*, (Paris 1959–), ii:972; iii:95; and iv:468, and Rousseau to the Comtesse de Wartensleben, 27 September 1766, *Correspondance complète de Rousseau*, ed. R. A. Leigh, (Geneva and Banbury, 1965–), 5450, xxx:384–8.
12. It is worth noting that in his *Cours de politique constitutionnelle* and elsewhere, Constant identified both Hobbes and Rousseau as purveyors of despotism on account of their shared conception, on his reading, of the absolute sovereignty of the people. The similarity between his own

contrast of ancient and modern liberty and that of Hobbes did not, so far as I am aware, attract his notice, perhaps in part because his distinction portrayed ancient liberty as practically unsuited to modern society, rather than as philosophically meaningless. *De la liberté des anciens comparée à celle des modernes* even ends with a plea for the reconciliation of both sorts of liberty, the one in its isolation judged incompatible with individual freedom, the other held to threaten the exercise of our right to participate in public affairs.

13. See, above all, *Emile*, Livre I (*OC*, IV:245) and *Rousseau juge de Jean-Jacques*, Troisième dialogue (*OC*, III:934).
14. I have pursued this subject at greater length in my 'Rousseau and Marx', in, David Miller and Larry Siedentop (eds), *The Nature of Political Theory* (Oxford, 1983) pp. 219–46. Some lines here, in the previous paragraph, and in the paragraph that follows, are adapted from that text.
15. See Rousseau's *Lettre à d'Alembert sur les spectacles*, ed. M. Fuchs (Bordeaux, 1968) pp. 154–5. Allan Bloom's English edition of this text, under the title *Politics and the Arts* (Glencoe, 1960), provides an invaluable guide to the place of Rousseau's philosophy of the theatre in his politics.
16. See Rousseau's *Essai sur l'origine des langues*, ed. Charles Porset, (Bordeaux, 1970) ch. xx, pp. 197–201. For an account of the place of Rousseau's philosophy of music in the context of his political theory, see my 'Rousseau on Rameau and Revolution', in R. F. Brissenden and J. C. Eade (eds), *Studies in the Eighteenth Century*, IV (Canberra, 1979) pp. 251–83.
17. See especially the *Rêveries du promeneur solitaire*, Sixième promenade; the *Contrat social*, I, viii and II, vii; and *Emile*, livre I (*OC*, I:1052; *OC*, III:364–5 and 381–2; and *OC*, IV:249). On the subject of mankind's denaturation in society, as Rousseau perceived that development, see especially Michèle Ansart-Dourlen's *Dénaturation et violence dans la pensée de J.-J. Rousseau* (Paris, 1975).
18. To my mind, it is the insufficient attention paid to this fundamental distinction between our natural and political existence which mars John Charvet's otherwise extremely perceptive *The Social Problem in the Philosophy of Rousseau* (Cambridge, 1974). For an exchange of views about it, see Charvet's 'Rousseau and the Ideal of Community' and my 'Reply to Charvet', in *History of Political Thought*, II (1980) pp. 69–90.
19. *Emile*, Livre III (*OC*, IV:311). A notable discussion of this passage, and its place in Rousseau's conception of natural discipline, can be found in the second chapter of John W. Chapman's *Rousseau – Totalitarian or Liberal?* (New York, 1956), still an illuminating treatment of the whole of Rousseau's political and social thought around the themes at issue here.
20. For Rousseau's praise of *Robinson Crusoe* as a most useful book of natural education, see especially *Emile*, Livre III (*OC*, IV:454–5).
21. Above all, Lester Crocker in vol. II, ch. 4 of his comprehensive biography, *Jean-Jacques Rousseau* (New York, 1968, 1973). For, in my judgement, a more perceptive account of the relation between Emile

and his tutor, see Judith N. Shklar's, 'Rousseau's Images of Authority', in Maurice Cranston and Richard S. Peters (eds), *Hobbes and Rousseau* (New York, 1972) pp. 333–65.

22. See, for instance, Livre IV (*OC*, IV:661).
23. See Rousseau's *Emile et Sophie* and Pierre Burgelin's introduction, in *OC*, IV:clxiii–clxvi and 879–924.
24. See especially *OC*, III:134–5 and 141–2.
25. I have dealt with some of the material in the next five paragraphs in the second and third section of my 'Rousseau's Perfectibilian Libertarianism', from which a number of sentences are recapitulated here.
26. See Berlin's 'Historical Inevitability', in *Four Essays on Liberty*, especially pp. 63–6 and 73–5, and the introduction, pp. xiii–xxv. Of course for Berlin the most appropriate (although not exclusive) place in which to identify Rousseau's main conceptions of freedom is in the tradition of positive liberty, not least because of Rousseau's conjunction of liberty with sovereignty. But I think it is worth noting how much closer to Berlin Rousseau appears with regard to the subject of determinism, on which Berlin parts company from the foremost philosopher of negative liberty, Hobbes.
27. *Discours sur l'inégalité* (*OC*, III:193). This idea can be found in different formulations throughout Rousseau's writings. For an excellent interpretation of his account of the social life we lead outside ourselves, see Jean Starobinski's classic *Jean-Jacques Rousseau: La transparence et l'obstacle* (2nd edn, Paris, 1971) chs 1–3.
28. See de Sade's *La Nouvelle Justine, ou Les Malheurs de la vertu*, in his *Oeuvres complètes* (Paris, 1966–7) VII:37.
29. See Rousseau's *Discours sur l'inégalité*, the *Manuscrit de Genève*, I, ii, and the 'Etat de guerre', in *OC*, III:184, 288 and 610; and *Emile*, Livre IV (*OC*, IV:524).
30. See Rousseau's *Confessions*, Livre Neuvième (*OC*, I:404–5); his 'Préface de *Narcisse*' (*OC*, II:969); and his *Discours sur l'économie politique* (*OC*, III:251).
31. *OC*, III:966. In his *Lumières de l'utopie* (Paris, 1978) ch. 2, Bronislaw Baczko provides an extraordinary interpretation of the utopian vision of Rousseau's *Considérations sur le gouvernement de Pologne*.
32. Livre I, ch. viii, (*OC*, III:364–5). See also Rousseau's *Manuscrit de Genève*, I, ii (*OC*, III:283).
33. L. G. Crocker, *Rousseau's 'Social Contract': An Interpretive Essay* (Cleveland, 1968) pp. 30, 61.
34. For a discussion of these passages, see Derathé's *Jean-Jacques Rousseau et la science politique de son temps*, pp. 151–71.
35. In the introduction to his own edition of Rousseau's *Social Contract*, reprinted in *The Mask of Politics* (see p. 73).
36. See Plamenatz, '"Ce qui ne signifie autre chose sinon qu'on le forcera d'être libre"', in *Hobbes and Rousseau*, pp. 318–32.
37. Rousseau's account of the substitution, in incremental stages, of the sovereign by the government in the Republic of Geneva bears some comparison with Trotsky's later charge, in *Our Political Tasks*, that Lenin's theory of party organization would give rise, in due course, to

the substitution of the Social Democratic Party for the revolutionary proletariat, followed by a Central Committee substituted for the party, and then a dictator for the Central Committee.

38. It should be noted that there has been much academic controversy about the nature and extent of the Genevan inspiration for Rousseau's *Contrat social*, with several scholars regarding that link as relatively insignificant by comparison with natural law and other philosophical sources. The principal evidence for the connection appears in several passages of the *Lettres de la montagne*, among them Rousseau's remark there (Sixième Lettre, *OC*, III:810) that in the *Contrat social* he had not written about utopian chimeras but about an existing object, bearing witness against the outrage soon to be committed in his native city. It was for this reason, he supposed, that it was in Geneva but nowhere else that the *Contrat social* had been banned and burnt. Rousseau's account of Genevan history in the *Lettres de la montagne*, nevertheless, is problematic, while the connection between the absolute sovereign of the *Contrat social* (from which no one is specifically excluded) and the Conseil Général described in the *Lettres* (which embraced by right only a fraction of the adult population of Geneva) remains similarly unclear. According to some of his critics, Rousseau's reflections on Geneva portray him as much less democratic than might be inferred from his remarks on popular sovereignty in the *Contrat social*, although it should be borne in mind that he speaks of democracy in the *Contrat* (mainly in Livre III, ch. iv) just as a (defective) form of government and not as a (perfect) form of sovereignty. On this much documented subject, see especially R. A. Leigh, 'Le *Contrat social*, oeuvre genevoise?', *Annales de la Société Jean-Jacques Rousseau*, XXXIX (1972–77) pp. 93–111.

39. *Jugement sur la Polysynodie (Écrits sur l'abbé de Saint-Pierre)*, (*OC*, III:643).

40. See also Rousseau's fragmentary 'Parallèle entre les deux républiques de Sparte et de Rome', in *OC*, III:538–43.

41. See the *Contrat social*, III, xv (*OC*, III:429). Cf. the *Projet de Constitution pour la Corse* and the *Considérations sur le gouvernement de Pologne* (*OC*, III:929 and 1004).

42. I leave aside the Italian term *indipendenza* and its derivatives, which throughout the history of their relatively modern usage have had a more specialised meaning in political discourse than 'liberty'. I also leave aside such German negations as '*Ungebundenheit*' and '*Unabhängigkeit*', which can hardly be said to have had a resounding impact upon the literature of freedom.

43. This is not the place to undertake a history of Western philosophy, but perhaps Kant's contrast between 'die Freiheit im innern Gebrauche' and 'die Freiheit im außern Gebrauche', may serve to illustrate my point. Among Rousseau's followers who have conceived his distinction as one between our 'higher' and 'lower' liberty, mention should at least be made of Bosanquet and his *Philosophical Theory of the State*.

44. For an introduction to this still relatively unexplored subject in the history of ideas, see Sergio Moravia's ' "Moral" – "physique": genesis and evolution of a "rapport" ', in Alfred J. Bingham and Virgil W. Topazio

100   *Rousseau's Two Concepts of Liberty*

(eds), *Enlightenment Studies in Honour of Lester G. Crocker* (Oxford, 1979) pp. 163–74. Moravia focuses his attention mainly upon late eighteenth-century contrasts of the two terms.

45. *Contrat social*, III, i (*OC*, III:395). See also, for instance, the *Discours sur l'inégalité* (*OC*, III:157) and the *Contrat social*, I, iii (*OC*, III:354).

46. See Maurice Cranston, *Jean-Jacques: The Early Life and Work of Jean-Jacques Rousseau (1712–1754)* (London, 1983).

47. About Rousseau's concept of the legislator – even just in connection with his doctrine of liberty – a good deal more needs to be said than space here permits. I have already abused my share, and must leave the subject for another occasion. A superb discussion of the concept can be found in Bronislaw Baczko's 'Moïse, législateur . . .', in Simon Harvey *et al.* (eds), *Reappraisals of Rousseau: Studies in Honour of R. A. Leigh* (Manchester, 1980) pp. 111–30.

48. This essay was written too late to benefit from any of the comments and criticism I should have sought from colleagues and friends. As well as from Maurice Cranston and William Pickles, however, who together first excited my interest in Rousseau twenty years ago when I was at the London School of Economics, I have drawn much inspiration from the writings of one woman and three men in particular – Judith Shklar, Bronislaw Baczko, Jean Starobinski and, above all, Ralph Leigh, I now see that I should have benefited too, from reading James Miller's *Rousseau: Dreamer of Democracy* (New Haven, 1984), but my text was sent to press before I could take stock of that work. Stephen Holmes's *Benjamin Constant and the Making of Modern Liberalism* (New Haven, 1984) also appeared too late for me to consult it. I am grateful to the Master and Fellows of Sidney Sussex College, Cambridge, for enabling me to write the essay there during the 1984 Michaelmas Term.

Addenda

References within the text:

p. 69, §1, 1.4: *OC*3.7/*CW*2.5
  Ibid., 1.13: *OC*3.184/*CW*3.59
  Ibid., §2, 1.10: *OC*3.177/*CW*3.54
p. 70, §1, 1.12: *OC*3.608–09/*CW*11.61;*OC*3.610/*CW*11.62
p. 71, §2, 1.6: *OC*3.7/*CW*2.5
  Ibid., 1.28: *OC*3.171/*CW*3.49
p. 72, §1, 1.2: *OC*3.202–208/*CW*3.75–80
p. 73, §2, ll.6–7: *OC*1.1059/*CW*8.56
  Ibid., §4, 1.4: *OC*4.309/*Em*.84
  Ibid., 1.7: *OC*4.857/*Em*.473
p. 74, §1, 1.14: *OC*4.491/*Em*.212
  Ibid., 1.17: *OC*4.323/*Em*.93
p. 78, §3, 1.8: *OC*3.966/*CW*11.179–80
  Ibid., 1.11: *OC*3.955/*CW*11.171
p. 79, §2, 1.7: *OC*3.259/*CW*3.154–55
  Ibid., §3, ll.8–9: *OC*3.414/*CW*4.181, *OC*3.415/*CW*4.182
p. 80, §1, 1.6: *OC*3.841–42/*CW*9.260–61
p. 81, §1, 1.14: *OC*3.364/*CW*4.141
  Ibid., 1.19: *OC*3.440n/*CW*4.200–201n (not as stated)
p. 82, §1, 1.4: *OC*3.373/*CW*4.149
  Ibid., 1.11: *OC*3.377/*CW*4.151–52, *OC*3.397/*CW*4.167
  Ibid., §2, 1.18: *OC*3.394/*CW*4.164
p. 83, §1, 1.5: *OC*3.364/*CW*4.141
  Ibid., §2, 1.9: *OC*3.430/*CW*4.192
  Ibid., ll.18–19: *OC*3.815/*CW*9.239
p. 84, §2, 1.6: *OC*3.365/*CW*4.142
p. 85, §1, 1.3: *OC*3.251/*CW*3.148
  Ibid., 1.5: *OC*3.361/*CW*4.139
  Ibid., 1.18: *OC*3.371/*CW*4.147
  Ibid., 1.22: *OC*3.363/*CW*4.140–41
  Ibid., 1.30: *OC*3.371/*CW*4.147
p. 86, §2, 1.10: *OC*3.959/*CW*11.173
  Ibid., 1.15: *OC*3.958/*CW*11.173
  Ibid., 1.16: *OC*5.93–94/*CW*10.326–27
  Ibid., 1.19: *OC*5.122/*CW*10.349
  Ibid., 1.22: *OC*5.114/*CW*10.343
  Ibid., 1.25: *OC*5.117/*CW*10.346
p. 87, §1, 1.4: *OC*5.121/*CW*10.349
Ibid., 1.12: *OC*3.968/*CW*11.181
  Ibid., §2, ll.7–8: *OC*3.391–92n/*CW*4.162–63n
  Ibid., 1.10: *OC*3.924/*CW*11.142–43
  Ibid., 1.14: *OC*2.607/*CW*6.496
  Ibid., 1.16: *OC*2.608–609/*CW*6.497–98
  Ibid., 1.20: *OC*2.608/*CW*6.497
  Ibid., 1.29: *OC*5.408/*CW*7.316, *OC*5.428/*CW*7.332
p. 88, §1, 1.11: *OC*3.428–29/*CW*4.192
  Ibid., §3, 1.4: *OC*3.903/*CW*11.123
p. 91, §1, 1.13: *OC*3.131/*CW*3.18
p. 92, §1, ll.3–4: *OC*3.364–65/*CW*4.141–42
  Ibid., §3, 1.4: *OC*3.510/*CW*4.41

100b

> *Ibid.*, §4, 1.16: *OC*3.431/*CW*4.193
p. 93, §2, 1.15: *OC*3.813/*CW*9.237
> *Ibid.*, ll.21–22: *OC*3.425/*CW*4.189
p. 94, §1, 1.2: *OC*4.549/*Em*.253
> *Ibid.*, §2, 1.9: *OC*4.1101/–
> *Ibid.*, 1.13: *OC*4.305/*Em*.81
> *Ibid.*, 1.17: *OC*4.912/–
> *Ibid.*, §3, ll.10–11: *OC*3.251/*CW*3.148
> *Ibid.*, 1.19: *OC*3.381–82/*CW*4.155

Endnotes:

11. *OC*2.972/*CW*2.196; *OC*3.95/*CW*2.128–129; *OC*4.468/*Em*.194
13. *OC*4.245/*Em*.37; *OC*3.934/*CW*1.213
15. –/–
16. *OC*5.424–427/*CW*7.329–331 (Chapter 19, not 20)
17. *OC*1.2052/*CW*8.50; *OC*3.364–365,381–382/*CW*4.141–142,155; *OC*4.249/*Em*.39–40
19. *OC*4.311/*Em*.85–86
20. *OC*4.454–455/*Em*.184–185
22. *OC*4.661/*Em*.332
23. *OC*4.clxiii–cixvi/–; *OC*4.879–924/–
24. *OC*3.134–135,141–142/*CW*3.20–21, 25–26
27. *OC*3.193/*CW*3.66
29. *OC*3.184/*CW*3.59–60; *OC*3.288/*CW*4.81–82; *OC*3.610/*CW*11.62
    *OC*4.524/*Em*.236
30. *OC*1.404–405/*CW*5.340; *OC*2.969/*CW*2.194; *OC*3.251/*CW*3.148
31. *OC*3. 966/*CW*11.179–80
32. *OC*3. 364–65/*CW*4.141–42; *OC*3.283/*CW*4.77–78
38. 1.7: *OC*3.810/*CW*9.234
39. *OC*3.643/*CW*11.97–98
40. *OC*3.538–43/*CW*4.59–64
41. *OC*3.429/*CW*4.192; *OC*3.929/*CW*11.146–47, *OC*3.1004/*CW*11.210.
42. *OC*3.395/*CW*4.166; *OC*3.157/*CW*3.38; *OC*3.354/*CW*4.133

[9]

INDIVIDUALS IN SOCIETY: ROUSSEAU'S REPUBLICAN VISION

John Hope Mason

I
The Social Theory

In his *Discours sur l'origine et les fondements de l'inégalité* (1755) (referred to hereafter as the *Inégalité*), Rousseau claimed to have presented 'the solution to an infinite number of problems in ethics and politics which philosophers are not able to resolve' (p. 192).[1] The problems were the central issues of moral and political philosophy — what is human nature? why do men behave as they do? how should we best organize our lives? — and the solution, briefly put, was that men are not everywhere and always the same (p. 212). They are the product of their histories and their societies and they vary accordingly. That is not to say that everything is relative, for there is such a thing as human nature; men, like other living creatures, have certain distinct qualities. But unlike other creatures they are susceptible to change, and only by understanding, firstly, what such changes have been and, secondly, how they have occurred, will we be able to settle 'the infinite number of problems'.

The story told by Rousseau in the *Inégalité* is, famously, one of disaster and loss. Although original man had had no reason, imagination or language (and was later described by Rousseau as 'a stupid and limited animal' (p. 364)), he had enjoyed 'a real happiness' (p. 132). He had been free, healthy and without worries. Rousseau particularly emphasized both the freedom he enjoyed and the limits to that freedom. Although the *sauvage* could do whatever he wanted, unconstrained by the impositions of others, what he wanted was limited, because his expectations extended no further than his knowledge of what he could himself accomplish. He had no experience of more, so he had no expectation of more (pp. 143–4). He lived therefore in a state of equilibrium, with a balance between his physical and mental life, his needs and desires, his abilities and hopes.

In civilized societies this original contentment has vanished. Unlike the *sauvage*, civilized man is prey to continual dissatisfaction and restlessness (pp. 193, 203), and

---

[1] Bracketed figures in the text refer to the pages of Volume Three — *Du Contrat social, Écrits politiques* — of Rousseau's *Oeuvres complètes*, edited under the direction of B. Gagnebin and M. Raymond (Paris, 1959–). Where the original French is quoted the spelling has been modernized. Other references to Rousseau's works in this edition are indicated by the letters *OC*, followed by the relevant volume number and page number. Like all modern readers of Rousseau I am indebted to these volumes and (for the texts discussed in this article) to the excellent introductions and notes by Jean Starobinski and Robert Derathé, as well as to Derathé's *J-J. Rousseau et la science politique de son temps* (Paris, 1950). I would also like to acknowledge my debt to R.A. Leigh's magnificent edition of the *Correspondance complète de J-J. Rousseau* (46 vols., Geneva, 1965–Oxford, 1987) (references to which are indicated by the letters *CC*). Professor Leigh, the greatest Rousseau scholar of this or any other generation, died while this article was being written, and I would like to dedicate it to his memory.

his life is dominated by feelings of envy or hostility towards others (pp. 175, 202). The *amour-de-soi* enjoyed by the first has become the *amour-propre* of the second (p. 219). In addition, *l'homme civilisé* inhabits a world of extreme injustice. Throughout the *Inégalité* there is a juxtaposition of 'the violence of powerful men and the oppression of the weak' (p. 127). The principal reason for this emphasis on contemporary inequality was that it was not simply an accompaniment to psychological malaise and moral bankruptcy, but rather the cause of it. Rousseau's fundamental insight, his *illumination*, had been that evil lay not in human nature but in 'all the contradictions of the social system . . . all the abuses of our institutions'.[2] Part Two of the *Inégalité* suggested how these bad social arrangements and bad political structures had arisen. By describing these, and indicating their results, the work showed 'all the changes which the sequence of times (*la succession des temps*) and of things must have produced in man's original constitution', the alterations which had been brought about by 'circumstances (*les circonstances*) and [man's] progress' (p. 122).

There were two key aspects of this process, one of which could be called *la succession des temps* and the other *les circonstances*. The first was the notion of gradual and irreversible change over time, what Rousseau elsewhere referred to as a 'genealogy' (pp. 49–50)[3] and what we now call evolution. Between the state of nature and civilized societies there was an 'immense distance' (p. 192). During that vast stretch of time had occurred a series of changes, few of them sudden, most of them slight, the cumulative effect of which had been a dramatic alteration in human feelings, aptitudes and behaviour. This process of evolution explained how what previous writers had taken to be essential, ineradicable human characteristics, were in fact the products of history.

The second element in Rousseau's account was a description of change not in terms either of an inner potential or 'nature' being realized, or of specific choices being made, but as the result of external *circonstances* (p. 143). Human faculties 'could never have developed by themselves . . . for that they needed the chance combination of several outside causes' (p. 162). It was specific *occasions* which led people to the exercise of their faculties (p. 152), and it was a new *situation* which led to 'the first developments of the heart' (p. 168). This presupposed that humans were capable of development and Rousseau did indeed regard such a quality as a distinctly human attribute. He called it *perfectibilité*, a term which he seems to have been the first to use.[4] By this he referred to both the active freedom a person has to change himself and the passive malleability which meant that he could be altered from without. The vast majority of changes which had taken place over time were, however, not the result of free choice; they were the product of specific social arrangements, 'the work of all these new relations' (p. 192).

[2] *OC*, I, p. 1135.

[3] See also *OC*, IV, pp. 935–6.

[4] See Starobinski's note (pp. 1317–19), and R. Wokler, 'Rousseau's Perfectibilian Libertarianism'. in *The Idea of Freedom*, ed. A. Ryan (Oxford, 1979), pp. 233–52.

ROUSSEAU'S REPUBLICAN VISION 91

In this way Rousseau's explanation combined a theory of social evolution with an embryonic sociology. Both notions were in the process of emerging at this time. The notion of *succession* occupied a central place in the accounts of the universe or the history of the earth in the first volume of Buffon's *Histoire naturelle* (1749), Diderot's *Lettre sur les aveugles* (1749) and Maupertuis' *Essai de cosmologie* (1750); and it occupied an equally important place in the speculation by the same writers on the development of living creatures.[5] In the latter, development was also explained mostly in terms of chance and the influence of external circumstances.[6] Locke's educational and epistemological writings, which encouraged the idea of human malleability, were massively influential among the *philosophes*; and the notion of behaviour, feelings and attitudes being affected by social circumstances could have been suggested to Rousseau by, among others, Condillac or d'Alembert,[7] as well as by the writings of Montesquieu.

In recent years much work has been done on this intellectual environment in which Rousseau was writing, as well as on the *Inégalité* itself, and as a result this text no longer presents major difficulties of interpretation.[8] It would be fair to say that there is a reasonable level of agreement about the meaning of Rousseau's theory of social development. With his political theory, however, the situation is completely the opposite. Much work has been done but disagreement still prevails. The argument which has raged since the French Revolution — his political thought being seen as either aristocratic or revolutionary, ancient or modern, collectivist or individualist, totalitarian or liberal — shows no signs of drawing to a close.[9]

---

[5] For accounts of the universe or history of the earth, see Buffon, *Histoire naturelle* (Paris, 1749), I, pp. 77–8, 85, 164, 611; Diderot, *Oeuvres philosophiques*, ed. P. Vernière (Paris, 1956), pp. 121–4; Maupertuis, *Oeuvres* (Lyons, 1756), I, pp. 73–4; (this passage does not use the word *succession* but it describes the same process). On living creatures, see Buffon, *Histoire naturelle*, IV (1753), p. 215; Diderot, *Oeuvres philosophiques*, pp. 238–40; Maupertuis, *Oeuvres*, II, p. 66. This is, of course, not meant to suggest that Rousseau was not indebted to other sources, such as the *Kulturgeschichte* contained in Lucretius, *De rerum natura*, Book V. Mandeville's *Fable of the Bees*, which Rousseau knew well, also contains an account of human change as a result of social developments which has some striking similarities to the *Inégalité*; see *The Fable of the Bees*, ed. F.B. Kaye (Oxford, 1924), I, pp. 183–5, 205–6, 231–2, 344, and II, pp. 129–39.

[6] Buffon, *Histoire naturelle*, III, p. 530 and IV, p. 215; Maupertuis, *Oeuvres*, II, pp. 110 and 148.

[7] See the texts cited in J. Hope Mason, 'Reading Rousseau's First Discourse', *Studies on Voltaire & the Eighteenth Century*, CCXLIX (1987), p. 263. On the relationship between Rousseau's ideas and those of Turgot and Adam Smith, whose four-stage theory of social evolution was also taking shape around this time, see R. Meek, *Social Science and the Ignoble Savage* (Cambridge, 1976), pp. 76–91.

[8] In addition to the introduction and notes by Starobinski, cited in Note 1, see the edition by H. Meier (Paderborn, 1984); R.G. Masters, *The Political Philosophy of Rousseau* (Princeton, 1968), pp. 106–204; V. Goldschmidt, *Anthropologie et politique: les principes du système de Rousseau* (Paris, 1974); M.F. Platten, *Rousseau's State of Nature* (Dekalb, 1979); R. Wokler, 'The *Discours sur l'inégalité* and its sources', *Studies on Voltaire & the Eighteenth Century* (forthcoming).

[9] L.G. Crocker has been the most notable proponent of the collectivist view, Derathé (and Leigh) of the individualist view. Two important studies of Rousseau's politics relevant to the subject-matter of this article are J. Shklar, *Men and Citizens* (Cambridge, 1969), Ch. 5, and B. Baczko, *J-J. Rousseau: solitude et communauté* (Paris, 1964), Part IV.

92   J. HOPE MASON

I believe that this argument is misconceived. We should not ask ourselves whether Rousseau was either one or the other but instead try to explain the reason why (or the manner in which) his writings contain ideas or statements which seem to be so contradictory. In other words, instead of asking 'is Rousseau's political theory collectivist or individualist?' we should ask 'why does Rousseau's political theory seem to be both collectivist and individualist?'; and it may be possible to arrive at an answer to this question if we see how his social theory underlay, or was incorporated into, his political thought.

I
La Succession Des Temps

The first clear expression of Rousseau's political views occurred in the long Dedication to the Republic of Geneva with which he prefaced the *Inégalité*. This praised the political system of his native city-republic. There, he claimed, could be found a real freedom, both in the sense of the city being independent (p. 113) and in the sense that the citizens lived under laws which they had approved of *en corps* (p. 114), administered by magistrates of their own choosing (p. 116). There, he stated, could be seen as much equality as any civil society could expect to have (p. 111). The city was so limited in size that all citizens knew one another (p. 112); and as a result of this, and the fact that the citizens were themselves active in the republic's defence, there was an effective *amour de la patrie* (pp. 112–13). Not only was Geneva limited in size, it was also limited in wealth (p. 116), and accordingly suffered none of the ill-effects that came with luxury (p. 120).

The terms in which Geneva was praised — for realizing freedom as self-government and as participation in government, equality under the law, a citizen militia, the dangers of luxury — were the standard terms of classical republicanism. When taken together with the rest of the *Inégalité*, however, these terms appear in a new light. In the first place, insofar as there could be a correspondence between the well-being of natural man and the situation of the republican citizen, the latter could be seen to enjoy a specifically emotional and psychological satisfaction. The republic, in other words, could meet not simply the requirements of justice but also some fundamental inner needs. Secondly, the social theory of the *Inégalité* gave politics a new pre-eminence. If our characters are decisively shaped by our history and our socio-political arrangements, if it was the case that 'everything depended radically on politics and . . . no people would ever be anything except what the nature of their government made them',[10] then the form of our politics becomes of paramount importance. For this determines what we are.

To some extent this had been true of earlier republican theory. In his *Discorsi* Machiavelli had attributed the success of the Roman republic to Rome's particular *leggi* and *ordini* (which included customs, education and religion, as well as political

---

[10] *OC*, I, p. 404.

ROUSSEAU'S REPUBLICAN VISION 93

institutions); it was these which had shaped the Romans' remarkable character.[11] This became a standard argument in favour of republican government. Hobbes singled out this notion in his attack on republican ideas[12] and it occurs regularly in (to take a text well-known to Rousseau) Algernon Sidney's *Discourses concerning Government*: 'Strength, wisdom, valour and good discipline . . . [never] have been found or subsisted anywhere, unless they were cultivated and nourished by a well-ordered government'; 'good order being once established, makes good men'.[13] Montesquieu, similarly, in his *Considérations sur les causes de la grandeur des Romains* (1734), had emphasized the importance of *institutions*,[14] of *la situation*,[15] of circumstances in general,[16] and this republican sociology provided the seeds out of which grew the more complex and extensive analysis of *De l'esprit des lois* (1748).

However, with none of these writers did the sense of the necessity for republican government have the same force as it did with Rousseau. This was either because of the belief that men have always been the same,[17] so that the scope of what could be different was more limited; or else because, as was the case with *De l'esprit des lois*, the republican ideal itself was not presented as being desirable. It involved self-denial, and in this respect a republic resembled a community of monks.[18]

For Rousseau, on the other hand, the republic alone made possible an inner contentment in a society with others. This may not have been clear in the *Inégalité* itself, since that gave a picture of social life which (with the exception of Genevan society in the Dedication) was entirely negative. But it began to be clear in the work of Rousseau's published soon after the *Inégalité*, the article *Économie politique*. (This first appeared in Volume Five of the *Encyclopédie* (1755).)

Here we find a blunt assertion of the importance of politics — 'it is certain that people are in the course of time what the government makes them' (p. 251) — coupled with an emphasis on the affective experience — a shared sense of '*le moi commun* . . . the reciprocal *sensibilité*' (p. 245) — on which good government must rest. To have such a sense would be to possess *l'amour de la patrie*, 'that sweet and

[11] Machiavelli, *Discorsi*, Bk. I, chs. 3, 11, 18; and Bk. II, ch. 2. Rousseau was familiar with Machiavelli's works. It is interesting to note that when the Genevan exile T.P. Lenieps wrote to Rousseau in 1763, advising him about republican principles in relation to the political crisis in Geneva, the three writers he quoted were Machiavelli, Sidney, and Montesquieu: *CC*, XVII, p. 45.

[12] Hobbes, *Leviathan*, Bk. I, ch. 29; ed. C.B. Macpherson (Harmondsworth, 1968), p. 369.

[13] A. Sidney, *Discourses concerning government* (London, 1698), pp. 114 and 167. A French translation appeared in 1702.

[14] *Oeuvres complètes*, ed. R. Caillois (Paris, 1951), II, p. 70; '*la force de son institution*' — II, pp. 81, 89, 122.

[15] *Ibid.*, II, p. 172.

[16] *Ibid.*, pp. 129 and 173. The importance of appropriate time and circumstances had featured in Machiavelli's *Discorsi* (Bk. III, chs. 8 and 9) and Sidney's *Discourses* (pp. 136, 366–7, 455).

[17] Machiavelli, *Discorsi*, Bk. I, ch. 39 and Bk. III, ch. 43.

[18] Montesquieu, *De l'esprit des lois*, Bk. IV, ch. 5 and Bk. V, ch. 2.

94   J. HOPE MASON

lively feeling which joins to the strength of *amour-propre* all the beauty of virtue, giving it an energy without disfiguring it and making it the most heroic of the passions'(p. 255). If we have this feeling, 'we gladly want what is wanted by the people whom we love' (p. 254). But this would only arise in the conditions outlined in the Dedication to the *Inégalité*. Firstly, in a republic of limited size, where there can be a real sense of the whole; where the 'feeling of humanity' is concentrated among the citizens and 'takes on a new strength among them by their habit of seeing one another and by [their awareness of] the common interest which keeps them together' (p. 254). Secondly, where there was the freedom of living under laws common to all, which established juridical equality among all (pp. 248, 258), and where a share in the public administration meant that the citizens felt that they 'were at home (*chez eux*), and that the laws in their eyes were only the guarantees of shared freedom' (p. 258). Thirdly, where there was a degree of economic equality, *la mediocrité*, with excesses of neither wealth nor poverty, so that all can feel a commonality (pp. 258–9). In other words, without luxury; for the result of luxury developing is 'private interest substituted for public interest . . . mutual hatred among the citizens . . . [and] their indifference to the common cause' (p. 259).

The corruption caused by luxury, and its corrosive effect in destroying *l' amour de la patrie*, was one of the oldest republican themes, then recently restated with particular clarity by Montesquieu in *De l' esprit de lois*.[19] Rousseau's theory of social evolution, in which increasing wealth and inequality generates increasing self-interest and the desire for more (thus bringing about an irremediable state of division and conflict), could be seen to owe as much to republican histories as his theory of sociology may have owed to republican theory.[20] On the question of luxury he was covering well-trodden ground, though he gave a new psychological depth and sociological range to what had been said before.

It was on the subject of republican experience before corruption had set in that Rousseau's account was most notable. Republican *vertu*, as Montesquieu had observed, was essentially a matter of *amour*, 'a feeling and not a collection of knowledge'.[21] To Rousseau — for whom 'to exist . . . is to feel'[22] — the affective basis of republican life was a central concern. It could not be engendered by repressing emotions: 'the performance of such a project would be no more desirable than it would be possible' (p. 259). It could only be done by providing future citizens from an early age with some positive image or experience on which they could focus their emotions.

---

[19] *Ibid.*, Bk. III, ch. 3; Bk. V, ch. 3 and Bk. VII, chs. 1–3.

[20] See, for example, Sallust, *De conjuratione Catilinae*, chs. 5, 9–12, and 52, probably derived from the elder Cato: D.C. Earl, *The Political Thought of Sallust* (Cambridge, 1961), p. 41. However, there was much in common between these republican views and a broad current of moral teaching in the ancient world which could be found in many sources.

[21] Montesquieu, *De l' esprit des lois*, Bk. IV, ch. 5 and Bk. V, ch. 2.

[22] *OC*, IV, p. 600. These words are put into the mouth of the *Vicaire Savoyard* but they undoubtedly reflect Rousseau's own view.

ROUSSEAU'S REPUBLICAN VISION 95

If, for example, they are trained as soon as possible never to regard their individual self except through their relations to the body of the state, and, as it were, to see their own existence only as a part of the state's existence; then they could eventually come to identify themselves in some way with this greater whole, to feel themselves members of the *patrie*, to love the *patrie* with that exquisite feeling which every isolated man only has for himself . . . and thus transform into a sublime virtue that dangerous disposition which gives rise to all our vices . . . It is too late to change our natural inclinations when they have taken their course and *amour-propre* is reinforced by habit; it is too late to draw us out of ourselves once *le moi humain*, concentrated in our hearts, has there developed that contemptible activity which absorbs all virtue and is the lifeblood of petty souls. How can *l'amour de la patrie* arise in the midst of so many other passions which stifle it? (pp. 259–60)

This passage is of major importance. Rousseau envisaged a process in which the young person transformed into 'a sublime virtue that dangerous disposition which gives rise to all our vices', i.e. *amour-propre*. Earlier he had described *l'amour de la patrie* as a feeling 'which joins the strength of *amour-propre* to all the beauty of virtue' (p. 255). He was not therefore suggesting the eradication of *amour-propre*, any more than the suppression of emotions generally. He stated explicitly: we 'should not look beyond the nature [of men] for a perfection to which they are not susceptible' (p. 259).[23] Rather, he wanted to prevent *amour-propre* from becoming dominant or all-absorbing. There is a time in a person's life when that can be done, the stage before natural inclinations have taken complete hold and *le moi humain* has become completely preoccupied with itself.

The passage contains an undeniable fatalism. Our inclinations will naturally lead us away from *l'amour de la patrie*; there is no hope once other passions have developed. We find a similar fatalism in a reply Rousseau wrote around this time to a critic of the *Inégalité*. The latter, the Genevan naturalist Charles Bonnet, maintained that human society was the product and reflection of human faculties. Rousseau replied that developed society (with arts, laws and governments) was as natural to the human species as *décrépitude* was to an individual.

The whole difference is that the state of old age arises from the nature of man alone, while that of society arises from the nature of mankind, not immediately, as you say, but only, as I have proved, with the aid of certain external circumstances which can or cannot occur, or at least can happen sooner or later, and therefore can hasten or slow down the progress. Several of these circumstances depend on the will of men . . . As the social condition has a final state, therefore, at which it is in men's power whether they arrive sooner or later, it is not useless to show them the danger of going so fast, and the miseries of a condition which they take to be the perfection of the species. (p. 232)

---

[23] Rousseau's emphatic rejection of perfection, here and elsewhere (*CC*, VI, p. 128 and XVII, pp. 63–4; *Lettre à d'Alembert*, ed. M. Fuchs (Geneva, 1948) (hereafter *LA*), p. 148), deserves more attention than it has generally received.

96   J. HOPE MASON

Rousseau here summarized the thesis of the *Inégalité* (adding the significant suggestion that individuals can consciously slow down the decline which social development brings). His observation that developed society, which is generally taken as the perfection of the species, is in fact comparable to the *décrépitude* of the individual brings to mind his comment in the *Inégalité* about progress being 'so many steps apparently towards the perfection of the individual and actually towards the *décrépitude* of the species' (p. 171). What he meant by the perfection of the individual was precisely that 'exquisite feeling which every isolated man has only for himself' (p. 259), that condition of '*le moi humain* concentrated in our hearts' (p. 260) to the exclusion of everyone else. The individual *qua* isolated individual is as fully developed as possible; simultaneously, social life in general has collapsed into a Hobbesian state of *homo homini lupus*.

The republic can only exist if its citizens have not reached this stage of development; and the best way to prevent that occurring is to raise children not in isolation, in different family units, but 'in common, in the heart of equality . . . surrounded by examples and objects which continually speak to them of the tender mother who nourishes them, of the love she has for them, of the priceless goods which they receive from her, and of what they owe her in return'. If that were the case the young would learn 'to cherish one another mutually as brothers, only ever to want what society wants, [and] to substitute actions of men and citizens for the fruitless and empty chatter of sophists' (p. 261). Rousseau concluded these comments about the benefits of republican education by observing that such an upbringing would contain 'within narrow limits that personal self-interest which so isolates individuals that the state is weakened by their power and has nothing to hope for from their good will' (p. 262). If private interest is limited, if there are experiences in common, if the young grow up with an awareness of the extent to which they are part of a greater unit, then *le moi humain* can feel part of *le moi commun*. But, Rousseau insists, this can only occur at a certain stage of development, a certain point in *la succession des temps*.

The *Inégalité* gave a general account of human development, from the original condition of being 'a stupid and limited animal' to the 'new order of things' which constituted a fully civilized life, in which we find people like ourselves today, with 'all our faculties developed, the memory and imagination in play, *amour-propre* aroused, reason made active and the mind arrived at almost the limit of the perfection which it can reach' (p. 174). This account was placed within a sweeping condemnation of the evils which accompanied the process and as a result its implications were somewhat obscured. That is to say, the extent to which man's development in society might be seen in a positive as well as a negative light was not clear. One of the reasons for this was undoubtedly the profound ambivalence which Rousseau felt about this development and about the relationship between mental and emotional life. In this ambivalence lay the cause of contradiction in his writing and of much subsequent confusion.

One of his most important statements about the process of development (a subject which he never fully elaborated) occurred in a text written soon after the *Économie politique* but not published until the late nineteenth century: the second chapter of the Geneva Manuscript (the first version of the *Contrat social*). (This was a reply to

Diderot's *Encyclopédie* article *Droit naturel* (1755).) The chapter opened with an account of how political institutions became necessary, as a result of the escalation of needs which followed men's living in groups and the division of labour: 'so it is that the same causes which make us evil also make us slaves, and bring us into subjection as into depravity. . . Our needs bring us together to the extent that our passions set us apart, and the more we become enemies of our fellows the less we can do without them' (p. 282). However, Rousseau then went on to point out that if men had always remained isolated they would have suffered from 'the absence of that *liaison* of the parts which constitutes the whole'; that would have been 'harmful to the progress of our most excellent faculties'. 'Our understanding could not have been developed; we would live without feeling anything, we would die without having lived . . . We would never have tasted the most wonderful feeling of the soul, which is the love of virtue' (p. 283).

Diderot had maintained that natural right was based on individuals' sense of *la volonté générale*, which he described as 'a pure act of the understanding which reasons in the silence of the passions on what man can demand of his fellow-man, and on what his fellow has a right to demand of him' (p. 286). In reply, Rousseau insisted that men had no innate reason or conscience. 'The art of generalising ideas in this way is one of the most difficult operations and the last [to develop] in the human understanding' (p. 286); conscience only grows up as a result of social life, so it cannot provide the basis for social life (p. 287). This analysis is, Rousseau pointed out, confirmed by history: the ideas of natural right and the common brotherhood of all men only arose at a certain stage in history and they only became widespread with Christianity (p. 287).

Personal evolution, social evolution, historical evolution; they could all be seen to follow the same course. Rousseau's constant argument against Hobbes, repeated at this point in the Geneva Manuscript, was that he assumed men to be naturally what in fact only applied to a particular stage of human development.

At the time he wrote the *Inégalité*, the *Économie politique*, and much (if not all) of the Geneva Manuscript, Rousseau had one particular contrast in mind — that of Geneva and Paris. This contrast was implicit in the Dedication to the *Inégalité*, and it became explicit three years later in the *Lettre à d'Alembert* (1758), written to prevent a French theatre being set up in the Swiss city-republic. What is suitable in one time and place, he observed, is not suitable in another: 'from people to people there is a prodigious variety of *moeurs*, temperaments, [and] characters . . . We should not look among ourselves for what is good for men in general, but for what is good for them at such a time or in such a place'.[24] In a large, wealthy city, theatre could be useful: it could keep the rich busy and distract the poor from their misery, 'in a word, it could prevent bad *moeurs* from degenerating into violent disorder (*brigandage*)'; but in a small, poor city it was otherwise: there it would serve only 'to destroy the love of work . . . to make the people inactive and irresolute [and] prevent them from seeing the public and private concerns with which they ought to be occupied'.[25] If a French theatre were introduced the effect would be to substitute 'for our ancient

---

[24] *LA*, p. 22.   [25] *Ibid.*, p. 86.

simplicity the pleasant life of Paris and the fine airs of France'. He warned: 'let us not imagine that we will retain our freedom when we abandon the *moeurs* which have acquired it for us'.[26] In other words, Rousseau's basic objection to the proposal was that Geneva had not yet reached the stage at which isolation and private interest had become dominant. In his native republic concord and *fraternité* were still a reality.[27]

There was a moment in *la succession des temps* when men could live together in republican freedom and equality. When he wrote the *Lettre à d'Alembert* Rousseau believed Geneva to be still at that point. Soon afterwards he was disillusioned: 'I was deceived in my *Lettre à d'Alembert*. I did not think our progress was so great or that our *moeurs* had gone so far. Our ills are now irremediable. Now we need only palliatives, and theatre is one'.[28] When he published the *Contrat social* (1762), he suggested that the only country in Europe still 'capable of legislation', at the stage where it could still become a good republic, was Corsica (p. 391).

As for France, that had long passed the point of no return. There was never any question in Rousseau's eyes of an inhabitant of Paris becoming a republican citizen. He made this crystal clear in his posthumously published *Rousseau Juge de Jean-Jacques* (1780). Writing about himself in the third person he stated that his intention was not 'to lead large populations or great states back to their first simplicity, but only, if it was possible, to arrest the progress of those states whose small size and situation have preserved them from such a swift advance towards the perfection of society and the deterioration of the species. These distinctions deserve to be made and have not been made'. His work had been 'for his *patrie* and for small states constituted like it'; and he added, to reinforce this point: 'in spite of these distinctions, so frequently and forcefully repeated, the bad faith of *gens de lettres* and the stupidity of *amour-propre*, which persuades everyone that one is concerned with him even when one is not, have had the effect that the great nations have taken to apply to them what was only intended for small republics'.[29]

The republican *forma* was only suitable to a certain *materia*, one which was still 'pliable (*maniable/docile*)' (pp. 319/85). Generally speaking, that occurred when a society, like an individual, was in its youth, when it still had 'the simplicity of nature in conjunction with the needs of society' (p. 391). History, in other words, is a one-way street: at a certain time a good socio-political order could be established, but once passed the possibility was forever lost. It was true that there could be exceptional crises when a state might be reborn, so to speak, from its ashes 'and in escaping from the arms of death regain the vigour of youth' (p. 385). This had happened in the past; but although Rousseau anticipated 'a condition of crisis and a century of revolutions',[30] there is little (if any) evidence that he thought such a restoration of youth could occur in the future of Europe. On the contrary, his remarks about Corsica and Poland make it clear that, in his view, wherever a modern economy developed the possibility of social integration disappeared (pp. 933, 1003–4).

---

[26] *Ibid.*, pp. 149 and 152.

[27] *Ibid.*, p. 178.

[28] *CC*, VII, p. 24.

[29] *OC*, I, p. 935.

[30] *Ibid.*, IV, p. 468.

ROUSSEAU'S REPUBLICAN VISION 99

III
Les Circonstances

In the *Économie politique* Rousseau compared the state to a human body: 'the body politic, taken by itself, can be considered as an organised, living body, similar to that of a man' (p. 244). He then compared the various parts of the state to parts of the body and concluded: 'the life of one and the other is *le moi commun* to the whole, the reciprocal *sensibilité* and the internal correspondence of all the parts. Does this communication come to a halt, the formal unity disappear, and the contiguous parts belong to one another no more than by juxtaposition? The man is dead or the state is dissolved' (p. 245).

This comparison was as old as political theory itself, but there was something new about its use here by Rousseau. He was not simply drawing on Hobbes's celebrated Introduction to the *Leviathan*.[31]

In the Geneva Manuscript he made another comparison which contains an emphasis on similar qualities; this was a comparison between an *être morale* and a chemical compound. (An *être morale*, or *personne morale*, was a legal term for an institutional entity brought into being by the union of its members, and was to be applied by Rousseau (as by his Natural Law predecessors) to the state.)[32] 'An *être*

---

[31] As suggested by Derathé (1394 n.7), G. Davy, 'Le Corps politique selon le *Contrat social* et ses antécédents chez Hobbes', *Études sur le Contrat social de J-J. Rousseau* (Paris, 1964), pp. 65–93, and, in effect, by A. Meyer, 'Mechanische und organische Metaphorik politischer Philosophie', *Archiv für Begriffsgeschichte*, XIII (1969), pp. 139–47.

[32] Pufendorf's *De jure naturae et gentium* opens with an account of *entia moralia* and *personnae morales*; the state in his taxonomy was a *personna moralis composita* (I, I ,13). On this subject see Derathé, *Rousseau et la science politique*, pp. 398–404.

Rousseau's purpose in this passage was to show the impossibility of thinking of the whole human race as an *être morale*, that is to say, as a single unit: 'the phrase *genre humain* only conveys a purely general idea, it does not presuppose any real union between the individuals who constitute it' (p. 283). The passage is crossed out in the manuscript, and the manuscript itself was not published by Rousseau. But there is no reason to think that this characterization of an *être morale* was one which he would have disowned, since these characteristics also appear elsewhere in his writings. What does not appear elsewhere is the specifically chemical comparison. One reason for this may have been the fact that chemistry dealt with the mineral realm, i.e. with substances which had no consciousness and about which therefore it was impossible to speak of a *moi commun*.

Rousseau had taken a keen interest in chemistry in the 1740s and, drawing on the work of Becher, Stahl, Boerhaave and others, wrote a treatise entitled *Institutions chymiques*. We find there the notion used in his comparison: 'new mixtures of a kind that two substances, which are intimately mixed and merged into a unity, compose a third substance which has a strong union and is different in nature from each of those which had composed it'. (*Institutions chymiques*, ed. M. Gautier, in *Annales de la Société Jean-Jacques Rousseau*, XIII (1921), p. 116. See also pp. 134–5, where the term used is not *mixtion* but *combinaison* or *composé*, and XII, pp. 26–36.) It should be remembered that the chemical vocabulary at this period was by no means fixed, and the contrast of aggregate (or mixture) and compound not generally defined as it came to be in the nineteenth century. For Rouelle, for instance, *composés* formed *agrégés*, in which there was *adhésion* or *cohérence* or *combinaison*, and which distinguished them from an *amas* in which there was merely contiguity among the parts, like a pile of sand. (See Diderot, *Oeuvres complètes*, ed. H. Dieckmann *et al*. (Paris, 1975–) IX, pp. 217–18.)

morale . . . would have particular and distinct qualities from those of the individual entities which constituted it, rather like chemical compounds have properties which they do not derive from the elements which compose them.' In such a compound unit there would be a common language which would make possible 'their mutual communication', and there would be 'a common sensorium which would allow the correspondence of all the parts. The public good or ill would not only be the sum of the individual goods and ills as in a simple *agrégation*, but it would lie in the *liaison* which unites them, it would be greater than this sum, and far from public happiness being established on the happiness of individuals, it is the public happiness which would be the source of that' (p. 284).

The emphasis in both these comparisons lay in the contrast between juxtaposition and communication, between an aggregate and a compound, the second of these terms being characterized by an internal reciprocity or *liaison* between the parts which is the source of its distinctive life. This reflected a conception of the relationship of the parts and whole which we also find among Rousseau's contemporaries, writing about living bodies.

In the change in scientific thinking which occurred in the middle years of the century (now generally characterized as a change from a mechanistic to a vitalist conception of nature),[33] one of the central issues was how complex living creatures arose. If such creatures were not, so to speak, programmed from the start, but developed by stages, subject to external influence, how did such developments actually occur? The atomistic conception of particles of matter coming together in particular combinations seemed quite inadequate to explain either the coherence or the complexity of living creatures. Instead, a process of assimilation and transformation was suggested.

Buffon, for example, put forward the idea that by *intussusception* each separate part could 'be incorporated internally' and 'assimilated into the whole'.[34] Maupertuis envisaged such a process taking place and asked: 'would each element, in losing its form and being accumulated into the body which it is going to make, also lose its perception? Would the small degree of feeling which it possessed be lost or weakened, or would it be increased by its union with the others, to the benefit of the whole?'[35] Working in a different context the Montpellier doctor Bordeu came to a similar view, suggesting that each different part of the body had 'its particular disposition' and 'particular action', and together all the parts work for 'the general life of the body . . . All contribute to form a solid body and yet each has its particular action'.[36] In all these accounts it was the interdependence of the parts, their dynamic

---

[33] See J. Roger, *Les sciences de la vie dans la pensée française du XVIIIe siècle* (Paris, 1963); S. Moravia, 'From *Homme Machine* to *Homme Sensible*', *Journal of the History of Ideas*, XXXIX (1978), pp. 45–60; P.H. Reill, 'Science and the Science of History in the *Spätaufklärung*', *Auflklärung und Geschichte*, ed. H.E. Boedeker *et al.* (Gottingen, 1986), pp. 430–51.

[34] Buffon, *Histoire naturelle*, II, pp. 43, 45 and 41.

[35] Maupertuis, *Oeuvres*, II, p. 155*. (First published in Latin in 1751 and in French in 1754.)

[36] Bordeu, *Oeuvres* (Paris, 1818), pp. 164, 186 and 187. (First published in 1752.)

ROUSSEAU'S REPUBLICAN VISION   101

interaction, described in terms of the *liaisons* and *rapports* between them, their reciprocal efforts,[37] which explained the life of the whole.

For Buffon, for Diderot (who enthusiastically elaborated the suggestions of Maupertuis and Bordeu[38]), and for doctors in the Montpellier school, these ideas were in sharp contrast to those of their mechanistic predecessors.[39] Firstly, the matter they were concerned with was not inert but self-animating; secondly, it changed over time; thirdly, in the formation of complex entities change involved internal transformation.[40] It is this last characteristic which also distinguished Rousseau's contrasts of juxtaposition and communication, aggregate and compound, or (in the *Contrat social*) *agrégation* and *association* (p. 359).[41] When he used these terms Rousseau was describing something qualitatively different from the contrast of *multitudo* and *civitas* which occurs in Hobbes and (with a varying terminology) in subsequent

---

[37] *Ibid.*, pp. 46, 145, 189 and 206.

[38] Diderot, *Oeuvres philosophiques*, pp. 228 (published in 1753), and pp. 289–93 (written in 1769, published in 1830).

[39] The contrast was expressed in terms of opposition either to mechanism itself or to mathematics or geometry as a model for scientific method. Buffon, *Histoire naturelle*, I, pp. 53–4, 58–9 and 60–1; Diderot, *Oeuvres philosophiques*, pp. 178–80; Ménuret de Chambaud, 'Oeconomie animale', *Encyclopédie* (Paris, 1765), XI, 364b. Likewise, Rousseau attacked the idea of applying geometrical analysis to politics 'because it does not relate enough to feeling' (*CC*, VIII, pp. 320–1). As much as his contemporaries in the life-sciences he was concerned with a living reality (Bordeu, *Oeuvres*, p. 47), an interior reality (Buffon, *Histoire naturelle*, I, p. 30 and II, pp. 34–5), characterized by an internal *sympathie* between the parts (Ménuret de Chambaud, *Encyclopédie*, XI, 318b and 362a). This did not prevent him, however, from referring to the state as a *machine* (see, on this point, Derathé's note: (1393–4), and A. Meyer, 'Mechanische und organische Metaphorik', pp. 131–2).

[40] Rousseau does not seem to have accepted the idea of self-animating matter, largely because of its materialist implications: see *OC*, IV, pp. 574 and 584–5n.

[41] In the *Contrat social*, Bk. I, ch. 6, Rousseau states: 'as men cannot engender new forces, but only unite and direct those which exist', they arrive at a situation in which 'they no longer have any means of preserving themselves except by forming by *agrégation* a sum of forces . . . and making them act together' (p. 360), i.e. undertaking some form of social contract. Rousseau's use of *agrégation* here stems from the fact that he is describing physical properties. This is clear from remarks elsewhere. 'Basically, the body politic, being only a *personne morale*, is only a creature of reason. Take away the public convention and at once the state is destroyed without the least alteration in everything which constitutes it; and all the conventions of men cannot change a thing in *le physique des choses*' (p. 608). 'In the *agrégation* of the body politic we should take into account how inferior the public force is to the sum of individual forces, how much friction there is in the play of the whole machine; then we will find that, making all necessary allowances, the weakest man has more strength for his own maintenance than the most robust state has for its maintenance.' This passage then continues: 'in order that the state survives, therefore, it is necessary that the liveliness of its passions supplements that of its movements, and that its *volonté* is animated to the same extent that its power grows slack'. By way of illustration he states that 'this is the reason why small states have proportionately more vigour than large states; because public *sensibilité* does not increase with territory; [on the contrary] the more extensive the territory, the cooler the *volonté*, and the feebler the movements' (p. 606). This passages indicates exactly how the moral and emotional aspects of political life, above all *l'amour de la patrie*, must supplement *le physique des choses* if an *agrégation* is to be transformed into an *association*.

102   J. HOPE MASON

Natural Law writers.[42] The latter was purely a legal change: dispersed individuals come together to form a collective entity which can function with one will and have specific rights. This entity will affect the individuals (that is its purpose), but it will not bring about an inner transformation. Hobbes likened the breakdown of a whole into its parts to what could be done with the mechanism of a watch;[43] the assembly of the various parts in such a case does not alter them individually.

The same observation could be made about another common idea of the parts and the whole which was applied to politics, the analogy with music. Like the comparison with the body this was ancient but well-known in the eighteenth century. Montesquieu used it in his *Considérations* . . . : 'what is called union in a body politic . . . is a union of harmony, which works so that all the parts, however opposed they may seem to us, contribute to the general good of the society; as dissonances, in music, contribute to the overall accord'.[44] As with the watch, each individual element, the musical line, has the same character *per se* before or after, with or without, its combination with the other lines.

There was a further notion of the whole and the parts which did contain the idea of inner transformation. This was the neo-Platonic conception familiarized by Pope: 'All are but parts of one stupendous whole, / Whose body Nature is, and God the Soul'.[45] If he transformed his life by turning away from material and earthly concerns, the Christian neo-Platonic believer could participate in the whole, know and love God, and so find the greatest possible human fulfilment. However, these parts

---

[42] *De Cive*, II, vi, 1 note; II, vii, 5 and 16; II, xii, 8; *Leviathan*, I, 17.

In his *Rousseau et la science politique*, pp. 410–13, Derathé takes issue with C.E. Vaughan for asserting that Rousseau put forward an 'organicist' theory of the state (in his edition of Rousseau's *Political Writings* (Cambridge, 1915), I, pp. 57–9 and 70, and his edition of the *Contrat social* (Manchester, 1918), pp. xxvii–xxix). Derathé points out that in his most extended use of the comparison Rousseau described it as 'commonplace and not very exact' (p. 244). However, Derathé does less than justice to Vaughan's treatment of this particular issue, for the latter wrote that although in spirit 'the analogy with the animal and the social organism . . . dominates the whole [*Contrat social*], . . . unless taken in the most vague and general sense, no analogy could be more misleading'. He went on to add: 'the union between the individual and the community must surely be not mechanical, nor even organic. It must involve not the absorption of the one in the other; but the reaction of each upon the other, the interpenetration of each by the other' (*Political Writings*, I, pp. 58–9). The analogy of the state with a natural organism, he stated in his edition of the *Contrat social*, cannot embody the subtlety of 'the essentially spiritual relation between the individual and the state' (p. xxix). On this specific point Vaughan's comments seem to me more accurate than those by Derathé.

Discussion of this question has in general been clouded by an inattention to the ways in which writings of the period from c.1750 to c.1790 were distinct from what preceeded and what came after them. For example, Kant was deeply impressed by the idea of the self-generating organism, in which parts and whole reciprocally affected each other. But there was a clear difference between his view of nature and that of Schelling, which was to provide the main inspiration for subsequent organic theories in political thought. (On these differences, see T. Lenoir, 'Generational factors in the origin of *Romantische Naturphilosophie*', *Journal of the History of Biology*, XI (1978), pp. 57–100.) This subject is, of course, part of the larger problem of the relationship between 'Enlightenment' and 'Romanticism'.

[43] Hobbes, *De Cive*, Preface.

[44] Montesquieu, *Oeuvres*, II, p. 119.

[45] Pope, *Essay on Man*, I, 267–8.

ROUSSEAU'S REPUBLICAN VISION 103

depended on an external and pre-existing agent, the divine Soul. They did not by their combination form a distinctly new entity. So this also was different from what Rousseau envisaged and, as we shall see, while he accepted this neo-Platonic conception in metaphysics he never applied it to politics.[46]

When Pufendorf described the act by which a multitude changed themselves into a civil society he wrote: ' each person commits himself with all the others to be joined together for ever in a single body and by a common consent to provide for their mutual security'.[47] (In Barbeyrac's translation: *'chacun s' engage avec tous les autres à se joindre ensemble pour toujours en un seul corps et à pourvoir d'un commun consentement à leur sûreté mutuelle'*.)[48] Rousseau described the contractual act as follows: 'each of us puts his person and all his power in common under the supreme direction of the *volonté générale*; and we receive *en corps* each member as an indivisible part of the whole. (*Chacun de nous met en commun sa personne et toute sa puissance sous la suprême direction de la volonté générale; et nous recevons en corps chaque membre comme partie indivisible du tout)*' (p. 361). The difference between these two is slight. Yet there is a difference, signalled by the sense of personal involvement (*chacun de nous . . . nous recevons . . .*) and by the phrase *volonté générale*.

The excessively dry, terse, legalistic language of the *Contrat social*, and its use of the conceptual framework of the Natural Law school, tends to obscure an essential dimension of Rousseau's political thought. That dimension was clearer in the *Économie politique* and the Geneva Manuscript, for there we find both the particular conception of the relation of the parts and the whole and clear statements of the emotional change possible in the just society. In the *Économie politique* these statements were in terms of *l' amour de la patrie*; in the Geneva Manuscript Rousseau wrote of the possibility of someone experiencing 'new feelings', 'multiplying his being and his happiness by sharing them with his fellow-men' (p. 288). These were essentially republican sentiments, and to understand the *Contrat social* it is necessary to be aware of the way these sentiments underpin (and subtly alter) the Natural Law framework. Although Rousseau emphasized the intellectual and moral gain which is achieved by the 'passage from the state of nature to the civil state' (p. 364), when he came to write of the different kinds of law he stated that the most important kind was that which exists 'in the hearts of the citizens. This forms the real constitution of the state' (p. 394). 'Law only works externally and rules actions: the *moeurs* alone reach within and direct the wills' (p. 555).

---

[46] The metaphysical view could and did lend itself to republican ideology. See, for example, James Thomson's poem *Liberty* (1734–6), in which he apostrophized republican freedom as 'The godlike passion! which, the bounds of self / Divinely bursting, the whole public takes / Into the heart, enlarged, and burning high / With the mixed ardour of unnumbered selves; / Of all who safe beneath the voted laws / Of the same parent state, fraternal, live' (III, 107 ff.). The idea of the self being 'enlarged' in this way was a neo-Platonic commonplace.

[47] *De jure naturae*, VII, ii, 7: *'necessum est, ut futuri cives primo omnium inter se singuli cum singulis pactum ineant, quod in unum et perpetuum coetum coire velint, suaeque salutis, ac securitatis rationes communi consilio ductuque administrare'*.

[48] *Le droit de la nature* (Amsterdam, 2nd edn., 1712), II, p. 231.

104   J. HOPE MASON

The *volonté générale* was, for Rousseau, the manifestation of, and intellectual counterpart to, *l'amour de la patrie*. As he made plain in his attack on Diderot's definition, Rousseau's idea of the *volonté générale* distinguished it clearly from an intellectual exercise, conducted in solitude, of a kind subsequently suggested by Kant. On the contrary, it depended on the experience of the people being *en corps*. The *volonté générale* was 'the will of the body of the people' (p. 369) and could only be expressed when the people were assembled (p. 425). That is why regular assem- ·blies were an essential feature of a legitimate state (p. 426), and· why the use of representatives (like the employment of professional soldiers) was a sign that the state was close to collapse (p. 428). 'Every law which the people has not ratified in person is null [and void]; it is not a law' (p. 430). It could not be taken to express the wish of the people as a whole because the people had not had the opportunity to experience themselves as a people, as a whole.

This view was a reflection of the empirical epistemology Rousseau shared with his contemporaries: knowledge is based on experience, without the experience there can be no knowledge. But it was also a reflection of the social theory of the *Inégalité*. (The first was, of course, integral to the second.) Inner feelings depend on external conditions. What we think or esteem or want is decisively affected by our relations with other people: 'the moral condition of a people is less a reflection of the absolute condition of its members than of their *rapports* among one another' (p. 511). Our relationships in turn are affected by the institutional framework (*les circonstances*) in which they take place. (This was Rousseau's fundamental insight.) This connection of the social theory to the political theory was suggested by Rousseau's comment in the *Inégalité* that children in a state of nature were treated as they later were to be in Sparta (p. 135), and by his comment in the *Contrat social* that the effect of good institutions would be that a people would be 'submitted to the laws of the state as to the laws of nature' (p. 383).

The idea of the creation of a new social order by individuals whose lives were transformed by their participation in that order was at the heart of Rousseau's political vision. As parts of this whole the individuals would in important respects be limited. That did not mean, however, that individual selves were eradicated or completely absorbed into a collectivity. Although there are some instances when Rousseau wrote as if he may have meant this,[49] it is abundantly clear that that cannot have been his intention.

Firstly, an individual's liberty and life were 'essential gifts of nature' (p. 184); to 'renounce one's liberty is to renounce your quality of being a man, the rights of humanity' (p. 356); the purpose of the contractual act was to institute an order in which each person remained after the contract 'as free as beforehand' (p. 360). Secondly, the aim of the *Contrat social* was to ally 'what right permits with what interest prescribes' (p. 351). *Intérêt* here, and on the two other occasions when

---

[49] For example, 'everything that destroys social unity is worthless; all institutions that put a man in contradiction with himself are worthless' (p. 464). But Rousseau's aim here, as Judith Shklar observed, 'is not social cohesion as an end in itself. The end is the unity within each man', Shklar, *Men and Citizens*, p. 167.

Rousseau repeated this point (pp. 363, 374), meant self-interest, and the remark would be meaningless if there were no individual selves. Thirdly, the obligations imposed by the *volonté générale* were reciprocal; 'the engagements which bind us to the social body are only obligatory because they are mutual, and their nature is such that in fulfilling them one cannot work for another without also working for oneself'. For this reason 'there is no one . . . who does not think of himself in voting for all' (p. 373).[50] Fourthly, individuals retained individual wishes and wills: 'each individual as a man can have a particular *volonté* contrary to or different from the *volonté générale* which he has as a citizen' (p. 363), hence the distinction between the *volonté générale* and the *volonté de tous* (p. 371). In a footnote Rousseau pointed out that it is precisely the difference between individuals which brings awareness of the common interest; 'if there were no different interests, the common interest, never finding any obstacle, would scarcely be felt' (p. 371n).

Fifthly, the social whole, created by the contractual act, was not an organic whole, in the sense in which that came to be understood in subsequent political thought. This is made clear by the distinction Rousseau made between politics and religious or metaphysical belief. In the latter the relation of the parts to the whole was different and it could be a case of 'All discord, harmony not understood; / All partial evil, universal good'.[51] Metaphysics is not a subject about which we can speak with authority; 'such knowledge is without doubt beyond human intelligence';[52] but if we believe in God and attribute certain qualities to him, then 'the system of this universe which produces, preserves and perpetuates all thinking and feeling creatures, should be dearer to [God] than a single one of these creatures. Therefore God can, in spite of his goodness (or, rather, through his very goodness) sacrifice something of the happiness of individuals to the preservation of the whole'.[53] In this respect, it can be that 'the private suffering of one individual contributes to the general good'.[54] If we adopt this belief (that 'the whole is good, or all is good for the whole') then we can accept that 'particular events here below are nothing in the eyes of the Master of the universe . . . that He is content . . . to preside over the whole without being worried about the way in which each individual passes this short life'.[55]

Rousseau never wrote in these terms about the social whole. He may have compared the two, to stress the interdependence of parts and whole (p. 554), or observed that 'the good man orders himself in relation to the whole and the bad man orders the whole in relation to himself'.[56] But man is not God, and what men can know or accomplish is different. For this reason, Rousseau stated, 'goodness in man is love of his fellow-men, and the goodness of God is the love of order'.[57] In the *Économie politique* he rejected in the clearest possible terms the application of optimist belief to political affairs:

[50] See also p. 438 and *OC*, IV, p. 936.

[51] Pope, *Essay on Man*, I, 292–3.

[52] *OC*, IV, p. 1068.

[53] *Ibid.*, p. 1067.

[54] *Ibid.*, p. 1068.

[55] *Ibid.*, p. 1069.

[56] *Ibid.*, p. 602.

[57] *Ibid.*, p. 593.

106   J. HOPE MASON

Is the safety of a single citizen less a matter of common concern than the safety of the whole state? If someone tells us that it is good that one person dies for everyone else, I will admire this remark in the mouth of a noble and virtuous patriot who voluntarily and through duty devotes himself to die for the safety of his country; but if it means that the government is permitted to sacrifice an innocent person for the safety of the multitude, then I regard this maxim as one of the most despicable that tyranny has ever invented, the most false . . . the most dangerous . . . and the most directly opposed to the fundamental laws of society. (p. 256)[58]

For all these reasons we can assert that Rousseau's political thought had an individualist core and an undeniable concern for individual freedom. However, we have also seen that the Rousseauian *association* was different from the Hobbesian *civitas*, and that to identify Rousseau with his Natural Law predecessors (in the manner of Hegel or Gierke or Derathé)[59] is mistaken. We cannot call Rousseau's ideas 'individualist' in the same way as we can those of previous social contract theorists, for that is to ignore the republican sentiments which were at the heart of his political vision, newly conceived in terms of an inner transformation in a just society.

The fact is, the social theory of the *Inégalité* drastically undermined the autonomy of individuals. While we all have a personal core of individuality, we are all also conditioned by our society. 'Our different situations determine and change *malgré nous* the affections of our hearts.'[60] This belief not only made socio-political arrangements a matter of the utmost importance. It also meant that the optimal condition of such arrangements could not be perceived in terms of simple individuals.[61] A proper assessment would pay attention to them but it would equally take account of the *rapports* and *liaisons* between them, their awareness of the *moi commun*, the reciprocal *sensibilité*; and those in turn would rest on the individuals' experience of being a whole, the opportunities they had to be *en corps*. Dependence on *les circonstances* meant that what we share collectively is, to a large measure, also what we are, individually.

[58] See also his remarks on *le bien public* (p. 511) and *le salut public* (*OC*, IV, p. 1126).

[59] Hegel, *Lectures on the History of Philosophy*, trans. E. Haldane (London, 1894), III, p. 503; O. Gierke, *Natural Law and the Theory of Society, 1500–1800*, trans. E. Barker (Cambridge, 1934), pp. 129–30, and *The Development of Political Thought*, trans. B. Freyd (London, 1939), pp. 109–10 and 180; Derathé, *Rousseau et la science politique*, pp. 237–8.

[60] *OC*, II, p. 1558.

[61] 'When it is a question of subjects as general as the *moeurs* and manners of a people, it is always necessary to beware of contracting one's views to individual examples. That would be the way never to perceive the sources of things . . . It is necessary to examine the *rapports*' (p. 53n). Buffon had made similar comments (with reference to observing the natural world) in his *Histoire naturelle*, I, pp. 21 and 25.

IV
The Intellect and The Emotions

Rousseau's social theory absolved man from original sin; it turned what had been primarily theological concerns into matters of politics and history, and it gave his political theory an extraordinary emotional charge. Yet it also seemed to leave man powerless to improve his actual condition. The importance of a particular stage in *la succession des temps* and dependence on *les circonstances* seemed to mean that the magnificent promise of inner transformation was, except by some happy accident, unattainable.

In the *Contrat social* Rousseau recognized this fact: 'in order that a people in the process of formation can appreciate the sound maxims of politics and follow the fundamental rules of statecraft, it would be necessary for the effect to become the cause, for the *esprit social* which should be the result of the institution to preside over the act of institution itself, and for men to be before laws were established what they should become by means of those laws' (p. 383). (He was here making the same point about *esprit social* that he had made in the Geneva Manuscript about conscience, see above, p. 97.)

Within the terms of his social theory there seemed to be no solution to this problem. The balance between human freedom (or *perfectibilité*), social conditions and evolutionary development, almost always seemed to favour the last two at the expense of the first. It was certainly true that the malleability of human beings, the artificial character of political institutions, and the uneven way in which development occurred, did open up the possibility of 'new associations' which could achieve 'by perfected art the repair of the ills which art initially did to nature' (p. 288). At one point in the *Inégalité* Rousseau wrote of 'revolutions' which might bring a government 'closer to its legitimate institution' (p. 187); but it was not at all clear how this possibility might be perceived, or acted upon.

At this point Rousseau had recourse to history. For the historical record differed from the 'hypothetical history' of the *Inégalité* (pp. 127, 133). In the ancient world, as in sixteenth-century Geneva, good republics had been established. Out of a political crisis a new socio-political order had been formed. This had been the work of a *Législateur*: an outstanding individual, an aberration in nature, who by virtue of being that was able to rise above circumstances and see what others could not. In adopting this idea Rousseau followed Machiavelli (and his reading of Plutarch) as succinctly restated by Montesquieu: 'at the birth of societies it is the leaders of republics who form the institution, and subsequently it is the institution which forms the leaders of republics' (p. 381).[62]

The *Législateur* was a freak in politics as well as in nature (p. 382). He had no role in the functioning of the republic. His task was, rather, to provide the institutional framework within which republican life could flourish. He did not impose such a framework on any people; that would be to deprive them of precisely that freedom which the republic was designed to promote (p. 316). There was a clear distinction

---

[62] Machiavelli, *Discorsi*, Bk. I, chs. 9, 10 and 11. Montesquieu, *Oeuvres*, II, p. 70.

between the *Législateur*'s proposals and the specific act by which a people, in adopting them, made them effective. This distinction, based on the example of antiquity, was well understood by republican writers. Sidney, for example, had observed: 'Solon did not make, but propose laws, and they were of no force till they were established by the authority of the people. The Spartans dealt in the same manner with Lycurgus: he invented their laws, but the people made them.'[63] If such a distinction were not made, Rousseau observed, the result would be tyranny (pp. 314, 382).

Here again, however, the comprehensive character of Rousseau's social theory generated grave problems. It was not simply a question of what could be known, but of how such knowledge could be communicated. The *Législateur* might perceive what political arrangements would most benefit a particular people, but how could he convince them he was right? 'There are a thousand kinds of ideas which it is impossible to translate into the language of the people.' (p. 383) He was faced with the problem of 'persuading without convincing' (p. 383). The record of history indicated that to do this he would need to invoke the gods and present himself as if he were their mouthpiece. Then the people would recognize 'the same power in the formation of the physical body [man] and in that of the moral body [the city]' (pp. 317, [383]). For this to be plausible he would need 'an eloquence and assurance which were more than human. The depths of wisdom and the firmness of virtue would have to be accompanied by the fire of enthusiasm' (p. 317).

The *Législateur*, in other words, was not simply Solon or Lycurgus, but also Amphion or Orpheus: the poet as legislator as extolled by writers from Aristophanes onwards.[64] This notion had been incorporated into the rhetorical tradition with Isocrates' suggestion that society had been founded by an orator,[65] and it is possible that Rousseau had drawn on this tradition in the *Inégalité* when he portrayed the institution of property and of legally sanctioned inequality as effected by deceitful speech seducing 'uncultivated men' (pp. 164, 177). If the 'true founder of civil society' was an evil orator, then the *Législateur* was precisely the opposite. While the former stimulated the egotistic and competitive tendencies, the latter's work was 'to transform each individual, who on his own is a perfect and solitary whole, into a part of a greater whole from which this individual in some way receives his life and being; to alter man's constitution in order to reinforce it; to substitute a partial and moral existence for the independent, physical existence which we have all received from nature' (p. 381). By so doing the *Législateur* would solve the difficulties presented by the social theory.

[63] Sidney, *Discourses*, p. 308.

[64] Aristophanes, *Frogs*, 1031 ff.; Horace, *Ars poetica*, 391 ff. For Rousseau's views about the first poets see his *Essai sur l'origine des langues*, Ch. 12, ed. C. Porset (Paris, 1970), pp. 139 ff. (In his poem *The First Anniversary of Government under O.C.* (1655), lines 35 ff., Andrew Marvell had compared Cromwell to Amphion: 'So when Amphion did his lute command, / Which the God gave him, with his gentle hand, / The rougher stones, unto his measures hewed, / Danced up in order from the quarries rude; / . . . Such was the wondrous order and consent, / When Cromwell tuned the ruling instrument. / . . . The Commonwealth then first together came, / And each one entered in the willing frame.')

[65] Isocrates, *Nicocles*, 5–8; *Antidosis*, 253–6; Cicero, *De inventione*, I, ii, 2.

At the same time, however, he created new problems in terms of the political theory. For the means by which he accomplished his task were those of deception and enchantment. He must pretend to be divinely inspired, even if he is not; while ostensibly being occupied with making laws he should 'in secret' be concerned with *moeurs* (p. 394); and he must so captivate his audience that they will be convinced of what he suggests. The result of his work would be that the citizens would 'obey with freedom' (p. 383). But what meaning can freedom have in such a context? The same could be asked about the 'wise administration', whom Rousseau described, in an unpublished fragment, as being wise insofar as it was able 'to form public *moeurs* by education and custom and so direct individuals' inclinations that in general they find themselves happier with the government under which they are living than they would be under any other, whether better or worse' (p. 513). Such passages inevitably bring to mind ideas of manipulation, conditioning or, in the chilling phrase our century has invented, brainwashing.

There is no way the principles set out in the *Contrat social* could justify such action. Indeed, the central thrust of that work is the protection of citizens from autocratic rule. Rousseau's refusal to transfer sovereignty from the citizenry to government and his insistence on the subjection of government to the citizen-body was uncompromising. The framework suggested was precisely designed to avoid any dependence on individual men or groups of men. His reiteration of these principles in subsequent writing, especially in the work occasioned by the political crisis in Geneva, the *Lettres écrites de la montagne*, with its explicit definition of freedom as 'not being submitted to the will of another' (p. 841), put this matter beyond reasonable doubt.[66] Yet it is in the *Contrat social* that we read of the *Législateur* so deceiving and enchanting the people that they are 'freely' obedient.

This contradiction arose from the difficulty which Rousseau expressed as a problem of the *esprit social* having to be known before the event. This was essentially a problem caused by his empirical epistemology: how could the parts know in advance what it would be like to be part of an as-yet-uncreated whole? But there was another difficulty here, which lay at the heart of Rousseau's ambivalence about social life generally. This was his feeling that the emotions and the intellect are at best uneasy partners and, at worst, natural enemies.

'The mind corrupts the senses' (p. 141). In the process of development described in the *Inégalité* the growth of intellectual activity is depicted as a loss of emotional well-being: 'it is reason which engenders *amour-propre* and it is reflection which reinforces it; it is that which turns a man in on himself . . . it is philosophy which isolates him' (p. 156). This was a constant theme in Rousseau's writing. He had expressed the point earlier in his *Préface à Narcisse* (1753)[67] and was to do so later in *Emile*: the philosophical state of mind 'concentrates all the passions in individual

---

[66] Rousseau's acute fear of the increase in the executive power of governments also found its sharpest expression in this work, as a result of his sociological perspective: 'justice among the people is a virtue of their condition; similarly violence and tyranny among leaders is a vice of their condition. If we were in their position we would become like them, violent, grasping and wicked' (p. 891n).

[67] *OC*, II, pp. 966–7.

110   J. HOPE MASON

self-interest, in the abjection of the *moi humain*, and in that way quietly undermines the true foundations of society'.[68] One of the most original aspects of Rousseau's work was precisely his attack on the claims made for reason by previous writers. 'The error of most moralists was always to take man to be essentially an *être raisonnable*. Man is merely an *être sensible*, who only consults his feelings to act.' (p. 554) Intellectual life, like literary life, distorts the feelings;[69] what fills the mind freezes the heart (p. 156).[70]

Yet we cannot renounce our mental faculties, once they have developed; and not all that they bring is harmful. It is, in fact, only by reason and imagination that we can recover a true idea of what is essential to our nature (p. 123), the project of the *Inégalité*. It is reason alone which can re-establish 'the rules of natural right' after the emotional bases of natural right have been destroyed (p. 126). It is reason likewise which determines the 'principles of political right' of the *Contrat social*. Such matters are not easily grasped. They need that 'superior intellect' which distinguishes a *Législateur* (p. 312).

We need the knowledge, but the qualities which make such knowledge possible are not those which will ensure the maintenance of the good society. 'Although it is necessary for philosophers, historians and scholars to enlighten the world and lead its blind inhabitants . . . I can think of nothing so mad as a people of wise men (*un peuple de sages*)' (p. 227). The sedentary, isolated life of the intellectual is the antithesis of that active, shared life in which *l' amour de la patrie* can flourish.[71] But the other side of this coin was, as Rousseau then observed, that 'if it is good that great *génies* instruct men, it is necessary that *le vulgaire* accept their instructions' (p. 227). In reading these lines we need to rid ourselves of the connotations which *le génie* and *le vulgaire* have for us today. In Rousseau's eyes each had something the other lacked, brilliant intellect or humane feelings. The first *voit* the good, the second always *veut* the good (p. 380). Only the first could establish the form of a good society, only the second could make it function.[72]

This distinction between intellect and emotions was reflected in the division of responsibility in the just society. The government is 'the brain of the state', the

---

[68] *Ibid.*, IV, p. 633n.

[69] *Ibid.*, p. 1063.

[70] Rousseau often wrote in praise of a life of minimal mental activity (see, for example, *OC*, I, pp. 43 and 849–50, and *ibid.*, IV, p. 1063). R.A. Leigh observed that there is a 'secret vein of aspiration to a Nirvana-like condition which runs underground in Rousseau's work, from the primitive man of the first part of the *Inégalité* to the *Rêveries du promeneur solitaire*', 'From *Inégalité* to *Candide*', *The Age of Enlightenment*, ed. W.H. Barber *et al.* (Edinburgh, 1967), p. 85. Although the Spartan Rousseau of the *Contrat social* is often opposed to the romantic Rousseau of *La Nouvelle Héloïse*, and the public world of the former to the intensely personal world of the *Rêveries*, there were important links between these texts: in the first pair, in terms of emotional *expansion*, in the second pair in terms of a *situation* which kept mental activity at a low level.

[71] *OC*, II, pp. 966–7.

[72] For other aspects of the problem which arose from this distinction see H. Meier's Introduction to his edition of the *Inégalité* (Paderborn, 1984), pp. xlviii–liii.

sovereign assembly is its 'heart' (p. 424). Only the government could propose a new law, but only the people *en corps*, by accepting or rejecting it, could make it law (p. 439). (They do so by expressing the *volonté générale* and it is unfortunate that this phrase is always translated as 'general will'; for *volonté* is as much a matter of emotional wish as it is of rationally-determined will.) It is also this distinction, I believe, which underlay Rousseau's brief comments on *liberté civile* and *liberté morale* (p. 365). The former, 'which is limited by the *volonté générale*' reflects the *moeurs* of a just society, where duties are not generally in opposition to inclinations. The latter, which is not connected by Rousseau to the *volonté générale* but is rather 'obedience to the law one prescribes to oneself', is a Stoic or Kantian rule of reason over the emotions.[73]

In considering the difference between *le génie* and *le vulgaire* it was always the condition of the latter which should determine whether or not a society was functioning well. 'People have had too much admiration for the centuries in which the arts and literature have been seen to flourish'; instead we should turn our attention to 'the well-being of whole nations and above all to that of the condition of the majority' (420n). *Le vulgaire* had need of *le génie* but it was their well-being which mattered most.

On this point Rousseau parted company with his republican predecessors. One of the principal arguments of republican writers, from Herodotus and Sallust to Machiavelli and Sidney, was that the republic alone fostered greatness. 'Athens never had an eminent man, after it felt the weight of the Macedonian yoke'; 'the strength, virtue, glory, weight, power and happiness of Rome, proceeding from [republican] liberty, did rise, grow and perish with it.'[74]

For Rousseau, on the other hand, greatness and glory were never the goal. On the contrary, they were signs of a society where the desire for personal distinction (*le fureur de se distinguer*) had taken preference over *l'amour de la patrie*, two emotions which in his view were incompatible.[75] The good society was one in which 'public *moeurs* make up for the *génie* of the leaders; . . . the more virtue reigns, the less talents are necessary' (p. 254; and see p. 940). They are necessary neither to fill what might be called the gaps in the social functioning, nor to meet the emotional needs of individual citizens. 'The better the state is constituted, the more public affairs count over private affairs in the minds of citizens. There are even a great many less private affairs. Because the amount of shared happiness provides considerably more

---

[73] Elsewhere Rousseau distinguished between *liberté commune*, which was an affair of the *patrie*, and *liberté particulière* 'that is to say, virtue. The virtuous man is always free, for in doing his duty he never does anything except what he wants' (*CC*, XXIV, p. 32). It is this virtue — individual, moral freedom — which Emile, a young man without a *patrie*, is taught to have (*OC*, IV, pp. 814 ff, especially pp. 817–18). For this reason it is wrong to see the *Contrat social* and *Emile* as having a common aim (as is suggested in my *The Indispensable Rousseau* (London, 1979), pp. 8 and 180–1, and I. Fetscher, *Rousseaus politische Philosophie* (Frankfurt, 1975), pp. 88–96.

[74] Sidney, *Discourses*, pp. 126 and 116.

[75] In the Dedication to the *Inégalité* Rousseau praised his father for the fact that 'he was not *distingué* among his fellow-citizens; he only was what they all are' (p. 118).

112   J. HOPE MASON

to each person than he obtains on his own, there is less need to look for happiness in individual concerns.' (p. 429)

When he was young Rousseau had read Plutarch's *Lives* and accounts of ancient Rome; these, he said, had 'opened that youthful heart to all the expansive and tender feelings'.[76] The just republic was for him above all the place where such emotions could be realized. It was not based on self-denial but, on the contrary, could give opportunity for the greatest self-fulfilment. Such a self would, of course, in important respects be limited. But it would accept such limits, gladly, in the awareness that only by means of such limits could this particular kind of happiness be achieved and sustained. 'The most wicked man is he who isolates himself the most, who most concentrates his heart in himself; the best man is he who shares his affections equally with all his fellows.'[77]

Although Rousseau wrote of this happiness sometimes in terms of unity and overcoming contradiction (pp. 464, 510), it would be better described as a balance — between 'the simplicity of nature' and 'the needs of society' (p. 391), between inner experience and external circumstance, between the private and the shared, needs and desires, freedom and limits. The principal reason for preferring balance to unity is that the latter was not, in Rousseau's own terms, attainable. Once men have left the state of nature and entered history they cannot escape contradiction. They can only hope to minimize it, and find an equilibrium, in a republic characterized, above all, by a shared feeling of *fraternité*.[78]

J. Hope Mason   ADELPHI UNIVERSITY

---

[76] *OC*, I, p. 819.

[77] *LA*, p. 158.

[78] Some aspects of this article were first presented in papers given to a Conference on the Enlightenment at the Wissenschaftskolleg, Berlin (where it benefitted from the contributions of Sergio Moravia, Peter Hanns Reill and Robert Wokler), to the Colloquium on the Enlightenment at New York University, and to the Seminar on Political Thought at Johns Hopkins University.

Addenda 112a

References within the text:

p. 89, §1, 1.4: *OC*3.192/*CW*3.65
  Ibid., 1.7: *OC*3.212/*CW*3.84–85
  Ibid., §2, 1.3: *OC*3.364/*CW*4.141
  Ibid., 1.4: *OC*3.132/*CW*3.18
  Ibid., 1.9: *OC*3.143–44/*CW*3.27–28
  Ibid., §3, 1.2: *OC*3.193/*CW*3.66, *OC*3.203/*CW*3.75–76
p. 90, §1, 1.1: *OC*3.175/*CW*3.51–52, *OC*3.202/*CW*3.74
  Ibid., 1.3: *OC*3.219/*CW*3.91
  Ibid., 1.5: *OC*3.127/*CW*3.15
  Ibid., 1.15: *OC*3.122/*CW*3.12
  Ibid., §2, 1.4: *OC*3.49–50/*CW*2.48
  Ibid., 1.5: *OC*3.192/*CW*3.65
  Ibid., §3, 1.3: *OC*3.143/*CW*3.27
  Ibid., 1.5: *OC*3.162/*CW*3.42
  Ibid., 1.6: *OC*3.152/*CW*3.34
  Ibid., 1.7: *OC*3.168/*CW*3.46
  Ibid., 1.14: *OC*3.192/*CW*3.66
p. 92, §2, 1.4: *OC*3.113/*CW*3.5
  Ibid., 1.5: *OC*3.114/*CW*3.6
  Ibid., §2, 1.6: *OC*3.116/*CW*3.7
  Ibid., 1.7: *OC*3.111/*CW*3.3
  Ibid., 1.8: *OC*3.112/*CW*3.3
  Ibid., 1.10: *OC*3.112–13/*CW*3.4–5
  Ibid., 1.11: *OC*3.116/*CW*3.7
  Ibid., 1.12: *OC*3.120/*CW*3.10
p. 93, §4, 1.2: *OC*3.251/*CW*3.148
  Ibid., 1.4: *OC*3.245/*CW*3.143
p. 94, §1, 1.3: *OC*3.255/*CW*3.151
  Ibid., 1.4: *OC*3.254/*CW*3.151
  Ibid., 1.9: *OC*3.254–55/*CW*3.151
  Ibid., 1.10: *OC*3.248/*CW*3.145–46, *OC*3.258/*CW*3.153–54
  Ibid., 1.13: *OC*3.258/*CW*3.154
  Ibid., 1.15: *OC*3.258–59/*CW*3.154
  Ibid., 1.17: *OC*3.259/*CW*3.154
  Ibid., §3, 1.7: *OC*3.259/*CW*3.155
p. 95, §1, 1.13: *OC*3.259–60/*CW*3.155
  Ibid., §2, 1.5: *OC*3.255/*CW*3.151
  Ibid., 1.8: *OC*3.259/*CW*3.154–55
  Ibid., §4, 1.9: *OC*3.232/*CW*3.128–29
p. 96, §1, 1.7: *OC*3.171/*CW*3.49
  Ibid., 1.9: *OC*3.259/*CW*3.155, *OC*3.260/*CW*3.155
  Ibid., §2, 1.9: *OC*3.261/*CW*3.156
  Ibid., 1.12: *OC*3.262/*CW*3.157
  Ibid., §3, 1.6: *OC*3.174/*CW*3.51
p. 97, §1, 1.7: *OC*3.282/*CW*4.76
  Ibid., 1.13: *OC*3.283/*CW*4.78
  Ibid., §2, 1.4: *OC*3.286/*CW*4.80
  Ibid., 1.7: *OC*3.286/*CW*4.80
  Ibid., 1.8: *OC*3.287/*CW*4.80–81
  Ibid., 1.11: *OC*3.287/*CW*4.81

112b

p. 98, §2, l.8: *OC*3.391/*CW*4.162
  Ibid., §4, l.2: *OC*3.319/*CW*4.105, *OC*3.385/*CW*4.157
  Ibid., l.4: *OC*3.391/*CW*4.162
  Ibid., l.8: *OC*3.385/*CW*4.158
  Ibid., l.13: *OC*3.933/*CW*11.150, *OC*3.1003–04/*CW*11.209–10
p. 99, §1, l.3: *OC*3.244/*CW*3.142
  Ibid., l.8: *OC*3.245/*CW*3.143
  Ibid., §3, ll.5–7: *OC*3.283–84/*CW*4.78–79
p. 100, §1, l.10: *OC*3.284/*CW*4.78–79
p. 101, §2, l.8: *OC*3.359/*CW*4.137
p. 103, §2, ll.7–11: *OC*3.361/*CW*4.139
  Ibid., §3, ll.8–9: *OC*3.288/*CW*4.82
  Ibid., §3, l.13: *OC*3.364/*CW*4.141
  Ibid., §3, l.16: *OC*3.394/*CW*4.164
  Ibid., §3, l.17: *OC*3.555/*CW*4.71
p. 104, §1, l.6: *OC*3.369/*CW*4.145
  Ibid., l.7: *OC*3.425/*CW*4.189
  Ibid., l.8: *OC*3.426/*CW*4.190
  Ibid., l.10: *OC*3.428/*CW*4.191–92
  Ibid., l.11: *OC*3.430/*CW*4.192
  Ibid., §2, l.7: *OC*3.511/*CW*4.41
  Ibid., l.12: *OC*3.135/*CW*3.21
  Ibid., l.14: *OC*3.383/*CW*4.156
  Ibid., §4, l.1: *OC*3.184/*CW*3.59
  Ibid., l.3: *OC*3.356/*CW*4.135
  Ibid., l.4: *OC*3.360/*CW*4.138
  Ibid., l.6: *OC*3.351/*CW*4.131
p. 105, §1, l.1: *OC*3.363/*CW*4.140, *OC*3.374/*CW*4.149
  Ibid., l.7: *OC*3.373/*CW*4.148–49
  Ibid., l.9: *OC*3.363/*CW*4.140–41
  Ibid., l.10: *OC*3.371/*CW*4.147
  Ibid., l.13: *OC*3.371n/*CW*4.147n
  Ibid., §3, l.2: *OC*3.554/*CW*4.71
p. 106, §1, l.9: *OC*3.256/*CW*3.152
p. 107, §2, l.6: *OC*3.383/*CW*4.156
  Ibid., §3, l.7: *OC*3.288/*CW*4.82
  Ibid., l.9: *OC*3.187/*CW*3.62
  Ibid., §4, l.2: *OC*3.127/*CW*3.16, *OC*3.133/*CW*3.19
  Ibid., l.10: *OC*3.381/*CW*4.155
  Ibid., §5, l.1: *OC*3.382/*CW*4.155
  Ibid., l.5: *OC*3.316/*CW*4.103
p. 108, §1, l.8: *OC*3.314/*CW*4.101, *OC*3.382/*CW*4.155
  Ibid., §2, l.6: *OC*3.383/*CW*4.156
  Ibid., l.7: *OC*3.383/*CW*4.156
  Ibid., l.11: *OC*3.317/*CW*4.104 [*OC*3.383/*CW*4.156]
  Ibid., l.13: *OC*3.317/*CW*4.104
  Ibid., §3, l.7: *OC*3.164/*CW*3.43, *OC*3.177/*CW*3.54
  Ibid., l.14: *OC*3.381/*CW*4.155
p. 109, §1, l.5: *OC*3.394/*CW*4.165
  Ibid., l.7: *OC*3.383/*CW*4.156
  Ibid., l.12: *OC*3.513/*CW*4.43
  Ibid., §2, l.9: *OC*3.841/*CW*9.260
  Ibid., §4, l.1: *OC*3.141/*CW*3.26
  Ibid., l.5: *OC*3.156/*CW*3.37

p. 110, §1, l.6: *OC*3.554/*CW*4.70
   Ibid., l.7: *OC*3.156/*CW*3.37
   Ibid., §2, l.3: *OC*3.123/*CW*3.13
   Ibid., l.5: *OC*3.126/*CW*3.15
   Ibid., l.8: *OC*3.312/*CW*4.100
   Ibid., §3, l.5: *OC*3.227/*CW*3.106
   Ibid., l.8: *OC*3.227/*CW*3.106
   Ibid., l.12: *OC*3.380/*CW*4.154
p. 111, §1, l.1: *OC*3.424/*CW*4.188
   Ibid., l.3: *OC*3.439/*CW*4.199–200
   Ibid., l.7: *OC*3. 365/*CW*4.141–42
   Ibid., §2, l.6: *OC*3.420n/*CW*4.185n
   Ibid., §4, l.6: *OC*3.254/*CW*3.150, *OC*3.940/*CW*11.156
p. 112, §1, l.2: *OC*3.429/*CW*4.192
   Ibid., §3, l.2: *OC*3.464/*CW*4.218–19, *OC*3.510/*CW*4.41
   Ibid., l.3: *OC*3.391/*CW*4.162

Endnotes:

2. *OC*1.1135/*CW*5.575
3. *OC*4.935–36/*CW*9.28
4. *OC*3.1317–19/–
10. *OC*1.404/*CW*5.340
22. *OC*4.600/*Em*.290
23. –/–; *OC*5.101/*CW*10.332
24. *OC*5.16/*CW*10.262–63
25. *OC*5.59/*CW*10.298
26. *OC*5.102/*CW*10.333
27. *OC*5.103/*CW*10.334
28. –/–
29. *OC*1.935/*CW*1.213
30. *OC*4.468/*Em*.194
31. *OC*3.1394n.7/–
32. §2, l.3: *OC*3.283/*CW*4.78
39. l.5: –/–; l.9: *OC*3.1393–94/–
40. *OC*4.574/*Em*.272, *OC*4.584–85n/*Em*.279n
41. l.4: *OC*3.360/*CW*4.138; l.8: *OC*3.608/*CW*11.73; l.17: *OC*3.606/*CW*11.68
49. *OC*3.464/*CW*4.219
50. *OC*3.438/*CW*4.198–99, *OC*4.936/*CW*9.28–29
52. *OC*4.1068/*CW*3.115
53. *OC*4.1067/*CW*3.114–15
54. *OC*4.1068/*CW*3.115
55. *OC*4.1069/*CW*3.116
56. *OC*4.602/*Em*.292
57. *OC*4.593/*Em*.285
58. *OC*3.511/*CW*4.41, *OC*4.1126/–
60. *OC*2.1558/*CW*6.688
61. *OC*3.53n/*CW*2.51
64. l.2: *OC*5.410ff/*CW*7.318ff
66. *OC*3.891n/*CW*9.301
67. *OC*2.966–67/*CW*2.191–92
68. *OC*4.633n/*Em*.312n
69. *OC*4.1063/*CW*3.111
70. *OC*1.43/*CW*5.36–37, *OC*1.849–50/*CW*5.146–47, *OC*4.1063/*CW*3.111
71. *OC*2.966–67/*CW*2.191–92

112d

73. –/–; *OC*4.814ff/*Em*.442ff, *OC*4.817–18/*Em*.444–45
75. *OC*3.118/*CW*3.9
76. *OC*1.819/*CW*1.123
77. *OC*5.107/*CW*10.337–38

[10]

Freedom, Dependence, and the General Will

Frederick Neuhouser

In his *Lectures on the History of Philosophy* Hegel credits Rousseau with an epoch-making innovation in the realm of practical philosophy, an innovation said to consist in the fact that Rousseau is the first thinker to recognize "the free will" as the fundamental principle of political philosophy.[1] Since Hegel's own practical philosophy is explicitly grounded in an account of the will and its freedom, Hegel's assertion is clearly intended as an acknowledgment of his deep indebtedness to Rousseau's social and political thought. What is not so clear, however, is how this indebtedness is to be understood: What precisely does it mean to say that the political theories of Hegel and Rousseau share the same first principle? In this paper I intend to follow up on this interpretive suggestion of Hegel's by elaborating, much more explicitly than he himself does, the sense in which Rousseau's political thought is founded on the principle of the "free will." While accomplishing this task will put us in a better position to clarify the obscure philosophical strategy behind Hegel's own social theory, my primary interest here is to illuminate the foundations of Rousseau's political thought, especially its account of the connection between freedom and the general will. I argue that it is necessary to distinguish two ways in which Rousseau takes the general will to secure, or realize, the freedom of individual citizens, namely, by functioning as an embodiment as well as a precondition of such freedom. Understanding both of these points will lead us to see that Rousseau's thought rests on two distinct, though not incompatible, accounts of how citizens whose actions are constrained by the general will are in fact subject only to their own wills and therefore free in their obedience to the general will. As we shall see, these two accounts are implicitly based upon distinct conceptions of political freedom,

---

[1]Georg Wilhelm Friedrich Hegel, *Werke* (Frankfurt am Main: Suhrkamp, 1986), vol. 20, 306. See also §258R of Hegel's *Philosophy of Right*.

FREDERICK NEUHOUSER

which, for reasons I discuss below, can be characterized respectively as "subjective" and "objective" conceptions of freedom. My claim is that to ignore either of these conceptions is to leave out an essential element of Rousseau's understanding of how citizens achieve their freedom within the rational state.

Hegel sets out his understanding of Rousseau's contribution to political philosophy in a brief summary of his predecessor's basic position:

> The human being is free, and this is certainly his substantial nature. This freedom is not something that is surrendered in the state; rather, it is first constituted therein. Natural freedom, the predisposition [*Anlage*] to freedom, is not real freedom, for only the state is the realization of freedom.[2]

Two points emerge from this characterization of Rousseau's view that are relevant to understanding what it means to found political philosophy on the principle of the free will. The first involves a claim about the essential nature of human beings, which is said to consist in *freedom*: Human beings live up to their true essence when they possess free wills; or, as Rousseau himself puts it, "to renounce one's freedom is to renounce one's status as a man" (SC 1.4.6).[3] The second point formulates the most basic principle of political philosophy by asserting an essential connection between human freedom and the state: "The state is the realization of freedom." The key to understanding Rousseau's political thought (and ultimately Hegel's as well) lies in grasping the nature of the relation that is said to hold between freedom and the state. Above all, what

---

[2]Hegel, *Werke* 20:307.
[3]'SC 1.4.6' refers to book 1, chapter 4, paragraph 6 of *On the Social Contract* (SC), ed. Roger D. Masters, trans. Judith R. Masters (New York: St. Martin's Press, 1978). Other works of Rousseau's are cited as follows: *Emile*, trans. Allan Bloom (New York: Basic Books, 1979); *Discourse on the Sciences and Arts* (DSA) and *Discourse on Inequality* (DI), in *The First and Second Discourses*, trans. Roger D. Masters and Judith R. Masters (New York: St. Martin's Press, 1964); *Geneva Manuscript* (GM) and *Political Economy* (PE), in *On the Social Contract*; *The Reveries of the Solitary Walker* (RSW), trans. Charles E. Butterworth (New York: Harper & Row, 1979); *The Government of Poland* (GP), trans. Willmoore Kendall (Indianapolis: Hackett, 1985); *Oeuvres Complètes* (OC), ed. Bernard Gagnebin and Marcel Raymond (Paris: Gallimard, Bibliothèque de la Pléiade, 1959–69), vol. 3.

FREEDOM, DEPENDENCE, THE GENERAL WILL

is meant by the claim that the state "realizes" freedom? To say that the state realizes freedom is to imply that without the state freedom is not real or actual—or, in the words of Hegel cited above, that human freedom is first constituted in the state. On this view, the role of the state with respect to freedom is not, as Locke would have it, one of simply preserving and extending a freedom that individuals can possess independently of their membership in a political community. For Rousseau the freedom that defines our nature as human beings is first constituted in the state and therefore depends upon the state for its very existence. Thus, the most basic thought of Rousseau's political philosophy can be formulated as follows: The justification of the rational state resides in the fact that such a state plays an indispensable role in constituting human beings as bearers of free wills and is therefore essential to the fulfillment of their true nature as free beings.

Elaborating this basic thought of Rousseau's will involve, above all, specifying how the rational state realizes the freedom of its members. There are at least two ways one might conceive of the relationship between the state and freedom. First, the state might be thought of as bringing about a set of determinate social conditions that *make possible* the freedom of its members. On this view, the state would realize freedom by fulfilling (at least some of) the conditions that enable individuals to possess a free will. Membership in a rational state would then be a precondition of one's essential freedom. A second possibility would be to understand political membership not as something that conditions, but remains external to, the freedom of citizens but rather as a mode of relating to the social world that is itself an instance of freedom. That is, being part of a rational state might be regarded as constitutive of, or as *embodying*, the freedom of the individuals who compose it. This is especially plausible if, as in the case of Rousseau, the rational state is held to be a democratic one in which (at least a part of) the freedom of citizens consists in their self-legislating activity. This set of conceptual possibilities can be summed up by saying that the rational state might relate to the freedom of its members either as a *precondition* or as an *embodiment* of that freedom.

An intriguing, and complicating, feature of Rousseau's political philosophy is that it views the state as standing in *both* of these relations to the freedom of its members: Membership in the rational state makes freedom real by being both its precondition and its

FREDERICK NEUHOUSER

embodiment. This interpretive claim immediately raises a question concerning the coherence of Rousseau's position: How can the state stand in both of these relations to one and the same thing? The key to answering this question in the case of Rousseau is to associate each of these relations with one of the two kinds of political freedom distinguished in the *Social Contract*, both of which are realized only in the state. In short, Rousseau's view will be that membership in the state *embodies* "moral freedom," which is defined as a species of autonomy, or as "obedience to the law one has prescribed for oneself" (SC 1.8.3).[4] At the same time, political membership is a *precondition* of "civil freedom," which Rousseau takes to be the ability of individuals to act unconstrained by the particular wills of others within a sphere of activity deemed by society to be external to the vital interests of the community as a whole. For now I shall consider moral and civil freedom simply to be two distinct kinds of freedom and only later ask about the relationship between them.

Freedom through the General Will

Having indicated the general direction in which my interpretation is headed, I turn now to a more detailed examination of Rousseau's views as he himself presents them. I shall be concerned to articulate not only Rousseau's understanding of how a rational state realizes the freedom of its members but also his reasons for maintaining that a free will can exist *only* as part of a rational political order. The place to begin such an investigation is the central concept of Rousseau's political theory, the general will. For the general will is both a *political* concept—it embodies the principles of political as-

---

[4]Rousseau's term *liberté morale* easily misleads twentieth-century readers, who are apt to take 'moral' to refer to the ethical, to that which has to do with right and wrong. Rousseau very often uses 'moral' in a broader sense that denotes the intellectual, mental, or spiritual aspects of human reality, in contrast to the material or physical. It might be better to call the autonomy Rousseau describes here "spiritual freedom" in order to avoid confusing it with Kant's notion of moral autonomy, which is moral in both the broad and narrow senses.

FREEDOM, DEPENDENCE, THE GENERAL WILL

sociation—and the principle that accounts for the *freedom* of the state's individual members. This dual function of the general will is expressed in the statement that "it is through the general will that [individuals] are citizens and free" (SC 4.2.8, translation amended). In what follows I begin to elucidate Rousseau's thought that it is through their political attachments, or "through the general will," that individuals exist as free.

Rousseau invokes the concept of the general will in order to solve what he takes to be the fundamental problem of political philosophy—namely, to devise a form of political association that reconciles the associates' need for social cooperation with their essential natures as free beings. The difficulty of this task lies in the fact that effective social cooperation must be regulated by a social will in accord with the common good, whereas the freedom of individuals requires that their wills be subject to no will other than their own. Since the need to cooperate with others requires individuals to adjust or curtail their actions in accord with interests beyond their own purely particular good, they seem to have no option but to submit their wills to a will other than their own and thus cease to be free. As is well known, the key to Rousseau's solution to this problem lies in his doctrine of the general will. If this solution is to succeed, the general will must regulate social cooperation in accord with the common good and at the same time be the will of the individuals whose behavior it governs. If the latter condition is met, then individuals whose actions are subject to the general will can be said to be free, for in doing so they obey only their own will. Thus, individuals can achieve freedom through the general will only if the general will is also their own will. But what is involved in the latter condition? In what sense and under what circumstances can the general will be understood as the will of each individual? It is this question, more than any other, that must be answered if we are to grasp the strategy behind Rousseau's solution to the fundamental problem of political philosophy.

The most straightforward way of understanding how the general will can be the will of individual citizens is offered by the "social autonomy" model of freedom.[5] This conception of the freedom

---

[5]This term, as well as much of the following description of this concep-

FREDERICK NEUHOUSER

that is realized in the rational state involves the thought of individuals who consciously identify with the general will in the sense that
they regularly recognize and embrace the common good as their
own deepest interest. Conceiving of freedom in this way depends
upon seeing the general will (and the legislation that derives from
it) as expressing a consciously shared conception of the common
good: if the general will is grounded in an understanding of the
common good that is both shared and affirmed by the individuals
who make up the state, then in submitting to laws that derive from
the general will they remain subject only to their own wills and
therefore free. This model requires not only that individuals be
able to come to a theoretical agreement as to what constitutes the
common good; it also requires that they be capable of *willing* the
common good. This requirement is based on the thought that if
one had theoretical insight into the common interest without any
conscious, voluntative relation to it—if one were able to discern the
common interest but unable to affirm or endorse it—then actions
regulated by a conception of the common good could not be said to
derive from one's own will. Thus, if individuals are to remain free
while subject to the general will, they must will the common good.
But what is involved in such willing? In the first place, individuals
must *have* a general will, which simply means that they can be
moved by considerations of the common good, that something's
being in the common interest can count for them as a reason for
acting to attain it. But having a general will in this minimal sense is
not sufficient to insure that one will be free (subject only to one's
own will) in a society where the general will prevails. The reason
for this is that one may have a general will without it being one's
dominant will. For individuals who have general wills do not therefore cease to have particular wills, and these particular wills can—
indeed, very often do—come into conflict with what the common
interest dictates. Thus, individuals who inhabit a state in which the
general will prevails (a society in which the general will, through
law, effectively regulates the actions of individuals) can be consid-

---

tion of freedom, comes from Joshua Cohen, "Reflections on Rousseau:
Autonomy and Democracy," *Philosophy and Public Affairs* 15 (1986): 276–
88.

FREEDOM, DEPENDENCE, THE GENERAL WILL

ered free only if, as individuals, they possess *properly ordered* wills— that is, wills that are disposed to subordinate purely particular interests to the common good in cases where the two conflict. Such wills belong to individuals whose identification with the shared ends of the association is sufficiently strong to outweigh, at least most of the time, their commitment to purely particular interests. Thus, according to the social autonomy model of freedom, individuals remain free in a society governed by the general will only if they are internally constituted as *citizens*, which requires both that they can be motivated by the common good and that, as a rule, their general will speaks to them in a louder voice than their particular will.

It is not difficult to see that the freedom depicted by the social autonomy model is an inherently political species of freedom that can be realized only within the rational state. Moreover, this model views the state as essentially involved in the realization of freedom not because political membership satisfies preconditions of being free but because such membership is itself an embodiment of freedom—more precisely, an embodiment of a form of "moral freedom," or autonomy, which consists in individuals governing their lives by laws they all help to frame in accord with a shared conception of the common good. Although this conception of freedom does play a prominent role in Rousseau's political thought, the relationship between the freedom of individuals and the general will is more complex than this model, taken by itself, can allow for. This point is brought out most forcefully by two troublesome passages of the *Social Contract*. The first of these is the site of Rousseau's well-known but poorly understood remark that "whoever refuses to obey the general will shall be constrained to do so by the entire body, which means only that he will be forced to be free" (SC 1.7.8). The second passage occurs in Rousseau's discussion of voting procedures in the assembly. There he asserts that the citizens of a well-constituted state are free, even when required to submit to particular laws that do not conform to their own understanding of what the common good prescribes: "when the opinion contrary to mine prevails, that proves nothing except that I was mistaken, and what I thought to be the general will was not. If my particular opinion had prevailed, I would have done something other than what I wanted. It is then that I would not have been free" (SC

FREDERICK NEUHOUSER

4.2.8).[6] Although these passages occur in different contexts, they both express the idea that one achieves freedom by being subject to the general will, even if one does not consciously recognize the general will as one's own. There must be, then, for Rousseau a sense in which the general will's being the will of each individual does not depend upon the individual's recognition of it as such— that is, there must be a sense in which the general will can be said to be my will (one might say: my deepest or truest will), even though I may lack the kind of subjective relation to it that is ordinarily taken to constitute willing. I may fail to discern the common good or to make it the object of my striving, and yet the general will is understood to be *my* will, and my subjection to its dictates freedom. That Rousseau intends to make such a claim seems to me incontrovertible; what is less certain is whether it is possible to make sense of this position, including its apparently perverse implication that an individual can be free even when required to act contrary to her own assessment of what she wants to do. The social autonomy model of freedom, however, is unable to make sense of such a position, and so, if we are to understand this aspect of Rousseau's view, we must look beyond this model for an alternative—or, better, a supplement—to the conception of freedom as social autonomy. The best way to do this is to examine more closely Rousseau's notorious claim that in the rational state it is possible for individuals to be forced to be free.

Let us begin by reviewing the passage in question in its entirety:

> [I]n order for the social compact not to be an ineffectual formula, it tacitly includes the following engagement, which alone can give force to the others: that whoever refuses to obey the general will shall be constrained to do so by the entire body; which means only that he will be forced to be free. For this is the condition that, by giving each citizen to the homeland, guarantees him against all personal dependence; a condition that creates the ingenuity and functioning of the political machine, and alone gives legitimacy to civil engagements which without it would be absurd, tyrannical, and subject to the most enormous abuses (SC 1.7.8).

---

[6] I have changed Masters's 'private will' (*avis particulier*) to 'particular opinion' in order to make it consistent with the translation of *avis* as 'opinion' in the previous sentence.

FREEDOM, DEPENDENCE, THE GENERAL WILL

The most common way of explicating this difficult passage is to take Rousseau simply to be arguing that citizens have a rightful obligation to obey the general will and that therefore the state's coercive power can be legitimately directed against them when they fail to do so.[7] This obligation to obey the general will is usually understood to derive from citizens' previous (actual) consent to the terms of the social contract, which include a promise to abide by those laws arrived at through agreed-upon procedural principles of majority rule. If Rousseau's passage is understood in this way, the issue it addresses appears to be not a distinctively Rousseauean problem but the problem faced by any social contract theory of providing an account of the citizen's obligation to comply with legitimately constituted legislation and of the state's corresponding right to use coercive force to ensure such compliance. Moreover, insofar as this interpretation views the *Social Contract* as grounding the citizen's obligation to obey the law in the obligation incurred through her original promise to do so, Rousseau's position comes out to be essentially indistinguishable from that of other social contract theorists, including Locke. But this reading, regardless of its merit as an account of the obligation citizens have to obey, fails to address the passage's central, and most puzzling, assertion— namely, that being forced to comply with the general will is nothing more than being "forced to be free." In other words, the most fundamental question raised by this assertion is not how citizens come to have an *obligation* to obey the general will but how their being forced to fulfill that obligation can be consistent with— indeed, constitutive of—their being *free*.[8] What sense can it possibly

---

[7] For examples of this way of interpreting Rousseau's passage see the editor's notes to *On the Social Contract*, 138, and W. T. Jones, "Rousseau's General Will and the Problem of Consent," *Journal of the History of Philosophy* 25 (1987): 115, 128.

[8] This distinction between the issues of obligation and freedom is also made in the second of the two passages cited above, most explicitly at SC 4.2.7. After establishing that "the vote of the majority always *obligates*" (my emphasis), Rousseau goes on to ask how being forced to obey the law to which one is obligated can be consistent with *freedom*. While it is essential to distinguish the issue of obligation from that of freedom, it is also important to note that Rousseau's solution to the former is parasitic on his account of the latter, since he intends to ground our obligation to obey the

FREDERICK NEUHOUSER

make to say that the would-be offender, forced to obey, is doing nothing other than following her own will?

It is sometimes said that the citizen who is forced to obey the general will can be thought of as simply being forced to follow his own will, insofar as the general will embodies those principles that he himself, in moments of undisturbed reflection, recognizes as the object of his own deepest commitment. In such a case the principles that define the general will would constitute the citizen's own constant (and therefore true) will, and the occasional impulse to follow his particular will in opposition to the general will would be a temptation to act contrary to what he, by his own acknowledgment, most wants to do.[9] Thus, disobedience to the law would represent a species of weakness of will, and one's original consent to the social contract—more specifically, one's agreement to subject oneself to the law-enforcing powers of the state—could be seen as the will's strategy for binding itself to a principle which it explicitly endorses but finds difficult to follow in every situation. Being forced to subordinate one's divergent particular will to the general will would then simply be to have one's actions brought into line with one's own constant will; but this would amount to nothing more than being forced to do what one most wants, which could also be described as being forced to be free.

This interpretation has the advantage of being able to give some meaning to the idea that one can be forced to be free; its disadvantage is that the explication it offers is not the one Rousseau himself suggests in the lines immediately following his famous utterance. Considering the amount of confusion that the phrase "forced to be free" has generated among interpreters, it is surprising to discover that Rousseau explicitly points out to us the thought that is supposed to make sense of his otherwise paradoxical formulation: "For this [the stipulation that individuals be constrained to follow the general will] is the condition that, by giving each

---

general will in the more fundamental imperative that exhorts us to realize our nature as free beings.

[9]This interpretation is suggested by a passage from the *Geneva Manuscript* (178) which was left out of the *Social Contract*, as well as by N. J. H. Dent in *Rousseau* (Oxford: Basil Blackwell, 1988), 179–80. Dent, however, goes on to give an account of the "forced to be free" passage that is much closer to the one I develop below.

FREEDOM, DEPENDENCE, THE GENERAL WILL

citizen to the homeland, *guarantees him against all personal dependence*" (SC 1.7.8, emphasis added). It is quite clear, I believe, that Rousseau intends for this sentence, which is linked to its predecessor by the explanatory 'for', to be recognized as holding the key to the riddle posed by the expression 'forced to be free'. That is, he means for us to take seriously the thought expressed by this sentence—namely, that universal compliance with the general will effectively safeguards citizens from personal dependence and that this protection from dependence is so bound up with their freedom that obedience to the general will can be said to make them free, even when their obedience is not voluntary in the ordinary sense of the term. My aim in what follows will be to make sense of this difficult thought and thereby to elucidate one of the ideas that lies at the heart of Rousseau's conception of freedom and its relation to the political order. Doing so will require a discussion of two sets of questions raised by Rousseau's claim: First, how are we to understand the notion of dependence, and in what relation does it stand to the concept of freedom? If freedom is not simply identical with independence, why does Rousseau believe the two concepts to be so closely connected? The second set of questions concerns the relation that allegedly holds between the general will and the independence of citizens—most importantly, What is behind the assertion that the general will, if adhered to, safeguards citizens from personal dependence?

Dependence and Freedom

Rousseau's claim that compliance with the general will makes citizens free because it safeguards them from personal dependence could be taken to imply that freedom simply consists in the absence of dependence and that therefore *independence* is synonymous with *freedom*. This view, which some interpreters have taken, appears to be reinforced by the fact that Rousseau more than once treats these two terms as though they were interchangeable.[10] But adopting

---

[10]John Plamenatz is one (otherwise reliable) interpreter who equates the two concepts ("Ce qui ne signifie autre chose qu'on le forcera d'être libre," in *Hobbes and Rousseau*, ed. Maurice Cranston and Richard S. Peters (Gar-

FREDERICK NEUHOUSER

this view will have serious consequences for any attempt to make sense of Rousseau's philosophical project. For the fundamental problem to which his project as a whole is directed can be coherently formulated only by distinguishing freedom from independence. That such a distinction is required becomes clear once we recognize that Rousseau starts from the supposition that dependence is a fundamental, ineliminable feature of human existence. Although, as we shall see, he regards this dependence as having negative implications for our ability to be free, dependence does not strictly preclude freedom's being realized. In fact, Rousseau's thought can be understood as aiming, above all, to show how the basic dependence of human beings can coexist with their freedom. If this task is to be anything other than a logical impossibility, it must presuppose a conceptual distinction between freedom and independence. That Rousseau's thought operates with such a distinction cannot be gathered from his actual usage of the terms *liberté* and *indépendance*. Yet a careful reading of his central works, especially his *Discourse on Inequality*, compels one to conclude that this distinction, if only implicit in Rousseau's texts, is indispensable to his philosophy of freedom.[11]

How, then, is the distinction between freedom and independence to be drawn? Rousseau's concept of independence is best understood as closely related to the notion of self-sufficiency. As such, it can be defined only with reference to the more basic concept of *need*: To be independent is to be self-sufficient with respect to the satisfaction of one's needs, and dependence is simply the lack of such self-sufficiency. Thus, human beings are dependent in the broadest sense of the term when they must rely on resources outside of themselves in order to have their needs satisfied. Although Rousseau recognizes two species of dependence in general—

---

den City, N.Y.: Doubleday, 1972), 323–24). Rousseau himself sometimes fails to distinguish freedom from independence (e.g., at *Emile*, 84). At other times he appears to make a distinction and to do so in a way that is consistent with my interpretation (DI, 156; GM, 159); in at least one other place he explicitly draws the distinction differently than I do (OC 3:841).

[11]Here I take seriously Rousseau's statement (*Emile*, 108n) that he does not always "give the same meanings to the same words" but that the thoughtful reader will always be able to discover the underlying coherence of his thought.

FREEDOM, DEPENDENCE, THE GENERAL WILL

dependence on things and dependence on other human beings—it is the latter category that is of primary importance to him. The reason for this can be traced back to his belief that dependence on things alone—that is, on things other than human individuals or groups—has little impact on one's ability to be free (*Emile*, 85). Thus, Rousseau portrays the independent individual as one who "has no need to put another's arms at the end of his own" (*Emile*, 84); in other words, he is able to satisfy his needs without the cooperation of other human beings. The primitive gatherer of fruit, reliant on the beneficence of nature but not on the assistance of others, is therefore not dependent in the sense that most interests Rousseau.

Thus, a consideration of Rousseau's concept of independence leads directly into his account of human needs. Although this aspect of Rousseau's thought is sufficiently rich to merit a lengthy treatment of its own, I shall restrict myself here to those points that are most relevant to elucidating the connection between dependence and freedom. It is important to note first that in this context the concept of need refers always, and only, to *perceived* needs. Characterizing a need as "perceived" does not imply that it is *merely* a perceived need (but not, say, a real or true need). Although Rousseau's texts do provide resources for distinguishing true (or real) needs from false (or illusory) needs,[12] this distinction is irrelevant here. What is important for understanding dependence is not some objective quality of needs (for example, whether they are in fact essential to one's well-being, properly understood) but their subjective character—that is, the way they present themselves to and influence the behavior of the subject to whom they belong. All

---

[12]Rousseau speaks of "true" or "natural" needs (e.g., *Emile*, 84, 86, 213, 333), but his use of these terms is inconstant. At DI, 137, he says that savage, as opposed to modern, man "felt only his true needs." The impression is often given that "true" (or "natural") means "given to the human by his biological nature" and hence that true needs are simply the primitive physical needs of the original state of nature. I suggest that Rousseau's notion of true needs is better understood as referring, roughly, to those goods that are essential to one's well-being properly understood, and that false needs are those that are perceived as such but are in fact destructive of, or not essential to, one's well-being properly understood. Thus, for Rousseau an essential feature of true needs is that they are compatible with one's being *free*.

FREDERICK NEUHOUSER

needs, whether real or illusory, have the potential to give rise to dependence, as long as they are perceived as needs by the subject.

There are two subjective qualities of needs that make them crucial to the phenomenon of dependence—namely, the *force* and the *constancy* with which they present themselves to subjects as inducements to action. First, needs are powerful determinants of behavior and psychological well-being. The feeling of lack that accompanies an unfulfilled need possesses an urgency that is not easily ignored or endured. An unquenched thirst or an unrequited love has the power to torment individuals and to drive them to desperate action. It is this forceful quality of needs that accounts for the nearly irresistible hold that relations of dependence come to have over individuals who become entangled in them. Second, needs possess a constancy that many inclinations do not; in contrast to whims or fleeting desires, needs constitute an enduring part of the subject's appetitive makeup: when needs go unsatisfied, the urges to which they give rise do not simply disappear but continue to make their demands felt by the subject. Moreover, satisfying a need once does not amount to extinguishing it, for needs typically give rise to recurrent feelings of lack, which demand that the process of satisfaction be repeated. Whether fulfilled or unfulfilled, needs are not easily gotten rid of. This feature of needs is important, because it is what makes dependence an enduring state rather than a merely momentary phenomenon.

The needs that figure most prominently in Rousseau's thought fall into two main classes. The first comprises those goods (for example, food, clothing, shelter) that are involved essentially in the reproduction of life and whose significance for the human being derives primarily from the requirements of his physical constitution. The second class is made up of needs that have their origin not in our biological nature but in a form of self-love that Rousseau calls *amour-propre*, a passion that gives rise to the distinctively human yearning "to have a position, to be a part, to count for something" (*Emile*, 160).[13] *Amour-propre*, which is fundamental to our

---

[13]The problems involved in finding a suitable English translation of *amour-propre* are well known. For an excellent discussion of Rousseau's frequently misunderstood view of *amour-propre*, see Dent, chapter 2.

FREEDOM, DEPENDENCE, THE GENERAL WILL

nature as spiritual (or moral) beings, is capable of manifesting itself in numerous ways and therefore of giving rise to an extremely diverse set of concrete needs. The need to be thought handsome or clever, the need to be loved, the need to have one's will and preferences respected—all are grounded in the promptings of *amour-propre* and can be understood as particular forms of the basic need generated by that passion: the need to have a recognized standing among beings of one's own kind or, in other words, the need to be acknowledged by one's fellow beings as possessing a value that makes one worthy of their esteem. This two-fold classification of needs is summed up by Rousseau in a footnote to the Second Discourse: "all our labors are directed to only two objects: namely, the commodities of life for oneself, and consideration among others" (DI, 223).[14]

These two kinds of needs give rise to the two main types of dependence with which Rousseau is concerned: *economic* and *psychological* (or psycho-moral) dependence.[15] The former consists in dependence on others in the production or acquisition of necessary commodities. It is a necessary consequence of the two most important economic facts of modern (and most of premodern) society: the material division of labor (for example, into tillers of the soil and workers of metal) and the division of society into economic classes of rich and poor (or, in more precise terminology, into owners and nonowners of the means of production). Psychological dependence is dependence on others for the recognition one needs in order for one's sense of one's value or standing among others to be reflected and thus confirmed in the external world. Rousseau's writings abound with sharply observed examples of dependence which he takes to be of this second type: the artist whose self-respect requires his audience's applause, the lover who

---

[14]Notice that the commodities of life are "for oneself," while the need for "consideration" inherently involves others. I explain and emphasize this feature of Rousseau's view below.

[15]Although the two types of needs appear to stand in a one-to-one correspondence to the two types of dependence, their relation is more complex, since, as we shall see, for civilized (as opposed to primitive) human beings *amour-propre* plays a significant role in constituting economic dependence.

FREDERICK NEUHOUSER

cannot endure being denied his beloved's affection, the citizen who values the honor of his countrymen more than his own life.[16]

It would be a mistake to conclude, as some interpreters have done, that Rousseau regards one species of dependence as of greater consequence than the other; on the contrary, he sees correctly that economic and psychological dependence pose equally serious threats to individuals' freedom. Yet one interesting feature of his view is that it ascribes far more importance to *amour-propre* than to biology in its explanation of human dependence. The explanatory primacy of *amour-propre* manifests itself in two ways. First, *amour-propre* has a more immediate connection to dependence than does purely physical need. In addition to his vivid depictions of human dependence, Rousseau offers accounts, usually in narrative form, of the conditions under which the fact of human need gives rise to a state of dependence. In the Second Discourse Rousseau argues that dependence, understood as an enduring condition, is not a necessary consequence of our biological nature alone.[17] Savage individuals, isolated and independent, are able to satisfy their purely physical needs without the regular cooperation of their fellow beings. Physical needs result in dependence only when the production of necessary commodities acquires certain *social* characteristics (which itself presupposes that these needs have become more complicated and less easy to satisfy). That is, it is only with the division of labor, occasioned by the advent of metallurgy and agriculture, and with the subsequent division of society into rich and poor that individuals become economically dependent on other humans for the satisfaction of their physical needs. In contrast, the relation between psychological dependence and the needs of *amour-propre* is more straightforward. For the object of *amour-propre*'s striving is such that its attainment requires by its very nature the involvement of others. The individual's yearning for a recognized standing among others cannot be satisfied by the indi-

---

[16]It is important to bear in mind that psychological dependence is not necessarily pathological; on the contrary, it is essential to being human. Emile is dependent on Sophie's regard (and vice versa), and this is as it should be.

[17]This point is echoed in *Emile*, 185: "So long as one knows only physical need, each man suffices unto himself."

FREEDOM, DEPENDENCE, THE GENERAL WILL

vidual herself, nor by subhuman beings.[18] Thus, in the case of *amour-propre* neediness is inseparable from dependence; the existence of psychological dependence presupposes no conditions beyond those of *amour-propre* itself: a simple awareness of oneself as an individual, a certain constancy of social intercourse, and the mental capacity to make comparisons between oneself and one's fellow beings.

Amour-propre has primacy over purely physical needs in Rousseau's account of dependence in a second sense: The needs of *amour-propre* not only give rise on their own to psychological dependence, they also play an important, perhaps dominant, role in the constitution of economic dependence. This is most easily seen in the fact that many of the needs that make us dependent on the labor of others (for example, the need for a sufficiently stylish wardrobe) stem directly from the promptings of *amour-propre*. Although the possession and consumption of things cannot by itself satisfy *amour-propre*, commodities frequently play a central role in individuals' strategies for gaining the respect of others. A less obvious but equally important point is that with the development of society, biologically based needs quickly cease to be purely biological in nature. What counts as a "commodity of life" is not determined by a fixed, strictly biological quantity (for example, the minimum required for survival and reproduction). Rather, our conception of the necessities of life changes with historical development and presupposes a conception of the minimal standard of living that is consistent with a humane existence. Thus, these biologically based needs come to be determined in part by considerations as to the kind of physical existence that it is *fitting* for human beings to have and hence by considerations that ultimately have their source in *amour-propre*. To fail to achieve this minimal standard is to lead a less than human existence, a circumstance which is incompatible with the recognized standing that *amour-propre* strives to attain. This blurring of the distinction between physical and psychological needs is due to the fact that for beings in whom *amour-propre* has begun to operate—and that includes all *human* beings—no aspect

---

[18]This is not to say that recognition by others cannot be, or is not typically, mediated by things.

FREDERICK NEUHOUSER

of one's existence remains untouched by the concern for one's standing among others. Even those needs that derive most immediately from our biological nature take on a psychological significance and become essential to achieving self-esteem, as well as the esteem of our fellow beings.

Freedom, in contrast to independence, is defined without reference to the concept of need. It refers, rather, to a condition of the *will*, and more precisely, to a particular relation between the will and the world. The meaning of freedom is captured in a rough way by Rousseau's characterization of the free being as "one who does his own will" (*Emile*, 84). Freedom, it would seem, consists in an agreement of will and action; individuals are free when they "do what accords with their will" (RSW, 84). At times, however, Rousseau insists upon a slight but significant revision of this formulation: "Freedom does not consist so much in doing one's will as in not being subjected to the will of others" (OC 3:841).[19] What is the import of defining freedom negatively (as the absence of subjection to a foreign will) rather than in the more straightforward manner suggested above? Rousseau's endorsement of the negative formulation implies that "doing one's will" is too exclusive a definition of freedom and, hence, that there are instances in which one does not do what one wants without therefore being unfree. What Rousseau must have in mind are instances in which the force that prevents me from doing my own will comes from the "necessity of things" rather than from a foreign will.[20] That is, I may fail to do what I want because I lack the requisite strength, or because of limits imposed by the laws of nature. In such cases Rousseau will agree that my will has been frustrated but deny that my freedom has been compromised.[21] Rousseau's concept of freedom, then, cannot

---

[19]See also RSW, 83.

[20]See *Emile*, 85: "Dependence on things, since it has no morality, is in no way detrimental to freedom. . . ."

[21]The view that natural necessity does not compromise human freedom is based on the idea that the world of things is ordered by natural laws, which have a constancy and necessity that the particular wills of individuals do not. This makes the natural world reliable (and predictable) in a way that particular wills are not. Moreover, Rousseau appears to believe that the fact that nature is ordered is sufficient to guarantee that it will be benign with respect to anything "natural," including human freedom (e.g., *Emile*, 37).

FREEDOM, DEPENDENCE, THE GENERAL WILL

be defined simply as a correspondence between an individual's will and her deeds. Such a definition equates freedom with the success- ful translation of will into action, and in doing so it overlooks a central characteristic of freedom, a characteristic that makes free- dom, for Rousseau, an inherently moral phenomenon, namely, that freedom (as well as its opposite) always refers to a relation between one will and another: To be unfree is to obey a foreign will, and freedom is always being free of the will of another. We can do justice to this aspect of Rousseau's conception of freedom by replacing our initial characterization of the free individual as "one who does his own will" with the following: The free individual is one who *obeys* only his own will, or more explicitly, one who *obeys no will* other than his own.

This rather meager formula is not, of course, Rousseau's final word on the topic of freedom. It would be more accurate to de- scribe it as his starting point. For although the thought of "obeying only one's own will" captures what is most essential to the idea of freedom, it is still a long way from a full account of what a free human existence would look like and how such an existence could be realized. It is no exaggeration to say that Rousseau's thought as a whole is devoted, above all else, to the task of providing just such an account. Central to this project is the question that could be said to inform each of Rousseau's major works: Under what conditions is human freedom possible? How must the world be constituted— both the external, social world and the inner, psychological world—in order for individuals to be able to obey only their own wills? It is in this context that the topic of dependence makes its entry into Rousseau's philosophy, for dependence on others rep- resents the most important obstacle to the realization of freedom.

With this thought we return to the question posed at the begin- ning of this section: What relation exists between freedom and dependence? Although, as we have seen, the concepts of freedom and independence can be distinguished in thought, the phenom- ena to which they refer are closely connected in reality. The gen- eral nature of this connection is expressed in Rousseau's remark that dependence on others is "detrimental to freedom" (*Emile*, 85). One could also say that dependence is the *source* of subjection and, more precisely, that it is the source of subjection in two distinct senses: First, dependence is a condition that makes possible the subjection of one will to another. It allows us to make sense of the

FREDERICK NEUHOUSER

otherwise puzzling phenomenon of obeying a foreign will instead of one's own.[22] For in certain, easily imaginable circumstances, requiring the cooperation of others for the satisfaction of one's needs makes it necessary, or gives one powerful incentives, to abandon one's will in favor of another's. But Rousseau makes the even stronger claim that dependence is *necessary* for subjection to arise: "since the bonds of servitude are formed only from the mutual dependence of men and the reciprocal needs that unite them, it is impossible to enslave a man without first putting him in the position of being unable to do without another" (DI, 140).[23] Rousseau's talk of "bonds of servitude" indicates that it is the enduring subjection of one will to another that requires dependence as its condition. For isolated instances of yielding to a foreign will can occur even in the absence of dependence; a simple threat of violence, for example, can result in obedience to another, and such encounters are conceivable even for the thoroughly independent beings of the original state of nature. The enduring subjection of individuals, however, is possible only for dependent beings—that is, for beings whose lack of self-sufficiency requires them to have ongoing interactions with others.

Second, dependence for Rousseau is more than just a necessary condition of subjection. Insofar as it is relatively extensive and exists in its natural form (that is, prior to being restructured in the ways advocated by Rousseau's philosophy),[24] dependence *virtually guarantees* that individuals will be unfree. This is to be attributed in part to the nearly irresistible force with which unsatisfied needs impel individuals to seek satisfaction. Beings who constantly have to choose between getting what they need and following their own wills cannot be expected to opt consistently for freedom over sat-

---

[22]Obedience to a foreign will is a phenomenon that calls for an explanation, because human beings by nature value being their own master and are *prima facie* strongly disinclined to cede to a will that is not their own. This is *one* of the claims implicit in Rousseau's view that human beings are naturally free.

[23]Or, more succinctly: "what yoke could be imposed on men who need nothing?" (DSA, 36n). See also DI, 139, where Rousseau depicts a state of perfect independence and asks, "[H]ow will [a man] ever succeed in making himself obeyed?"

[24]The unrestructured dependence referred to here is "natural" in the sense that it is the result of a development which, as a whole, was not an object of human foresight, plan, or will.

FREEDOM, DEPENDENCE, THE GENERAL WILL

isfaction. But dependent individuals will regularly find themselves in this unhappy position only if their relations of dependence are so constituted that they give rise to systematic conflicts among wills. Hence Rousseau's view that the loss of freedom is a virtually unavoidable consequence of unrestructured dependence is also based on a supposition about the inevitability of conflict among the desires and particular interests—and hence among the wills—of interdependent individuals in the absence of an imposed order that harmonizes those interests. The division of society into economic classes which have directly antithetical material interests is but one of Rousseau's examples of a common form of dependence that guarantees a systematic conflict among wills.[25]

We are now in a position to consider how Rousseau's understanding of the relation between freedom and dependence dictates the basic terms of his solution to the fundamental problem of political theory, that of devising a structure for the ongoing social cooperation of human beings that allows for each individual to exist as free. First, however, it is important to note that Rousseau's formulation of his task—his specification of freedom as the end to be realized—bears witness to the important fact that freedom, not independence, is the supreme value of his political thought (and, indeed, of his philosophy in general). Rousseau's view is not merely that freedom stands above independence in the hierarchy of values but that independence has no intrinsic value at all. Indeed, whatever value Rousseau ascribes to independence is completely parasitic on the value of freedom. Thus, to the extent that Rousseau considers independence to be good, he does so not because it is intrinsically valuable, nor because self-sufficiency is the surest means to the satisfaction of one's needs, but solely because of the positive contribution independence can make to the ability of individuals to avoid subjection to foreign wills. By the same token, dependence is regarded not as bad in itself but as bad only insofar as it is detrimental to the freedom of the dependent individual.

Rousseau's view of dependence as the source of subjection suggests one obvious response to his central question concerning the

---

[25]Another important example is Rousseau's analysis of how the needs generated by inflamed *amour-propre* lead to inevitable clashes among wills. For a discussion of this and the distinction between inflamed and benign *amour-propre*, see Dent, chapter 2.

FREDERICK NEUHOUSER

conditions under which freedom can be realized, namely, the perfect independence of all individuals. Further, it suggests that a
political solution to the problem of subjection could be found in
eradicating dependence on others in all of its forms, since to eradi-
cate dependence would be to eliminate the condition which both
makes subjection possible and virtually ensures that it will come
about. Indeed, the link between dependence and subjection is a
theme which occurs so frequently and with such urgency in Rousseau's texts that it is easy to get the impression that the eradication
of dependence is the *only* possible remedy for the subjection of
individuals. In the Second Discourse, however, Rousseau in effect
considers, and emphatically rejects, just this solution. His portrayal
of the original state of nature can be seen as an attempt to imagine
what life would be like for beings who enjoyed a freedom predi-
cated on the complete self-sufficiency of individuals. The beings
Rousseau depicts are perfectly "free and independent" (DI, 156)
(and free *because* they are independent); they obey no wills other
than their own and are able to do so only because they are self-
sufficient. Yet Rousseau makes it clear that such freedom, even if
it were practically possible, would be achieved at too high a cost.
His refusal to look to the original state of nature for the solution to
dependence is based less on his belief about the impracticality of
returning to the state of nature than on his view that such a solution would not be a desirable alternative. For the radical independence that makes such freedom possible can be maintained only in
the absence of all enduring attachments to others. But, as Rousseau
makes clear, the unencumbered beings of the original state of nature are not, and cannot be, *human* beings, for the absence of
enduring social bonds precludes the existence of a wide variety of
goods and capacities which are essential to being human and which
are of sufficient intrinsic value that freedom may not be obtained
at their expense: Perfect independence makes impossible not only
conjugal love (one of "the sweetest sentiments known to men") but
also language, reason, virtue, and subjectivity itself.[26]

---

[26]This interpretation of the Second Discourse is confirmed at GM, 159.
There Rousseau also rules out a return to the "golden age" (described at
DI, 151) as a possible solution to the problem of dependence. In this case,
too, he rejects the idea of returning to a more primitive society not because

FREEDOM, DEPENDENCE, THE GENERAL WILL

In accord with this view, Rousseau's strategy for reconciling the ineliminable dependence of human beings with the freedom which constitutes their essential nature will focus less on the eradication of dependence than on its restructuring. This strategy implies that human dependence admits of being reorganized in such a way that it ceases to be incompatible with the freedom of individuals. The principles that are to guide the restructuring of dependence—at least the political component of this restructuring[27]—can be found in Rousseau's conception of the general will. For, as we have seen, Rousseau claims that it is the individual's (forced or voluntary) compliance with the general will that "guarantees him against all personal dependence." Thus, Rousseau intends for the general will to be understood as willing a set of social and political institutions which alter the nature of individuals' dependence on others so as to eliminate, or at least significantly reduce, those aspects of dependence that make it inimical to freedom. Our task now is to understand how Rousseau's conception of the general will accomplishes this.

Dependence and the General Will

A clue to the basic idea behind Rousseau's proposed restructuring of dependence can be found in the statement, cited above, in which the general will is said to guarantee individuals against "personal" dependence. This suggests that Rousseau's political solution to the problem of freedom involves transforming the dependence on individual persons into a dependence on the community as a whole. This suggestion is confirmed by Rousseau's remark later in the *Social Contract* that in the rational polity "each citizen is in a position of perfect independence from all the others and of excessive dependence upon the city" (SC 2.12.3). But what does it mean to

---

such a return would be impossible but because the golden age is "a state foreign to the human race."

[27]It is important to bear in mind that the sociopolitical measures espoused in the *Social Contract* are not in themselves a sufficient response to the problem of dependence. Individuals must also be internally constituted in accord with the principles outlined in *Emile*, if their psychological dependence is to admit of being structured in a way that is compatible with freedom. The most important consideration here is whether *amour-propre* appears primarily in its benign or inflamed form.

FREDERICK NEUHOUSER

depend upon the city, as opposed to the individual persons who compose it, and how does depersonalizing dependence in this way make it possible for individuals to be free? In another context Rousseau says that the only social remedy for "dependence on men" is "to substitute law for man" (*Emile*, 85). Hence the "dependence upon the city" Rousseau envisages can be described more accurately as a dependence on the well-constituted republic, that is, on a community effectively governed by law that faithfully reflects the general will. As we shall see below, however, it is best to characterize the social arrangement endorsed by Rousseau, not as one in which one species of dependence (dependence on other individuals) is *replaced* by another (dependence on the law-governed republic), but rather as a social order in which the ineliminable relations of dependence among individuals are preserved but *mediated* by a system of well-founded law and thereby made less injurious to freedom.

The question to be answered, then, is how the rule of law orders the dependence of individuals such that dependence on others can coexist with freedom. A great deal could be said about Rousseau's view of the rule of law and its virtues; in what follows I merely outline three ways in which Rousseau believes law to be capable of restructuring dependence such that the freedom of individuals can be realized. Although these three points can, and should, be distinguished from one another, they all share one fundamental attribute: In each case law mitigates the harmful consequences of dependence by establishing *equality* (again, in various senses) among citizens. This close connection between law and equality is explicitly recognized by Rousseau: "[law] reestablishes, as a right, the natural equality among men" (PE, 214).[28] He also acknowledges the deeper philosophical point which my interpretation of his position emphasizes, namely, that law aims at the equality of citizens, not because equality is valuable in itself, but because it furthers the end of freedom.[29] Each of the following three points, then, can serve as a particular illustration of the general idea that

---

[28] See also Rousseau's advice to the Corsicans: "The fundamental law of your constitution must be equality" (OC 3:909–10).

[29] See SC 2.11.1, where equality is said to be one of the two principal objects of law for the reason that "freedom cannot last without it."

FREEDOM, DEPENDENCE, THE GENERAL WILL

bringing equality to mutually dependent individuals helps to safeguard them from the subjection into which their dependence is otherwise likely to deliver them.

The first way that law is to restructure dependence is by ensuring that citizens enjoy a significant (but not fully specified) level of *material equality*. The legislation of a well-constituted republic does not seek to establish an absolute equality of wealth among its citizens but only to impede the development of great material inequalities that are the inevitable consequence of unregulated economic activity.[30] Rousseau's concrete proposals range from laws that restrict inheritance or levy taxes on luxury goods to the suggestion that the existence of a class of propertyless individuals—more precisely, a class of individuals who own no means of production other than their own labor power—is incompatible with the freedom of citizens.[31] More important than the details of Rousseau's proposals is the idea behind them: Narrowing the distance between the extremes of wealth alleviates the economic dependence of the less advantaged and thereby reduces the likelihood that they will have to submit to the will of another in order to satisfy their material needs. Yet lessening, or even eliminating, the differences between classes does not do away with all economic dependence, for as long as there is a material division of labor within society, individuals will rely upon the cooperation of others in order to obtain the necessities of life. What distinguishes the material division of labor from the division of society into economic classes is that the former is compatible with a high level of equality among individuals, whereas the latter is not. Moreover, it is this difference that makes the material division of labor a less harmful form of dependence than the existence of classes, for interactions among

---

[30]Rousseau advises the Poles: "The tendency of your laws should be toward a continuous reduction of large inequalities of wealth and power, . . . a chasm that the cumulative operation of natural forces tends unavoidably to widen further" (GP, 65). See also SC 2.11.2.

[31]The first two proposals are made at OC 3:945 and PE, 234. Rousseau's critique of capitalist class relations is explicit at SC 2.11.2 ("no citizen should be so opulent that he can buy another, and none so poor that he is constrained to sell himself") and implicit in his depiction of a golden age without economic classes (DI, especially 151). For a detailed discussion of these themes in Rousseau, see Andrew Levine, *The Politics of Autonomy* (Amherst: University of Massachusetts Press, 1976), chap. 5.

FREDERICK NEUHOUSER

mutually dependent individuals who meet on an equal footing are
less likely to result in the sacrifice of freedom than those among
highly unequal beings. Thus, legislation directed at bringing about
the material equality of individuals should be understood as aiming
not so much at a lessening or eradication of economic dependence
as at its equalization.

In this first instance the capacity of law to restructure dependence is due not to a formal feature of law in general but to a
particular end that Rousseau ascribes to law, the promotion of
material equality. That law can be said to have such a content for
Rousseau is a reflection of the fact that the general will (of which
law is simply a determinate expression) is more than a set of purely
formal criteria for the legitimacy of legislation; the general will, as
Rousseau conceives it, also has a content in the sense that it wills
certain broadly defined but nonvacuous ends. In some places, however Rousseau implies that the rule of law per se, regardless of the
law's particular content, shields citizens from some of the pernicious consequences of dependence on others.[32] This suggests that
Rousseau sees law as capable of restructuring dependence in a
second way that relies solely on the formal character of law as such.
The feature of law that Rousseau draws on in this context is its
universality. Although more will need to be said about the kind of
universality that is relevant here, it will involve some form of the
idea of "bearing equally on all." Thus, the universality of law implies that those who are under it enjoy a species of equality, distinct
from the material equality discussed above, which can be characterized as the *formal equality of citizens before the law.* The nature of
this equality is roughly captured in the idea that the law is no
respecter of persons; it regards individual citizens as abstract units
that (in a sense to be specified) count as equals. This raises two
questions in need of further attention: In what precise sense do
citizens count as equals before the law, and how does this formal
equality function as an antidote to dependence?

Although Rousseau's claim here is difficult to pin down precisely, the general thrust of his idea is that the rule of law helps to
protect individuals from the capricious wills of those on whom they

---

[32]E.g., OC 3:491–92, 842–43.

FREEDOM, DEPENDENCE, THE GENERAL WILL

depend.[33] Capricious wills are (for the most part) unconstrained by principles and are therefore inconstant, unpredictable, and arbitrary. Being dependent on capricious individuals poses a serious threat to one's freedom, because it is virtually inevitable that wills exhibiting only random motion will come into frequent collisions with other (random or nonrandom) wills. Rousseau's idea, then, must be that the laws of a rational state effectively order capricious wills by placing external constraints on what those wills may demand of others. Thus, without decreasing the level of their interdependence, the rule of law helps to preserve the freedom of individuals by shielding them from one of the most freedom-endangering consequences of dependence. While the basic thought here is plain enough, it is not at all evident why Rousseau believes that this capacity of law follows simply from its formal character as *universal* law. This claim is tersely formulated in Rousseau's remark that "any condition imposed on each by all can be onerous to no one" (OC 3:842). Here law is said to be universal in two distinct senses: it is imposed *on each* and *by all*. Not surprisingly, these two kinds of universality reappear in Rousseau's statement of what makes a general will general, namely, that it "applies to all" and "comes from all" (SC 2.4.5). But how can the universality of law in either of these senses account for its ability to protect individuals from the capricious wills of those on whom they depend?

In a number of passages Rousseau appeals only to the first kind of universality—the universal *applicability* of law—when making the point that law protects individuals from capricious wills. An example of this is his statement that "the worst of laws is worth even more than the best master, because every master has preferences and the law never does" (OC 3:842–43). Law, in both its formulation and enforcement, applies to all and tolerates no exceptions; "magistrates themselves are obliged to obey them" (OC 3:491). By making no distinctions among particular individuals, the law effectively creates a kind of equality among citizens—a guarantee of equal treatment under the law—which, at least within the domain

---

[33]This formulation is suggested by Frederick Barnard, *Self-Direction and Political Legitimacy: Rousseau and Herder* (New York: Oxford University Press, 1988), 27.

FREDERICK NEUHOUSER

of activity governed by law, deters one of the modes of behavior characteristic of capricious wills: the differential treatment of individuals on the basis of arbitrary preferences. But the universality of law in this sense alone still leaves plenty of room for what we would consider arbitrary treatment, not perhaps of particular individuals, but of classes of individuals.[34] For the law 'Only property owners may have access to the means of public communication' can be scrupulously applied to all citizens and still be arbitrary in an important sense. For this reason it is important to take into account the second sense in which law is said to be universal, namely, that it is imposed by, or comes from, all. The universality referred to here is best understood not as the actual participation of all citizens in the process of framing laws but as a condition that places a constraint on the content of admissible legislation by requiring that laws be possible objects of the rational consent of all citizens.[35] Since laws (like the one suggested above) which violate a fundamental interest of a class of citizens cannot be regarded as capable of gaining the rational consent of those citizens, they lack universality in this sense. The requirement that laws come from all implies a kind of equality of citizens before the law that consists in the fact that each citizen is regarded as having fundamental interests which no law may violate and which count as equal to the fundamental interests of every other citizen in the framing of legislation. Laws that are universal in this sense can be seen as a response to the problem posed by dependence on others, because by safeguarding (at least some of) the fundamental interests of individuals, such laws block one important kind of arbitrary treatment by capricious wills to which dependent individuals are otherwise susceptible.

The third way in which the rule of law transforms personal dependence into dependence on the republic is by making the community itself into a source of the esteem sought by individuals as a consequence of their *amour-propre*. Law accomplishes this by ensuring that individuals enjoy an *equality of respect* as citizens. This func-

---

[34]Rousseau acknowledges that the universal applicability of law (the sense under consideration here) does not preclude distinctions among classes of citizens but only references to particular individuals (SC 2.6.6).

[35]My understanding of Rousseau's statement that legitimate law must "come from all" is indebted to Dent's excellent treatment of this topic (179–84).

FREEDOM, DEPENDENCE, THE GENERAL WILL

tion of law is a direct consequence of its universality in the sense discussed immediately above. For safeguarding the fundamental interests of individuals has the effect of securing for them a kind of recognized standing within the community that is itself a form of respect. Moreover, the availability of this respect is not contingent on the mutable opinions of particular individuals but is assured by a guarantee as reliable as the rule of law itself. Rousseau, of course, does not believe that the recognized standing individuals achieve as citizens of a law-governed community is sufficient to satiate *amour-propre* in all of its manifestations. His view, rather, is that one's standing as a citizen represents a partial but not insignificant confirmation of one's value for others, which, because it relies only on the institution of law, makes individuals less dependent on particular persons for the satisfaction of their need to possess a standing among their fellow beings.

Concluding Remarks: On the Possibility (and Impossibility) of Being Forced to Be Free

Having examined the connections between freedom and dependence, on the one hand, and between dependence and the general will, on the other, we are now in a position to reconstruct Rousseau's response to the central question that arises from his claim that being constrained to follow the general will is nothing more than being "forced to be free": In what sense do the dictates of the general will constitute one's own will as an individual, even when one fails to recognize them as such? Rousseau's answer consists in the following thought: By restructuring human dependence such that subjection to the will of others ceases to be a virtually inevitable consequence of dependence, the general will brings about the objective social conditions that must be present if individuals are to be able to avoid subjection to a foreign will. The general will, then, can be said to be the individual's own *true* will, even when she does not consciously recognize it as such, because the general will wills the conditions necessary in order for her freedom (along with the freedom of all others) to be realized. Identifying the general will with the true will of each individual is based on the idea that the individual will, apart from whatever particular ends it may embrace, necessarily, and most fundamentally, wills its own freedom. But in

FREDERICK NEUHOUSER

willing a certain end (its freedom) it must also will the conditions
that make that end attainable. A will that chooses to act in ways that
are inconsistent with what is required for the realization of its own
freedom cannot be regarded as "doing its own will" and therefore
cannot be considered truly free. Such a will—one which in effect
wills its own subjection—is a self-negating, therefore contradictory,
will.

This set of claims rests upon an understanding of how freedom
is realized through the general will—call it the "freedom-through-
personal-independence" model—which, in contrast to the social
autonomy interpretation, views the rule of laws informed by the
general will not as itself an embodiment of citizens' freedom but as
the latter's precondition. Moreover, the kind of freedom that is
claimed to be realized on this view is not moral freedom (because it
does not necessarily involve determining one's actions in accord
with self-given laws) but rather the negatively defined freedom that
Rousseau calls civil freedom. That is, the general will's restructuring of dependence creates for individuals, not merely the abstract
right, but the real possibility to act unconstrained by the will of
others within a sphere of activity external to the community's vital
interests. Rousseau's political thought, then, contains two distinct
accounts of how individuals realize their freedom through the general will, accounts that differ with respect to both (i) the nature of
the relation claimed to hold between freedom and the general will
and (ii) the type of freedom said to be realized: According to the
first, membership in the state is (i) a *precondition* of (ii) a negatively
defined *civil freedom*, insofar as the rule of law effectively mitigates
the freedom-endangering consequences of dependence; according
to the second, membership in the state is (i) an *embodiment* of (ii)
moral freedom (or social autonomy), insofar as citizens are ruled by
laws they construct for themselves in accord with a shared conception of the common good.

Can Rousseau consistently maintain both of these accounts of
how freedom is realized through the general will, or are the two
views incompatible? In order to answer this question we must first
locate more precisely the point at which the two views threaten to
collide. The fact that Rousseau ascribes two kinds of freedom to the
members of a rational state is not itself problematic. For civil and
moral freedom are to be understood not as two rival conceptions of
freedom but simply as two different forms that the freedom of

FREEDOM, DEPENDENCE, THE GENERAL WILL

citizens assumes. Being free of constraints imposed by the wills of other individuals and being subject only to self-given laws are merely two different ways of satisfying the basic condition of freedom, which stipulates that one obey no will other than one's own. Neither is there a problem in Rousseau's assertion that the two kinds of freedom exist side by side within a single state. Since the sphere of moral freedom can extend only as far as the domain of law itself, and since the latter is not so extensive as to determine everything individuals do, the limits of the domain of law demarcate a sphere within which citizens enjoy a freedom that can be characterized only negatively, as a condition of not being constrained to obey the particular wills of other individuals.

If there is a tension between these two accounts, it resides not in the distinction between civil and moral freedom itself but in the way each account conceives of the relation that must hold between individual wills and the general will, if the general will is to be considered the will of each individual. In other words, the point of difference concerns the kind of relation that individuals who are in fact subject to the general will must have to that will if their subjection to it is to count as obedience to their own will and therefore as freedom. According to the social autonomy model, the general will counts as the will of individuals only by virtue of a certain *subjective* relation individuals can have to the general will, a relation that consists in a conscious affirmation of the principles that inform the general will. For this reason the freedom depicted by the social autonomy model could be characterized as a species of "subjective freedom." For the freedom-through-personal-independence model, however, the general will's being the will of each individual depends not on a subjective quality of individual wills but on an *objective* feature of the general will itself, namely, that what it wills is a set of conditions which, if realized, has the effect of freeing individuals from their otherwise necessary subjection to the arbitrary wills of others. Because the freedom one enjoys on this scenario is independent of one's subjective relation to the principles that structure the social world, it could be termed a kind of "objective freedom."[36] Thus, the tension between these two accounts

---

[36]It is worth pointing out that Hegel, in an appropriation of Rousseau's political thought, uses precisely these terms, 'objective freedom' and 'sub-

FREDERICK NEUHOUSER

comes to the fore when the requirements of objective and subjective freedom come into conflict—that is, in those instances where individual citizens of a well-constituted state do not consciously affirm the principles by which they are governed, principles which, objectively speaking, are necessary for their own freedom. In other words, the conflict becomes manifest in precisely those situations where Rousseau speaks of individuals being forced to be free.

The question to be answered, then, is whether it is possible to bring together Rousseau's distinct accounts of freedom into a single coherent theory. The key to resolving the tension between these two models of political freedom lies not in embracing one at the expense of the other but in recognizing that, while each on its own represents a genuine species of freedom, each is also, in the absence of the other, a limited or merely partial freedom. This is obvious enough in the case of being forced to be free: to fail to affirm the principles which in fact constrain one's actions is to fall short, in an important way, of the ideal of being subject only to one's own will. While the notion of objective freedom provides the conceptual resources that make it possible to speak coherently of being forced to be free, such one-sided freedom remains a kind of unfreedom from the point of view of the subjective requirements of free willing. But the claim that each of the two conceptions is only partial freedom is no less true for the purely subjective freedom envisaged by the social autonomy model. The full freedom of citizens must consist in more than their simply having the appropriate subjective attitude to the principles by which they are governed, since to affirm principles that are ultimately destructive of one's freedom is itself a kind of unfreedom—that is, a failure to will in accord with one's own true will and its fundamental aspiration to be able to pursue its ends in the world free of external determination. Thus, the basic point underlying Rousseau's dual account of how citizens realize their freedom through the general will can be formulated as the claim that each of the two conceptions of freedom isolated here constitutes a necessary but not sufficient condi-

---

jective freedom', to refer to the two principal components of the conception of freedom that grounds his theory of *Sittlichkeit*. I intend to develop this insight in future work aimed at reconstructing the philosophical foundations of that theory.

FREEDOM, DEPENDENCE, THE GENERAL WILL

tion of achieving what Rousseau regards as full political freedom. According to this reconstruction, then, two independent conditions, one subjective and one objective, must be met in order for individuals to realize full political freedom: (i) the laws that govern citizens must be objectively liberating—they must effectively mitigate the freedom-endangering consequences of dependence on other individuals; and (ii) citizens must also stand in the appropriate subjective relation to the laws that govern them—that is, the principles that inform the laws must be consciously embraced by citizens as their own.[37]

Harvard University

[37]I would like to thank Bill Bristow, Steve Engstrom, Raymond Geuss, Delia Graff, Andrew Levine, and Allen Wood for their helpful comments on earlier drafts of this paper. I am also indebted to the Alexander von Humboldt-Stiftung for its generous financial support of this work.

Addenda

References within the text:

p. 364, §4, l.7: *OC*3.356/*CW*4.135
p. 366, §1, l.10: *OC*3.365/*CW*4.142
p. 367, §1, l.4: *OC*3.440/*CW*4.200
p. 369, §2, ll.18–19: *OC*3.364/*CW*4.141
p. 370, §1, l.1: *OC*3.441/*CW*4.201
  Ibid., §3, l.10: *OC*3.364/*CW*4.141
p. 373, §1, l.2: *OC*3.364/*CW*4.141
p. 375, §1, l.5: *OC*4.311/*Em*.85
  Ibid., ll.7–8: *OC*4.309/*Em*.84
p. 376, §3, l.10: *OC*4.421/*Em*.160
p. 377, §1, l.14: *OC*3.220/*CW*3.92
p. 380, §2, l.6: *OC*4.309/*Em*.84
  Ibid., l.8: –/–
  Ibid., l.11: *OC*3.841/*CW*9.260
p. 381, §3, l.7: *OC*4.311/*Em*.85
p. 382, §1, l.10: *OC*3.162/*CW*3.42
p. 384, l.16: *OC*3.174/*CW*3.51
p. 385, §2, l.10: *OC*3.394/*CW*4.164
p. 386, §1, l.5: *OC*4.311/*Em*.85
  Ibid., §2, l.13: *OC*3.248/*CW*3.146
p. 389, §1, l.17: *OC*3.842/*CW*9.261
  Ibid., l.21: *OC*3.373/*CW*4.149
  Ibid., §2, l.6: *OC*3.842–43/*CW*9.261
  Ibid., l.8: *OC*3.491/*CW*4.28

Endnotes:

8. l.3: *OC*3.440/*CW*4.200
9. l.2: *OC*3.310–11/*CW*4.99–100
11. *OC*4.345n/*Em*.108n
12. l.1: *OC*4.310/*Em*.84, *OC*4.312/*Em*.86, *OC*4.491/*Em*.213
    l.2: *OC*4.662/*Em*.333; *OC*3.160/*CW*3.40
17. *OC*4.456/*Em*.185
19. –/–
20. *OC*4.311/*Em*.85
21. *OC*4.245/*Em*.37
23. *OC*3.7/*CW*.5; *OC*3.161/*CW*3.41
26. l.1: *OC*3.283/*CW*4.77–78
    l.3: *OC*3.171/*CW*3.48–49
28. *OC*3.909–10/*CW*11.130
29. *OC*3.391/*CW*4.162
30. *OC*3.1002/*CW*11.208–09; *OC*3.391–92/*CW*4.162–63
31. l.1: *OC*3.945/*CW*11.160–61, *OC*3.275–76/*CW*3.168–69
    l.2: *OC*3.391–92/*CW*4.162
    l.5: *OC*3.171/*CW*3.48–49
32. *OC*3.491–92/*CW*4.28, *OC*3.842–43/*CW*9.261
34. *OC*3.379/*CW*4.153

Part IV
Anticipations of Game Theory

[11]

GAMES, JUSTICE AND THE GENERAL WILL

By W. G. Runciman and Amartya K. Sen

In this paper, we argue that a useful sense may be given to the
" General Will " and the " Common Good " by reference to the
theory of non-zero-sum non-cooperative games, and we suggest
some possible implications of this for the notion of social justice.

I

We begin by looking at the two-person, non-zero-sum, non-
cooperative game known as the " prisoner's dilemma ".[1] Two
persons are thought to be jointly guilty of a serious crime, but
the evidence is not adequate to convict them at a trial. The
district attorney tells the prisoners that he will take them
separately and ask them whether they would like' to confess,
though of course they need not. If both of them confess, they
will be prosecuted, but he will recommend a lighter sentence than
is usual for such a crime, say 6 years of imprisonment rather than
10 years. If neither confesses, the attorney will put them up
only for a minor charge of illegally possessing a weapon, of which
there is conclusive evidence, and they can expect to get 2 years
each. If, however, one confesses and the other does not, the
one who confesses receives lenient treatment for providing
evidence to the state and gets only 1 year, and the one who does
not receives the full punishment of 10 years. From an egoistic
point of view, the strategy of confession for either of the prisoners " strictly dominates " over the strategy of non-confession,
i.e. no matter what the other prisoner is assumed to do it is
always better for this prisoner to confess. If, for example, this
prisoner thinks that the other one is going to confess, then by
confessing himself he gets only 6 years rather than the full 10
years which he will receive if he does not confess. If, on the other
hand, he assumes that the other prisoner will not confess, then
by confessing he gets only 1 year and by not confessing he
receives 2 years. So no matter what this prisoner assumes
about the other's behaviour, it is always in his interest to confess.
The same, of course, holds for the other prisoner. Therefore,
assuming egoism, both will confess and receive 6 years each,
but if neither confessed, they would have received only 2 years

---

[1] First devised by A. W. Tucker, and discussed in R. Duncan Luce and
Howard Raiffa, *Games and Decisions* (New York, 1957), pp. 94-102.

each. So what seems rational from an individualistic point of view, *i.e.* each taking the other person's actions as given, produces a relatively worse overall result.

To clarify the picture for ready reference, we reproduce below in a summary form the consequence of alternative policies for the two prisoners. The rows represent Prisoner 1's policies and the columns Prisoner 2's policies. We can find the overall result by looking at the item that belongs to the appropriate row and, the appropriate column. The first figure within each pair of brackets represents the consequences for Prisoner 1 and the second those for Prisoner 2, *e.g.* (10, 1) represents 10 years for the first and 1 year for the second.

PRISONER 2

	Not confess	*Confess*
NOT CONFESS	(2, 2)	(10, 1)
CONFESS	(1, 10)	(6, 6)

PRISONER 1

As is clear, for Prisoner 1 the second row is better than the first, no matter which column he is in, and for Prisoner 2 the second column is better than the first, no matter which row he is in. So the self-seeking of the two will lead them to (6, 6), as a consequence of confession by each, whereas they would have been both better off at (2, 2), the consequence of neither confessing.[1]

It is important to recognize that even if the two prisoners are allowed to talk to each other and to conspire, this will not affect the outcome. Since both prisoners are self-seekers, and since the confession takes place separately, it will be in the interest of each to break the contract not to confess which they might have made ; and it will be in the interest of each to do this quite irrespective of whether each assumes that the other prisoner will also break his contract or not.

This conflict between what seems individually better and what seems to produce the best over-all result contains, in our view,

---

[1] Repetitions of this game over time, under certain circumstances, may take the two to the mutually beneficial solution, but this is not always the case (Luce and Raiffa, pp. 97-102). Besides, such pure repetitions are normally not possible in social games, with which we shall be concerned in the rest of the paper. In fact, in the case of the " prisoner's dilemma " itself, pure repetitions will be difficult and many repetitions unlikely.

556 W. G. RUNCIMAN AND A. K. SEN:

the essence of Rousseau's distinction between the " will of all " and the " general will ". The " general will " of the prisoners, we can say, is to avoid confession, but each person's " particular will " is to confess. Since, in the absence of successful collusion their self-seeking will take them to a situation worse for both, what is needed is an enforceable contract between them. They would both be ready to appoint an agent who would see to it that neither of them confessed. In the absence of sanction (or, we might even say, of a Sovereign), each prisoner may be driven by rational self-seeking to break the contract which is to the common advantage of both.

This gives an immediate and plausible sense to Rousseau's notion of the members of a society being " forced to be free ", and can be claimed to correspond with what Rousseau says in the *Social Contract* about the general will. It is not our purpose to offer yet another reinterpretation of Rousseau as either totalitarian or liberal ; but it seems worthwhile to point out how Rousseau's notion can be given a valid sense by reference to the model of the prisoner's dilemma. The purpose of the general will, says Rousseau,[1] is the good of all, or common good : the general will " always tends to the public advantage ". What makes the general will general is not the number of citizens involved, but " the common interest by which they are united ". The divergence between the general will and the will of all arises because the individual's personal interest " may dictate a line of action quite other than that demanded by the interest of all ". The general will, though remaining unalterable, becomes subordinated to the encroachment of individual wills when " each, separating his interest from the interest of all, sees that such separation cannot be complete, yet the part he plays in the general damage seems to him as nothing compared with the exclusive good which he seeks to appropriate "—an account which fits exactly the case of the prisoner who seeks to gain an advantage by breaking the contract. The general will is general not only in its origins but its objects, and is " applicable to all as well as operated by all ". It tends always to equality : and all citizens being equal by virtue of the contract, " none has the right to demand that another should do what he does not do himself ". It is, finally, the legislator who must persuade the people of their true interest : the average man " finds it difficult to see what benefit he is likely to derive from the ceaseless privations which good laws will impose upon him ", so that the good

[1] The quotations which follow are taken from the translation in *Social Contract* (ed. Barker), World's Classics edition (London, 1947).

legislator is the legislator who will lead those " to whom mere
mortal prudence would ever be a stumbling block " (or who
would, in other words, pursue what might well be their rational
individual strategy, but at the cost of their real benefit).

These remarks of Rousseau's seem to us to make it possible
for an interpretation to be given to the general will on the model
of the prisoner's dilemma. This interpretation requires, however, to be distinguished from the interpretation of the general
will given by Arrow in *Social Choice and Individual Values*.
According to Arrow, " The idealistic doctrine may then be
summed up by saying that each individual has two orderings,
one which governs him in his everyday actions and one which
would be relevant under some ideal conditions and is in some
sense truer than the first ordering ".[1] Our interpretation, by
contrast, does not require us to impute to each person more than
a single set of orderings. On our view, each person has (as in
Rousseau) a single and consistent aim. The conflict between the
will of all and the general will arises not because the individual
must be required to change his preference orderings, but because
of the difference between the outcome of individual strategy and
of enforced collusion which arises under the conditions of the
non-cooperative, non-zero-sum game.

We thus further assume that a substantive sense may be given
to the common good (again, as in Rousseau). This is not to say
that the general will enjoins a set of specific practices on specific
persons. Rousseau makes clear at several points that this is not
so. It does, however, mean more than the sense to which, it
has been argued by Benn and Peters, the common good must be
restricted, namely that all claims should have been impartially
considered before legislation is passed.[2] The limit which must
be imposed on the meaning of the common good is rather that
it loses its meaning where there is a conflict of " real " interests
even in Rousseau's sense. That is to say, the common good may
be taken to be substantively embodied in what the general will
wills : but the general will does not will anything which requires
that any person should be (in terms of his own preference ordering) the long-term loser, although it may, of course, require him
to forego the pursuit of an individual advantage which, without
enforced collusion, would leave him in the end worse off. We
may say, if you like, that the general will always fulfils the

[1] Kenneth J. Arrow, *Social Choice and Individual Values* (New York,
1951), pp. 82-83.
[2] S. I. Benn and R. S. Peters, *Social Principles and the Democratic State*
(London, 1959), p. 227.

conditions of Pareto optimality, although it is not suggested thereby that Pareto optimality is a sufficient criterion of justice. Whether or how far it may be useful to say that the general will wills justice will be considered in the second section of this paper.

There is, however, a difficulty which may arise even where Pareto optimality is satisfied. Even where a set of social arrangements may be envisaged whereby all individuals would benefit, there may be a choice where one class of persons would be better off under one possible set of arrangements and another class under another. Consider, for example, a country where some people have cars with a left-hand drive and others with a right-hand drive, so that the former would prefer a rule of driving on the right and the latter of driving on the left. Which law does the general will enjoin ? It will be in the interest of both the two classes to have either of the two laws in preference to none at all, but one class will prefer one law and the other class another. We are here faced with a choice of cooperative solutions to a non-zero-sum game, and there does not appear to be any criterion by which one solution better embodies the general will (or, we may say, is more just) than the other. In other words, the appeal to the general will appears to yield weak but not strong orderings of aggregated preferences.

The problem, therefore, in such cases as these is to settle in advance the rules of a fair game by which the choice of cooperative solutions to a non-zero-sum non-cooperative game may be made. In the example offered, it could be claimed that the general will might require an appeal to the majority principle (with, perhaps, an agreement in the case of a tie to abide by the toss of a coin). Everyone could be assumed to be ready to accept a general method of resolving deadlocks which would be preferable to the pursuit by everyone of his atomistic rational strategy. The implementation of the law enacted on this basis would be consistent with the general will. In such a case, it could be said not only that the general will wills the common interest (either of two alternative laws being demonstrable as in the common interest in preference to no enforced collusion at all), but also that the general will wills the just resolution of conflicting interests. This formulation, however, directly raises the relation of the general will to the notion of justice, and the limits of the scope of the general will when applied to problems traditionally associated with the concept of social justice. It is to these questions that we turn in the following section.

GAMES, JUSTICE AND THE GENERAL WILL   559

II

For this purpose it will be convenient to start from the contractual model of justice as fairness as developed by John Rawls.[1] It is the notion of the contract which, on Rawls's model as on Rousseau's, must link any notion of the general will to that of justice, since it is by virtue of the contract that all persons are to be viewed as equally subject to the general will, and it is by reference to the contract that assessment is made of the justice of demanding that the individual should surrender the right to act purely according to his atomistic strategy. As used by Rawls, the contract implicit in justice as fairness is not, of course, a historical contract. But it is a contract in that all parties seeking a " just " aggregation or resolution of their individual interests are to be envisaged as having made, in Rawls's phrase, a " firm commitment in advance ". This commitment is not on specific practices, but on " principles of appraisal " mutually acknowledged by " free persons who have no authority over each other " ; and it is according to these principles that their competing claims are to be settled. This means, in effect, that every member of a society might as well have been party to a fictitious contract to abide by decisions of social policy to the extent that he would expect his own claims to be vindicated when in accordance with the principles agreed in advance. That this is the essence of justice, and that the social contract (in a modified form) does provide the model for it, seems to us to be adequately demonstrated by Rawls. It remains to consider the relation of the general will as we see it to this conception of justice.

On the model of the prisoner's dilemma, both prisoners partially share a common preference ordering—both, that is, prefer (2, 2) to (6, 6), since both wish to minimize their joint and equal sentences. Extending this, therefore, we must say that the model only applies to cases where social aims are up to a point unanimous.[2] However, even where aims may be said to conflict in that people may have conflicting preferences between cooperative solutions to a non-zero-sum non-cooperative game, but where each cooperative solution is better than no cooperation at all, we have seen that the general will may will a solution acceptable

[1] John Rawls, " Justice as Fairness ", *Philosophical Review*, lxvii (1958), 164-194.

[2] Cases of this kind vary from such civic rules as not dumping rubbish on the street, to important national economic decisions. For an example of the last, see A. K. Sen, " On Optimizing the Rate of Saving ", *Economic Journal*, lxxi (1961), esp. pp. 487-489.

to both parties. The real difficulty comes when we are confronted with a case where cooperation cannot make everybody better off. Take, for example, zero-sum social games—games, that is, where the gain of one person or group must be the loss of another. By our sense of the general will, a person cannot here be " forced to be free ", except where his own long-run preference ordering can be shown to be better realized by his acceptance of the loss in this particular case. What this means is that when the rules of a zero-sum game are to be settled then the general will may be described as enjoining the rules of a game of " fair " division to the extent that such rules can be shown to be in the long-term or " real " interest of all the players relative to the outcome which would result without such rules. A " fair " zero-sum game, to accord with the requirements of our sense of the general will, must in this sense accord with the preference orderings of all the players.

What will it mean, therefore, to say that (as Rousseau seems sometimes to imply) the general will wills social juśtice ? It is clear that on our analysis the justification of either enforced collusion or of " fair " rules for zero-sum social games will cover fewer cases than could be appealed to by Rawlsian justice. If justice is interpreted in Rawls's sense—and a case could perhaps be made for thus interpreting Rousseau's " true principle of equity "—then justice corresponds to such solutions to zero-sum games as accord with principles to which the players, had they met before the game under conditions of primordial equality, *would have* jointly agreed to. Our view of the " general will ", which rather follows Rousseau's emphasis on common interests than his implication of common principles, does not offer any way of establishing principles by which some players must accept to be losers except in so far as the acceptance of rules entailing loss accords with the players' long-term interest or preference. Interest does not mean here that terms of " fair " contracts depend purely upon the threat-advantage of individual players —an objection effectively raised by Rawls against Braithwaite's *Theory of Games as a Tool for the Moral Philosopher.* But it does mean that we do not extend the general will so far as to allow persons to be " forced to be free " by the criterion of any principle to which they could be supposed, if rational, to have been prepared to assent from the state of nature.

The initial difficulty in fitting the notion of a " game of fair division " even to our limited sense of the general will is that there are occasions when such games as formally defined by game theory are manifestly unfair. This is the difficulty inherent in

GAMES, JUSTICE AND THE GENERAL WILL   561

the attempt to apply the theory of games to the resolution of
conflicting claims without (as Rawls shows to be necessary)
introducing some further concept of fairness. The difficulty
most obviously arises when one player in a game of " fair "
division is initially very rich and the other very poor. Nor,
unless unanimity already exists, is it possible without a regress
to make the rules of the game themselves a part of the players'
desired outcome. By Rawlsian justice, we could perhaps settle
the matter by establishing the principles by which rational
persons would, before knowing if they would be rich or poor,
have agreed to decide when a game of " fair " division was in
fact appropriate. But this involves the assumption, which we
do not ourselves wish to make, that there are no conflicts between
the principles of, say, needs and deserts, except those dictated
by a vested position.[1] We can, however, demonstrate that
persons can be " forced to be free " in the cases where their
preference ordering of social states will be better realized as a
result of their willingness not to pursue their atomistic strategy.

With the concept of " social justice " which follows from
Rawls's model of justice and that of the " general will " as
developed above, it becomes possible to make the following
statements about their relationships in the context of rules that
are used to compel individuals. The set of rules that satisfy the
criterion of " social justice " we refer to as S, and the set of
rules that conform to an unambiguous " general will " we refer
to as G. Our contentions are the following :

(I) G is a sub-set of S.
(II) The " complement " of G in S, *i.e.* the set of rules that
belong to S but not to G, may be non-empty. This means
that it is possible that some rules may be socially " just "
without conforming to an unambiguous " general will ".
(III) Because of the possibility of a genuine conflict of
principles about who should gain and who should lose, it
may be difficult to decide whether a rule belongs to S or
not, if it does not belong to G.

Statement (I) says that if a particular rule conforms to an
unambiguous " general will ", it will pass Rawls's test of " social
justice ". If a certain contract will lead the persons concerned
to a situation where everyone would be better off than they would

---

[1] See, on this, Brian M. Barry, " Justice and the Common Good ",
Analysis, xxxi (1961), 86-90 ; and W. G. Runciman, " Sociological Evid-
ence and Political Theory ", in P. Laslett and W. G. Runciman (ed.),
Philosophy, Politics and Society, Second Series (Oxford, 1962), p. 35.

be if they followed atomistic strategy, then it will be correct to say that everyone, if rational (as defined by Rawls), will accept the contract in a situation of primordial equality, *i.e.* even without knowing his own exact position in the game. In the example of the " prisoner's dilemma ", the contract of non-confession will conform to " social justice " from the point of view of the two prisoners. Breaking this contract, moreover, can be regarded as " unjust ", and if either prisoner tries to break the contract he may be justly " forced to be free ".

Statement (II) can be understood by visualizing a case where it is known that everybody concerned would have accepted a rule in a state of primordial equality, even though the rule in practice leads to the greater detriment of somebody than would result if he were to follow his atomistic strategy. If, for example, it were known that everybody would have supported a certain system of progressive taxation in a state where they had absolutely no idea what their own pre-tax income would be, then such a system of taxation would satisfy the Rawlsian requirement of justice, even though there might not be the necessary partial unanimity of interests required for the existence of a " general will ".

Statement (III) can be illustrated with the same example. Since there exist genuine conflicts of principles, *e.g.* between " needs " and " deserts ", it will become difficult beyond a certain point to establish what principles people would have subscribed to in a state of primordial equality. Whether, therefore, a particular person's argument is attributable to his vested interest in the situation in which he finds himself, or whether it is attributable to a principle he would (if rational) have accepted even when he had no such vested interest, may be difficult to resolve. In contrast with this, cases that fit the " general will " pose no special difficulty, since irrespective of a person's vested position, the enforceable contract is to his advantage.

We do not, therefore, wish to restrict the use of the notion of " social justice " to the cases that conform to a " general will " ; but we do want to point out that in these cases there is no possibility of ambiguity in the interpretation of " social justice ", unlike the cases where the model of a " general will " cannot be applied.

[12]

THE STAG HUNT

BRIAN SKYRMS

I: THE STAG HUNT

The Stag Hunt is a story that became a game. The game is a prototype of the social contract. The story is briefly told by Rousseau, in *A Discourse on Inequality*:

> If it was a matter of hunting a deer, everyone well realized that he must remain faithful to his post; but if a hare happened to pass within reach of one of them, we cannot doubt that he would have gone off in pursuit of it without scruple..."

Rousseau's story of the hunt leaves many questions open. What are the values of a hare and of an individual's share of the deer given a successful hunt? What is the probability that the hunt will be successful if all participants remain faithful to the hunt? Might two deer hunters decide to chase the hare?

Let us suppose that the hunters each have just the choice of hunting hare or hunting deer. The chances of getting a hare are independent of what others do. There is no chance of bagging a deer by oneself, but the chances of a successful deer hunt go up sharply with the number of hunters. A deer is much more valuable than a hare. Then we have the kind of interaction that is now generally known as the Stag Hunt.

Once you have formed this abstract representation of the Stag Hunt game, you can see Stag Hunts in many places. David Hume also has the Stag Hunt. His most famous illustration of a convention has the structure of a two-person Stag Hunt game:

> Two men who pull at the oars of a boat, do it by an agreement or convention, tho' they have never given promises to each other...

Both men can either row or not row. If both row, they get the outcome that is best for each - just as in Rousseau's example, when both hunt the stag. If one decides not to row then it makes no difference if the other does or not - they don't get anywhere. The worst outcome for you is if you row and the other doesn't, for then you lose your effort for nothing, just as the worst outcome for you in the Stag Hunt is if you hunt stag by yourself.

We meet the Stag Hunt again in the meadow-draining problem of Hume's *Treatise*:

> Two neighbors may agree to drain a meadow, which they possess in common; because 'tis easy for them to know each others mind, and each may perceive that the immediate consequence of failing in his part is the abandoning of the whole project. But 'tis difficult, and indeed impossible, that a thousand persons shou'd agree in any such action ...

where Hume observes that achieving cooperation in a many-person Stag Hunt is more difficult than achieving cooperation in a two-person Stag Hunt.[1]

The Stag Hunt does not have the same melodramatic quality as the Prisoner's Dilemma. It raises its own set of issues, which are at least as worthy of serious consideration. Let us focus, for the moment, on a two-person Stag Hunt for comparison to the familiar two-person Prisoner's Dilemma.

If two people cooperate in Prisoner's Dilemma, each is choosing less rather than more. In Prisoner's Dilemma, there is a conflict between individual rationality and mutual benefit.

In the Stag Hunt, what is rational for one player to choose depends on his beliefs about what the other will choose. Both stag hunting and hare hunting are *equilibria*. That is just to say that it is best to hunt stag if the other player hunts stag and it is best to hunt hare if the other player hunts hare. A player who chooses to hunt stag takes a risk that the other will choose not to cooperate in the Stag Hunt. A player who chooses to hunt hare runs no such risk, since his payoff does not depend on the choice of action of the other player, but he foregoes the potential payoff of a successful Stag Hunt. Here rational players are pulled in one direction by considerations of mutual benefit and in the other by considerations of personal risk.

Suppose that hunting hare has an expected payoff of 3, no matter what the other does. Hunting stag with another has an expected payoff of 4. Hunting Stag alone is doomed to failure and has a payoff of zero. It is clear that a pessimist, who always expects the worst, would hunt hare. But it is also true with these payoffs that a cautious player, who was so uncertain that he thought the other player was as likely to do one thing as another, would also hunt hare.[2] That is not to say that rational players could not coordinate on the stag hunt equilibrium that gives them both better payoff, but it is to say that they need a measure of trust to do so.

I told the story so that the payoff of hunting hare is absolutely independent of how others act. We could vary this slightly without affecting the underlying theme. Perhaps if you hunt hare, it is even better for you if the other hunts stag for you avoid competition for the hare. If the effect is small we still have an interaction that is much like the Stag Hunt. It displays the same tension between risk and mutual benefit. It raises the same question of trust. This small variation on the Stag Hunt is sometimes also called a Stag Hunt[3] and we will follow this more inclusive usage here.

Compared to the Prisoner's Dilemma, the Stag Hunt has received relatively little discussion in contemporary social philosophy – although there are some notable exceptions.[4] But I think that the Stag Hunt should be a focal point for social contract theory.

The two mentioned games, Prisoner's Dilemma and the Stag Hunt, are not unrelated. Considerations raised by both Hobbes and Hume can show that a seeming Prisoner's Dilemma is really a Stag Hunt. Suppose that Prisoner's Dilemma is repeated. Then your actions on one play may affect your partner's actions on other plays, and considerations of reputation may assume an importance that they cannot have if there is no repetition. Such considerations form the substance of Hobbes' reply to the Foole. Hobbes does not believe that the Foole has made a mistake concerning the nature of rational decision. Rather, he accuses the Foole of a shortsighted mis-specification of the relevant game:

> He, therefore, that breaketh his Covenant, and consequently declareth that he think that he may with reason do so, cannot be received into any society that unite themselves for Peace and Defense, but by the error of them that receive him.[5]

According to Hobbes, the Foole's mistake is to ignore the future.

David Hume invokes the same considerations in a more general setting:

> Hence I learn to do a service to another, without bearing him any real kindness; because I foresee, that he will return my service, in expectation of another of the same kind, and in order to maintain the same correspondence of good offices with me and with others.[6]

Hobbes and Hume are invoking the *shadow of the future*.

How can we analyze the shadow of the future? We can use the theory of indefinitely repeated games. Suppose that the probability that the Prisoner's Dilemma is will be repeated another time is constant. In the repeated game, the Foole has the strategy *Always Defect*. Hobbes argues that if someone defects, others will never cooperate with him. Those who initially cooperate, but who retaliate as Hobbes suggests against defectors, have a *Trigger* strategy.

If we suppose that *Always Defect* and *Trigger* are the only strategies available in the repeated game and that the probability of another trial is .6, then the Shadow of the Future transforms the two-person Prisoner's Dilemma:

	Cooperate	Defect
Cooperate	3	1
Defect	4	2

into the two-person Stag Hunt:[7]

	Trigger	All Defect
Trigger	7.5	4
All Defect	7	5

This is an exact version of the informal arguments of Hume and Hobbes.[8]

But for the argument to be effective against a fool, he must believe that the others with whom he interacts are not fools. Those who play it safe will choose *Always Defect*. Rawls' maximin player is Hobbes' Foole.[9] The Shadow of the Future has not solved the problem of cooperation in the Prisoner's Dilemma; it has transformed it into the problem of cooperation in the Stag Hunt.

In a larger sense, the whole problem of adopting or modifying the social contract for mutual benefit can be seen as a Stag Hunt. For a social contract theory to make sense, the state of nature must be an equilibrium. Otherwise there would not be the problem of transcending it. And the state where the social contract has been adopted must also be an equilibrium. Otherwise, the social contract would not be viable. Suppose that you can either *devote energy to instituting the new social contract* or not. If everyone takes the first course the social contract equilibrium is achieved; if everyone takes the second course the state of nature equilibrium results. But the second course carries no risk, while the first does. This is all quite nicely illustrated in miniature by the meadow-draining problem of Hume.

The problem of reforming the social contract has the same structure. Here, following Binmore, we can then take the relevant "state of nature" to be the *status quo*, and the relevant social contract to be the projected reform. The problem of instituting, or improving, the social contract can be thought of as the problem of moving from riskless Hunt Hare equilibrium to the risky but rewarding Stag Hunt equilibrium.

II: GAME DYNAMICS

How do we get from the Hunt Hare equilibrium to the Stag Hunt equilibrium? We could approach the problem in two different ways. We could follow Hobbes in asking the question in terms of rational self-interest. Or we could follow Hume by asking the question in a dynamic setting. We can ask these questions using modern tools – which are more that Hobbes and Hume had available, but still less than we need for fully adequate answers. The news from the frontiers of game theory is rather pessimistic about the transition from hare hunting to stag hunting.

The modern embodiment of Hobbes' approach is rational choice based game theory. It tells us that what a rational player will do in the Stag Hunt depends on what he thinks the other will do. It agrees with Hume's contention that a thousand-person Stag Hunt would be more difficult to achieve than a two-person Stag Hunt, because – assuming that everyone must cooperate for a successful outcome to the hunt – the problem of trust is multiplied. But if we ask how people can get from a Hare Hunt equilibrium to a Stag Hunt equilibrium, it does not have much to offer. From the standpoint of rational choice, for the Hare Hunters to decide to be Stag Hunters, each must *change her beliefs* about what the other will do. But rational choice based game theory as usually conceived, has nothing to say about how or why such a change of mind might take place.

Let us turn to the tradition of Hume. Hume emphasized that social norms can evolve slowly:

> Nor is the rule regarding the stability of possession the less derived from human conventions, that it arises gradually, and acquires force by a slow progression...

We can reframe our problem in terms of the most thoroughly studied model of cultural evolution, the replicator dynamics. If we ask in this framework, how one can get from the Hunt Hare equilibrium to the Hunt Stag equilibrium, the answer is that you can't! In the vicinity of the state where all hunt hare, hunting hare has the greatest payoff. If you are close to it, the dynamics carries you back to it. This reasoning holds good over a large class of adaptive dynamics. The transition from non-cooperation to cooperation seems impossible.

Perhaps the restriction to deterministic dynamics is the problem. We may just need to add some chance variation. We could add some chance shocks to the replicator dynamics[10] or look at a finite population where people have some chance of doing the wrong thing, or just experimenting to see what will happen.[11] If we wait long enough, chance variation will bounce the population out of hare hunting and into stag hunting.

But in the same way, chance variation can bounce the population out of stag hunting into hare hunting. Can we say anything more than that the population bounces between these two states? Yes, we know how to analyze this system[12] but the news is not good. When the chance variation is small, the population spends almost all its time in a state where everyone hunts hare.[13] It seems that all we have achieved so far is to show how the social contract might degenerate spontaneously into the state of nature.

Social contracts do sometime spontaneously dissolve. But social contracts also form. And there is experimental evidence that people will hunt stag even when it is a risk to do so.[14] This suggests the need for a richer theory.

III: LOCAL INTERACTION

The foregoing discussion proceeded in terms of models designed for random encounters in large populations. But cooperation in the Stag Hunt may well have originated in small populations with non-random encounters. How should we think about this setting?

Perhaps, instead of interacting at random with other members of the population, we interact with our neighbors. Can local interaction make a difference? We know that it can, from investigations the dynamics of other games played with neighbors. Philosophers have contributed these developments and in this regard I would like to mention Jason Alexander, Peter Danielson, Patrick Grim, Bill Harms, Rainer Hegselmann, Gary Mar, and Elliott Sober. In some cases local interactions make a spectacular difference in the outcome of the evolutionary (or learning) process.

Does local interaction make a difference in the Stag Hunt? Can it explain the institution of the social contract? The news gets worse. Glenn Ellison (1993) investigates the dynamics of the Stag Hunt played with neighbors, where the players are arranged on a circle. He finds limiting behavior not much different than that in the large population with random encounters. With a small chance of error, the population spends most of its time hunting hare. The difference in the dynamics of the two cases is that given local interaction, the population approaches its long run behavior much more rapidly. The moral for us, if any, is that in small groups with local interaction the degeneration of the social contract into the state of nature can occur with great rapidity.[15]

There is, however, a small glimmer of light from the following fable.[16] There is a central figure in the group, who interacts (pairwise) with all others and with whom they interact - you might think of him as the Boatman in honor of Hume or the Huntsman in honor of Rousseau.

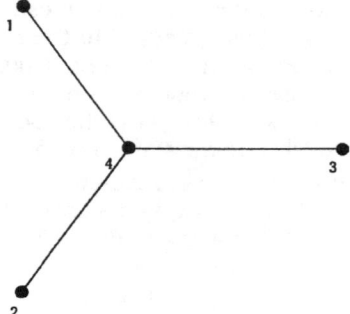

Every round, players revise their strategies by choosing the best response to their partners' prior play, with the exception that the Huntsman revises his strategy much less often. We add a small chance of spontaneously changing strategy for each player. If everyone hunts stag and the Huntsman spontaneously switches to hunting hare, in two rounds probably everyone will hunt hare. But conversely, if everyone is hunting hare and the Huntsman spontaneously switches to hunting stag, in two rounds probably everyone will hunt stag. In the long run the population spends approximately half its time hunting hare and half its time hunting stag. The story does not speak to all our concerns, but at least it shows that the social contract need not have negligible probability in the long run and that the *structure* of local interaction can make a difference.[17]

IV: DYNAMICS OF INTERACTION STRUCTURE

Still, it is hard not to feel that there must be something fundamental that is missing from our analysis. I would like to suggest that what is missing is an account of the evolution of the structure of interactions. Game theory takes the interaction structure as fixed. But in real life individuals adjust with whom they interact on the basis of past experience. This as a fundamental aspect of social behavior that is completely absent from the theory of games.

Let me show you how the analysis of the Stag Hunt is changed if individuals can learn with whom to interact. What follows is the result of joint work with Robin Pemantle.[18] Suppose that we have a small group of agents, some disposed to hunt stag and some disposed to hunt hare. They start out interacting at random, but when agents interact they are reinforced for interaction with the same agent by the payoff that they receive from the interaction. Reinforcement modifies the probability that one agent will choose to interact with another.

How do these interaction probabilities evolve? It can be shown, both by simulation and analytically, that stag hunters learn to interact with other stag hunters. This, perhaps, should come as no great surprise. It is not quite so obvious that hare hunters will end up interacting with other hare hunters. Hare hunters do not care with whom they interact. Nevertheless it is so.[19] Learning dynamics leads to a structure of interaction probabilities quite different from that of a random pairing model. In this environment, stag hunters prosper.

Now we can add the further consideration of players revising their strategies. Suppose that once in a while a player looks around the little group, sees who is doing best, and imitates that strategy. If interaction structure were fixed at random pairing, we would be back were we started and the most likely outcome would be that everyone would end up hunting hare. But if structure is fluid and the learning dynamics for structure is fast relative to the strategy revision dynamics, stag hunters will find each other and then imitation will slowly convert the hare hunters to stag hunters. This conclusion is robust to the addition of a little chance. Here, we finally have a model that can explain the institution of a modest social contract.

In between the extremes, the limiting outcome in a small group may be either all hare hunters or all stag hunters. Which outcome one gets depends somewhat on the vicissitudes of chance in the early stages of the evolution of the group. But it is also strongly influenced by the relative speeds of structure and strategy dynamics. Rapid structural adaptation favors the stag hunters. Our social contract may form in some circumstances but not in others.

We can consider different strategy revision dynamics. Suppose, as before, that structure dynamics is fast relative to strategy revision, but that the individuals never look around the group for successful models, but rather choose the best response to the strategy that they have encountered on the last play. Then the ultimate outcome will be that the group is divided into two stable classes, the stag hunters and the hare hunters, which never interact with one another. A different kind of strategy revision leads to a different social contract. There are other interesting possibilities to explore.

CONCLUSION

We should pay more attention to the Stag Hunt. There is a lot to think about. Real Stag Hunts are complex interactions between more than two people. So are the social contracts - large and small - that we have used the Stag Hunt to represent. In our analysis of two-person Stag Hunts we finally focused on the coevolution of strategy and interaction structure. I believe that this is a key to the larger question of the emergence of social structure.

REFERENCES

Alexander, Jason and Brian Skyrms (1999) "Bargaining with Neighbors: Is Justice Contagious?" *Journal of Philosophy* 96 588-598.

Axelrod, Robert (1984) *The Evolution of Cooperation* New York: Basic Books.

Binmore, Ken (1993) *Playing Fair: Game Theory and the Social Contract I.* Cambridge: MIT Press.

Binmore, Ken (1998) *Just Playing: Game Theory and the Social Contract II.* Cambridge:MIT Press.

Danielson, Peter (1992) *Artificial Morality* London:Routledge.

Ellison, Glenn (1993) "Learning, Local Interaction and Coordination" *Econometrica* 61, 1047-1071.

Epstein, Joshua and Axtell, Robert (1996) *Growing Artificial Societes: Social Science From the Bottom Up.* Cambridge:MIT Press.

Foster, Dean P, and H. Peyton Young (1990) "Stochastic Evolutionary Game Dynamics" *Theoretical Population Biology* 28:219-32.

Grim, Patrick, Gary Mar, Paul St. Denis (1998) *The Philosophical Computer: Exploratory Essays in Philosophical Computer Modeling* Cambridge: MIT Press.

Hampton, Jean. (1997) *Hobbes and the Social Contract Tradition.* N.Y.: Cambridge.

Harms, William (2000) "The Evolution of Cooperation in Hostile Environments" *Journal of Consciousness Studies* 7, 308-313.

Harsanyi, J. and R. Selten (1988) *A General Theory of Equilibrium Selection in Games* Cambridge: MIT Press.

Hegselmann, Rainer (1996)"Social Dilemmas in Lineland and Flatland" In Wim B. G. Liebrand and David. Messick (eds) *Frontiers in Social Dilemmas Research*. Berlin: Springer, 337-362.

Hobbes, Thomas. (1668) *Leviathan.* ed. & tr. E. Curley (1994) Indianapolis: Hackett.

Hume, David. (1739) *A Treatise of Human Nature.* ed. Selby-Bigge (1978) Oxford: Clarendon.

Jackson, Matthew and Alison Watts (working paper) "On the Formation of Interaction Networks in Social Coordination Games".

Jervis, Robert (1978) "Cooperation under the Security Dilemma" *World Politics* 30: 167-214.

Jiborn, Magnus. (1999) *Voluntary Coercion.* Lund: Lund University.

Kandori, Michihiro, George Mailath, and Rafael Rob (1993) "Learning, Mutation and Long-Run Equilibria in Games" *Econometrica* 61:29-56.

Luce, Duncan and Howard Raiffa (1957) *Games and Decisions* New York:Wiley.

Rankin, Frederick W., John B. Van Huyck and Raymond Battalio (2000) "Strategic Similarity and Emergent Conventions: Evidence from Similar Stag Hunt Games" *Games and Economic Behavior* 32, 315-337.

Sen, Amartya (1967) "Isolation, Assurance, and the Social Rate of Discount" *Quarterly Journal of Economics* 81:112-124.

Skyrms, Brian (1998) "The Shadow of the Future" In *Rational Commitment and Social Justice: Essays for Gregory Kavka*. Ed. Jules Coleman and Christopher Morris. Cambridge: Cambridge University Press, 12-22.

Skyrms, Brian and Pemantle, Robin (2000) "A Dynamic Model of Social Network Formation" *Proceedings of the National Academy of Sciences of the USA* 97, 9340-9346.

Skyrms, Brian and Vanderschraaf, Peter (1997) "Game Theory" in *The Handbook of Practical Logic*. Ed. Philippe Smets. Dordrecht:Kluwer.

40   *Proceedings and Addresses of the APA.* 75:2

Sober, Elliott and David Sloan Wilson (1998) *Unto Others: The Evolution and Psychology of Unselfish Behavior* Cambridge: Harvard University Press.

Vanderschraaf, Peter (1998) "The Informal Game Theory in Hume's Account of Convention" *Economics and Philosophy* 14:251-257.

Vanderschraaf, Peter (2001) *Learning and Coordination: Inductive Deliberation, Equilibrium and Convention.* London: Routledge.

Van Huyck, J. B., R. C. Battalio and R. O. Beil (1990) "Tacit Coordination Games, Strategic Uncertainty and Coordination Failure" *The American Economic Review* 80:234-248.

Young, H. Peyton (1998) *Individual Strategy and Social Structure* Princeton: Princeton University Press.

ENDNOTES

1. For evidence that this is true in laboratory experiments, see Van Huyck, Battalio and Beil (1990).

2. Hunting hare is said to be the *risk dominant* equilibrium.

3. Sometimes it is called an Assurance Game, following Sen (1967).

4. Ed Curley, Jean Hampton, Magnus Jiborn, and Peter Vanderschraaf.

5. Hobbes, *Leviathan*, xv,5, 205.

6. Hume, *Treatise*, 521.

7. If the probability of repetition is less than .5, the repeated game is still a Prisoner's Dilemma. If the probability of repetition is high enough, the stag hunting equilibrium becomes risk dominant.

8. And of Curley's remarks in his introduction to his edition of the Leviathan, p. xxviii.

9. Rawls recommends that agents choose a social contract according to the maximin principle which would have each agent play it safe by maximizing her minimum gain. If agents followed this advice here, they would choose *Always Defect*.

10. Foster and Young (1990).

11. Kandori, Mailath and Rob (1993).

12. Kandori, Mailath and Rob (1993), Young (1998).

13. In the risk dominant equilibrium.

14. See Van Huyck, Battalio and Beil (1990).

15. Peyton Young (1998) finds the same story true much more generally for local interaction on structures different from the circle.

16. Adapted from an example of Jackson and Watts.

17. If the huntsman were not patient, then the population would spend a smaller proportion of its time hunting stag, but that proportion would still not be negligible and it would still be true that structure makes a difference. That is the form of the example in Jackson and Watts.

18. For details and analysis, see Skyrms and Pemantle (2000).

19. Skyrms and Pemantle (2000).

Part V
Strategies of Redemption

[13]

THE ANTIDOTE IN THE POISON: THE THOUGHT OF JEAN-JACQUES ROUSSEAU

Jean Starobinski

I. Achilles' Spear

Rousseau, speaking of his childhood, found affliction inherent in it from the beginning: "I was born weak and sick; I cost my mother her life, and my birth was the first of my misfortunes."[1] This initial injury (or, rather, conviction and narration of injury) elicits and mobilizes all available reparative energies, all the faculties of compensation. An entire life is not too much to devote to the search for a cure when the disease is intimately bound up with one's arrival in the world. Afflicted with a congenital malformation and guilty of having killed his mother, Rousseau is at once the victim and the cause of an evil fate, yet it is a malady that he neither deserved nor wanted. In recounting his life with the intention of "telling all," he immediately blames his destiny on his initial injury, whose primary presence he would continue to feel at times owing to its aggravated effects, at other times to its surprising disappearance during intervals of good health. The reader is implicitly invited to pity a man afflicted by misfortune from the first yet also to feel amazement at all that was gloriously accomplished in spite of illness and in the face of an adversity that marked Jean-Jacques's existence in its very commencement.

In the *Confessions* the theme of a primitive injury is almost immediately coupled with that of therapy (in the broad sense of the term). Disease and its treatment enter into combination. The very possibility of survival depended on a saving intervention, yet this same intervention allowed the disease to persist. Rousseau does not hesitate to yoke opposites in his narrative, to join them inextricably. Aunt Suzon's care saves him, but the initial evil is only reinforced. Jean-Jacques barely escapes death; his survival is a miracle. But at the same time his sickness only gets worse. Astonishment and compassion are doubly warranted: "I was almost born dead. They had little hope of saving me. I carried the germ of a disorder that the years have reinforced and that now allows me moments of respite only so that I may suffer more cruelly in some other way. One of my father's sisters, a woman kindly and wise, took such good care of me that I survived."[2]

Rousseau wants very much to be able to mention in the same breath both the saving of his newborn life and the implacable crescendo of the illness he brought with him into the world. He invites us to envision in a single glance images of disease along with images of attempted remedies and cures. It is therefore essential that we try to understand how he compares, contrasts, and combines these images in a work that is among the most astonishing accounts we have of the *curable* and the *incurable*.

THE ILLS OF CIVILIZATION

The *Discourse on the Sciences and the Arts,* which marked the debut of Rousseau's literary career, is an indictment of the disease—the poison—that overtakes civilized societies as "fatal enlightenment" and "idle knowledge" progress. Can the progress of this disease be reversed? For a while Rousseau allows us to believe that it cannot, but he is only setting the stage for a final effect. In his conclusion he mentions the possibility of extracting a therapeutic principle from the poison itself, and since he has written the essay in the hope of winning a prize offered by the Academy of Dijon, he uses this as an argument to justify the existence of academies. But even though Rousseau's purpose here was to compliment the academicians who would sit in judgment of his work, his argument was of the utmost importance and would later serve him in very different contexts: "I admit, however, that the evil is not as great as it might become. Eternal providence, by placing salutary simples alongside noxious plants, and by endowing the substance of certain harmful animals with remedies for their wounds, has taught the sovereigns who are its ministers to imitate its wisdom."[3]

The idea is expressed in the broadest possible terms: remedies are to be found near where poisonous plants grow and in the very flesh of dangerous animals. In one case the noxious agent attracts its antidote; in the other it contains it. The intervention of a therapist—in this case Louis XIV, the protector and founder of the Academies—is required to *extract* the remedy from the poison. By following the example of Providence, Rousseau asserts, "this great monarch drew from the very bosom of the sciences and arts, the sources of a thousand aberrations, . . . those celebrated societies charged with the safekeeping of human knowledge and with the sacred trust of morals."[4] The image of the remedy is here patterned after that of a select society of men bound by a mutual insistence on purity of morals and concern to safeguard a perilous treasure.[5] Thus the remedy is to entrust the ambiguous privilege of knowledge to a small number of men, who will seek to perpetuate and even increase that knowledge while limiting its diffusion. We recognize the Rousseauist ideal of a closed community, which can be as large as a city-state but which can equally well be limited to a small "elite society" of noble souls *(belles âmes)*. The antidote is the poison itself, provided it is kept under strict surveillance by exceptional men certain not to be corrupted by its deleterious power. The society of Clarens is a perfect example.

The evil of which Rousseau accused the sciences and the arts was that of dissolving the truth of human relations. By contrast, one could reconstitute an island of transparency by gathering together a community of equal individuals, all virtuous, who would form a select society devoting itself to "cultivation of the sciences." Of primary importance was that each member of this society should be a *true* scholar. The members of academies, as idealized by Rousseau, were people in possession of abundant and authentic knowledge, radically different from the "idle science" he denounced as the work of "charlatans." This deceptive and pretentious brand of learning had only the appearance of knowledge. Around it the gap between appearance and reality spread like an epidemic. The true science of the academicians repaired, among themselves at any rate, this ontological tear; it overcame alienation and restored the unity of external appearance and internal reality.

Was the remedy reliable, however? Was it powerful enough to overcome the disease? Because Rousseau does not wish to diminish the pathos of his indictment, he hints that the outcome may be uncertain and of limited effectiveness. At a time when medicine had few effective weapons at its disposal, the metaphor of a "remedy" left the way clear for skepticism: "The intensity of the care only demonstrates the need, and no one looks for remedies for nonexistent diseases. To be sure, the available remedies are inadequate. But is that not the case with all common remedies?"[6]

Indeed, there was a danger that the prestige of the academies might make the sciences attractive and thus, rather than confine them within a safe zone, help spread them dangerously abroad, leading to relapse. Rousseau refuses to retract his accusatory warning that the disease may be irremediable, but he is equally unwilling to relinquish whatever appeal he may exercise on the reader who, having been made to feel his guilt, is instructed on the means of achieving a difficult salvation and the price that must be paid. In the course of the lengthy polemic triggered by the first discourse, Rousseau continually invoked the remedy metaphor, but he varied it in every possible way as if experimenting with its latent possibilities. In one text he starts out by stating that "no more remedies can be hoped for," but ultimately he leaves the question open.[7] He leaves it to others to provide an answer: "I have seen the ill and tried to find its causes; others bolder or more foolhardy than I may search for a remedy."[8]

In the *Observations* (which Rousseau addressed to the king of Poland, who had ventured to take part in the debate) and later in the preface of *Narcissus*, the remedy was downgraded to the status of a palliative. Compromise with the disease is the only hope that remains:

> I have praised the academies and their illustrious founders, and I gladly repeat that praise. When the disease is incurable, the physician applies palliatives and administers remedies in proportion not so much to the patient's needs as to his temperament.[9]

> The same causes that have corrupted peoples serve sometimes to prevent even greater corruption. Thus a person who has ruined his temperament by unwarranted use of medicine must look once more to the physicians to save his life. And the arts and sciences, having given birth to many vices, are needed to prevent them from turning into crimes. At least they cover them with a varnish that prevents the poison from being exhaled so freely . . . My advice is therefore . . . to allow academies, colleges, universities, libraries, spectacles, and all the other amusements that may divert men from their wickedness to exist, and even to devote much care to their maintenance.[10]

THE ANTIDOTE IN THE POISON 121

Note that here the recourse to medicine (and its remedies) is itself described as a kind of poison; the palliative extracted from the primary poison is a drug of the second degree. But the relation between illness and remedy can also be cast in more dramatic fashion as a choice between incurable disease and heroic cure, now called "revolution," which risks provoking a disease even more serious than the one it is meant to treat. Is Rousseau proposing a potential cure, or is he pushing pessimism to an extreme by suggesting that the heroic cure magnifies the disease to the ultimate degree?

> No one has ever seen a corrupted people return to virtue. You may pretend to destroy the sources of the disease, but to no avail . . . You may restore men to the primordial condition of equality, but in vain . . . Their hearts, once spoiled, will remain so always. No remedy is possible, except perhaps some great revolution almost as much to be feared as the disease it is meant to cure, and which it is blameworthy to desire and impossible to foresee.[11]

Note the rhetorical precautions employed here to evoke, hypothetically, a remedy that can be described only in terms of the ambivalent feelings it inspires before the fact. Rousseau does not tell us whether a "revolution" that by some miracle does exert a curative effect is derived from the substance of the poison itself. It may rather be one of those dramatic changes that take place when things are at their worst: a reversal brought about by the disease but not necessarily of the same nature. But it makes no difference: Rousseau sees the malady as reintroducing itself via the "revolution," so that an intimate relation persists between disease and response.

It is a matter of some moment, however, whether the remedy is conceived on the homeopathic model as being inherent *in* the cause of the disease itself or on the allopathic model as coming from *outside* to combat the disease through administration of a contrary agent. If, through improvements of a practical order, the disease can somehow be made to cure itself, the way is open to a great reconciliation, and none of what human beings have acquired over the course of history need be totally rejected. If not, the disease must progress to a point of crisis before a liberating rupture can occur and a new order be established to replace the one that has succumbed to terminal corruption. In either case the disease will have been useful, but in the former it will have demonstrated its aptitude for transformation from evil into good, whereas in the latter its very severity will have called down the forces of destruction and led to its replacement by an antagonistic power.

LITERATURE JUSTIFIED

One of the first objections raised by Rousseau's adversaries (who in so doing availed themselves of a familiar figure of legal rhetoric known as retortion) was to ask how it was, since he condemned the arts and sciences, that he came to write such eloquent discourses. Rousseau defended himself by invoking the image of using evil to combat evil, a theme on which he rang countless changes:

> On this subject I might mention what the Church Fathers said about the worldly sciences they despised yet used to combat the pagan philosophers. I might cite the comparison they made with the Egyptian vases stolen by the Israelites. But I shall limit my final response to this single question: if someone came to kill me and I were lucky enough to catch hold of his weapon, would I be forbidden to use it to drive him from my home before disposing of it?[12]

When he published the comedy *Narcissus,* however, Rousseau could not avoid explaining his participation in an activity that he had so loudly condemned. Among the reasons he gives at least two belong to the order of argument that concerns us here. He says, first of all, that what he is doing is merely a diversion, a palliative. For once he expresses this in a nonmedical metaphor: "The question is no longer to induce people to do good but simply to distract them from doing ill. They must be occupied with foolishness in order to dissuade them from wickedness. They have to be amused, not preached to."[13] Yet soon the figures of injury, venom, and poison are again being invoked as metaphors for the disease in question, which must therefore be treated with the appropriate therapy, namely, the poison itself: "Although these things have done much harm to society, today it is highly essential that they be used as a medicine for the ills they have caused, or in the manner of those harmful animals that must be crushed on the very wound they inflict as they bite."[14] Later he addressed Voltaire: "But there comes a time when the illness is such that the causes from which it stems are necessary to prevent it from increasing. It is like the arrow that must be left in the wound lest the victim die from plucking it out. As for myself, if I had followed my original vocation and neither read nor written, I would no doubt have been happier. If letters were now abolished, however, I would be deprived of the only pleasure I have left."[15]

In the dialogue that serves as a second preface to *La Nouvelle Héloïse*, Rousseau has his interlocutor pose the following questions: "Is it enough that [the moral of your book] goes to the source of the ill? Are you not afraid that it will cause further harm?" Rousseau answers: "The source of the ill? Whose ill? In a time of epidemic and contagion should the distribution of drugs helpful to the sick be prevented on the grounds that they may be harmful to healthy people?"[16] The novel is indeed an ill, as the first of the two prefaces states: "No chaste girl ever read novels . . . Any girl who, despite this title, dares to read a single page is lost."[17] Yet Saint-Preux writes Julie: "Novels are the only instruction that remains for a people so corrupt that no other instruction can do it any good."[18]

Rousseau develops a similar casuistry when he considers the value of theater in various types of society. Though pernicious for states that have preserved their moral health, the theater may be useful in large cities, where it interferes with more harmful activities:

> Reason demands that amusements of people whose occupations are harmful be encouraged and that those whose occupations are useful be dissuaded from partaking of those same amusements. Another general consideration is that it is not good to allow idle and corrupt men to choose their own amusements lest they conceive them in the image of their vicious inclinations and become as obnoxious in their pleasures as in their affairs.[19]

Clearly Rousseau has in mind some form of government intervention, and it is difficult to say whether that intervention would have had more in common with old-fashioned religious censorship or with the state-sponsored cultural policies of our own day. But this voluntaristic conception is itself a consequence (or corollary) of the idea of history as decline or as the progress of evil. The virtually constant metaphor of a remedy administered by a therapist is linked to the metaphor of social change as decline, as akin to the decay of a living organism. The "morals" of a people are subject to "the inevitable accidents that attack them," to "the natural tendency that deforms them."[20] When salutary action is possible, it consists essentially in prohibiting certain things or delaying certain changes: "All that human wisdom can do is to prevent changes, to halt long in advance everything that brings them on."[21] If the disease is not too advanced, preventive measures can be recommended. But by the time corruption has progressed in "large cities," it is too late for anything but diversion, carried out in deliberate fashion by an informed government:

> Government policies *(la police)* cannot do enough to increase the number of permissible pleasures or to make them even more agreeable so that private individuals are not tempted to seek out even more dangerous recreations.[22]

> In some places [theatrical spectacles] may be useful for attracting foreigners; for increasing the circulation of currency; for stimulating artists; for varying fashions; for occupying those who are or aspire to be excessively wealthy; for making them less harmful; for distracting the common people from their miseries; for turning their attention to mountebanks and away from their leaders; for preserving and improving taste when decency is lost; for varnishing over the ugliness of vice; in short, for preventing bad morals from degenerating into brigandage.[23]

In other words, having stated that "the moral effect of plays and theaters can never be good or salutary in itself," Rousseau now admits that "when the people are corrupt, spectacles are good for them."[24] Concerning Geneva, the final pages of the *Letter to d'Alembert* begin with what appears to be a definitive denunciation: "With plays, all that may be useful to those for whom they are created may become harmful to us."[25] But just when it seems that Rousseau has banished the theater from Geneva once and for all (on the grounds that the people of the city still have "morals" and would therefore stand to lose if they tolerated such a seedbed of corruption), he proposes a surprising remedy, and one that relies on the dramatic art, that is, on the disease itself. The therapeutic approach is to accept the evil inherent in the theater (which is distortion, alienation, separation of consciences) and use it to effect a reconciliation of the self *(retour à soi):*

> I see only one remedy for so many drawbacks: in order to appropriate the dramas of our theater, we must write them ourselves, and we

THE ANTIDOTE IN THE POISON   125

must have playwrights before we have actors. It is not good for us to
be shown all sorts of imitations; it is good for us to be shown only
those decent things appropriate to free men. It is certain that plays
derived, like those of the Greeks, from the past misfortunes of the
fatherland or the present defects of the people could offer useful
lessons to their spectators.[26]

It will, however, be difficult, Rousseau admits, to build a great national theater, since the heroes that it would celebrate would be obscure
men with "common names." At his wits' end, Rousseau therefore asks
Voltaire (who is the implicit enemy throughout the *Letter to
d'Alembert*) to write new tragedies on Roman and republican themes.
Voltaire is thus invoked against Voltaire himself. This part of the text
is not intended simply to mollify the great man. As usual it proposes
treating the disease with a remedy derived from the disease itself: "May
M. de Voltaire deign to compose tragedies on the model of *The Death
of Caesar* or the first act of *Brutus*. If we absolutely must have a theater,
let him pledge to fill it always with his genius, and to live as much as
his plays do."[27]
Ultimately Rousseau comes to favor other kinds of spectacle: popular celebrations in the open air (for summer) and dances (for winter).
Is the festival really the negation of the theater, however? Isn't it rather
the generalization, the extension of the theater to the entire community? If so, then Rousseau is proposing to treat the disease of exclusive
theatrical presentations not by eliminating the theater but by transforming it into something more inclusive. In that way it can incorpo-
rate the entire population of the city, as each person becomes simultaneously actor and spectator. The festival is the theatricalized version
of the act of voluntary alienation performed by the parties to the social
contract: obedience and submission, which are evils as long as they
remain partial, become the cornerstone of legitimacy when no one is
exempted. The alienating effects of the theater can be eliminated by
transforming the theater into something like a "group in fusion" [to
borrow Sartre's terminology—TRANS.]. The effects of appearance and
imitation could be denounced as corrupting as long as they implied
isolated consciousnesses. As if by a stroke of the magic wand, however,
appearance becomes beneficial as soon as everyone is drawn into the
business of viewing everyone else in a universal exchange of gazes.

THE ANTIDOTE IN THE POISON   126

Clearly, the terms of the problem had simply been shifted. Evil—*true evil*—revealed itself most fully in the guise of non-reciprocity. In the development of Rousseau's thinking, non-reciprocity vanished when the theater, initially stigmatized as a perverse entertainment, was generalized to a universally shared experience. In other words, the remedy's medicinal value lay in the move toward self-reconciliation (which is what Rousseau has in mind when he speaks of "appropriating the dramas of our theater") and egalitarian universalism. This move strikes at the root of the illness and opens up a new perspective. Read the celebrated exhortation that inspired Robespierre and many others in more recent times: "Go one better: make the spectators themselves the spectacle. Make them actors themselves, see to it that they see and love themselves in one another for the greater unity of all . . . All societies are one, all things are common to all men."[28] Compare this with the doctrine attributed the the Gnostics, that the best way to free oneself from evil is to extend it, to push it to the limit. In Tertullian's *De pudicitia* (I, 16) we read: "Incontinence is necessary to continence; fight fire with fire."

EXTENSION OF THE SYSTEM

It should come as no surprise, therefore, that, twice and in almost identical terms (in the *Political Fragments* and in the Geneva manuscript of the *Social Contract*), Rousseau used the metaphor of "the antidote in the poison" to formulate the fundamental insight of his political philosophy: "Let us strive to draw from the poison itself the antidote needed to counteract it. If possible let us correct through new associations the defect in the general association . . . Let us demonstrate . . . in perfected art the cure for the ills that inchoate art *(l'art commencé)* inflicts on nature."[29] Although Rousseau blames human history for having developed the alienating faculties of reflection, amour-propre, abstraction, imagination, and intellectual dependence, he expressly warns against any attempt to turn back the clock. The development that has made us unhappy must be carried even further: reflection must be perfected, amour-propre put to work, the imagination channeled. Alienation must be made reciprocal and complete. This is our only chance of rediscovering in a new (political and moral) form our original (natural and animal) wholeness, which has been destroyed by the onset of our affliction. In *Emile* he writes: "It requires a great deal of art to prevent social man from being entirely artificial."[30] And: "Our only grip on passion is through the passions. Their tyranny must be combatted through their power."[31] The name for the disease is also the name for the antagonistic force.

The imagination, which is to be feared if it obtrudes on life too early, takes on a positive value when it serves to distract Emile from "real objects," namely, women encountered "in the world." In book IV of *Emile* Rousseau recommends smothering "the first flames of the imagination." But later, in order to prevent his adolescent pupil from succumbing to corrupting influences, he calls upon the imagination to invent an ideal "model." Initially suspect because of its power to "awaken the senses," the imagination is now invested with the power to "repress the senses." There is nothing contradictory about this. The argument is based in large part on a therapeutic model: an active substance ceases to be dangerous depending on the individual, the time, the danger to be met, and so on.

In fact, the whole ethical program that immediately precedes the discussion of religious education in book IV of *Emile* is aimed at assigning amour-propre the positive role it was absolutely denied at the beginning of the same book. Earlier Rousseau wrote that "love of self, which looks only at myself, is content when my true needs are satisfied; but amour-propre, which compares, is never and can never be content, because in preferring myself to others this sentiment also requires that others prefer me over themselves, which is impossible. Thus the gentle and affectionate passions stem from love of self, and the hateful and irascible passions from amour-propre."[32] But Emile cannot be prevented from making comparisons, and he thus comes to experience amour-propre. The reader then learns, not without surprise, that not all the passions stemming from amour-propre are hateful and irascible. Some of them may be "humane and gentle" and can develop in the direction of "benevolence" and "commiseration."[33] Emile's education thus enters a new phase, which makes use of a properly guided amour-propre. Accordingly, an activity that had been described as harmful in an earlier stage can now be useful, namely, profiting from the "experience of others" by reading history.[34] Emile can now be permitted to covet first place, to prefer himself to others, and thus to expose himself to flattery (thus justifying the reading of fables, which in book II was considered pointless and pernicious).

·Emile may now feel pity not as natural man does, through spontaneous identification with suffering creatures, but in a detached way, contemplating the human spectacle from on high or at a distance. Though still in certain respects a "savage," Emile brings knowledge and judgment to bear in order to put himself "in the place of others." Reflection, so harmful if allowed to operate prematurely, now enables him to feel compassion for their misery. Just as theatrical pretense loses its harmful effects when generalized to the entire population, so, too, does amour-propre cease to be harmful through generalization:

> People who never deal with any affairs other than their own are too impassioned to form healthy judgments. Seeing everything in relation to themselves alone and shaping their ideas of good and evil to suit their own interest, they fill their minds with a thousand ridiculous prejudices, and in anything that is in the slightest degree inimical to their own advantage they see a threat to the whole universe.
>
> *If we extend amour-propre to other individuals, we transform it into a virtue,* and there is not a single human heart in which this virtue has no root. The less the object of our attention has to do directly with us, the less the illusion of self-interest is to be feared, the more that interest is generalized, the more equitable it becomes.[35]

The transmutation of poison into antidote, of what was a source of vice and conflict into a "virtue," is accomplished by changing the point of application; the sentiment of amour-propre is the same, but its structure and distribution are different.

The poison/disease metaphor when applied to the sociopolitical sphere implies, as in the medical model, that the antidote/remedy must be administered at the proper moment. It must comfort and strengthen *(conforter)* the suffering body at the moment of truth, when the disease, having attained its natural limit, is *judged* in its evolution toward death or recovery: the power of a medicine manifests itself at the *critical* moment in the combat between nature and disease. A crisis is always an alternative: recovery is simply the more favorable of two possible outcomes. Lexicographically and semantically the concepts of *crisis* and *revolution* are of course similar and sometimes linked.[36]

In discussing the rise of inequality Rousseau describes how societies develop until they reach a "terminal point" at which "further revolutions either dissolve the government entirely or move it closer to the legitimate institution." This alternative is a crisis, analogous to the ones described in the *Social Contract*, where the two similar terms are explicitly linked:

> Just as certain diseases confuse the mind and obliterate all memory of the past, in the lives of states there are sometimes violent epochs in which revolutions do to peoples what certain crises do to individuals, in which horror of the past is tantamount to loss of memory, and in which the state, inflamed by civil war, is in a manner of speaking reborn from its ashes and, escaping from the arms of death, regains the vigor of youth.[37]

The same idea can be found in *Judgment on Polysynody*, where Rousseau speaks of the "moment of anarchy and crisis that necessarily precedes a new establishment."[38] In the ninth of the *Letters from the Mountain* he compares the legitimate government of Geneva with the arbitrary rule of a patrician oligarchy:

> But compare, and you will find on the one hand definite ills, terrible evils, unlimited and endless, and on the other hand difficulty even with mere abuse, so that if the abuse is great it will be brief and when it occurs it always brings its own remedy with it . . . There will always be this difference between the one and the other, that abuse of liberty will harm the community guilty of it and, punishing it for its wrong, will force it to seek a remedy; so that in this case the affliction is never anything other than a crisis; it cannot be a permanent condition.[39]

As terrible as the ills of arbitrary government may be (and Rousseau envisions the worst case), there is still reason for hope in the very severity of the ailment: "The worst of conditions has but one advantage: things can only get better. This is the sole resource of extreme afflictions."[40] (At the end of his life Rousseau would describe his own situation in the very same terms.) The following passage from the *Considerations on the Government of Poland* attests to the persistence of this type of argument: "Extreme afflictions call for violent remedies; one must try to heal them whatever the cost . . . Any free state that fails to foresee great crises stands in peril of death at every storm. Only the Poles have deduced from the crises themselves a new way of preserving the Constitution."[41]

Even Oriental despotism contains the remedy for its own failings:

"Oriental despotism subsists because it is harder on the grandees than on the people: it thus takes from itself its own remedy."[42] Striking as such assertions are, they are not Rousseau's final word. They merely temper the pessimistic vision of human social evolution that predominates in his work. Crises and revolutions are themselves fraught with fatal danger. Thinking to administer a remedy for disorder, one only hastens disaster: "When will men learn that there is no disorder so harmful as the arbitrary power by which they attempt to administer a remedy? This power is itself the worst of all disorders. To prevent them by such means is to kill people in order to cure their fever."[43] Here Rousseau is harking back to antimedical tradition, which he frequently invokes: the use of remedies is the worst of all maladies. The remedy in the disease is provided either by nature or by *perfected* art. Imperfect art can only do harm if it resorts to drugs.

IMAGINARY CURES

Emile and the *Social Contract* are grand theories based on the principle of using poison against itself. This same principle also governs Rousseau's affective imagination and even his behavior. It is therefore worth digressing a moment to examine some of his favorite fictions.

Valère is a fop who spends too much time in front of a mirror. On his wedding day his sister attempts to "cure him of a weakness that exposed him to ridicule."[44] She therefore orders a portrait of her brother dressed in female finery and made to look like a woman. He falls in love with the unknown woman in the portrait and tries to delay his marriage. His affliction thus attains its paroxysm. Disabused of his error, Valère, alias Narcissus, claims to be "cured of a silly affectation that was the shame of his youth."[45]

The Village Soothsayer is, taken in the broadest sense, also a story of healing. Following a traditional formula of comedy, the soothsayer advises Colette to feign infidelity and claim to love "a gentleman from town" so as to arouse the jealousy of her fickle lover Colin, whereupon he will leave "the lady of the castle" and beg her forgiveness. Colette grasps the point of the advice at once: "I will pretend to imitate the example he has set." Equal but opposite, the two infidelities will cancel each other out, and everyone will live happily ever after.

A well-meaning fairy tells the Phoenix King how he can win back the affections of the Fairy Queen: "Your best hope of curing your wife of her extravagances is to emulate them."[46] Rousseau offers the same advice to tutors of the young: "Show your pupil your weaknesses in order to cure him of his own. Let him see in you the same battles that are raging within himself."[47]

La Nouvelle Héloïse, a vast panorama of fantasy, is a novel whose characters, never fully cured of their afflictions, are condemned always to imagine newer and better remedies. Whenever a cure seems imminent or certain, it turns out to be illusory, incomplete, or temporary. Julie informs Saint-Preux that she is pregnant in these mysterious terms: "The love that caused our ills must give us the remedy for them" (part 1, letter 33). Ultimately this hope too will vanish. Otherwise the healing—marriage—would have come too easily. Rousseau's imagination requires greater sacrifices and reinforces the image of prohibition.

Of the various characters in the book, M. de Wolmar stands for self-assured rationality. He is the one character capable of manipulating the others for their own good, the clairvoyant therapist in all realms except the religious. His role is that of the demanding superego. After marrying Julie, he invites the man she had loved passionately a few years earlier to come to Clarens. His plan is to complete the cure of the former lovers. Convinced that they "are more in love than ever" yet "fully cured,"[48] he intends to eliminate the contradiction in this situation by rooting out what remains of their love. To the perspicacious Wolmar it is obvious that Saint-Preux loves Julie "in the past." In his words: "Their highly stimulated imaginations continually portrayed each to the other as they were during their separation." Present reality must therefore be substituted for the illusions that hold them in thrall. (This is the reverse of Rousseau's usual method, which is to invent an imaginary world to compensate for the inadequacy of real objects. Only after his imaginative powers dry up does he seek to moor his mind to the objective details of the plant world.[49] Then, however, the purpose of the reconciliation with reality is to preserve a sphere of activity, to perpetuate what is intended to be an innocent intellectual occupation, and not to exorcise a guilty imagination.) Saint-Preux allows himself to be persuaded: "M. de Wolmar's explanations fully reassured me as to the true state of my heart. Though all too weak, that heart was as fully cured as it could be . . . My heart is as filled with peace as is the room in which I am living . . . Although I do not enjoy all the authority of a master, I experience even greater pleasure in looking upon myself as the child of the house" (V, 2). Wolmar has apparently been able to dupe (in French: *donner le change à*) Saint-Preux's imagination by substituting one object for another: "Instead of his mistress I force him always to see the wife of a respectable man and the mother of my children; I erase one portrait with another, and cover the past with the present." Wolmar, by staying away, proposes to remove himself as an obstacle standing between the two former lovers: "The more they see each other alone, the more readily they will understand their error as they compare what they feel with what they would once have felt in a similar situation." The danger is heightened, the better to overcome it. If the malady (in the eyes of conventional morality) was previously the "meeting" of Julie and Saint-Preux, the remedy chosen by Wolmar is to bring them together again so as to root out the effects of passion: Wolmar removes himself from the scene so that the former lovers can internalize his image and accept the reality of a present in which they no longer belong to each other.

We are, however, in the realm of passionate love, and it would be to step outside love's magic circle to assume that this attempt at a rational cure is entirely successful. In love it is the incurable that is fascinating. To the end of the novel Julie remains "virtuous" but not "cured."[50] On the brink of death she confesses the continued existence of her love, for it is too late to do any harm: "For a long time I remained under an illusion. That illusion was good for me. Now that I longer need it, it has destroyed itself. You believed that I was cured, and so did I. Let us give thanks to the one who caused that error to last as long as it was useful."[51] Thus the imminence of death reveals that passion remains unhealed, that the deliberate struggle to subdue it has failed, but it also reveals a higher order in which the law of sublimated passion reigns supreme and in which another ill—the lovers' *separation*—will be definitively cured. Thus the non-healing of illegitimate love (according to the laws of reason and society) corresponds to the healing of separation (according to the law of passion). And virtue, which in this world was the handmaiden of social taboo, in the other world accomplishes the couple's eternal union: "The virtue that separated us on earth will reunite us in our eternal abode."[52] Wolmar's half-successful cure allowed the disease (in this case guilty passion, repressed but not eliminated by virtue) to persist, but in the end the tables are turned: once an ontological divide is crossed, the sickness of love becomes the supreme good. In the complex game that Rousseau's imagination is playing, forces of frustration are transformed into curative powers. Virtue and death are no longer the negation of pleasure but its pre-conditions. The worst misfortune that can befall desire can take on new value as an antidote. In Rousseau, one might even say, faith in the other world is not so much an act of disinterested belief as the hollowing out of a space in which the transmutation of sickness into remedy can take place. The crucial thing is the will to consolation: it demands an afterlife.

An Epistolary Therapy

Henriette, one of many total strangers who corresponded with Rousseau, wrote to tell him of her suffering and to ask for his advice. After the success of his major works, Rousseau accepted the role of confessor and spiritual guide. He did his best to live up to the expectations of the countless readers who wrote because they had not found happiness in their lives.[53] Not without irritation, and at times with suspicion, Rousseau took on the role of master of happiness, healer of souls, and dispenser of useful remedies. To judge from his responses, this therapist's role did not displease him. Instinctively, one might say, he alluded to his own ills, both to protect himself from correspondents who wanted too much from him and to heighten his charismatic powers. He was aware of his precursors in myth and religion and knew the prestige that attached to the figure of the suffering healer. A healer who had been touched by an affliction himself was more apt to dispense a useful remedy than one who had never suffered. In other words, Rousseau was qualified to serve as a guide because he himself had gone astray.

Henriette began her letter with a feminist protest against Rousseau's sarcastic remarks on the subject of educated women. Elderly, impoverished, afflicted with many ills, she viewed literary studies as her only solace, her best hope for fleeing her woes. One cannot doubt the reality of her (depressive) suffering after hearing her describe the ordeal of waking up (in a style that has no precedent):

> It is a long time since I have known the happiness of waking up with the sweet tranquillity that makes one glad to exist with the prospect of a quiet and pleasant day in store. The moment of awakening is

the most terrifying moment of my life. A sharp twinge in my heart snatches me from sleep, a piercing arrow of pain rouses my senses from their stupor, and the fear and terror of awakening finishes the job.

After being awakened and returned to life by such painful feelings, I find myself all alone in nature. A thousand sad and confused ideas gather and form a thick cloud that seems to envelop me. I try to get away, I struggle, I look around, I gaze upon the things around me, I see nothing to console me, I call upon reason, I see it, I hear it, but nothing speaks to my heart. Regret at not being able to sleep through the rest of my sad existence only adds to my woes. What an effort it is, Sir, to finish with any greater sense of security days begun amid such shadows! . . . What I try is to put [my heart] to sleep by fixing my mind on objects apt to hold its attention. At first there may not be much interest in them, but with time habit, reawakened curiosity, and a tincture of vanity can sometimes conspire to form a passion that is not without effect. I would be so happy if only I could find some peace, even at the cost of looking foolish.

The opportunity to write all these things down on paper is already the source of some relief:

Since I gave in to the desire to write to you and took up my unfamiliar pen, I feel that I have passed some quieter hours. Preoccupied with what I wanted to write to you, wanting to say enough and fearing to say too much, anxious about the impression that my writing would make on you, torn between the fear of looking foolish and the hope of finding a reliable and indulgent guide, daring and not daring, constant only in the feelings of esteem and admiration that the reading of your works has inspired in me, my imagination wraps you in a variety of forms. When it allows me to see only the philosopher, I am frightened; I tear everything up and burn it. When it endows you with all the kindly traits of goodness and humanity, I regain my confidence, I feel comfortable again, and I write. In the end, all of this has given me something to occupy my mind, something lively enough and strong enough to distract me from my usual thoughts and from that inner feeling that I would be so glad to lose.[54]

Rousseau's response is singular. He could hardly have failed to recognize the tone of melancholy suffering in the letter, but oddly enough he is convinced that his correspondent has disguised her true identity and that the letter is really from Suzanne Curchod (a *belle penseuse,* "a woman who courts notoriety"[55]—Gibbon wanted to marry her, Necker did so, and she became the hostess of a Paris salon). Accordingly, his response takes the tone of a man who refuses to be taken in, who will not rise to the bait. He castigates amour-propre, vanity, and wit. His suspicions are ill founded, yet despite his error about the identity of his correspondent, Rousseau's rude tone may not have been entirely out of place. In a manner reminiscent of a fairly common psychoanalytic technique, he looks beyond the explicit message to its implicit intention: "Above each of your lines I read these words in large characters: *Let us see if you will have the audacity to condemn a person who thinks and writes in this way not to think or read any more.* This interpretation is assuredly not a criticism, and I can only feel gratitude that you count me among those whose judgment matters to you." More to the point, Rousseau, in an attempt at individual guidance, rehearses arguments from his philosophy of history:

> One can no more regain simplicity than one can regain childhood. The mind, once in effervescence, remains so forever, and anyone who has thought will think for the rest of his life. Therein lies the greatest misfortune of the reflective state: the more one is aware of its ills, the more one increases them, and all our efforts to escape from this condition only serve to bog us down that much more deeply.
>   Let us speak not of changing our condition but of what benefit you may derive from yours. That condition is unhappy and must always remain so. Your ills are serious and without remedies . . . And to make them bearable you are looking for at least a palliative. Is that not the purpose of your study plans and occupations?

Rousseau begins by stating that the woman's present illness is incurable: there is no turning back. He makes her condition sound even bleaker than she does and offers not the slightest reason for hope, as if he knew by instinct that it is wise to be rude to people in depression and that merely *answering* her plea is already enough of a gift. He attempts to trace the illness back to its source (but blindly, since he believes that the woman at the other end is Suzanne Curchod): "But what is this vaunted sensibility? Do you want to know, Henriette? In the final analysis it is a form of amour-propre, which makes comparisons. I have put my finger on the seat of the disease." Rousseau adopts the same tactic he used in the first discourse: Henriette's chosen remedy, he says initially, is nothing but a more acute form of her affliction: "On the pretext of working for independence, you work for domination. Hence far from alleviating the burden of opinion that makes you so unhappy, you increase its weight. That is not the way to make your waking up more serene." Later, however, Rousseau offers, as he has hinted he would, his approval of Henriette's decision. Study, which is her affliction, can also cure it, but on one condition: that it is not a distraction or a diversion but a means of self-reconciliation:

> Although my ideas in this respect differ greatly from yours, we are almost in agreement as to what you must do. For you, study is now the Achilles' spear that must heal the wound it made. But you want merely to nullify the pain, and I would like to remove its cause. You want to distract your attention from yourself by means of philosophy. I would like philosophy to detach you from everything and return you to yourself. . . . Then, content with yourself yet incapable of being discontent with others, you will sleep peacefully and awake with pleasure.

TELEPHUS AND THE SPEAR OF ACHILLES

At the beginning of the *Remedia Amoris* Ovid plays with the same allusion to Achilles: "I have already taught you the art of love. Now learn the art of how to love no longer. The hand that wounded you can also heal you. The same soil often produces both healthy and harmful herbs. The rose grows close to the nettle, and Achilles' spear itself closed the wound it inflicted on Hercules' son."[56]

In the *Metamorphoses* Ovid has Achilles say: "Telephus twice felt the power of my spear."[57] And in the *Tristia* he mentions Telephus again: "Telephus would have died of an incurable wound if the hand that wounded him had not also healed him."[58] In the ancient world the name of Telephus, healed by the spear that wounded him, symbolized "healing by the weapon that inflicted the wound." The erotic uses of this concept are not difficult to imagine: the object of desire inflicts a wound that cannot be healed except by possession of that same object. Consider the following two epigrams from the *Greek Anthology:*

I carry my love as a wound. Instead of blood tears flow from my wound, which never runs dry. My affliction leaves me helpless, and Machaon himself has no balm to soothe my distress. I am Telephus, young lady. And you, you be my loyal Achilles: may your beauty slake my desire, just as it smote me.[59]

If your present to me [a pair of apples] is a symbol of your breasts, I greatly appreciate the favor. But if you stop there, how wicked of you, having touched off such a violent conflagration, to refuse to put it out. The man who wounded Telephus also healed him. Do not treat me, little girl, more cruelly than one would treat an enemy.[60]

Even more striking, however, was the use of this myth element to denote the ambiguity of literary language. Ovid, as we have seen, used it to evoke the double power of his poetry—erotic and anti-erotic. In a more edifying context, Plutarch uses the image of Telephus to describe the effects of philosophical language:

When some wise dictum has bitten you and made you suffer, why not take advantage of what is useful in it? Telephus's wound, healed according to Euripides by "rust scraped from the spear," is not the only wound to be cured in that way. The wounds that the incisive words of the philosophers inflict on the souls of well-born youths are to be cured by the very same words that caused them. One must accept this suffering, these nips, without being crushed or discouraged by the criticism . . . Let us bear with these early purifications, these first disruptions, in the hope that such torments and trials will bring us compensations as sweet as they are glorious.[61]

The legend of Telephus is known to us through the mythographers as well as through surviving fragments of the tragedy Euripides devoted to him. It is worth pausing a moment to examine it in greater detail. Telephus's childhood can be read as a variant of the Oedipus myth (Rank includes it in his collection[62]) in which the incestuous marriage of son and mother is prevented in the nick of time by divine intervention. The story can be summarized as follows:

Telephus, the son of Hercules and Auge, was exposed immediately after his birth and raised by a doe . . . When the boy grew up, he obeyed the oracle's orders and went to the court of Mysia to look for his parents. Teuthras, the king of Mysia, was at that time involved in a foreign war that was going badly for him. He announced that he would give his adoptive daughter Auge and his crown to anyone who could deliver him from his enemies. Telephus took command of the Mysian troops and after leading them to total victory was recognized as heir to the Mysian kingdom.[63] Teuthras awarded him Auge's hand in marriage, but when he entered her bedroom she threatened to kill him unless he left at once. As Telephus was prepared to use force, the gods sent a dragon, which separated the two and frightened Auge so badly that she threw down the sword she was holding. Telephus again insisted on his rights. Auge called for help to her lover, Hercules, and they then recognized one another.[64]

It is hard to be sure that there is any necessary connection between the legend of Telephus's childhood and the story of the adult hero, but one can obviously let one's imagination play freely with the intervention of the dragon and the appearance of the strong father prior to the infliction of a wound that will take some time to heal.

The story, as reconstructed from available sources by the compiler Chompré, continues as follows:

> The Greeks on their way to Troy wished to land in Telephus's territory, but he opposed them with armed force, resulting in a fierce battle . . . Telephus was wounded in the hip by Achilles . . . The oracle he consulted told him that he could be healed only by the same hand that had inflicted the wound. Since it did not seem likely that his enemy Achilles would want to help him, Clytemnestra (according to Hyginus) advised him to abduct Orestes in order to force Agamemnon to make Achilles agree to take part in the healing. But the hero could not be moved, so Ulysses said that the meaning of the oracle was that the spear that had caused the wound must serve as the remedy. He therefore removed some rust from the tip of the spear and used it to make a poultice, which he sent to Telephus, who was soon healed.[65]

Pliny the Elder interpreted this use of rust quite literally as a demonstration of the hemostatic and scar-inducing qualities of certain metallic filings. He might have meditated more allegorically on the fact that the medicinal substance was not the same as the substance that caused the injury. Between the wound and the healing the metal had been altered. Time had done its work. When applied the second time, the iron was nothing but a powder. The repetition was remedial only because the spear had in the meantime suffered its own affliction, as it were.

More generally, one might think of coining the word *telephism* to refer to a heightening of the ambivalence or ambiguity of the sado-masochistic personality structure. Briefly, using Freud's description of sado-masochism,[66] I would distinguish three variants of telephism:

a. An active, sadistic (Achillean) variant: first inflict a wound, then agree to heal it. Or invest an intense libidinal charge in the care lavished on an object that one has previously injured. Beat, then cajole; set a fire, then (to borrow Rousseau's expression) "set the pumps to working." The Kleinian notion of *reparation* captures this sequence of attitudes.

b. A moderate, reflexive variant: subject oneself to suffering in order to participate later in a gratifying exercise of self-consolation, of narcissistic reintegration of the wounded ego. Here, obsessionality can manifest itself doubly, first in the search for suffering, then in the labor of reparation.

c. A passive variant: to expose oneself to injury so as to be comforted later, if possible by those responsible for the injury. Subject oneself to beating in order to attract the active compassion of one's persecutor. Provoke the hatred of others and ask that it be turned into love.

The myth of Telephus is important, I think, because one can derive from it a psychological structure homologous to certain theological and cosmological themes (Gnostic, Christian, and revolutionary): the alleged cause of evil can be reinterpreted as the cause of a future good, and violence inflicted (or endured) is presented as a harbinger of future healing. *Felix culpa!* It is a fortunate malady that leads to a healing of all ills.[67] The blood of the Grail, which flows from the spear of Longinus that pierces Christ's flank, will heal the ailing King. The words of the oracle to Telephus, that the wounder shall be the healer *(ho trosas iassetai),* can be invoked by the most diverse theodicies. Of course Rousseau offers the most fully developed example of a Telephian philosophy of history and a Telephian existentialism, which are at once spontaneously experienced and clearly spelled out. That is what is so interesting about the exchange of letters between Rousseau and Henriette. The philosophy of Rousseau can be seen offering healing to the unknown correspondent, but Rousseau speaks to the distant letter-writer as he would later speak to himself in the *Reveries*. His method is the very one that will later oblige him to forsake philosophical writing for autobiography. Remember that Rousseau came to think of his philosophical works as an evil he had been induced to inflict upon the world, an evil whose consequences he would continue to suffer until the end of his days but that he would attempt to repair by new writing.

Henriette wrote twice, and Rousseau answered both letters. With this abundant source material we can make out two forms of Telephism: an intellectual form, having to do with the dangers and healing powers of study, and another, much more profound version.

When Rousseau wrote Henriette that "anyone who has thought will think for the rest of his life" and that, for her, "study is now Achilles' spear," he was applying to the destiny of an individual what he had already asserted about human history and proper social institutions, namely, that they are "most apt to denature man in a favorable way."[68] Culture, itself a malady, if developed to perfection becomes the new good, the agent of healing.

Something else that Rousseau says is more directly relevant to the sphere of the emotions. Henriette must be willing to give up other people, to break her ties with them, to forgo her "need of them." She must become "sufficient unto herself": "You say that you have enjoyed hours of calm while writing to me and telling me about yourself. It is surprising that this experience has not shown you the way and taught you where you must look to find, if not happiness, then at least peace."[69]

For Rousseau, the saving resource is thus the monologue of the soul, which, having broken all its ties, converses inwardly with itself. This is not what Henriette had in mind: she had not renounced communication with others, had not abandoned that hope. Hence in the second letter she resists Rousseau's interpretation: she wrote to him not to observe and console herself but to arouse his interest, to be heard. Why, she asks, were the hours spent in writing so precious? "Not, as you believe, because I was telling you about myself, but because I was speaking to you and preoccupied with what I was saying."[70] The desire for a meeting of the minds could hardly be better expressed. Henriette was successful in her aim in any case, because Rousseau ended his first letter by saying: "The most important thing was to make you aware of how much you interest me."[71] Later he also said: "What I promise you, and it is a promise I shall keep, is to think about you always and never to forget you."[72] But Henriette expressed her desire for communication as a desire to flee herself, to forget herself, and thus opened herself up to Rousseau's reproach. She hoped to "distract herself from that deep and painful feeling that follows her everywhere." She was afraid of anything that brought her "too close to herself." She would have liked to "wrest herself free" of her self, to "lose herself in this inward feeling," to "distract herself there." Rousseau answered that she must not seek to wrest herself free of her self but hold on to her self by wresting herself free of people and things. Against the centrifugal impulses of a soul that seeks escape into the world he offers the traditional (Stoic and Christian) lesson: *redi in te ipsum* (go back into yourself). Note his tactics. First he alludes to a feeling of impasse, of failure of the therapeutic relation, of incurability:

> I thought I glimpsed a plan for rescuing you from the anxieties you describe without recourse to the distractions that according to you are the only possible remedy and that according to me are not even a palliative. You tell me that I am wrong and that what I thought I saw was not the case. How could I possibly find a remedy for your condition when that condition is inconceivable to me? To me you are a distressing and humiliating enigma. I thought I knew the human heart, and I know nothing of yours. You are suffering, and I cannot give you solace.[73]

This further refusal of treatment (which can be interpreted as aggressive, as indicating a desire to wound) is followed by a discussion, initially in a questioning mode, of the remedy approved by Rousseau. As comparison with other, similar examples would show, Rousseau's therapeutic practice was first to wound or frustrate so as to be in a position to follow up with a caress or with salutary advice. Furthermore, the remedy, when he finally agrees to administer it, turns out to involve the neutral (or partially passive) form of Telephism: break with others or accept the distressing reality of their "insensitivity" in order to savor in oneself, and starting with oneself, the pleasure of *compensation:*

What? Because nothing outside yourself satisfies you, you want to flee yourself, and because you have reason to complain of others, because you despise them, because they have given you the right to do so, because you feel in yourself a soul worthy of esteem, you do not wish to console yourself with it for the contempt inspired in you by other souls that do not resemble yours? No, I cannot understand anything so bizarre, it passes me by.

This sensitivity that makes everything so unsatisfactory to you— should it not retreat into itself, should it not fill your heart with a sublime and delicious feeling of amour-propre, and haven't you always in it a resource against injustice and a compensation for insensitivity? It is so rare, you say, to encounter a soul. That is true, but how is it that you can have one and not be satisfied with it? If one were to probe people of a narrow and constricted sort, one would recoil from them, push them away, but after feeling so uncomfortable visiting others, what a pleasure it is to return home. I know how much the need for attachment makes it distressing to sensitive hearts that attachments are impossible to form. I know how sad that state is, but I also know that it is not without its pleasures. It causes rivulets of tears to be shed; it produces a melancholy that bears witness about ourselves that we should not wish to forgo. It causes us to seek solitude as the only refuge, where we find ourselves alone with all that we have reason to love. I cannot state this too strongly: I know neither happiness nor rest in estrangement from my self. On the contrary, I am every day more certain that one cannot be happy on earth except insofar as one shuns things and explores the self.[74]

For the edification of his correspondent Rousseau preaches by example, as he would later preach, in the *Reveries,* for the edification of posterity. The answer to one question remains unclear, however. Is Rousseau suggesting that we are wounded by the insensitivity of others or that we wound ourselves by shunning "things"? This is a point about which he needs to maintain confusion. Once I suffer such a loss, however, it is clear that my only recourse is to fasten amorously on my self, to labor long and hard on consolations drawn from my inner resources, to invest the bulk of my passionate energy in closing a wound that I simultaneously work to keep open. If the remedy lies in the exercise of my sensibility, its calming virtue stems from the fact that I can *interpret* suffering as a consequence of the characteristic superiority of the sensitive soul. To be sure, the malady arises out of other people's incomprehension and even hostility, but it is easy to give consoling and flattering reasons for those hateful sentiments. The victim thus has direct proof of his worth. Illness becomes a distinction that guarantees his superiority. The extravagance of the affliction is a necessary condition for the subject to take full pleasure in himself as the one exception from an otherwise universal malady. Rousseau of course prefers to ignore that he may himself have been an agent of the disease, may have lent it a helping hand. In the reflexive mode Telephus wounds himself so as to "compensate" himself later on. But for one who is fond of deep wounds, the trick is to persuade oneself that the injury was caused by Achilles' shaft. Recall that Rousseau invariably needs to construct an external, exculpatory genealogy of evil.[75] That is why he needs to convince himself that the reparative effect of reverie is the complete *opposite* of the ill. Even if the mind of the dreamer is aware that it depends on evil and its "shadows" to produce certainty of its own transparency, it does not consider itself to be implicated in the evil to which it responds. The projective mechanism ensures that it believes itself to be wounded by *others* and healed by itself. The wound is indicted for coming from outside, and healing is praised as coming from within. How could it be otherwise? The full power of compensation cannot be brought to bear without the conviction of facing up to an unknown power. If it were too clear that the subject was the cause of his own wound, the reparative effort would be hobbled at its very source. Now we can understand Rousseau's endlessly repeated assertions that he is "happy in spite of his enemies," assertions intended to convince himself that, in elaborating the compensation, the "supplement," the substitute activity, he is fully successful in his aims.

FURTHER EVIDENCE

Rousseau uses the same phrase on two separate, and noteworthy, occasions in the *Confessions:* "What might have ruined me saved me" (or "preserved me"). The first use is in connection with the spanking administered by Mademoiselle Lambercier and Jean-Jacques's concomitant discovery of masochistic pleasure: "But when the passing of the years had finally made me a man, it came to pass that *what might have ruined me preserved me.* Instead of disappearing, my former childish taste became so strongly associated with the other that I could never separate it from the desires kindled by my senses."[76] An earlier version of this passage reads: "*What might have ruined me saved me* for a long time from myself. At the age of puberty the object with which I was occupied diverted me from the one I had to fear. One idea, substituted for the other, stirred me without corrupting me."[77]

The same phrase occurs again almost verbatim when Rousseau describes the beginning of his stay at the home of Mme de Warens and his recourse to the "dangerous supplement that deceives nature": "What stimulants! The reader who imagines them must look upon me as if I were already half dead. On the contrary: *what might have ruined me saved me*, at least for a time."[78]

In other words, evil (perversity, autoeroticism) turns out to have saving graces: "vice" turns out to contain its own antidote—according to an interpretation dictated by the conscience, which stigmatizes carnal commerce as the supreme evil, compared with which any diversion or perversion reflected onto the self is beneficial.

The memory of Mademoiselle Lambercier is closely connected with the idea I have been developing in this essay. The episode of the broken comb completes the "salutary" effect that Rousseau ascribes to the spanking: "Who would believe, for example, that one of my soul's most vigorous resources was tempered in the same spring where lust and weakness flowed in my blood?" And in speaking of the "execution" administered by Uncle Bernard, Rousseau adds: "It was terrible. If, seeking the remedy in the disease itself, he had wished to deaden my depraved senses forever, he could not have found a better way to go about it."

At times Rousseau compares the effervescence of love to a disease and paradoxically attributes curative value to the misfortunes that stem from it. Consider, for example, the curious relation between misfortune and healing implicit in these lines on the origin of *La Nouvelle Héloïse:* "The intoxication that took hold of me, though lively and wild, was so durable and powerful that to recover from it took nothing less than the unforeseen and dreadful crisis of the misfortunes into which it plunged me."[79]

Consider these lines of youthful verse, composed at Chambéry:

THE ANTIDOTE IN THE POISON   145

Et le mal dont mon corps se sent presque abattu
N'est pour moi qu'un sujet d'affermir ma vertu.[80]

[And the disease that has all but overwhelmed my body
is but an occasion for me to bolster my virtue.]

At first sight these lines seem to express a commonplace idea: the
soul, by resisting a disease, can derive spiritual benefit from it. A
psychoanalyst would speak of "secondary gain." When Jean-Jacques,
afflicted with fever, seeks refuge in Madame de Warens's bedroom, the
pleasure of his tears yields the same therapeutic benefit: "As if tears
were my nourishment and remedy, I fortified myself on those which I
shed in her presence, with her, seated on her bed and holding her
hands in mine."[81]

Consider now the account in book VI of the *Confessions* in which
Rousseau describes his extenuated and anxious state, which ends with
a sudden, violent auditory disturbance:

Imagine my surprise and my fright. I thought I was dead. I crawled
into bed. The doctor was called. Trembling, I described my case,
assuming there was no remedy for it . . . This accident, which might
have killed my body, killed only my passions, and I thank heaven
every day for the beneficial effects it had on my soul. I can truly say
that I did not begin to live until I looked upon myself as a dead man
. . . Finally, in spite or rather because of my condition I felt irresistibly impelled toward study, and though I continued to look upon
each day as my last I studied with as much ardor as if I were
supposed to live forever. People said that it did me harm; I believe
that it did me good.[82]

Significantly, Rousseau is not sure whether to say he took to study
"in spite of" or "because of" his condition: the benefits of study are
first considered to be an antidote to his disease, but he corrects himself
immediately and presents them instead as a direct, if paradoxical,
benefit of his affliction. Note, moreover, the indication of passivity: "I
felt irresistibly impelled," implying that the passion for study was as
much an involuntary affliction as the illness that preceded it. Immediately thereafter, however, we encounter the verb *to study* in an
active, intransitive form: "I studied." Here we have a perfect example
of a reversal of the kind pointed out by J.-B. Pontalis, in which Rous-

seau responds with voluntary action to a situation of abandonment or rejection. Rousseau's attitude toward what he believes to be his imminent death is reminiscent, moreover, of his attitude on the night of his flight from Geneva, when the gates of the city close behind him: "The turnabout occurs at once: *he* is leaving, as if anticipating and dismissing in advance any possibility of rejection."[83] For evidence, consider this striking sentence in which death, the expulsion from life as the drawbridges of earthly existence are raised behind, is described as if it were a journey: "Whether it seemed good to go on learning right up to my final hour, or whether a glimmer of hope that I might go on living remained hidden in the depths of my heart, my anticipation of death, so far from diminishing my zeal for study, seemed to stimulate it, and I hastened to amass a few goods for the other world, as if I believed that all I would have there was what I brought with me."[84] A sense of impending death triggered an intense effort of narcissistic enrichment in a desexualized and therefore less anxiety-ridden domain.

The service that this conviction of impending death rendered to Jean-Jacques's intellectual apprenticeship will later find its counterpart in the service that a conviction of universal conspiracy renders to therapeutic reverie. Once again, extreme affliction becomes an occasion for happy "working through" *(perlaboration)*. Rousseau's unhappiness is so severe that his condition cannot possibly worsen, and therefore he can devote himself entirely to an effort of compensation. The word appears on virtually every page of the *Reveries*, not in the religious sense in which it was used in *Emile* (compensation awarded by God) but in the sense of a substitute or "supplement" that the ego produces from its own substance. Rousseau was often conscious of, and admitted his predilection for, seeking desperate situations. In the preface to *La Nouvelle Héloïse* he wrote: "I have already accused myself of worse things, perhaps, than anyone else will accuse me of."[85] In a letter to his editor he admitted: "I am well aware that my constant inclination is to put things in the worst possible light" (13 September 1758).

In the *Dialogues* he has "the Frenchman" say the worst possible things that can be said about him. He plunges the sharpest of weapons deep into his own flesh. He explains why in his introduction: "I took the only course available to explain myself: among the various possible suppositions, I chose the worst for myself and the best for my adversaries . . . To say everything that could be said in their favor was my only way of finding out what they were actually saying."[86] In this relatively little-known text Rousseau tortures himself in order to reproduce as accurately as possible accusations he has not heard directly but has mysteriously divined from the signs on people's faces. He wants to demonstrate as quickly as possible that things could not possibly be any worse and therefore that he has nothing more to fear or to lose. The consequence that he does not fail to draw from this is of course once again double-edged: his persecutors, thinking to do him harm, have actually done him good. The dialogue form makes it possible to alternate between the injurious discourse of the Frenchman and the compensatory discourse of Rousseau.

At times Rousseau simply modifies his interpretation of an event, to which he gives first one meaning, then another. On the day he tried unsuccessfully to leave the manuscript of the *Dialogues* on the altar of Notre-Dame he thought he saw "heaven itself conspire in the iniquity of men."[87] Later, however, he ascribes a diametrically opposite meaning to the event:

> Gradually overcoming my initial shock, I began to reflect more calmly on what had happened to me, and, my cast of mind being such that I am as quick to console myself for a past misfortune as to take fright at an anticipated one, it did not take long before I began to look at the failure of my attempt in a new light . . . In the end, the miscarriage of my plan, which had affected me so profoundly, upon reflection came to seem a boon from heaven, which had prevented me from carrying out a design so contrary to my interests.[88]

Rousseau usually accepts the affliction as irrevocable so that he may enumerate the resulting benefits: he was "delivered from the anxiety of hope";[89] he was reduced to relying on himself, which was all he asked; consigned to solitude, he found that nothing could disturb his tranquillity, and he was free "to forge consolations" to his heart's content.[90] He put the finishing touches on the exclusion to which he found himself subjected and thus put himself in a position to take his revenge in the most narcissistic way possible. Were he not surrounded by an "edifice of shadows," he would not be able to claim for himself "the transparency of crystal." His exclusion by wicked men becomes irrefutable proof of the persistence of his innate goodness:

> What have I still to fear, since all is done? Now that they can no longer make my condition any worse, they can no longer cause me any alarm. Anxiety and fear are evils from which they have delivered me once and for all . . . Such is the good that my persecutors have done me by using up all the arrows of their animosity. They have deprived themselves of any further hold on me, and now I can mock them.[91]

> Let us learn, therefore, to seize these advantages in compensation for the wrong they have done me. By inuring me to adversity they have done me more good than if they had spared me its afflictions . . . Instinctively surrendering to the emotions that attract me, my heart still feeds on the feelings for which it was born, and I rejoice along with the imaginary beings that produce and share them as if those beings really existed.[92]

In the introduction to the *Dialogues* Rousseau decided to say "all that could be said" in favor of his persecutors. Now he says that *they* have "used up all the arrows of their animosity." Those hostile arrows are tantamount to the initial thrust of Achilles' spear. But the Rousseau of the *Reveries* ignores, or pretends to ignore, what the Rousseau of the *Dialogues* knew: that he himself forged and launched the arrows that rain down upon him, that he imagined the accusatory discourse as a way of uncovering a plausible cause for the signs of hostility he detected all around him. "Tell me what crimes I have committed and how and by whom I was judged!"[93] These words appear in a pamphlet that Rousseau attempted to distribute in the streets after completing the *Dialogues*, as if he had completely forgotten that it was he himself who reconstructed and mimicked the imagined discourse of his accusers. This paranoid forgetfulness, which transforms a self-inflicted wound into a wound inflicted by others, is no doubt part of the healing process. It opens up a space in the writing where the text can believe that it is working purely to heal the wound, when in reality it was the same text that inflicted the wound in the first place by striking a blow that is now carefully concealed.

THE ANTIDOTE IN THE POISON 149

In Book II of *Emile* Rousseau alludes to his childhood fear of the dark. He wants his fictional pupil Emile to overcome this fear through training and habit. "The cause of the affliction, once discovered, indicates the remedy . . . So do not argue with a boy whose fear of the dark you want to cure. Take him there often, and rest assured that no philosophical argument can do as much good as this habituation."[94] Rousseau dealt with the darkness of conspiracy in the same way, though without ever familiarizing himself with the thing he feared.

In the tenth reverie the description of the encounter with Mme de Warens is scarcely begun when it is interrupted by a Telephus who has healed his self-inflicted wound. The final, purely elegiac image is of "the one short period" in his life when he was "loved by a woman full of tenderness and sweetness." A key idea in this passage is *plenitude*— of a finite kind, to be sure, threatened by inadequacy and soon troubled by anxiety but still intact in memory.

The reverie of Easter 1778, in which the presence of *maman* predominates, no longer speaks of affliction or celebrates compensation. Rousseau would die a few weeks later. Rousseau said of himself: "I was born almost dead." One is tempted to reverse the formula and say: he died almost cured, in the resurrection of his first great happiness. Is there a connection between the tranquillity of this final reverie (which differs from the earlier ones in that it does not speak of regaining peace as a goal) and the imminence of Rousseau's death? The point, if there is one, is this: when the malady disappears along with the concomitant need to search for a remedy, it is because vital energy has all but run dry. This serenity, this peace, this apparent healing are premonitory signs of death.

II. The Social Aspects of Music

To Jacek Wozniakowski

"All matter is colored, but sounds reveal movement and the voice reveals a sentient being. Only animate bodies sing." In the context of other remarks, this statement is revealing. The distinction among colors, sounds, and voices, which is found in chapter 16 of the *Essay on the Origin of Languages*, shows clearly that Rousseau regarded music as an art of vital expression and communication. The implications of this are considerable: music theory becomes a vast subject, which includes such other modes of communication as speech and the organization of families, peoples, and governments. The comprehensive theory that can be deduced from Rousseau's writings establishes a close relation among music, politics, and the history of language. The development of that theory can be followed by tracing the images of human togetherness (French: *rassemblement*) that Rousseau propounds in his work.

The basic outlines of the subject are to be found in the *Discourse on Equality*. Everything begins, in the protective bosom of nature, in solitude and silence. The initial dispersion that Rousseau envisions is the exact opposite of congregation. But natural man is not condemned to absolute solitude: occasionally he meets another person for brief bouts of combat or sex. These momentary encounters are accompanied by an equally fleeting vocal sign, the cry, which intermittently disrupts the primordial silence. Rousseau points out the usefulness of the cry in the time before articulate speech became necessary to the functioning of a society that did not yet exist:

> Man's first, most universal, most energetic language, and the only one he needed before it became necessary to persuade men gathered together in assemblies, was the cry of nature. Since this cry was elicited only in response to a kind of instinct on urgent occasions, to ask for help in time of great danger or for relief in time of violent ills, it was not of much use in the ordinary course of life, during which more moderate sentiments predominate.[95]

The contrast is stark between a passive and passionate prelanguage (the elicited cry) and polished speech, which manifests its power in oratory, that is, in the political act par excellence ("to persuade men gathered together in assemblies"). As Rousseau develops his argument in a series of conjectures, he considers what obstacles might have impeded the emergence of articulate speech. He hints, however, that language would over the course of the centuries become what we know it is: a system of signs possessing "a constant form" and thanks to which it becomes possible "to speak in public" and "influence society."

In the second part of the *Discourse on Inequality* Rousseau outlines the development of social life and language. He then draws attention to the importance of song in festivals, whose purpose is to celebrate

THE ANTIDOTE IN THE POISON 151

the happiness of life in a "state of nascent society." But these festivals contain the seeds of future ills: they are an occasion for making comparisons and formulating preferences and thus permit the awakening of amour-propre, from which stem "repulsive and cruel" passions along with the earliest form of inequality:

> As ideas and sentiments followed one after another, and as minds and hearts exercised their powers, the human race became increasingly tame, relations expanded, and bonds grew tighter. People formed the custom of gathering in front of their huts or around a large tree: song and dance, true children of love and leisure, became the amusement or, rather, the occupation of idle men and women gathered together in groups. Each person began to look at the others and to want to be looked at himself, and public esteem was valued. The one who sang or danced the best, the handsomest, the strongest, the most adroit or eloquent became the most esteemed, and this was the first step toward inequality.[96]

In the *Essay on the Origin of Languages* the same festive scene is described but its role in Rousseau's argument has changed: the festival, he now maintains, was the "origin of societies and languages in the hot countries."[97] It was simultaneously the source of song, accent, speech, amorous feelings, and exogamic. marriage. In contrast to the second discourse, no shadow mars this pastoral scene à la Claude Lorrain. Everything began when shepherds and maidens came together at watering holes, described in prose that itself rises to lyrical musicality:

> The first family bonds were formed there; the first encounters of the sexes took place there. Young maidens came looking for water for the household, and young men came to water their flocks. There, eyes accustomed to the same sights since childhood now began to see sweeter things. These stirred the heart; their unfamiliar allure made it less savage, and it felt pleasure at not being alone. Imperceptibly water became more necessary. The animals became thirsty more often. One hastened to the place and, once there, was reluctant to leave. In that happy time, when nothing marked the hours, there was no need to count them. Time had no other measure than amusement and boredom. Beneath ancient oaks, the conquerors of time, ardent youth forgot its ferocity by degrees, as little by little each tamed the other. Through striving to make themselves understood, people learned to explain themselves to others.[98]

THE ANTIDOTE IN THE POISON 152

The repetition of *there* insistently marks a place of happiness (like a dancing foot stamping on the ground), a repeated commencement. How long the prelude—a mute pantomime of arrivals, glances, departures, returns—goes on! Rousseau deliberately delays the emergence of the need to "explain oneself" to others in order to emphasize the simultaneity of the sentiments that underlie all expression, sentiments that are crowned immediately by a pleasure that does not lead, as pleasure does among the corrupt and civilized, to the death of desire. The paragraph ends with a transmutation of water into fire and work into celebration: "There the first festivals were celebrated, feet jumped for joy, and eager gestures no longer sufficed. Voices accompanied gestures with impassioned accents; pleasure and desire, merged into one, were felt at once. There, finally, was the true birthplace of nations, and from the pure crystal of the fountains sprang the first fires of love."[99]

This often cited passage could well be analyzed for its rhythmic, phonic, and accentual structure as well as for its shrewd mixing of inchoative past tenses with iterative imperfects, the result of which is to make language begin its long history in prolonged moments during which no time was kept.

Thus a model is provided of a primitive language that was at the same time a pure and original melody. "The first languages were melodious and passionate; only later did they become simple and methodical." Rousseau works variations on this theme: "One would sing rather than speak."[100] An integrated musical language composed of signs indistinguishable from the sentiments they express permitted communication in which the intended message was infallibly transmitted to its recipient: unity, emotional oneness, manifested itself at all levels.

But that unity was fragile, and it disappeared as accents faded and melody and passion subsided. Once the unity was destroyed, music and words, both degenerate, became strangers to one another. Chilled to the core, language was now useless for anything but acts of tyranny and indirect communication. As "articulations" (consonants) took on greater importance, the speech of the civilized nations grew fainter; it lost the accent and sonority that had been its only means of "persuading an assembled people." Meanwhile, music, led astray by the development of harmony, deprived of its melodic plenitude, still offered superficial pleasure to the ears but could no longer touch the heart. Thus the "moral effects" of primitive language were lost. The cooling of language was accompanied by a loss of liberty. "Noise" invaded music, thwarting all communication of emotion.

As is well known, Rousseau in his debate with Rameau honed his arguments against the primacy of harmony, which he considered a "barbarous" invention. When Rousseau's first attempt at musical composition debuted in Paris in 1744, he had been treated rather "brutally" by the composer, whom he had previously admired and whose theoretical works he had assiduously read. Rousseau definitely had grounds for resentment, and he may have indulged his hostility to Rameau by developing a theory of music at odds with the master's. He took the side of Italian proponents of opera buffa who attacked the "din" of French music and attacked Rameau in articles that Diderot commissioned for the *Encyclopedia*. He continued the attack first in *La Nouvelle Héloïse*, then in the *Essay on the Origin of Languages* (not published until after his death), and finally in the *Dictionary of Music*. Personal grievance thus played a considerable role. But why did Rousseau feel so wronged? By denying the originality and value of Rousseau's music Rameau had barred his access to Parisian society, where Rousseau had hoped to "make a name for himself." Rameau had intervened just as Rousseau was about to emerge from obscurity into the limelight, or so he believed. Jean-Jacques hoped to win the approval of connoisseurs while preserving his "independence." He staked his all on winning notoriety and esteem with his opera *The Galant Muses* in 1744: "Now that my opera was finished, the time had come to profit by it. That was a far more difficult 'opera.' No one can make it in Paris who lives in isolation. I thought of asking M. de la Poplinière to produce my work . . . M. de la Poplinière was Rameau's Maecenas."[101] It is hardly surprising, therefore, that Rousseau saw the rival responsible for his continued isolation as the apostle of an art of non-communication, a music-obstacle.

Rousseau's revenge is central to the next book of the *Confessions*, which tells the story of the staging of his opera *The Village Soothsayer* at Fontainebleau in the presence of the king and court.[102] He is fully compensated for the humiliation he had suffered at the hands of Rameau. As dramatized in the autobiographical text, this compensation comes in the form of an approving murmur that runs through the entire audience, gathering strength as it rises to the loge where Rousseau is seated. All the emotion felt by the assembled crowd is concentrated in this murmur:

> From the first scene, which is truly a scene of touching naïveté, I heard high up in the loges a murmur of surprise and applause unprecedented in performances of this genre. The growing ferment was soon perceptible throughout the hall and, as Montesquieu might put it, its effect only enhanced its effect. That effect was at its height in the scene of the two brave little lovers. Because there is no clapping in the king's presence, every note could be heard, and both the piece and its author benefited. All around me women who to me seemed as beautiful as angels spoke in half-whispers: "This is charming, this is delightful. There is not a sound in it that does not speak to the heart." The pleasure of giving emotion to so many kind people moved me to tears myself, and at the first duet, when I noticed that I was not the only person crying, I could no longer contain myself.
>
> I am nevertheless certain that at that moment the concupiscence of sex had much more to do with my feelings than did the vanity of the author, and surely if only men had been present I would not have been consumed, as I was continuously, by the desire to gather up with my lips the delicious tears that I caused to flow. I have seen works elicit deeper sighs of admiration but never have I seen a rapture so complete, so sweet, or so touching prevail throughout a performance, and especially in a first presentation at court. Those who saw it must remember it, for the effect was unique.[103]

What is happening here is nothing less than a repeat of the fusion accomplished by the primitive festival, of the exchange of glances and loving sighs in which pleasure and desire flourish freely in innocent suspense. But the pleasure is no longer that of the first encounters under ancient oaks: Rousseau savors a joy that he has deliberately shaped, that of being the indirect cause of "a rapture so complete, so sweet." The labor of art was required to make this happen. Rousseau becomes an author in order to forget—supreme reward—his literary glory and experience only the immortal desire to slake his thirst: to gather up tears with his lips, thereby stanching the primitive thirst that drew flocks, shepherds, and maidens together around the ancient watering holes.

THE ANTIDOTE IN THE POISON   155

Under certain conditions, therefore, a disease that has grown steadily worse throughout human history can find its remedy. Instead of the incomprehensible "ruckus" of the French opera, proof of the decadence of a society given to artifice, it is possible to create another kind of music, a music that flows from the heart, that is the product of a truer taste. In no less a hotbed of civilized perversion than a court theater, that music, by setting peasant lovers singing and reciting, is capable of awakening the true passion of the beginning of time, and even jaded courtiers are capable of receiving the revelation in their hearts.

Rousseau did not advocate a straightforward "return to nature" in either his philosophy of culture or his political philosophy. To be educated Emile must first be completely denatured. Rousseau was convinced that we must look to "perfected art for the cure for the ills that inchoate art *(l'art commencé)* inflicts on nature."[104] When Henriette, the mysterious letter-writer, asks Rousseau if she is to be condemned for seeking consolation in literature, he answers, as we have seen, that since the harm has already been done, literature will be her "Achilles' spear," the allusion of course being to Telephus's wound, caused but also cured by Achilles' spear.[105]

Is there perhaps a similar tendency in Rousseau's philosophy of language and music? If a malady that has afflicted generations cannot be totally cured, can't there at least be some form of reconciliation that would reestablish the lost plenitude, or a vivid image of it, without repudiating the knowledge, technology, and instrumental means developed by civilized reason? Of course music and language are now separate arts, and this division cannot be forgotten any more than the nostalgic image of primary unity. But the conflict can be mollified, and the separate realms need not remain ignorant of or hostile to each other. Rhetoric, altered by the influence of writing and the muted tone of evolved language, can be revived in both literary style and solid philosophical argument: the effect on the reader's heart is then the guarantee of a rediscovered power, a restored communication. Rousseau, of course, worked hard toward that end.

The power of music could be regenerated in a similar way. Words and song, melody and harmony need not always be in opposition, as shown by the shared pleasure and emotion of the audience at the first performance of *The Village Soothsayer*. Further evidence can be found in a well-known note to the *Letter to d'Alembert* in which Rousseau describes a festival in the Saint-Gervais district of Geneva, where the celebrating populace dances with a regiment of soldiers. The unforgettable images of collective emotion can be explained by Rousseau's music theory: simple melodies, composed to touch the heart and remind it of its true attachments, bring tears in the one case and set the crowd to dancing in the other.

It is impossible to exaggerate the importance in Rousseau's thought of symbols of regeneration, which open a breach of hope and point the way to possible repatriation. These images are all the more striking because they stand out against the disastrous present, which is radically condemned. At the end of the *Essay on the Origin of Languages* the worst apparently prevails: nothing is left of the bonds responsible for the happiness of primitive societies and virtuous republics. In chapters 19 and 20 Rousseau deplores first the death of music and then the death of eloquence:

> In this way song became, by degrees, an art entirely divorced from speech, in which it originated; the harmonics of the tones obscured the inflections of the voice; and finally, limited to the purely physical effect of the concurrence of vibrations, music was deprived of the moral effects it had produced when it was doubly the voice of nature.[106]

> Societies have assumed their final form: only cannon or cash could change them now. And since there is nothing more to say to the people other than "Give money," it is said with placards on street corners or with soldiers in homes. No one need assemble for that. On the contrary, the subjects must be kept apart: that is the first maxim of modern politics.[107]

Yet despite this definitive fall into moral dispersion and civil servitude, Rousseau's personal conviction keeps up its demands, its exhortations to search for compensation, to turn language and music, such as they are, into means of assembling men again, in a new, possibly imaginary, setting.

Let us therefore examine Rousseau's writings on music more closely. *The Village Soothsayer* is an opera. What is an opera? Rousseau gives his definition in one of the *Dictionary of Music*'s key articles: "The elements of opera are poetry, music, scenery. Poetry speaks to the mind; music, to the ear; painting, to the eyes; and all must join together to move the heart, to impress upon it óne impression conveyed via several organs."[108] Moving the heart had been the central event of the first festivals, back in the time when speech and music were still unified. But these two means of expression had evolved in different ways and were now strangers to one another. The purpose of opera was precisely to reunite them and thus to achieve, in a work of late civilization, the unanimous joy that people had once experienced in the exchange of glances, in dancing, in the truthful effusion of amorous voices, in the simultaneity of pleasure and desire. According to Rousseau, Greek theater, which relied on "accented language" (unlike French), had been able to preserve something of the prior unity: "All their poetry was musical, and all their music declamatory . . . I take it for granted that Greek music was true recitative."[109] We moderns, however, must find other ways to reconcile music and words in the lyrical performance. Unity, no longer spontaneous, must be created. And it can be created by art, just as political unity can be the result of "social art." Art is nothing but the invention of substitutes or "supplements" for the privileges of the primary human associations, now forever lost. When those substitutes are imperfect, they merely aggravate the lack they are meant to compensate: "The less one is able to touch the heart, the more one must flatter the ear. We are forced to seek in sensation the pleasure that sentiment refuses. Therein lies the origin of airs, of symphony, and of that enchanting melody that so often embellishes modern music at the expense of poetry, but which, in the theater, the man of taste rejects when it flatters but does not move him."[110] Just as the opera must reconcile poetry, music, and painting, music itself must make sure that airs, choruses, symphony, and melody combine in proper proportion to find the way to the "heart." That way is filled with numerous obstacles, with "bad substitutes." In primitive festivals "joyful movement" preceded voice and called it forth, but in modern opera ballet is added after the fact. Dramatic dance and pantomime are superfluous elements in opera. Rousseau (in the article entitled "Opera") rejects them in the name of stylistic unity. The celebrations that are ingeniously introduced into opera almost invariably disrupt the unity of action. They are mere "disconnected leaps" and "pointless dances." Movement, now a separate language, ought to be reserved for additional entertainments: "A very agreeable way to end the show is to stage a ballet after the opera, just as a minor play is staged after a tragedy. The new performance has nothing to do with the one that comes before, so one can choose a different language; another nation appears on stage."[111] Nor does Rousseau have anything kind to say about the constant use of mythology in French opera from Lully to Rameau: this was but another unfortunate palliative, along with overlavish scenery and elaborate mechanical devices. Such subterfuges are necessary to hold the audience's attention when one attempts to "apply" music to languages like French, which lack sufficient accent and inflection.

In order to avoid a surfeit of artifice, language and music ought to fit together. Unfortunately this is not the case with French, which imposes intolerable constraints: "When the language has neither sweetness nor flexibility, the rough character of the poetry keeps it from serving the song, the very sweetness of the melody prevents it from aiding in proper recitation of the verse, and one senses in the forced union of the two arts a perpetual constraint that is an affront to the ear and destroys both the allure of the melody and the effect of the declamation." Carrying his condemnation of French music even further, Rousseau adds: "This defect is without remedy, and to attempt strenuously to apply music to a language that is not musical is to make that language even cruder than it would have been otherwise."[112] In extraordinary circumstances, however, this situation is subject to change. Such is the privilege of genius, to which Rousseau devotes an entry in his *Dictionary of Music.* Here Italian opera is held up as a model that the French musician might imitate, as if it were possible— with the aid of genius—to transfer to French the virtues of a more sonorous language, a language more suitable for melodic invention. Rousseau avails himself of the opportunity to summarize his theory of the mimetic, expressive, and communicative effects of music. If conceived by genius, music has the power to represent and translate all external objects and to transmute all internal events by raising them to the highest degree of emotive incandescence. Although it is in the very nature of music to depend on chronological succession, its "moral effect" is to annihilate time, almost to eternalize momentary emotions—an oxymoron as surprising as the "heat" bestowed on "frost":

The genius of the musician subjects the whole world to his art. He paints all pictures with his sounds. He makes even silence speak. He renders ideas by feelings, feelings by accents, and the passion he expresses he stirs in the depths of the heart. Desire, through him, takes on new charms. The pain he sets moaning calls forth cries. He burns always and is never consumed. He expresses frost and ice with heat. Even in painting the horrors of death he carries in his soul that feeling for life that never leaves him and that he communicates to hearts made to feel it. But, alas, he can say nothing to those where its seed does not exist, and his prodigies are scarcely perceptible to those incapable of imitating them. Do you therefore wish to know whether some spark of this devouring flame animates you? Run, fly to Naples to hear the masterpieces of Leo, Durante, Jomelli, and Pergolesi. If your eyes fill with tears, if you feel your heart palpitate, if shudders run through you, if emotion takes your breath away, take Metastasio and work. His genius will kindle yours, you will create after his example. That is how genius is made, and other eyes will soon yield up the tears that the masters have made you shed.[113]

The privilege of genius is to reawaken the primitive cry, but now wrested from the spectator by a perfectly imitated moan. Here again is the communion in tears that Rousseau made the climax, almost the epiphany, of the first performance of the *The Village Soothsayer* as recounted in the *Confessions*. Here, however, the communion is even broader, embracing first the disciple and his model and then extending to the public at large. The criterion of genius is not so much originality as it is capacity to feel emotion, frenzy, and rapture, which—from Paris to Naples, from admired master to inspired pupil, from Italian to French—cross all boundaries to ensure the union of hearts and to fashion the invisible society composed of those who rise above the "vulgar herd."

Such communion is possible solely because of the unifying intuition typical of the production of works of genius. To designate this power Rousseau employs an Italian expression, which he makes an entry in his *Dictionary: prima intenzione*. I have deliberately introduced the notion of intuition, thinking of the faculty that the neo-Platonists, most notably Marsilio Ficino, attributed to the sharp tip of the soul *(mens)*. Along with the angels the soul enjoys the privilege of taking in at a single glance *(uno intuitu)* the totality of being and time *(totum simul)*. Rousseau offers a sentimental—that is, aestheticized and deintellectualized—version of this doctrine:

> An air or piece *di prima intenzione* is one that takes shape suddenly and completely and with all its parts in the mind of the composer, just as Pallas lept fully armed from the brow of Jupiter. Pieces *di prima intenzione* are among those rare strokes of genius whose ideas are so closely related that they form, as it were, a single idea, and none could have come to mind without the others. In music, pieces *di prima intenzione* are the only ones that can cause those ecstatic, rapturous, and exalted feelings that transport listeners outside themselves: one feels them, divines them instantly. Connoisseurs never mistake them.[114]

This entry echoes the one on "the unity of melody," one of Rousseau's most important theoretical texts. On this score Rousseau is dissatisfied with an aesthetic assumption widely shared by his contemporaries, which he characterizes in these terms: "There is in music a successive unity that relates to the subject and by which all the duly linked parts compose a single whole, which we perceive in its entirety and in all its relations." This first kind of unity concerns the global composition of the work. Later, however, Rousseau reflects on another kind of unity: "A unity of more subtle, more simultaneous substances, which imperceptibly gives music its energy and force of expression." This unity involves the components of "modern" music, namely, melody and harmony, which Rousseau elsewhere criticizes for having become antagonistic. Here, however, he asserts that this opposition, in which he has hitherto taken the part of melody, is only temporary. Genius can reconcile the superficial *(de sensation)* and fleeting pleasure of harmony with the more profound *(de sentiment)* pleasure of melody, which constantly demands a new kind of attention. By effecting a happy fusion of both genius can avoid the overly simplistic unison quality that is nevertheless so touching in popular tunes as well as the surfeit of polyphony that Rousseau rejects:

> Music, therefore, must necessarily sing in order to touch, to please, to sustain interest and attention. But how, in our systems of chords and harmony, is music to go about singing? If each part has its own

melody, all those melodies heard at once will cancel one another out, leaving no melody at all. And if all the parts use the same melody, one no longer has harmony, and the concert will be all in unison.

The manner in which a musical instinct, a certain unspoken sentiment of genius, unwittingly overcame this difficulty and even profited by it is quite remarkable. Harmony, which might have stifled melody, animates it, reinforces it, determines it: the diverse parts, without merging with one another, contribute to a single effect, and though each one seems to have its own melody, one hears only a single melody emerging from the assembled parts. That is what I call *unity of melody*.[115]

Rousseau clearly credits himself with superior knowledge, capable of discerning processes that proceed unbeknownst to us and unbeknownst even to genius. Expressions such as "unaware" and "unwittingly" allude rhetorically to unsuspected feelings, to intuitive apperceptions. These unnoticed processes—detected only by Rousseau—are good: they lead toward a salvation of sorts. Of course in that respect the advantage remains with the Italians: "It is in this principle of the unity of melody, which the Italians sensed and obeyed without understanding it but which the French neither obeyed nor understood—it is, I was saying, in this great principle that the essential difference between the two musics lies."[116] Once again Rousseau presents himself as an exceptional individual: the principle that went unobeyed in one case and unobserved though instinctively obeyed in the other did not escape his scrutiny; he alone perceived it clearly. Later in the same text he says that, having "discovered" this principle, he immediately attempted an "application" in *The Village Soothsayer* (1752) and shortly thereafter formulated the theory in his *Letter on French Music* (1753). The series of events follows an empirical order: first the illuminating intuition, then the practical proof with the success of the *Soothsayer,* and finally the theoretical statement, formulated only after the fact and supported by irrefutable evidence. In the *Letter on French Music* Rousseau states that unity of melody is, in his view, an "indispensable rule, no less important in music than unity of action in a tragedy, because it is based on the same principle and aimed at the same objective."[117]

Another invention that Rousseau claims as his own, in French music at least, and which he says he tried out in *The Village Soothsayer,* is that of the obbligato recitative. Recitative is first defined as "the means of unifying song and speech."[118] Thanks to recitative, accent, which was paramount in primitive language, again assumes its proper place in more highly developed musical forms. If the recitative is obbligato, that is, intimately associated with an instrumental part, its power may be even greater. It can then be a unifying factor in the piece, ensuring that the declamation, shared by the actor who speaks the lines and the orchestra that plays the melody, serves a single goal. Because the actor overcome by emotion cannot express himself fully, the orchestra helps out by substituting music for the ineffable message. It then becomes possible to "tell all," as the halting voice is backed up by the instruments:

> *Obbligato recitative:* A recitative combined with ritornellos and symphonic devices which, as it were, oblige both actor and orchestra so that each must be attentive to and wait for the other.
>
>   These passages, alternating recitative with melody embellished by all the splendor of the orchestra, are the most touching, most ravishing, most energetic in all modern music. The actor, agitated, carried away by a passion that does not allow him to tell all, interrupts himself, halts, holds back, and during these pauses the orchestra speaks for him. Silences filled in this way affect the listener infinitely more than if the actor himself were to say all that the music suggests. Until now French music has made no use of the obbligato recitative. An attempt was made to give some idea of the technique in one scene of *The Village Soothsayer.*

Although unity of melody might create a more "simultaneous order," the obbligato recitative, based on the mutual obligation of the reciting voice and the orchestral melody, ensured that the recitative would have a coherent temporal structure by filling in the silences that extreme passion imposed on the spoken voice. In both cases art introduces a complement, an adjunct: harmony "adds" to the expressiveness of the melody, and the orchestra "fills" the silent moments. (In the "melodrama" *Pygmalion* the complementarity of the *spoken* voice and the orchestral music stems from the same principle, once again meeting the demand for full emotional expression.)

   To formulate principles, define bonds and "obligations" capable of assuring the unity of the work, and thereby to establish communion among composer, performers, and public: this program irresistibly calls to mind the program that Rousseau would later formulate in his "principles of political justice," the *Social Contract*.

Musical rules and political structures had of course long been seen as analogues, and a metaphorical system had been created as the repository of this "kinship": the happiness or internal peace of a society might be referred to as symmetry, harmony, accord, concert, and so on. Rousseau made use of this metaphorical system, which can be traced back to Plato and the Pythagoreans, but in a flexible fashion and without explicitly reflecting on its significance. More significantly, Rousseau presents both his musical beliefs and his political ideas as the result of a conversion or illumination. According to the account in the *Confessions*, it was in Venice that Rousseau had the "first idea for [his] *Institutions Politiques*." Then, on the road to Vincennes, in a famous moment of "bedazzlement," he had a vision of his "sad and grand system" in its entirety. Now, it so happens, he also dates his conversion to Italian music from the time of his stay in Venice. According to the *Confessions*, this change of opinion came about in a short period of time owing to the extraordinary consequences of several revealing events: "I had brought with me from Paris the Parisian prejudice against Italian music, but I had also received from nature a sensibility against which prejudices cannot stand. I soon felt for that music all the passion it inspires in those made to judge it. As I listened to the barcaroles I discovered that I had never heard singing before."[119]

In the fictional account given in *La Nouvelle Héloïse*, however, the conversion is the effect of a single evening of music. Saint-Preux listens to the castrato Reggianino, and, immediately won over by the truth, renounces all his earlier illusions:

> How mistaken I have been until now about the products of this charming art. I felt that they had little effect and blamed this on the weakness of the music. I told myself that music was nothing but empty sound, which can only flatter the ear and which affects the soul only slightly and indirectly. The impression of chords is purely mechanical and physical. What does it have to do with feeling, and why should I hope to be more moved by a beautiful harmony than by a beautiful accord of colors? I did not perceive, in the accents of melody applied to those of language, the powerful and secret link between passions and sounds. I did not see that the imitation of the various tones with which the emotions animate the speaking voice

gives the singing voice the power to stir the heart, and that the energetic portrait that the person performing gives of the movements of his soul is what charms his listeners.[120]

The decisive experience is a series of surprises and discoveries:

> I soon felt, in the emotions this art caused in me, that it possessed greater power than I had imagined. I scarcely know what delightful sensation imperceptibly took hold of me. The music was no longer a pointless series of sounds, as in our recitals. With each phrase some image entered my mind or some sentiment entered my heart. The pleasure did not stop at the ear but penetrated to the soul. The performance flowed effortlessly, with charming ease. All the performers seemed animated by the same spirit.[121]

The alert reader will notice a parallel: the "same spirit" that animates the performers is a variant of the general will, the key concept of the *Social Contract*. To be sure, the spirit of the musicians is a general will of brief duration, limited to a single night and to a small circle of performers. Still, one can hardly escape the comparison with the celebrated formulation of the social contract and its consequences:

> If we exclude all that is not essential from the social pact, it can be reduced to the following terms: each of us jointly subjects his person and capabilities to the supreme direction of the general will, and we receive, as a body, each member an indivisible part of the whole.
>
> Instantly, in place of the individual person of each party to the contract, this act of association produces a moral and collective body composed of as many members as the assembly has voices *(voix)*, and that body receives from the selfsame act its unity, its common *ego*, its life, and its will.[122]

Note that the word *voix*, which can mean either voices or votes and which here alludes to universal suffrage, is one of those multivalent terms that can be understood either in a "literal" (linguistic, musical) sense or a "figurative" (political) sense. The use of the word in the political vocabulary is sufficiently unequivocal that there is no need to add to what has been said thus far about the social aspects of music a discussion of the musicalization of society. Still, it is impossible to avoid the conclusion that the notion of unity, whose emergence we have just examined, establishes a link between Rousseau's aesthetics and his politics: each one in its own sphere provides an answer to the fundamental question of how individuals communicate. Thus the history of societies can be looked at as a history of voices.

In the *Essay on the Origin of Languages* Rousseau maintains that the effect of the "first voices" was to "bring men together." Among the peoples of the south it was passion, working through inarticulate, musical voices, that established the first human convention. Celebration around the watering hole was, as we have seen, the "birthplace of nations." In the north, by contrast, need was paramount: there, articulate voices (harsher and more broken up by consonants) called for help, uttered the formula of the contract, and exhibited the will of the political "body." Contractual *concertation* brought remedies and substitutes: it produced civil liberty in place of natural independence; it put an end to the war of all against all, which pitted individuals now unequal against one another; and it thus reestablished, in the form of a voluntary organization, the unity primitive men and women had known when they gathered in spontaneous, festive assemblies.

Consider, in this connection, a key passage from the *Social Contract*: "The more *concert* prevails in the assemblies, or, in other words, the closer opinions are to unanimity, the more the general will predominates; but lengthy debates, dissent, and tumult presage the ascendancy of particular interests and the decline of the State."[123] There is danger in the multiplicity of voices, each of which expresses a particular interest instead of the general interest. The desired unanimity is compromised when factions proliferate and "small societies influence the larger society." Then, Rousseau adds, "the general will becomes mute."[124]

It is striking that Rousseau characterizes what is wrong in terms very similar to those he uses to criticize the deleterious effects of making harmony and polyphony preeminent in music. "Any music in which one can make out more than one melody at once is bad, and . . . the effect is the same as that of two or more speeches delivered at once in the same tone. There are no exceptions to this rule, hence there is no question what one ought to think about those marvelous musical forms in which one tune serves as accompaniment to another."[125] The danger, analogous to the danger of factions within a state, is one of destruction: "If each part has its own melody, so many melodies heard simultaneously will destroy one another."[126] When Rousseau hears "four-part psalms" sung in the Protestant churches of his native land, he at first feels rapture, but this is soon followed by a very different feeling: "Little by little the noise numbs me."[127] Noise, analogous to the tumult that Rousseau fears in the city, is what he allegedly dislikes in Rameau's operas and in French music generally: such music does not "speak" to the heart. In other words, it becomes "mute," like the general will in a state riven by particular interests. Rousseau claimed to feel greater affection for the unison structure of popular songs. Such songs, he says, are not without harmony, because each note calls forth its harmonics. Clearly, there is a parallel between these unison songs and the unanimity of peoples in the grip of an overwhelming patriotic fervor.

One further remark needs to be made. Genius, the product of a powerful instinct, should be employed in blending melody with harmony, that is, in assuring the unity of melody, the composition *di prima intenzione*. The function of genius in music is therefore not without analogy to the role that Rousseau, in the *Social Contract*, ascribes to the legislator, whose "great soul" is constantly employed in persuading individuals to sacrifice their particular interest to the general interest; his mission is to assemble men so as to obtain from them "the union of understanding and will."[128]

In the historical situation in which Rousseau found himself, political unity could be achieved only by transforming the system or by resisting the forces corrupting society. What was needed was a "mechanic to invent the machine."[129] Just as the musical genius is alone capable of composing a great work, a body politic, at its inception, needs a man who feels "capable of changing human nature, as it were, a man capable of transforming each individual and who by himself is a perfect and solitary whole yet part of a greater whole from which he somehow receives his life and his being."[130]

As we saw earlier, *The Village Soothsayer* proved to Rousseau's satisfaction the usefulness of his musical principles. But proof of his legislative principles was less easy to come by. Rousseau did not become the lawgiver of the Corsicans or the Poles. He never got beyond the stage of consultant to "peoples in need of institutions." Primitive festivals and regenerated societies would remain postulates of speculative reason or goads to the imagination.

If he could not unify a nation, it was within Rousseau's powers as a

musician to unite the members of a "small society." He had enjoyed
that privilege in his youth at Annecy in Mme de Warens's soirées. In
such a setting it was not necessary to compose an entire opera. With
an intimate group of friends it was enough to compose a tune or a
song to fill everyone's heart with joy and bring the group closer together. These days of happiness, which Rousseau described so well,
almost always ended with an evening song. Take, for example, the day
on the Isle of Saint-Pierre that is described in the fifth reverie: "After
supper, if the evening was fair, we would all go together for a walk
around the grounds to breathe the cool lake air. We would rest in the
pavilion, laugh, converse, or sing some old song easily as good as your
modern ditties, and finally we would go to bed content with the day
and desiring nothing but the same for the morrow."[131]

To breathe "the lake air": again, water, which Rousseau says he
always loved passionately. In the *Essay on the Origin of Languages* he
made watering holes the place where couples met and primitive festivals were held. But this lakeside sojourn is a final moment, almost an
end to a story that Rousseau is enjoying for his own personal benefit.
The ardor of amorous youth has given way to tranquillity. The evening
song, laden with memory (it is an "old song"), substitutes for the great
event of language's inception. A quiet walk with friends takes the place
of primitive dances. Yet once again, the spirit of music infuses the
communal life, the life of "all together." It attests to the unity of a small
community that hopes to go on living in just the same way: "After a
nice tune one feels satisfied. The ear desires nothing more. The tune
remains in the imagination. You take it with you and repeat it at will
. . . The true music-lover never forgets the beautiful tunes he hears
during his lifetime."[132] And so Rousseau suggests that time has come
to a halt in a paradise regained of plenitude and repetition, which,
standing at the end of history and through the power of art, echoes
the uncounted hours beneath clear skies and "ancient oaks, the con-
querors of time," when pleasure and desire were, by nature, one.

5. The Antidote in the Poison:
The Thought of Jean-Jacques Rousseau

1. Jean-Jacques Rousseau, *Oeuvres complètes* (Paris: Pléiade, 1959–1969), vol. I, p. 7. Hereafter referred to as *O.C.*

2. *O.C.*, I, pp. 7–8.

3. *O.C.*, III, p. 26.

4. Ibid.

5. See F. Baker, "Remarques sur la notion de dépôt," *Annales Jean-Jacques Rousseau* 37 (1966–1968):57–93.

6. *O.C.*, III, p. 27.

7. *O.C.*, III, p. 76.

8. *O.C.*, III, p. 95.

9. *O.C.*, III, p. 56.

10. *O.C.*, II, p. 972.

11. *O.C.*, III, p. 56.

12. *O.C.*, III, p. 39.

13. *O.C.*, II, p. 972.

14. *O.C.*, II, p. 974; compare Pliny the Elder, *Naturalis Historia* XXIX, 32. Homeopathic remedies were employed in medicine throughout the centuries. Montaigne disapproved: "I do not like to cure the disease by the disease" (*Essais*, III, 13). Hahnemann, the theorist of homeopathic medicine, developed the ancient principle. In paragraph 132 of his *Organon* (1810) we read that the first ingestion of homeopathic medicine is followed by "a homeopathic aggravation of the disease," because "the disease caused by the medication must of course be, to some degree, stronger than the disease one wants to cure in order to overcome (*überstimmen*) and extinguish it."

15. *O.C.*, III, p. 227.

16. *O.C.*, II, p. 25. Rousseau hoped to succeed where he believed Richardson had failed. In a letter to Duclos dated 19 September 1760 he wrote: "I still think that such reading is dangerous for girls. I even think that Richardson was sadly mistaken in wishing to instruct them through novels. That is like setting fire to the house in order to set the pumps to working."

17. *O.C.*, II, p. 6.

18. *O.C.*, II, p. 227.

19. *Lettre à d'Alembert* (Paris, 1967), p. 130.

20. Ibid., p. 155.

21. Ibid.

22. Ibid., p. 131.

23. Ibid., p. 139.

24. Ibid., p. 140.

25. Ibid., p. 223.

26. Ibid., p. 225.

27. Ibid., p. 227. On the history of relations between Rousseau and Voltaire, see Henri Gouhier, *Rousseau et Voltaire. Portraits dans deux miroirs* (Paris: Vrin, 1983); Jean Starobinski, "Rousseau et Voltaire," *Critique* 449 (October 1984).

28. Ibid., p. 234.

29. *O.C.*, III, pp. 288, 479.

30. *O.C.*, IV, p. 640.

31. *O.C.*, IV, p. 654. Mme de Staël in 1798 proved herself to be a good student of Rousseau: "The same creature, the same tree, that contains the poison often contains the remedy as well, and in correcting a man's character one finds in the passion that leads him astray the resources necessary to guide him. Moralists and legislators will always go wrong if they seek remedies in contraries rather than in the very principle that has been denatured by circumstance." Germaine de Staël, *Des circonstances . . .* (Geneva: Droz, 1979), p. 273.

32. *Emile*, book 4, *O.C.*, IV, p. 493.

33. Ibid., p. 523.

34. Ibid., p. 535.

35. Ibid., p. 547.

36. *Emile*, book 3, *O.C.*, IV, p. 187. The notion of *crisis* can of course be traced back to Hippocrates.

37. *Social Contract*, II, 8, *O.C.*, III, p. 385.

38. *O.C.*, III, p. 638.

39. *O.C.*, III, p. 891.

40. *O.C.*, III, p. 895.

41. *O.C.*, III, p. 998.

42. *O.C.*, III, p. 843.

43. *O.C.*, III, p. 828.

44. *O.C.*, II, p. 980.

45. *O.C.*, II, p. 1018.

46. *O.C.*, II, p. 1181.

47. *O.C.*, IV, p. 664.

48. *O.C.*, II, p. 508 (letter 14 of part 4). Etienne Gilson has commented on this letter in a detailed study, "La méthode de M. de Wolmar," in *Les idées et les lettres* (Paris, 1955), pp. 275–298.

49. "The deeper the solitude in which I live, the more I need some object to fill the void, and those that my imagination refuses to give me or that my memory rejects are provided by the spontaneous productions that the earth, unforced by men, presents to me wherever my eyes turn" (VII, *Rêverie*, *O.C.*, I, p. 1070).

50. Rousseau likes to describe incomplete cures. He was never able to "cure himself fully" from the temptation to commit petty thefts (*O.C.*, I, p. 32) or masturbation (*O.C.*, I, pp. 594–595, and variant, p. 1569). The virtuous Savoyard vicar was "not especially well disciplined" with respect to the temptations of the flesh (*O.C.*, IV, p. 563).

51. *O.C.*, II, p. 740.

52. *O.C.*, II, p. 743.

53. I touch on this subject in "Rousseau en 1764" in *Ecriture 13* (Vevey, 1977), pp. 123–131, rpt. in *Questions sur l'autorité* (Lausanne: L'Age d'Homme, 1989).

54. Letter no. 3192 in R. A. Leigh, ed., *Correspondance complète de Rousseau* (Geneva and Oxford, 1965–1989), vol. 19.

55. These are the terms Rousseau uses in his response dated 7 May 1764. See ibid., vol. 20, pp. 18–24. The editor, R. A. Leigh, points out the affinities between this letter and the argument of *The Discourse on Inequality*.

56. Ovid, *Remedia amoris*, lines 43–48; *Amores*, IX. Other Latin examples

include Horace, *Epodes,* 17, 8; Propertius, II, 1, 63–64. The hero was known from tragedies of Aeschylus, Euripides, Ennius, and others, now lost. In the Renaissance the legend was part of common knowledge. The formula remained proverbial until the middle of the nineteenth century. To cite several examples at random: "The great remedy for the license of the press lies in the freedom of the press; it is Achilles' spear, which heals the wounds it has made" (Camille Desmoulins, *Le Vieux Cordelier,* no. 7, text edited and introduced by Pierre Pachet [Paris: Belin, 1987], p. 13). Did Balzac have Desmoulins's text in mind in *Les Illusions perdues* when he had Lucien de Rubempré say, "The newspaper is most definitely like Achilles' spear, which healed the wounds it made" (Balzac, *La Comédie humaine,* ed. P.-G. Castex [Paris: Gallimard-Pléiade, 1977], vol. 5, p. 462). In an 1815 article Benjamin Constant wrote: "Violence is not like Achilles' spear; it does not heal the wounds it causes" (Benjamin Constant, *Recueil d'articles, 1795–1817,* ed. E. Harpaz [Geneva: Droz, 1978]).

57. *Metamorphoses,* XII, 112.

58. *Tristia,* V, 2, 15.

59. From Makedonios, *Greek Anthology,* V, 225. The English translation here is based on the French translation by P. Waltz ("Les Belles-Lettres").

60. From Paul the Silentiary, *Greek Anthology,* V, 291.

61. Plutarch, *How One Must Listen,* 16.

62. Otto Rank, *Der Mythus von der Geburt des Helden* (Deuticke, 1909), pp. 21–22. The essential facts can be found in Carl Robert, *Die griechische Heldensage* (Berlin, 1923), pp. 1138–1160.

63. F. Noël, *Dictionnaire de la Fable,* 3rd ed. (Paris, 1810).

64. Chompré, *Dictionnaire portatif de la Fable,* new ed. (Paris, 1801).

65. Ibid.

66. Freud, *Gesammelte Werke,* X: *Triebe und Triebschicksale,* pp. 210–232.

67. In *De doctrina christiana* Augustine sees divine wisdom as a therapeutic treatment that works sometimes by opposition and sometimes by the effect of like on like: *Morte mortuos liberavit* (I, XIV, 13). Pascal uses this as an argument in his *Prière pour le bon usage des maladies.* In a "Sermon for Ash Wednesday" Fénelon writes: "This ash . . . although it represents death . . . is a remedy that yields immortality." Baudelaire, in a translation of Thomas De Quincey's *The Opium Eaters,* adds to the English text's description of the torments of "troubled sleep": "Until, finding a remedy in the very intensity of the pain, human nature explodes in a loud cry" (chap. 2).

68. *O.C.,* IV, p. 249.

69. *Correspondance complète,* vol. 20, p. 21.

70. Ibid., p. 123.

71. Ibid., vol. 20, p. 22.

72. Ibid., vol. 22, p. 10.

73. Ibid., pp. 8–9.

74. Ibid.

75. As I showed in "Le dîner de Turin," *La Relation critique* (Paris: Gallimard, 1970); English translation: "The Dinner at Turin," in *The Living Eye,* trans. Arthur Goldhammer (Cambridge, Mass.: Harvard University Press, 1989).

76. *O.C.,* I, p. 17.

77. *O.C.*, I, pp. 1156. See Philippe Lejeune, "La punition des enfants, lecture d'un aveu de Rousseau," in *Le Pacte autobiographique* (Paris, 1975), pp. 49–85, and "Le peigne cassé," *Poétique* 25 (1976):1–30.

78. *O.C.*, I, p. 109; see Philippe Lejeune, "Le 'dangereux supplément,' lecture d'un aveu de Rousseau," *Annales Economies, Sociétés, Civilisations* 4 (1974):1009–1022; and the chapter entitled "Ce dangereux supplément," in Jacques Derrida, *De la grammatologie* (Paris, 1967), pp. 203–234.

79. *Confessions*, IX, *O.C.*, I, p. 427.

80. *O.C.*, II, p. 1129.

81. *Confessions*, V, *O.C.*, I, p. 222.

82. *O.C.*, I, pp. 227–232. On this episode and other problems touched on above, see the excellent commentary by Pierre-Paul Clément, *Jean-Jacques Rousseau, de l'éros coupable à l'éros glorieux* (Neuchâtel, 1976), esp. pp. 188–202.

83. J.-B. Pontalis, *Entre le rêve et la douleur* (Paris, 1977), p. 150.

84. *O.C.*, I, pp. 232–233.

85. *O.C.*, II, p. 27.

86. *O.C.*, I, pp. 662–663.

87. *O.C.*, I, p. 980.

88. *O.C.*, I, p. 981.

89. *O.C.*, I, p. 986, repeated p. 997.

90. *O.C.*, I, p. 132.

91. *O.C.*, I, p. 997.

92. *O.C.*, I, p. 1081.

93. *O.C.*, I, p. 990.

94. *O.C.*, IV, p. 384.

95. *Discours de l'inégalité*, *O.C.*, III, p. 148.

96. *O.C.*, III, p. 169.

97. *Essai sur l'origine des langues*, chap. 9, new critical edition by Jean Starobinski (Paris: Gallimard, 1991), p. 106, cited hereafter as *E.O.L.* For a complete English translation, see Jean-Jacques Rousseau, *The First and Second Discourses . . . and Essay on the Origin of Languages*, edited, translated, and annotated by Victor Gourevitch (New York: Harper and Row, 1986). The languages of the north stem from a different source (chap. 10).

98. *E.O.L.*, p. 106.

99. *E.O.L.*, p. 107.

100. *E.O.L.*, p. 70.

101. *Confessions*, book VII, *O.C.*, I, p. 333.

102. Ibid., book VIII, *O.C.*, I, pp. 378–379.

103. Ibid.

104. *Fragments politiques*, *O.C.*, III, p. 479. The formula also occurs in the first version of *The Social Contract*, *O.C.*, I, p. 288.

105. See the first part of this chapter.

106. *E.O.L.*

107. *E.O.L.*

108. *Dictionnaire de musique*, article "Opéra." (The only editions of this work date from the eighteenth and nineteenth centuries. References are therefore to articles only, pagination omitted.)

109. Ibid.

110. Ibid.

111. Ibid.

112. Ibid.

113. Ibid., article "Génie."

114. Ibid., article "Prima intenzione."

115. Ibid., article "Unité de mélodie."

116. Ibid.

117. *E.O.L.*

118. *Dictionnaire de musique*, article "Récitatif." Gluck's use of the device is familiar, as, of course, is the even more ingenious use by Mozart in *Idomeneo*.

119. *Confessions*, book VII, *O.C.*, I, pp. 313–314.

120. *La Nouvelle Héloïse*, I, letter 48, *O.C.*, II, pp. 131–132.

121. Ibid., p. 133.

122. *Contrat social*, I, chap. 6, *O.C.*, III, p. 361.

123. Ibid., IV, chap. 2, *O.C.*, III, p. 439.

124. Ibid., IV, chap. 1, *O.C.*, III, p. 438. Compare n. 3, p. 1491.

125. *Dictionnaire de musique*, article "Unité de mélodie."

126. Ibid.

127. Ibid.

128. *Contrat social*, II, chap. 7, p. 384.

129. Ibid., p. 381.

130. Ibid.

131. *Rêveries*, fifth walk, *O.C.*, I, p. 1045.

132. *Dictionnaire de musique*, article "Air." This study owes a great deal to those of my colleagues and students at the University of Geneva who took part in a seminar devoted to Rousseau's writings on music in the winter of 1983–84. I would like to thank Samuel Baud-Bovy, Alain Grosrichard, and Jean-Jacques Eigeldinger for their valuable suggestions.

Addenda

1. *OC*1.7/*CW*5–6
2. *OC*1.7–8/*CW*5.7
3. *OC*3.26/*CW*2.19
4. *OC*3.26/*CW*2.19
6. *OC*3.27/*CW*2.19–20
7. *OC*3.76/*CW*2.114
8. *OC*3.95/*CW*2.129
9. *OC*3.56/*CW*2.53
10. *OC*2.972/*CW*2.196
11. *OC*3.56/*CW*2.53
12. *OC*3.39/*CW*2.40
13. *OC*2.972/*CW*2.196
14. *OC*2.974f./*CW*2.198f.
15. *OC*3.227/*CW*3.106
16. *OC*2.25/*CW*6.18
17. *OC*2.6/*CW*6.3–4
18. *OC*2.277 (not 227)/*CW*6.227
19. *OC*5.53/*CW*10.293
20. *OC*5.68/*CW*10.305
21. *OC*5.68/*CW*10.305
22. *OC*5.54/*CW*10.294
23. *OC*5.59/*CW*10.298
24. *OC*5.60/*CW*10.298
25. *OC*5.108/*CW*10.338
26. *OC*5.109–110/*CW*10.339
27. *OC*5.111/*CW*10.340–341
28. *OC*5.115,116/*CW*10.344,345
29. *OC*3.288,479/*CW*4.82,20
30. *OC*4.640/*Em*.317
31. *OC*4.654/*Em*.327
32. *OC*4.493/*Em*.213–214
33. *OC*4.523/*Em*.235
34. *OC*4.535/*Em*.243
35. *OC*4.547/*Em*.252
36. *OC*4.187/*Em*.182
37. *OC*3.385/*CW*4.158
38. *OC*3.638/*CW*11.93
39. *OC*3.891/*CW*9.301
40. *OC*3.895/*CW*9.304
41. *OC*3.998/*CW*11.205
42. *OC*3.843f./*CW*9.262f.
43. *OC*3.828/*CW*9.249
44. *OC*2.980/*CW*10.127
45. *OC*2.1018/*CW*10.160
46. *OC*2.1181/–
47. *OC*4.664/*Em*.334
48. *OC*2.508/*CW*6.417
49. *OC*1.1070/*CW*8.65
50. *OC*1.32/*CW*5.27; *OC*1.594–595/*CW*5.497–498; *OC*1.1569/–; *OC*4.563/*Em*.264
51. *OC*2.740–741/*CW*6.608
52. *OC*2.743/*CW*6.610
68. *OC*4.249/*Em*.40

228b

76. *OC*1.17/*CW*5.15
77. *OC*1.1156/–
78. *OC*1.109/*CW*5.91
79. *OC*1.427/*CW*5.359
80. *OC*2.1129/–
81. *OC*1.222/*CW*5.186
82. *OC*1.227–232/*CW*5.190–195
84. *OC*1.232–233/*CW*5.195
85. *OC*2.27/*CW*6.20
86. *OC*1.662–663/*CW*1.4
87. *OC*1.980/*CW*1.248
88. *OC*1.980–981/*CW*1.248–249
89. *OC*1.986/*CW*1.253; *OC*1.997/*CW*8.5
90. *OC*1.132/*CW*5.111
91. *OC*1.997/*CW*8.4–5
92. *OC*1.1081/*CW*8.74
93. *OC*1.990/*CW*1.256
94. *OC*4.384/*Em*.135
95. *OC*3.148/*CW*3.31
96. *OC*3.169/*CW*3.47
97. *OC*5.405/*CW*7.314
98. *OC*5.405–406/*CW*7.314
99. *OC*5.407/*CW*7.314
100. *OC*5.383/*CW*7.296
101. *OC*1.333/*CW*5.280
102. *OC*1.378–379/*CW*5.317–318
103. *OC*1.378–379/*CW*5.317–318
104. *OC*3.479/*CW*4.20; *OC*3.288/*CW*4.82
106. *OC*5.427/*CW*7.331
107. *OC*5.428/*CW*7.332
117. *OC*5.305/*CW*7.155
119. *OC*1.313–314/*CW*5.263
120. *OC*2.131–132/*CW*6.107–108
121. *OC*2.133/*CW*6.109
122. *OC*3.361/*CW*4.139
123. *OC*3.439/*CW*4.199
124. *OC*3.438/*CW*4.198; *OC*3.1491/–
128. *OC*3.384/*CW*4.157
129. *OC*3.381/*CW*4.155
130. *OC*3.381/*CW*4.155
131. *OC*1.1045/*CW*8.45

[14]

Making Jean-Jacques*

David Gauthier

'It is necessary to choose between making a man or a citizen' (OC IV, p. 248). Rousseau's distinction between man, solitary, 'numerical unity' (ibid., p. 249) with a 'physical and independent existence' (OC III, p. 381), and citizen, civil man, 'a fractional unity that depends on the denominator' (OC IV, p. 249) with a 'partial and moral existence' (OC III, p. 381), seems to lie at the root of his thought. 'Man's first sentiment [is] that of his existence' (ibid., p. 165); natural man senses his existence within himself, the citizen 'believes himself no longer one but part of the whole' (OC IV, p. 249) and senses his existence only as an integral part of his society. Natural man is free insofar as his powers are adequate to his needs, so that he is independent of the will of any other being. The citizen is free insofar as his individual will is subsumed entirely in the general will of his society, whose collective powers are adequate to its collective needs.

If man is naturally a unity, independent, self-sufficient, and solitary, then the citizen is, as Rousseau insists, man denatured, deprived of his own independent forces, given forces foreign to him that he can use only in company with his fellows. The citizen must be made. But why does Rousseau speak also of making a man – of making what is natural? The answer, of course, is that human beings no longer exist in their natural condition. Neither men nor citizens, neither self-sufficient nor integral parts of a self-sufficient whole, human beings live in a condition of slavish dependence. The division of labour makes each dependent on his fellows for his physical existence. But beyond this, each is dependent on others for his psychological existence. Each lives 'only in the opinion of others, and ... derives the sentiment of his own existence solely from their judgement' (OC III, p. 193). Each senses his existence neither within himself nor as part of a larger whole from which he can not dissociate himself, but rather outside himself, in others whose judgements and wills are alien to his own. From this unnatural condition of dependence Rousseau seems to recognize only two possible ways of escape, neither of which can be achieved by the efforts of the dependent individuals. In the hands of the Tutor, Emile is raised to enjoy the physical and psychological self-sufficiency and so the freedom, although not the solitude, of natural man. In the hands of the Legislator, human beings dependent on others alien to them are transformed into citizens dependent entirely but only on the society with which they identify – their dependence, in being perfected, is transformed into new forms of freedom, civil and moral. Or so Rousseau claims.

Human beings cannot return to their natural and original solitude. The long course of human development has led to the emergence of needs and powers that did not and could not exist in their initial condition. But finding their powers falling ever short of their new needs, they have spoken the fatal words, 'aidez-moi', 'help me' – the first words, Rousseau insists, of the northern languages, 'sad daughters of necessity' (OL pp. 527, 526). To speak the words 'aidez-moi' is to renounce one's freedom, to recognize one's dependence on what is alien. The Tutor seeks to create an Emile who will find no occasion to say such words; the Legislator seeks to create citizens who will say only 'aidons-nous', none thinking of himself or any of his fellows except as one of us.

How do the Tutor and the Legislator accomplish their tasks? Rousseau advises the Tutor:

> [T]ake an opposite route with your pupil. Let him believe always that he is the master, and let it be always you who are. There is no subjection so perfect than that which sustains the appearance of liberty. Thus one captures the will itself ... Doubtless he should do only what he wants; but he should want only what you want him to do (OC IV, pp. 362–3).

Later the Tutor says, '[A]s long as I could not make myself master of his will I stayed master of his person; I didn't part from him by a step. Now I leave him sometimes to himself because I rule him always' (ibid., p. 661). And we may treat what Rousseau says in the *Discourse on Political Economy* as advice to the Legislator:

> [I]f it is good to know how to use men as they are, it is worth far more to make them as one needs them to be; the most absolute authority is that which reaches deeply into man and is not exerted less on his will than on his actions (OC III, p. 251).

Rousseau's answer to our question – how do the Tutor and Legislator accomplish their tasks – is very clear; they must master the will of those they would transform. Only through such mastery can they penetrate deeply enough into a human being to annul the fatal words, 'aidez-moi', and effect the radical changes required to make him either into a man or into a citizen. And only through such mastery can they bring about these changes through the will of the person whom they transform, so that he identifies with the transformation of his nature and is restored to a sense of his own freedom.

There is an evident and not unfamiliar paradox at the heart of Rousseau's account – the will must be made captive so that the person may be free. The notorious phrase in the *Social Contract* 'forced to be free' (ibid., p. 364) suggests that Rousseau was not altogether unmindful of it, although the forcing to which Rousseau refers is relatively superficial, the constraint exercised on each to obey the general will, rather than the shaping of the individual will so that it expresses the general will. But Rousseau's autobiographical writings, in particular the *Dialogues* and the *Rêveries*, display a more profound awareness. Without denying Rousseau's paranoia, I should want to claim that his sense of persecution at the hands of a universal conspiracy directed against him is not unrelated to his recognition that 'I have never been truly fit for civil society, where all is trouble, obligation, duty, and ... my independent nature makes me incapable of the submission necessary for whoever would live among men' (OC I, p. 1059). Note that the constraints Rousseau rejects are not the those of opinion, but of duty – not the constraints imposed by taking one's sentiment of existence from the alien regard of others, but those required in taking that sentiment from the general will. Rousseau refuses to have his will mastered, and in his paranoia he represents his fellows as responding to his refusal by 'forcing him to be free'.

I have offered some of the textual justification for this interpretation of parts of the autobiographical writings elsewhere (see Gauthier, 1990, pp. 35–8); here I have only stated dogmatically what I recognize to be quite controversial so that I may pass on to my main theme. In Rousseau's account in the *Dialogues* of the plight of Jean-Jacques, and in his account in the *Rêveries* of his return to solitude, we have his own immanent critique of his social theories, his rejection in his own person of the activities of the Tutor and the Legislator. But in the first part of the *Confessions*, and in the last *Promenade* of the *Rêveries*, we have Rousseau's account, in his own person, of a self very different from either Emile or the citizen. And it is that self whom I want to consider here. Like Emile and the citizen, this self is also a construction, and so I shall speak of making Jean-Jacques. And I shall ask whether in making Jean-Jacques, Rousseau claims to find a third way of escape from the slavish dependence that constitutes modern society.

In his *Essay on the Origin of Languages*, Rousseau distinguishes the southern languages of passion from the northern languages of need. As I have noted, the first expression of need is 'aidez-moi', expressing the loss of self-sufficiency that made human beings physically and then psychologically dependent on their fellows. But in the southern languages, the first expression of passion is 'aimez-moi', (OL p. 527) directly expressing psychological

3

dependence, but, as we shall see, of a very different kind. And it is from the demand for love that the making of Jean-Jacques begins. In the *Confessions*, speaking of himself as a child, Rousseau says, '[T]o be loved by all about me was the liveliest of my desires' (OC I, p. 14). But this desire for love, diffuse, without a determinate object, gave little structure to the character of the young Jean-Jacques. He had yet to meet and place himself in the service of the person who played the role in shaping his nature that the Tutor plays for Emile, or the Legislator for the citizen. He had yet to meet the woman he would always call 'Maman', Madame de Warens.

Rousseau was in no doubt about the effects of maman on his life. In the *Confessions* he says, '[F]inally I arrived; I saw Madame de Warens', and then, rather than describing either her or their meeting, he insists, '[T]his stage of my life has determined my character', and then immediately offers, for the first time, a sketch of his own appearance (ibid., p. 48). It is as if his first sight of Madame de Warens was the catalyst to bring his latent amour-propre into act. He began to exist as an object for others, although after describing himself he notes, '[U]nfortunately I knew nothing of all this' (ibid.) – he had yet to sense himself as an object. But only after this retrospective account of his appearance does he resume his narrative, describing in detail his first encounter with maman, and acknowledging 'For I became hers in an instant, certain that a faith preached by such missionaries could not fail to lead to paradise' (ibid., p. 49).

In the tenth *Promenade* Rousseau notes, '[M]y soul ... had not yet taken on any determinate form. It waited with some impatience the moment that should give it that form' (*Rêveries*, ibid., p. 1098) – a moment that was yet to come. We need not pursue the comings and goings in Rousseau's relationship with Madame de Warens, but we should focus on that period when the two lived and loved together in the country at Les Charmettes. For,

> without this short but precious time, I should perhaps have remained uncertain about myself, for all the rest of my life, weak and without resistance, I have been so shaken, tossed and turned to and fro by the passions of others that ... I should scarcely have distinguished what there was of myself in my own behaviour, ... But during these few years, loved by a woman overflowing with goodwill and affection, I did what I would do, I was what I would be, and by the use that I made of my leisure, helped by her teaching and her example, I was able to give my soul, still simple and new, the form most appropriate to it and which it has always retained (ibid., p. 1099).

In this passage Rousseau contrasts his normal passivity with what may seem to be his activity in forming his soul under maman's influence. But I suggest that we should rather distinguish two forms of passivity. 'I lived no more but

4

in her and for her' (ibid., p. 1098), he says in the last *Promenade*, and 'she knew that I did not think, did not feel, did not breathe save through her', he insists in the *Confessions* (ibid., p. 201). I suggest that we should contrast passivity in relation to the other – to what is experienced as alien to oneself, with passivity in relation to what is experienced as united with oneself. In the *Dialogues*, Rousseau says of Jean-Jacques, 'he can not say a word, or take a step, or lift a finger, without their knowing and willing it' (ibid., p. 710) – 'they' being the anonymous authors of the universal conspiracy against Jean-Jacques. This is the total passivity that represents dependence on what one experiences as alien; we should pause to note that the language is exactly that of Emile's dependence on the Tutor: 'he shouldn't take a step that you haven't foreseen; he shouldn't open his mouth without your knowing what he is going to say' (OC IV, p. 363).

Rousseau's dependence on Madame de Warens is very different. I shall quote at length and with interspersed comments the passage from the *Confessions* in which it is most fully expressed:

> [O]ur mutual attachment did not increase; that was not possible. But it took on an indefinable sense of increased intimacy, of increased tenderness in its great simplicity. I became altogether her work, altogether her child, more than if she had been my true mother. [Need I emphasize the passivity explicitly acknowledged in the child-mother relationship?] We began, all unawares, no longer to distinguish ourselves one from the other, and in some sense to share our existence in common. [The *sharing* of existence should be contrasted to the various other ways in which Rousseau claims that we may experience our existence.] Feeling that we were not only reciprocally necessary but sufficient, we became accustomed to think no more of anything beyond ourselves, to limit totally our happiness and all our desires to a mutual possession perhaps unique among human kind, [here Rousseau specifies the psychologically sufficient entity – in this case the pair, Jean-Jacques and maman, which we should contrast with the unit, natural man, and the whole, the society of citizens] which was not ... that of love, but a more essential possession that depends, not on the senses, on sex, on age, on external appearance, but on all that makes one oneself, and that one cannot lose but by ceasing to be (OC I, p. 222).

This last sentence raises two distinct and difficult problems. The first is to clarify Rousseau's view of love, for he both applies and withholds the term in characterizing his relationship with Madame de Warens. And the second is to understand the connection between possession and existence. For Rousseau's claim is not only that his relationship with maman was one of mutual possession dependent on their true selves – an intelligible enough claim, whether actually true or not – but that the continuation of this

5

relationship had become necessary to the existence of these selves. Since Rousseau admits that mutual possession was lost, does he then suppose that he and Madame de Warens had in some manner ceased to be? And even if we can make sense of Rousseau's apparent hyperbole, we should no doubt ask ourselves how *maman* might have regarded the words of her 'little one'. We may suspect that she did not regard her existence as merged with his.

Let us begin with love. And here we are seeking the real meaning of our first words – of the magical 'aimez-moi' in which our primary psychological dependence is expressed. Rousseau's first mention of love in relation to Madame de Warens should prepare us for the ambiguities to come.

> Let us suppose that what I felt for her was truly love, which will appear at least doubtful to anyone who follows the story of our liaisons, how could that passion have been accompanied from its birth with the sentiments that it least inspires – peace of heart, calmness, serenity, security, assurance? ... Can one have love, I do not say without desires, for those I had, but without disquietude and jealousy? (ibid., p. 52).

The association of love with disquiet and jealousy would suggest that, for Rousseau, it would be natural to identify or at least to correlate love with a desire for the exclusive possession of the beloved and her affections – for control over her desires and will. But we may, I think, understand Rousseau's desire as being, certainly for possession of *maman*, but as identification with her rather than control over her. In the fusion of persons that Rousseau seems to envisage, there is but one set of desires and one will. And this fusion has no place for disquiet or jealousy – the presence of either would reveal that the appearance of fusion was illusory. We might then suppose that Rousseau's ambiguous reference to love should lead us to recognize the imperfection in the ordinary form of that emotion – the dependence of the lover on the desires and will of his beloved, which are beyond his control. Such a lover is unfree in his psychological dependence on that which remains alien to him. Rousseau, on the other hand, depends only on that with which he is one, and so is free in his relationship with Madame de Warens.

Later, Rousseau, after referring to 'the sweet habit of affectionate sentiments that she [Madame de Warens] inspired in me', tells us, 'I shall make bold to say that anyone who feels only love does not feel what is sweetest in life. I am acquainted with another sentiment' (ibid., p. 104), and after attempting to describe it he concludes, '[T]his is not clear, but it will become so in what follows; sentiments are described well only by their effects.' The effects to which he refers are surely found in the description he gives of his life with Madame de Warens, and especially the passage that I have quoted, and that gave rise to this discussion of love. What goes beyond love is 'a more essential possession' in which the two 'share [their] existence in common'.

6

Two more references to love in the *Confessions* demand our attention. These both occur between Rousseau's first mention of 'another sentiment' and his later clarification. In the first, Rousseau notes that

> [M]y attachment to [Madame de Warens] ... did not prevent me loving others, but it was not in the same way. All equally owed my affection to their charms. But with the others it depended solely on these, ... whereas Mamma could have become old and plain without my loving her less tenderly. My heart had fully transferred to her person the devotion that it gave at first to her beauty ...

And Rousseau goes on to note that although he 'owed her gratitude', yet '[W]hatever she had done or not done for me, it would always have been the same. I loved her neither for duty, nor for interest, nor for convenience; I loved her because I was born to love her' (ibid., p. 151).

The man who feels no more than love is smitten by the charms of his beloved, and is enslaved by the desire to possess them, but the man who loves the *person* of his beloved seeks identification with her, and this expresses his true self – he is by nature 'born to love her' as man is by nature 'born free' (OC III, p. 353). The third way to seek to escape from slavish dependence is the way of the lover – if we understand the lover as expressing the desire to exist as one with the person of the beloved.

The second reference to love relates it to sexual desire. Rousseau's relationship with Madame de Warens was more than a communion of souls; he came to share her bed – although at first not exclusively. But physical possession was never at the core of their relationship – at least insofar as Rousseau represented it. Rousseau first met Madame de Warens at Annecy where he 'was in a state of intoxication'; later,

> at Chambéry, I was so no longer. I always loved her with all possible passion, but I loved her more for herself and less for myself, or at least I sought my happiness more than my pleasure in her company. ... To conclude, I loved her too much to desire her; that is what is clearest in my ideas (OC I, pp. 196–7).

When Rousseau did possess her physically, he tells us, 'I imagined [a mistress] in her place' (ibid., p. 219). The moment of sexual possession was not one of existential identification.

Indeed, there are passages in the *Confessions* that may suggest that the very physical presence of Madame de Warens impeded Rousseau's identification with her. Writing of the period when he first lived with her, though not yet sharing her bed, Rousseau tells us, 'I felt all the force of my attachment for her only when I did not see her. When I could see her I was

7

only content, but my unease in her absence became positively painful' (ibid., p. 107). Later, when he is about to share her bed, he writes 'I was well only when beside her; ... I went away from her only to think of her' (ibid., p. 195). But in this later passage there is no suggestion that he was *merely* happy when beside her. And later still, at the time at which he represents them as sharing their 'existence in common', their presence to each other is clearly essential. We should not think that a true existential union between Jean-Jacques and maman could be primarily an exercise of imagination, even if the mutual identification that would constitute it does not require, and is even impeded, by sexual possession. But of course we may wonder whether Rousseau himself only imagined that he enjoyed such a union with Madame de Warens, and the liveliness of this imagining might be enhanced by her absence.

I have distinguished between two forms of love in the *Confessions* – love as the desire to possess the affections of the beloved and love as the desire to identify one's existence with that of the beloved. But in *Emile* the Tutor discusses love in quite different terms.

> And what is true love itself if it is not a chimera, a lie, an illusion? One loves better the image that one creates for oneself than the object to which one applies it. If one saw what one loves exactly as it is, there would no more be love on earth (OC IV, p. 656).

And in the *Second Preface* to *La Nouvelle Héloïse*, Rousseau himself says, '[L]ove is only illusion; it makes itself, so to speak, another universe; it surrounds itself with objects that do not exist, or to which it alone gives existence. ... It sees only paradise ... the delights of our heavenly sojourn' (OC II, pp. 15–6). Elsewhere, illusion is grouped by Rousseau with slavery and prestige as contraries to liberty. But here the illusion is not condemned; the Tutor has more to say.

> All is but illusion in love; I admit it. But what is real are the sentiments with which it inspires us for the true beauty that it makes us love. This beauty is not in the object that one loves; it is the work of our errors. So, what does that matter? Does one sacrifice less of one's base sentiments to this imaginary model? ... Does one detach oneself less from the baseness of the human self? Where is the true lover who is not ready to sacrifice his life for his mistress ...? (OC IV, p. 743).

In these passages love as possession of the affections of the beloved is transcended and idealized; it becomes love of the truly beautiful, and only through illusion does the lover see the truly beautiful in his beloved. But we should not take this as Rousseau's final or deepest view of love. We might

8

better turn from Rousseau's *Preface* to *La Nouvelle Héloïse* itself, and to the words of the dying heroine, Julie, in her last letter to Saint-Preux, 'in this moment when the heart conceals nothing', and when the 'vous', with which she has faithfully addressed him through the years since their affair ended, becomes once more 'tu'.

> But should my soul exist without you, without you what happiness should I taste? No, I am not leaving you, I go to wait for you. Virtue which separated us on earth will unite us in our eternal sojourn. I die in this sweet expectation – too happy to purchase with my life the right to love you forever without sin, and to say it to you one more time (OC II, p. 743).

Here again we find the unity of the lovers – a unity to endure forever. We should not suppose that illusion can endure through our eternal sojourn; what Julie loves is not an ideal of true beauty but the person with whom she seeks to unite her existence through all eternity.

And so we have the perfect ending. Reading her dying words of undying love, Saint-Preux could well devote the rest of his life to living in and for his Julie. He could speak the magic words 'aimez-moi', and know that his plea would be met, that the absence of his beloved ensured the permanence of her love. But this is a novelistic ending, and while it may – and I think does – reflect the core of Rousseau's deepest view of the human self, it exists only in imagination. We should return to the real relationship with Madame de Warens. And here we find imagination and reality, dream and waking, interrelated. Immediately after recounting his painful disquiet in her absence, Rousseau proceeds to relate a solitary walk he took:

> my heart filled with her image and with the ardent desire to pass my days beside her. I had enough sense to see that for the present this was not possible, and that a happiness that I tasted so fully would be short. This gave my reverie a sadness, lacking however any somber aspect and tempered by a flattering hope. ... I saw myself as in ecstasy transported into that happy time and that happy stay, ... I do not remember ever being thrust into the future with greater force and illusion than I was then. And what has struck me most in the memory of this dream now that it has been realized, is to have found things exactly as I had imagined them. ... I was deceived only in its imaginary duration, for days and years and my entire life passed in a changeless tranquillity, whereas actually all that has lasted but a moment. (OC I, pp. 107–8).

So how did it end, this perfect union, the sharing of 'our existence in common'? 'It was not my doing,' Rousseau tells us, 'I can offer myself that

9

consoling testimony. It was not hers either, or at least not her will. It was decreed that soon invincible nature would reassert its empire' (OC I, pp. 222–3). If we descend from these abstract musings to something more nearly resembling actual events, we find that Rousseau found himself ill, and imagined himself to have a polypus on the heart. Allegedly, a doctor in Montpellier had cured such an ailment; encouraged by Madame de Warens, Rousseau set out to Montpellier in search of a similar cure. But as he remarks, 'I did not need to go so far to find the doctor that I needed' (ibid., p. 248) – a certain Madame de Larnage, whom he, pretending to be an Englishman named Dudding, encountered in his travels, who succeeded in making her desires known to him, and with whom he had the one truly passionate relationship in his life.

But she was bound to Bourg-Saint-Andéol and so they separated, Rousseau promising to visit her in the winter. But when the time came for him to leave Montpellier, feelings of remorse returned, 'so lively that, balancing the love of pleasure, they fixed my attention on the voice of reason alone'. And reason advised him that to continue to play an English gentleman without knowing a word of English was risky, that Madame de Larnage had a daughter, to whom Rousseau's thoughts kept turning although he had not met her, and led him to wonder if he was 'to return the mother's acts of kindness by seeking to corrupt her daughter', and that his 'Mamma, so good and generous, already burdened with debt [was] sinking deeper for his foolish expenses' although he 'was deceiving [her] most disgracefully' (ibid., pp. 259–60). These edifying words of 'reason alone' led him to hasten home to Chambéry rather than detouring to Bourg-Saint-Andéol carefully advising Madame de Warens of the exact hour of his arrival.

> I arrived then exactly at the hour. ... . I saw no one in the yard, at the door, at the window. ... The servant appeared surprised to see me ... . I went upstairs, I saw her at last, my dear Mamma whom I loved so tenderly, so ardently, so purely. I came running, I threw myself at her feet. ... A young man was with her. I recognized him, having seen him in the house before I departed. But now he seemed to be established there; he was. In short I found my place taken (ibid., p. 261).

Years later Rousseau would write, 'Ah! if I had satisfied her heart as she satisfied mine!' (ibid., p. 1098). The idyll in Chambéry had ended, and soon Rousseau was to depart for Paris; the author would take the place of the lover.

With the events – at least as described by Rousseau – before us, we may return to the self. Rousseau had claimed that one could not lose the 'essential possession' that united himself and Madame de Warens 'except by ceasing to be'. And now he says,

10

[W]hat a sudden and complete convulsion in all of my being! ... I, who since childhood was able to see my existence only with hers, saw myself alone for the first time. ... From that time, my senses and feelings have been half dead. ... if sometimes again an image of happiness touched my desires, this happiness was no more my own (ibid., p. 263).

'I lived no more but in her and for her.' The loss of Madame de Warens was, for Rousseau, the loss of his true self. And in that true self there is no trace of the independent natural man. The man who is made in the first part of the *Confessions* and who reappears in the last *Promenade* of the *Rêveries*, is no solitary, but a lover. He becomes a solitary, but not by choice. In the *Dialogues*, commenting on the solitude of Jean-Jacques, Rousseau writes, 'I know also that absolute solitude is a sad state, contrary to nature; sentiments of affection nourish the soul, the communication of ideas activates the spirit. Our sweetest existence is relative and collective, and our true self is not entirely within us' (ibid., p. 813). In this passage Rousseau seems to contradict many of his most familiar doctrines. Man is represented as a naturally solitary being in the *Discourse on Inequality*. In *Emile* natural man is 'all for himself' (OC IV, p. 249). It is the corrupted man of our times whose sense of existence has been externalized. Can we reconcile the sense of self that Rousseau develops in his social theory with this passage from the *Dialogues*?

Perhaps we should not try; perhaps we should write off the *Dialogues* as merely expressing paranoia. But in my view this would be deeply mistaken. I have mentioned previously my claim that in the *Dialogues* Rousseau implicitly reveals his rejection of the work of the Tutor and the Legislator. I read his statement about the self as showing his acceptance of the third way to be freed from the chains which he saw as binding his contemporaries – the way that he reveals in his account of himself as lover. The key is the replacement of the dependence expressed by 'aidez-moi' – the dependence of need, with the dependence expressed by 'aimez-moi' – the dependence of passion. For this dependence gives rise, not to the artificial unity of society manifested in a general will that constrains the citizens by law and duty, but to the natural unity of man and woman manifested in sharing their 'existence in common'.

If my reading of the first part of the *Confessions* and the tenth *Promenade* can be sustained, then a single pattern of thought may be found in Rousseau's principal writings. The first two discourses offer an account of the slavish dependence into which human beings, of his time and no doubt of our own, have fallen. The sentiment of existence, which for Rousseau is the primary constituent of the self, which is natural to man and associated with the self-sufficiency of the first human beings, has become alienated, in ways that Rousseau characterizes primarily in the second *Discourse*, so that each has become dependent for his sentiment of existence on the opinions of his fellows. The self exists only in its recognition by others.

11

Rousseau seeks to trace a way out of this dependence. He recognizes that a return to the primal human condition is impossible; the development of reason and feeling that Rousseau terms perfectibility is a one-way street. The acquisition of language changes human beings irrevocably, and the basic words 'aimez-moi' and 'aidez-moi' can not be unsaid. *Emile* is Rousseau's attempt to recreate a self-sufficient individual within society – an individual who need not say 'aidez-moi'. Avoiding physical dependence, he is able to avoid psychological dependence as well. Whatever Rousseau's explicit intentions, the unfinished sequel, *Emile et Sophie: ou les solitaires* casts evident doubt on the success of the project of recreation, and the *Dialogues: Rousseau juge de Jean-Jacques* reveal the totalitarian role of the Tutor in endeavouring to carry it out. Several works, of which the *Political Economy*, the *Social Contract*, and the *Government of Poland* are the most important, constitute Rousseau's attempt to make the chains of society legitimate, to free the individual by making him dependent for his sense of existence, not on recognition by others, but on identification with the general will of the society of which as a citizen he is indivisibly and inalienably a part. Far from avoiding physical and consequent psychological dependence, the citizen embraces them, so that he 'is nothing, and can do nothing, except with all the others' (OC III, p. 382) – but he depends not on what is alien, but only on the society that, we might say, is his extended self. I read key parts of the *Rêveries* as revealing both the totalitarian role of the Legislator or his equivalent in trying to make citizens and, in the person of Rousseau himself, the moral impossibility of dissolving the individual into a collective whole.

Rousseau never explicitly acknowledges an alternative to these two ways out of dependence, nor of course does he explicitly acknowledge their failure. But I have read the first part of the *Confessions* and the tenth *Promenade* as showing a third way, beginning not from 'aidez-moi' but from 'aimez-moi'. Although the desire to be loved makes one dependent on the beloved, if this dependence is mutual, it may develop into a full possession that constitutes identification, so that each senses his or her existence only with that of the beloved. Each self exists only in its union with the other, so that the two lovers become one. The idea is not an unfamiliar one; Rousseau was not the first to suppose that the self is realized in union with its beloved. But whether this realization is possible, and whether, if it is possible, it became actual for Rousseau and Madame de Warens, are of course questions that I have not tried to answer.

I have credited Rousseau with an imaginative awareness of the true implications of making a man and making a citizen that reveals the endeavours of Tutor and Legislator to be exercises in totalitarian control rather than, as Rousseau intends, strivings toward liberation. This awareness appears not only in his autobiographical writings but also in *La Nouvelle Héloïse*. Wolmar, Julie's husband, is the embodiment of Rousseau's figures of control and

Clarens, the household that he and Julie have created, is a realization of Rousseau's ideal of society. Describing Wolmar's work, Julie says,

> the order that he has established in his house ... seems to imitate in a small household the order established in the government of the universe. ... Everywhere one recognizes the hand of the master, but one never feels it; he has ordered the initial arrangement so well that now all goes by itself, and one profits from both regulation and liberty at the same time (OC II, pp. 371–2).

And she represents herself as involved in it: '[E]ach of us two is precisely what the other needs; he enlightens me and I animate him: we are worth more together, and it seems that we are destined to make between us only a single soul, of which he is the understanding and I the will' (ibid., pp. 373–4). Julie and Wolmar would seem to be one, as Madame de Warens and Rousseau, and together they rule over a household of which Saint-Preux says, 'I have never seen a house where each serves better, and less imagines himself as serving' (ibid., p. 445). And how is this control achieved? Saint-Preux tells us, 'All the art of the master is in concealing this control under the wing of pleasure or interest, so that they think that they want all that one obliges them to do' (ibid., p. 453).

But we have already read Julie's deathbed letter in which she makes implicitly clear that her destiny is not to be a single soul with Wolmar, as she envisages her eternal union with Saint-Preux. Julie and Saint-Preux, not Julie and Wolmar, are the pair who correspond to Madame de Warens and Rousseau. In the 'moment when the heart conceals nothing', Julie reaches her final and true self-understanding, and the idea of what she needs gives way to the expectation of union with whom she loves. As I have said, Rousseau offers the perfect novelistic ending.

And in real life? I want to conclude with Rousseau's other ending – the tenth, unfinished *Promenade* of the *Rêveries*. In the first promenade Rousseau has asked, 'What am I myself?' (OC I, p. 995). And the answer that he has constructed in the following walks seems to be that he is the true solitary, 'with no other sentiment, whether of privation or satisfaction, of pleasure or pain, of desire or fear, save that alone of [his] existence', a sentiment that 'entirely fills the soul' (ibid., p. 1046). Whoever finds himself in this state, Rousseau tells us,

> may call himself happy, not with an imperfect, poor and relative happiness as one finds in the pleasures of this life, but with a happiness sufficient, perfect, and full, which leaves no emptiness in the soul that it feels the need to fill. Such is the state in which often I found myself during my solitary reveries on the island of St Peter, whether lying in my boat which

13

I let the water carry whither it will, or seated on the shores of the troubled lake, or on the banks of a lovely river or a brook murmuring over its gravel bed (ibid., pp. 1046–7).

But this condition of solitude is not Rousseau's real truth. His nature, like Julie's, is that of a lover. Remembering his idylls on the island of St Peter, Rousseau may have passed beyond the incessant demand, 'aidez-moi', but only in the end to return him to the deeper demand, 'aimez-moi'.

I encouraged Mamma to live in the country. An isolated house on the side of a valley was our asylum, and it is there that during four or five years I enjoyed a century of life and a pure and complete happiness ... . I needed a female friend in accord with my own heart, and I possessed one. ... I could not suffer subjection, I was perfectly free, and better than free because subjected only by my own affections, I did only what I would do. All my hours were filled with loving cares or country pursuits (ibid., p. 1099).

'Better than free'. Rousseau's final self-understanding reveals the self as subject to the rule of loving cares. But such a rule does not last. Julie dies in hope, and Jean-Jacques in reverie. He has rediscovered his true nature, but it exists for him only in recollection. Yet he recognizes that this recollection 'covers by its charm all that is appalling in my present lot' (ibid., p. 1099). The union of lover and beloved is precarious, fleeting, but the epiphany of love suffices to realize the self.

One might query this conclusion, suggesting that the deeper message conveyed through the 'moment[s] when the heart conceals nothing' is the Tutor's view that love is, after all, illusion. Solitary, citizen, and lover would then all stand exposed as failures. But I want to leave such an interpretation open, and conclude with an observation. The tension in modern ethical and political thought lies between an individualism that is accused of treating human beings as natural solitaries who join together so that each may better promote his own ends, and a communitarianism that is accused of treating human beings as organic bearers of a tradition with ends that transcend those of actual individuals. Both of these views may be found in Rousseau, but, if I am right, both are rejected in favour of what we might call a dualism, in which love grounds a substantive union of man and woman as complementary individuals. Whether this account bears on our own ethical and political concerns is, fortunately, another question.

14

Note

* I am grateful to All Souls College, Oxford, and the John Simon Guggenheim Memorial Foundation, for support at the time this paper was written. Quotations from Rousseau are my own translation. References are to the *Oeuvres Complètes* (OC) and to the *Essai sur l'origine des langues* (OL).

References

Gauthier, D. (1990), '*Le promeneur solitaire*: Rousseau and the Emergence of the Post-Social Self', *Social Philosophy & Policy*, 8, , pp. 35–58 and (1991) Paul, E.F., Miller, Jr., F.D. and Paul. J. (eds.), *Ethics, Politics, and Human Nature*, Oxford: Blackwell.

Rousseau, J-J. (1959–69), *Oeuvres Complètes*, (4 vols.) Gagnebin, B., reprinted in Raymond, M. (eds.), Paris: Gallimard (Bibliothèque de la Pléiade).

Rousseau, J-J. (no date), *Essai sur l'origine des langues*, Paris: Bibliothèque du Graphe.

15

Addenda

p. 1, §1, ll.1–2: *OC*4.248/*Em*.39
   Ibid., ll.2–3: *OC*4.249/*Em*.39
   Ibid., l.3: *OC*3.381/*CW*4.155
   Ibid., ll.4–5: *OC*4.249/*Em*.39
   Ibid., l.5: *OC*3.381/*CW*4.155
   Ibid., l.7: *OC*3.165/*CW*3.43
   Ibid., l.8: *OC*4.249/*Em*.40
   Ibid., §2, l.12: *OC*3.193/*CW*3.66
p. 2, §2, l.6: *OC*5.408/*CW*7.316, *OC*5.407/*CW*7.315
   Ibid., §4, l.5: *OC*4.362–63/*Em*.120
   Ibid., §5, l.3: *OC*4.661/*Em*.332
   Ibid., §6, l.4: *OC*3.251/*CW*3.148
p. 3, §2, l.3: *OC*3.364/*CW*4.141
   Ibid., l.14: *OC*1.1059/*CW*8.56
   Ibid., §4, l.6: *OC*5.408/*CW*7.316
p. 4, §1, l.4: *OC*1.14/*CW*5.12
   Ibid., §2, l.5: *OC*1.48/*CW*5.40
   Ibid., l.8: *OC*1.48/*CW*5.40
   Ibid., l.13: *OC*1.49/*CW*5.41
   Ibid., §3, l.3: *OC*1.1098/*CW*8.89
   Ibid., §4, l.10: *OC*1.1099/*CW*8.89–90
p. 5, §1, l.1: *OC*1.1098/*CW*8.89
   Ibid., l.3: *OC*1.201/*CW*5.169
   Ibid., l.7: *OC*1.710/*CW*1.39–40
   Ibid., l.13: *OC*4.363/*Em*.120
   Ibid., §3, l.18: *OC*1.222/*CW*5.186
p. 6, §3, l.6: *OC*1.52/*CW*5.43–44
   Ibid., §5, l.4: *OC*1.104/*CW*5.87
p. 7, §3, l.4: *OC*1.151/*CW*5.126
   Ibid., §4, l.5: *OC*3.353/*CW*4.132
   Ibid., §6, l.5: *OC*1.196–97/*CW*5.165
   Ibid., §7, l.2: *OC*1.219/*CW*5.183
p. 8, §1, l.2: *OC*1.107/*CW*5.90
   Ibid., l.3: *OC*1.195/*CW*5.163
   Ibid., §3, l.4: *OC*4.656/*Em*.329
   Ibid., §4, l.5: *OC*2.15–16/*CW*6.10
   Ibid., §5, l.7: *OC*4.743/*Em*.391
p. 9, §2, ll.5–6: *OC*2.743/*CW*6.610
   Ibid., §5, l.12: *OC*1.107–108/*CW*5.90
p. 10, §1, ll.2–3: *OC*1.222–23/*CW*5.186
   Ibid., l.8: *OC*1.248/*CW*5.208
   Ibid., §2, l.11: *OC*1.259–60/*CW*5.217
   Ibid., §3, l.7: *OC*1.261/*CW*5.218–19
   Ibid., §4, l.2: *OC*1.1098/*CW*8.89
p. 11, §1, l.5: *OC*1.263/*CW*5.220
   Ibid., §2, l.10: *OC*1.813/*CW*1.118
   Ibid., l.13: *OC*4.249/*Em*.39
p. 12, §1, l.20: *OC*3.382/*CW*4.155
p. 13, §2, ll.5–6: *OC*2.371–72/*CW*6.305–306
   Ibid., §3, ll.4–5: *OC*2.373–74/*CW*6.307
   Ibid., l.8: *OC*2.445/*CW*6.367
   Ibid., l.11: *OC*2.453/*CW*6.373
   Ibid., §5, l.3: *OC*1.995/*CW*8.3

Ibid., 1.7: *OC*1.1046/*CW*8.46
p. 14, §1, 1.3: *OC*1.1046–47/*CW*8.46
Ibid., §3, ll.7–8: *OC*1.1099/*CW*8.90
Ibid., §4, 1.5: *OC*1.1099/*CW*8.90

Name Index